Racial Divide

Racial Divide

Racial and Ethnic Bias in the Criminal Justice System

edited by
Michael J. Lynch,
E. Britt Patterson &
Kristina K. Childs

LYNNE
RIENNER
PUBLISHERS

BOULDER
LONDON

Published in the United States of America in 2010 by
Lynne Rienner Publishers, Inc.
1800 30th Street, Boulder, Colorado 80301
www.rienner.com

and in the United Kingdom by
Lynne Rienner Publishers, Inc.
3 Henrietta Street, Covent Garden, London WC2E 8LU

ISBN: 978-1-881798-86-6 (pb : alk. paper)

First published in 2008 by Criminal Justice Press.
Reprinted here from the original edition.

Printed and bound in the United States of America

∞ The paper used in this publication meets the requirements
of the American National Standard for Permanence of
Paper for Printed Library Materials Z39.48-1992.

5   4   3   2   1

Table of Contents

continued

Table of Contents

About the Authors

Donna M. Bishop is a professor in the College of Criminal Justice at Northeastern University. For over two decades, her research and scholarship have focused primarily on juvenile justice and youth policy. She is the author of a book, over 60 articles, and numerous monographs, including major works on: racial and gender disparities in juvenile court processing; juvenile detention reform; and juvenile transfer policy and practice. Her current work focuses on the implications of incarceration for adolescent development, the role of organizational factors in justice decision making, the link between features of juvenile correctional institutions and inmate misconduct, and racial stereotyping in the juvenile justice system.

Beth Bjerregaard is an associate professor at the University of North Carolina, Charlotte. Her research interests include the study of gang membership and its relationship to delinquent behaviors, capital punishment, and family violence. Her publications have appeared in several criminological journals, and include the book *Criminal Law in North Carolina* (Thompson Publishing, 2004).

Kristina K. Childs is a doctoral candidate in the Department of Criminology at the University of South Florida. Her research interests include improving front-end intervention strategies for juvenile offenders and identifying the risk and protective factors associated with risky sexual practices and substance use among this population. Recent publications have appeared in *The Journal of Child and Adolescent Substance Abuse, Sexually Transmitted Diseases,* and *Behavioral Sciences and the Law.*

Billy R. Close, Ph.D. is currently an assistant professor of criminology and criminal justice at Florida State University (FSU) and Founder & Executive Director of Beyond The Athlete®, Inc. Close has also served as assistant director of FSU's Black Studies Program, and as a member of Florida's Council on the Social Status of Black Men & Boys. His research examines theory and dynamics of racism and crime, racial profiling, sports and crime, black crimmythology, conflict reduction, and multiculturalism. Close belongs to several professional organizations and has numerous publications to his credit.

John K. Cochran is a professor of criminology and Associate Dean for Faculty Affairs in the College of Arts and Sciences at the University of South Florida. His research interests include tests of micro-social theories of criminal and deviant behavior, tests of macro-social theories of crime and crime control, and empirical examinations of the various issues underlying the death penalty debate.

Amy Farrell is an assistant professor in the College of Criminal Justice and the Associate Director of the Institute on Race and Justice at Northeastern University. Her research focuses on disparity in the criminal justice system. Her primary interests include racial and gender differences in traffic enforcement, disparate prosecution and sentencing outcomes in state and federal criminal justice, and bias crime reporting. She has recently conducted research on local law enforcement responses to human trafficking and is currently leading the development of a national human trafficking data collection program for the Bureau of Justice Statistics. Dr. Farrell is a co-recipient of the National Institute of Justice's W.E.B. DuBois Fellowship on crime justice and culture.

Sondra J. Fogel is an associate professor in the School of Social Work at the University of South Florida, and currently serves as Associate Editor of the journal *Families in Society*. Her interests include crime and poverty, as well as mitigation in capital murder trials. Her co-authored articles and chapters on these topics have appeared in several publications, including *Homicide Studies, Justice Quarterly*, and *Key Correctional Issues, 2nd edition* (R. Muraskin, editor; Prentice Hall, 2008).

Lorie Fridell is an associate professor in the Department of Criminology at the University of South Florida (USF). Prior to joining USF in August of 2005, she served for six years as the Director of Research at the Police Executive Research Forum (PERF). Dr. Fridell is a national expert on racial profiling. She is the first author of *Racially Biased Policing: A Principled Response* and the author of *By the Numbers: A Guide for Analyzing Race Data From Vehicle Stops*. Dr. Fridell speaks nationally, trains command staff, and consults with agencies on the topic of racially biased policing.

Shaun L. Gabbidon is a professor of criminal justice in the School of Public Affairs at Penn State Harrisburg. He earned his Ph.D. in criminology at Indiana University of Pennsylvania. His specialty areas include race and crime, private security, and criminology and criminal justice pedagogy. In addition to having authored 30 peer-reviewed articles, he is the author or editor of seven books. Professor Gabbidon's most recent book is *Criminological Perspectives on Race and Crime* (2007) published by Routledge. In 2007, Dr. Gabbidon was the recipient of Penn State Harrisburg's Excellence in Research and Scholarly Activity Award.

George E. Higgins is an assistant professor in the Department of Criminal Justice at the University of Louisville. Dr. Higgins is interested in issues related to race and crime as well as the testing of criminological theories. Dr. Higgins has published over 31 peer-reviewed articles in these areas since 2002.

Judith Kavanaugh-Earl is currently a doctoral student in criminology at the University of South Florida. She has practiced law in both Texas and Florida since 1976, specializing in Section 1983 civil right claims. She also served as a Special Prosecutor for the 12th Judicial Circuit in Florida, as the Commissioner of the Florida Human Relations Commission, Chair of the Florida Environmental/Land Use Law Section and on the Editorial Board of *The Florida Bar Journal*. She has previously published on federal and state environmental law enforcement. Her research interests include constitutional issues and race and the death penalty.

Michael J. Leiber is a professor in the L. Douglas Wilder School of Government and Public Affairs at Virginia Commonwealth University. His articles have appeared in leading journals in sociology and criminology, including the *American Sociological Review, Criminology, Justice Quarterly, Journal of Research in Crime and Delinquency, Crime & Delinquency,* and *Quantitative Criminology*. He has served as a consultant and advisor to more than 30 states and localities on the overrepresentation of minority youth in secure facilities, and on the evaluation of treatment programs and case management information systems.

Michael J. Lynch is a professor of criminology at the University of South Florida. His research examines radical criminology, environmental and corporate crime and regulation, environmental justice and racial bias in criminal justice processes. His recent books include *Environmental Crime, Law and Justice* (2008; with R.G. Burns and P. B. Stretesky); *Big Prisons, Big Dreams: Crime and the Failure of American's Prison System* (2007); *Primer in*

Radical Criminology (2006; with R. J. Michalowski); and *Environmental Crime: A Sourcebook* (2004; with R. G. Burns). He is a recipient of a William R. Jones Outstanding Mentor Award for contributions to the McKnight Doctoral Fellowship Program.

Tom Mieczkowski is professor and chair in the Department of Criminology at the University of South Florida. His research focuses on forensic issues, especially hair analysis, drug use and drug testing. His has published articles in journals representing criminology, criminal justice, law, addiction studies, medicine, pharmacology and forensics. His books include *Drug Testing in the Criminal Justice System* (Hazelden Press, Minneapolis, 2005).

E. Britt Patterson is an associate professor at Shippensburg University. His research interests are race and crime and criminal justice processing; drug and alcohol use and criminal justice response; and ecological explanations of crime. His publications have appeared in several criminological journals.

M. Dwayne Smith is a professor in the Department of Criminology and Senior Vice Provost at University of South Florida. He was formerly a faculty member and chair of departments at Tulane University and the University of North Carolina at Charlotte. His current research involves exploring structural and case-related predictors of death sentencing in North Carolina. He is the founding editor of *Homicide Studies*, and has published in journals such as *American Journal of Sociology*, *American Sociological Review*, *Justice Quarterly*, *Journal of Crime & Delinquency*, and *Social Forces*.

Paul B. Stretesky is an associate professor of sociology at the Colorado State University. He received his Ph.D. from the School of Criminology and Criminal Justice at The Florida State University. His publications have appeared in several science and social science journals including *Social Problems*, *Archives of Pediatrics and Adolescent Medicine*, *Social Science Quarterly*, *Sociological Quarterly*, and *Rural Sociology*. His primary research interests include corporate crime and environmental justice. He is coauthor of *Environmental Crime, Law and Justice* (LFB Scholarly, 2008).

About the Authors

Brian N. Williams is an assistant professor in the Department of Public Administration and Policy in the School of Public and International Affairs at Georgia State University. In addition, he is also a Certified Ethics Trainer (Department of Justice/Federal Law Enforcement Training Center), a faculty member with the Illinois Law Enforcement Executive Institute, and a trainer and instructor with the Regional Community Policing Institute at Eastern Kentucky University. His previous publications include *Citizen Perspectives on Community Policing: A Case Study in Athens, Georgia* (State University of New York Press).

1. Racial Divide: The Context of Racial and Ethnic Bias in Criminal Justice Processes

Michael J. Lynch
E. Britt Patterson
Kristina K. Childs

This book examines the racial divide that characterizes American society as it is played out in the practice of criminal justice and the dispensation of justice in America.

There can be little doubt that, despite efforts to create a fair and equal system of justice, the American system of criminal justice remains beset by a variety of persistent patterns of racial and ethnic discrimination, and not simply, as some believe, by isolated, unconnected, non-recurring individual acts of injustice where the affected individuals are minorities. In contrast to that latter view, typified, for example, by Wilbanks's (1987) book *The Myth of a Racist Criminal Justice System*, we have argued that the appearance of racial bias across time and geographic locations, and at various stages of the criminal justice and legal process, is too persistent to be viewed as aberrational, but rather must be understood as part of the institutionalized nature of bias in criminal justice processes in America (Lynch and Patterson, 1996, 1991, 1990; Patterson and Lynch, 1991; Lynch, 2007, 1990). The chapters that follow in this book provide examples of the widespread nature of racial and ethnic discrimination that plague the practice of criminal justice in America.

It is, in our view, unfortunate that in the 21st century it is still necessary to explore and write about these issues. But, as Cornell West (1994) pointed out in his classic book, race still matters in America. This view is supported by a number of other important discussions of race in America. Andrew Hacker (1995) noted: "blacks must endure a segregation that is far from freely chosen. So America may be seen as two separate nations. Of course, there are places where the races mingle. Yet in most significant respects, the separation is pervasive and penetrating. As a social and human division, it surpasses all others — even gender — in intensity and subordination" (pp. 3-4).

In their book *American Apartheid,* Massey and Denton (1994) summarized this situation when they argued that the extreme racial isolation experienced by Black Americans[1] "did not just happen; it was manufactured by whites through a series of self-conscious actions and purposeful institutional arrangements that continue today" (p. 2). Martin Carnoy (1994) reinforced this interpretation, pointing out that racial inequities have been justified not only by race-linked stereotypes, but by economic and social policies which reinforce the idea that "racial inequity is embedded in deep-seated differences between blacks and whites" (p. 2).

These are important points which highlight the fact that not only does race matter in American society, it matters because it has been made to matter — because racial differences have become part of American culture, institutionalized in American society through various processes, assumptions, rules, and practices. To understand why race and ethnicity still matter, it is necessary to examine the context of racial and ethnic bias in America.

The Context of Racial and Ethnic Bias in America

In order to understand racial and ethnic biases in criminal justice processes and law, one must first come to grips with these biases within the larger context of American society. By placing legal and criminal justice bias into a broader context, it becomes obvious that such biases are not unusual, and that *they reflect the kinds of racial and ethnic biases prevalent in society at large.* In other words, the kinds of biases that are played out in criminal justice processes are not unique or extraordinary — they are reflections of the racial divide that remains evident in many aspects of American life and society. This is not to say, however, that such biases should be acceptable on these grounds. Rather, relating criminal justice to broader patterns of bias is one way to explain why legal and criminal justice processes are not immune from these forms of bias.

As the chapters in this book illustrate, criminal justice and legal processes are replete with numerous racial and ethnic biases. Racial and ethnic biases remain in legal and criminal justice processes despite many special efforts undertaken to eliminate or minimize unequal treatment. Racial and ethnic biases are so deeply ingrained in American society that in 1964 the U.S. Congress enacted the Civil Rights Act in an effort to remedy such abuses. Today, the widespread persistence of criminal justice processing biases is widely recognized and is regularly the subject of state commissions on racial and ethnic bias. The creation of these commissions constitutes empirical evidence that racial and ethnic biases persist in criminal justice processes. Currently, 15 states and the District of Columbia operate active committees or commissions on racial and ethnic bias that primarily examine the relationship between race, ethnicity, and fairness in court proceedings. At some point in the recent past, nearly every state has established a similar commission (see Table 1.1 and the website of the National Consortium on Racial and Ethnic Fairness in the Courts; *www.consortiumonline.net*).

Before we can make sense of racial and ethnic biases in criminal justice processes, it is useful to discuss some of the ways in which these biases appear in other aspects of society, and to understand the extent of these biases.

The Context of Racial Bias

The extent or context of racial and ethnic biases in American society can be illustrated with reference to a number of different indicators. A commonly employed indicator is the distribution of income across racial and ethnic groups. As an indicator of equality, income also reflects several other factors that may influence one's income, such as educational attainment, access to employment, the geographic distribution of racial and ethnic groups and employment opportunities, and even the history of racial and ethnic bias in employment. Thus, the income distribution is not a perfect indicator of racial and ethnic bias, but it does illustrate a general pattern that has been fairly evident within American society.

Income. Let us first consider household income distribution. Because we want to discuss both racial and ethnic bias, and measures of ethnicity are not considered reliable in older Census data, we begin this discussion with data from 1975. In 1975, Black median income was 60% of White median income, while Hispanic median income was nearly 72% of White median income. Thirty years later, in 2005, one would expect these differentials to have diminished fairly substantially given educational advancements among the Black and Hispanic population (see below), and the impact of various affirmative action programs, *especially if those programs were effective* in minimizing racial and ethnic biases (Schmidt, 2007; Carnoy, 1994). Yet, by 2005, things had changed very little: Black median income was nearly

Table 1.1. State Commissions and Committees on Racial and Ethnic Bias in Criminal Justice Processes

State	Title, Area, Year Established, Web-link or contact number
Arizona	The Commission on Minorities in the Judiciary[a] (2001). *www.supreme.state.az.us/courtserv/ComMinorities/minorities.htm*
California	Access & Fairness Advisory Committee, Courts (1994). *www.courtinfo.ca.gov/programs/access/about.htm*
Colorado	Fairness and Diversity Committee, Courts (1990). *www.courts.state.co.us/supct/committees/fairnessdiversitycomm.htm*
District of Columbia	Standing Committee on Fairness and Access to DC Courts (1990). *www.dccourts.gov/dccourts/about/standing.jsp*
Georgia	Access and Fairness in the Courts Committee (1993). *www.georgiacourts.org/agencies/gcafc/index.html*
Hawaii	Supreme Court Committee on Gender and Other Fairness, Courts (1989). *(phone 808-522-6475)*
Idaho	Supreme Court Fairness and Equality Committee (1992). *(phone 208-334-2246)*
Indiana	Indiana Supreme Court Commission on Race & Gender Fairness, Courts. *www.in.gov/judiciary/fairness/*
Iowa	Supreme Court Monitoring & Implementation Committee of the Equality in the Court Task Force (1995). *(phone 515-281-5241)*
Maryland	Commission on Racial and Ethnic Fairness in the Judicial Process (2002). *www.msa.md.gov/msa/mdmanual/33jud/defunct/html/25racial.html*
New Jersey	Supreme Court Standing Committee on Minority Concerns, Courts. *www.judiciary.state.nj.us/hudson/minority/njsupreme.htm*
Oregon	Access to Justice, Courts (1997) *www.ojd.state.or.us/osca/cpsd/courtimprovement/access/aboutus.htm*
Pennsylvania	Committee on Racial and Gender Bias in the Justice System, Courts (1999). *www.courts.state.pa.us/Index/SupCtCmtes/bias.asp*
Rhode Island	Permanent Committee on Women and Minorities in the Courts (1984). *www.courts.state.ri.us/supreme/womenincourts.htm*

Table 1.1. *(continued)*

State	Title, Area, Year Established, Web-link or contact number
Utah	Commission on Racial and Ethnic Fairness in the Criminal and Juvenile Justice System (2003). *www.utcourts.gov/specproj/retaskforce/index.htm*
Washington	Minorities and Justice Commission (1987). *www.courts.wa.gov/committee/?fa=committee.home&committee_id=84*
West Virginia	Task Force to Study Perceived Racial Disparity in the Juvenile Justice System (2002). *www.state.wv.us/wvsca/JuvJus/covercss.htm*

a. No longer active.

64% of White median income, while Hispanic median income was approximately 74% of White median income.

The evidence of racial economic disparity can also be highlighted by examining the distribution of income in other ways. For example, according to the 2000 Census, about 88% of households in the top 5% of income earners were headed by a person identified as White. In the top 40% of households, 86% of households were headed by a person identified as White. Households headed by a Black or Hispanic individual were overrepresented in the bottom two quintiles, or 40% of the lowest income earning households.

Education. The modest gains in income made by minorities during this period are partially explained by the rising educational levels across all groups, and by the accelerated educational gains among Black Americans compared to White or Hispanic Americans (for those 25 years of age and older). Between 1975 and 2007, for example, the proportion of Whites with a high school or college degree increased by 26.1%; for Hispanics, the figure was 22.4%; but for Black Americans, the gain was 39.8%. In 2007, 90.6% of White, 60.3% of Hispanic and 82.3% of Black Americans had a high school or college degree (U.S. Census Bureau, 2007a, Historical Tables, Table A-2).

While African Americans have made substantial educational gains over the past 30 years, they have done so in a context of expanding educational segregation. This is especially true in inner cities, where educational segregation remains as extensive as it had been in the 1960s (Kozol, 2005). In several major American cities, public schools have become highly segregated as White students became more likely to attend private schools (Kozol,

Table 1.2. Occupation by Race and Ethnicity, 2006, for Employed Persons over 16 Years of Age, U.S. Bureau of Labor Statistics (in percentages)

Occupation	White	Black	Hispanic
Management and Professional	35.5	27.0	17.0
Service	15.4	24.1	23.7
Sales and Office	25.1	25.7	21.2
Natural Resources, Construction, and Maintenance	11.8	6.8	19.8
Production, Transportation, and Material moving	12.2	16.4	18.3

2005). The idea and reality of racial segregation is thus reinforced in the minds of today's youth. In addition, it should be noted that at every level of educational attainment (e.g., high school graduate; some college; college graduate; college graduate plus advanced degree), Whites continue to earn more than Black Americans (U.S. Census, 2007b, Table A-3).

Occupation. Income differentials may also be a product of occupational differences. The Bureau of Labor Statistics (*www.bls.gov/cps/cpsaat10.pdf*) keeps data on occupational employment by race and ethnicity (Table 1.2). Over all, management and professional occupations are dominated by Whites, while lower paid service employment occupations are dominated by minorities. This distribution may help explain some of the variation in income by race and ethnicity. While these data may be useful for this purpose, they fail to account for the forms of racial and ethnic biases that might produce variations in the distribution of occupations across racial and ethnic groups.

Unemployment also contributes to income differentials. Here, too, differences in race and ethnicity can be noted. In May of 2008, the Bureau of Labor Statistics reported unemployment rates of 4.3% for Whites, 5.9% for Hispanics, and 8.6% for Blacks. These data are consistent with racial and ethnic income differentials, but not with racial and ethnic variations in educational attainment. Why, for instance, should Hispanics have lower unemployment levels and higher income levels than Blacks when Hispanic educational attainment lags far behind Black educational attainment? In addition, we should ask why Black unemployment is much more extensive than White unemployment, and why Black income levels lag so far behind

White income levels when Blacks have made extraordinary educational gains.

Poverty. Racial and ethnic differences are also evident in the distribution of poverty. Indeed, poverty rates show rather large racial and ethnic differences. The poverty rate for Whites (10.1%) is less than half the poverty rate for African Americans (nearly 25.3%) or Hispanics (21.5%; U.S. Census Bureau, 2007c). These differences impact other dimensions of racial and ethnic segregation, including residential segregation, and these two social problems (poverty and segregation) appear to be intimately related.

Segregation. Community segregation remains extensive in the United States. In effect, residentially, America remains a nation that is racially divided. While racial neighborhood segregation has declined somewhat over the past decade and a half, and is impacted by socio-economic characteristics, race remains the most important determinant of residential segregation (Iceland, Sharpe and Steinmetz, 2004; Iceland and Wilkes, 2006). Higher income groups experience less residential segregation and isolation than lower income groups (Iceland and Wilkes, 2006). Thus, while low socioeconomic status (SES) explains a portion of residential segregation, lower SES is itself partially explained by racial discrimination (Iceland and Wilkes, 2006, p. 269).

Residential segregation is not only widespread and related to racial and ethnic characteristics, it has also been related to a wide array of other negative outcomes including: a higher incidence of crime in segregated minority communities; diminished service provision and restricted access to banking and insurance; differential economic development patterns and access to consumer goods and retail establishments; mortgage discrimination and housing redlining; and differential access to health care (Clayton and Byrd, 2001; Eisenhauer, 2001; Squires, 2003; Massey and Denton, 1994). Communities marked by racial segregation also experience welfare dependency, concentrated poverty, poor educational access, elevated mortality rates, joblessness, an expanded likelihood of family disruption (Akins, 2007) and environmental injustice (see chapter by Stretesky, this volume). A number of these negative outcomes contribute to or reinforce racial and ethnic disparities and discrimination. For example, minorities living in low income urban areas have a lower probability of finding employment than those living in suburban areas.

Institutional racial and ethnic discrimination in the insurance, housing, and mortgage industries have contributed to community racial and ethnic segregation. Research indicates that these forms of discrimination contribute to inequities in the labor market and to more general patterns of economic inequality across racial and ethnic groups (Squires, 2007). For example, housing values in segregated communities tend to remain suppressed. Since house value is a significant aspect of wealth, minorities living in segregated communities tend to benefit the least from increases in housing market values, leading to an inability to move to more desirable locations. Furthermore, federal and state policies that foster segregation by locating subsidized housing in segregated and low income communities contribute to suppressed housing market values in these communities (Squires, 2007). According to Squires (2007) these processes facilitate racial inequality.

It is also important to recall Massey and Denton's (1994) summary of the effects of racial segregation. They argued that, "The effect of segregation on black well-being is structural, not individual. Residential segregation lies beyond the ability of any individual to change. It constrains black life chances irrespective of personal traits, individual motivations, or private achievements. . . . [T]his fundamental fact has been swept under the rug by policymakers, scholars, and theorists of the urban underclass. . . . As long as blacks continue to be segregated in American cities, the United States cannot be called a race-blind society" (pp. 2-3).

Crime. Racial and ethnic segregation also influence crime patterns, including, not surprisingly, the racial similarities between victims and offenders. In 2005, for example, the U.S. Bureau of Justice Statistics (*www.oj-p.usdoj.gov/bjs/pub/pdf/cvus0502.pdf*) reported that nearly 64% of White victims of violence (threatened, attempted and completed) able to identify their offender's race noted that the offender was White, 17% identified the offender as Black, and 13% noted that the offender was of "another" racial category (6% could not identify the offender's race). Among Black victims, 73% of offenders were identified as Black, 10% as White, 9% as other, and 8% as unknown. Not surprisingly, given the broad extent of racial segregation in American communities, victims and offenders tend to be from the same racial group.

Culture. The enduring social structural inequities explored above (poverty, educational/occupational obstacles, segregation, crime and discrimination) have helped shape life experiences and thus individuals' understanding of the world. Coupled with the long-standing popular cultural belief that race is a genetic rather than a social construct (see the chapter by Mieczkowski in this volume), the racial experience (historically and presently) for many Blacks and other minorities is one of persistent social degradation, with little or no control over their destinies (see the chapter by Gabbidon and Higgins in this volume for the reaction of Whites to inequitable treatment). Consequently, day-to-day information is filtered through a cognitive framework of inequality (see, for example, this volume's chapters by Williams and Close and by Fridell on policing and racial profiling). Differences in opinions and perceptions thus arise across groups experiencing different realities (see Tonry, 2004, on "sensibility" differences; and Hagan et al., 2005, on "comparative conflict theory"). Over time, as stated earlier, "two separate nations," White and Black, have emerged (Hacker, 1995). This division is sustained through socialization and everyday experiences that reinforce existing differences.

This cultural divide is reflected in opinions regarding issues ranging from those of national concern to those issues faced daily by individuals. For example, according to a Gallup Poll (Carroll, 2004), there are considerable differences in how Blacks and Whites view U.S. involvement in the Iraq War. To the question "*In view of the developments since we first sent our troops to Iraq, do you think the United States made a mistake in sending troops to Iraq, or not?*," 76% of Blacks indicated that it was a mistake, while 42% of non-Hispanic Whites believed the U.S. made a mistake.

Racial experiences are different, and thus racial perceptions are different. Table 1.3 presents an examination of perceptions of equal treatment over time among Whites and Blacks. Consistently, a larger percentage of Whites perceive that Blacks are treated the same as Whites, while the majority of Blacks feel they are treated less well.

Again, these differences in opinions should be no surprise. A poll by CNN in 2006 found that direct experience with differential treatment remains a reality for many (Public Agenda, 2008). When asked about their experiences with discrimination, 51% of Blacks indicated that they had been a victim of discrimination because of being Black/African American. A Pew Hispanic Center poll (2007) found that the experience of Hispanics parallels that of Blacks. When asked, "*During the past 5 years, have you, a family member, or close friend experienced discrimination because of your race or ethnic background, or not?*," 41% of Hispanic respondents indicated "yes."

Discrimination by our system of justice, as described in this book, is a significant contributor to this racial divide — both directly and indirectly.

The Chapters in This Book

The ten chapters that follow address a number of issues relevant to the study of racial and ethnic bias in criminal justice processes. Each of these

Table 1.3. Percent of Respondents Indicating Blacks Are Treated the Same as Whites, by Race (1963-1998)

	BLACKS		WHITES		
	Same as Whites	Sample Size	Same as Whites	Sample Size	Diff
1963	23%	177	62%	1,388	39%
1964	19%	181	57%	1,478	38%
1965	25%	126	69%	1,531	44%
1967	44%	99	74%	1,402	30%
1968	26%	108	73%	1,392	47%
1978	26%	204	71%	1,336	45%
1980	35%	149	67%	1,381	32%
1987	44%	150	64%	1,385	20%
1990	37%	96	66%	1,062	29%
1997	49%	1,269	76%	1,680	27%
1998	43%	996	76%	942	33%

Adapted from Newport et al. (1999).

chapters stands on its own as a discussion of racial and ethnic biases, but each was included as part of the design of this book to present a well rounded examination of the various dimensions of racial and ethnic bias.

Chapter 2, by Michael Leiber, presents a thorough discussion of the theoretical perspectives used to study, understand and explain the extent and emergence of biases in the criminal justice process. Leiber's chapter examines traditional explanations, such as consensus and conflict theories, as well as more recent studies that focus attention on the contextual factors that interfere with the ability of criminal justice decision-making processes to yield rational, unbiased outcomes. These contextual factors include the relationship between urbanization and bias, the roles of perceived minority group "threat" and racial/ethnic stereotyping, the effects of racial inequality and poverty, and the influence of the "court community" — that is, the various community factors that influence criminal justice decision making at local levels, and the effect of cognitive biases and attributions. The perspectives described in Leiber's chapter also provide a useful background for reading the remaining chapters in this book.

Lorie Fridell, the former director of research at the Police Executive Research Forum, examines racially biased policing in Chapter 3. Much of Fridell's chapter analyzes the research on unconscious racial bias — that is, how assumptions stored in the unconscious mind can impact behavior despite an individual's best intentions. Given that the unconscious can exert an influence over behavior and produce biases even where the individual does not intend to be biased, the question becomes: is it possible to remedy this situation? To address this question, Fridell reviews policies that can be implemented in criminal justice agencies to lessen the influence of unconscious bias on criminal justice outcomes.

Do citizens and police perceive racial bias differently? More specifically, do African-American citizens and African-American police officers view policing in the same way? These questions are probed by Brian N. Williams and Billy R. Close in Chapter 4. Using data obtained from interviews with police officers and residents in a community where community policing was practiced, Williams and Close present original research employing open-ended probe questions to stimulate discussions of racial bias in the community. Like Fridell, Williams and Close employ their data to discuss policies that could be implemented to reduce racial biases in policing.

In Chapter 5, Amy Farrell and Donna M. Bishop take on a large task: reviewing the extensive literature on sentencing outcomes and racial bias. In addition to making sense of this large literature and reducing it to useable and clear summaries, Farrell and Bishop also discuss sentencing reform policies and their effects on racial equity in sentencing outcomes. Like Leiber, Farrell and Bishop speak to the ways in which macro-and micro-level factors interact with defendant characteristics to produce outcome bias. Finally, Farrell and Bishop highlight the policy implications of research on sentencing and racial and ethnic bias.

Over the past three decades, a significant literature has emerged examining the relationship between drug laws and drug enforcement practices and racial and ethnic bias. This issue is explored in Chapter 6, in E. Britt Patterson's original study of the effect of race and ethnicity on the processing of juveniles for drug-related offenses. The data for this study represent drug cases processed nationally (185,482 cases processed in 2002) and in the state of Pennsylvania (2,059 cases from 2002). Both the national and the Pennsylvania data illustrate racial and ethnic differences in case processing and outcomes.

In Chapter 7, Michael J. Lynch analyzes the issue of minority overrepresentation in the U.S. prison system. Until the early 1990s, Whites constituted the majority of inmates in U.S. prisons, but today the U.S. prison population is only 34% White. This chapter explores: whether the racial and ethnic composition of the prison population results from justice system processing biases; how these differences might be explained and their variation over time and across states; and the differential impact of imprisonment on the life-course of those with different racial and ethnic identities.

One of the most controversial and long-standing types of racial bias studies focuses on relationship between race and use of the death penalty. The relationship between race and the death penalty varies over time and from state to state, is affected by the racial composition of the victim-offender pairing (e.g., Black offender-White victim versus White offender-Black victim), and has been affected by important policies and legal decisions. These issues are expertly reviewed in an extraordinarily comprehensive analysis of the death penalty literature in Chapter 8, written by Judith Kavanaugh-Earl and her colleagues. As their review indicates, despite the implementation of legal rules designed to eliminate racial bias in criminal justice processes, and in the death penalty in particular, evidence continues to suggest that race influences what is perhaps the most important of criminal justice decisions — the state's decision to take a life.

The last three chapters of this book present unique examinations of racial bias that are often omitted from criminological discussions and that have not previously appeared in a collection of essays examining racial bias and criminal justice.

In Chapter 9, Shaun L. Gabbidon and George E. Higgins make two primary and important contributions to the criminological literature. First, they extend the study of racial profiling beyond its traditional application to police departments by exploring the use of racial profiling and stereotyping in a retail establishment. Second, while the vast majority of studies examine the impact of racial profiling on African Americans, Gabbidon and Higgins employ survey data from the Philadelphia area to explore White shoppers' perceptions of whether they have been racially profiled while in stores. To place the perceptions of White shoppers in perspective, Gabbidon and Higgins also review earlier studies on consumer racial profiling.

In Chapter 10, Tom Mieczkowski provides an extraordinary examination of the use of race and racial identification in forensic sciences. The question "how is race measured?" has long been debated. Mieczkowski reviews the social legacy of definitions of race (the social construction of race) and the earliest scientific efforts to define race. In addition, he explores modern efforts to define race, and the attempt to use modern scientific techniques to identify the race of individuals from biological samples. As Mieczkowski ably illustrates, in contrast to common and even scientific assumptions, scientific methods — including hair, blood and DNA analysis — sometimes fail to provide accurate mechanisms for determining the racial identity of persons. To our knowledge, this is the first time this issue has been discussed by criminologists in relation to racial and ethnic bias research.

In the final chapter, Paul Stretesky explores the important issue of racial disparity in residents' proximity to environmental hazards and in the enforcement of environmental regulations. These issues — more commonly referred to as the study of "environmental justice" — have not been widely studied within criminology. The majority of environmental justice studies are found within the literatures of sociology, geography, political science and, to a lesser extent, environmental studies. Why should criminologists and criminology students be interested in environmental justice? First, because environmental justice studies explore the important issue of how racial bias impacts legal processes outside the criminal justice system — specifically in the regulatory system that enforces laws against environmental crime. Second, because this literature includes the use of research methods of that are sometimes vastly different from the techniques employed by criminologists to study racial bias. And finally because the study of environmental justice provides examples of persistent racial biases that also exist in other types of legal responses to crime.

CONCLUSION

As the chapters in this volume illustrate, American society continues to be marked by a deep and persistent racial divide. This racial divide exists on numerous dimensions: as a perception of others or in the form of stereotypes; in vastly different access to health care and education; and in the unequal distribution of economic goods and access to employment. And, despite society's best interests and intentions, there appear to be unconscious processes that continue to facilitate racial bias in criminal justice processes.

Unfortunately, numerous legal remedies and policies — ranging from civil rights laws to affirmative action programs and to enforcement efforts by agencies such as the U.S. Equal Employment Opportunity Commission — have failed to eliminate America's racial divide. Policies to help achieve this objective, however, must be informed by an understanding of the nature and extent of racial bias in American society and its institutions, which, in turn, highlights the need for continued study of this issue within criminology as well as other disciplines.

NOTES

1. The contributors to this volume use different approaches to capitalizing the names of racial and ethnic groups, such as "Black" — versus "black" — Americans. Since there is no single "correct" approach to capitalizing these group names, the editors of this volume have opted to retain the varying methods of capitalization used by the contributing authors.

2. Theories of Racial and Ethnic Bias in Juvenile and Criminal Justice

Michael J. Leiber

There are a number of explanations for understanding the relationship between race and the enforcement of societal norms and values, which is referred to as "social control." The "consensus" perspective, for example, explains the relationship between race and social control as a function of normative standards where legal factors, such as crime severity, are emphasized to explain the differential contact and involvement of minorities with the juvenile justice and/or the criminal justice system. Another view, the "conflict" perspective (and its derivatives), emphasizes the relationship between race, power and social control to explain differential justice system processing, which is attributed either to minorities' inability to influence the creation of laws that disproportionately impact them and/or to minorities' inability to resist state action in the form of arrest or the application of harsh sanctions. Finally, there are other more specific theoretical approaches that focus on the contexts of decision making and that stress the importance of contextual factors in determining when race matters in the criminal justice system. Emphasized within contextual approaches are community features, such as the percentage of minorities in a community, and organizational features of local police and/or the courts (e.g., expenditure levels, and characteristics of decision makers, such as their reliance on racial stereotypes). In this chapter, each of these approaches to the understanding of the race/social control relationship is discussed.

TRADITIONAL EXPLANATIONS

Base Assumptions

Traditional approaches used to guide research on race and juvenile or criminal justice processing usually draw on one or more theories based on consensus or conflict perspectives (Hagan, 1974; Tittle and Curran, 1988). According to the consensus tradition, founded by the 19th century French sociologist Emil Durkheim, law, punishment, and treatment derive from a broad consensus of societal norms and values (Durkheim, 1964). State intervention into people's lives, and the incarceration of individuals, result primarily from the occurrence, distribution and severity of criminal behavior. In later versions of this consensus theory, social structure has an indirect effect on social control by creating and sustaining inequality in the distribution of resources (i.e., money or lack thereof) that are conducive to criminality (Merton, 1957; Langan, 1985). Racial bias in criminal justice is seen as a random occurrence since legally relevant criteria constrain the discretion of decision makers and promote objective and egalitarian decisions (e.g., Wilbanks, 1987). Thus, differences between whites and minorities in case processing and outcomes are attributed to differential involvement in crime (Tracy, 2002).

"Labeling" and other conflict theories, in contrast, presume a lack of consensus in society. Majority groups are able to serve and protect their own interests by manipulating the law, law enforcement practices, and the courts. Both labeling and other conflict perspectives contend that "crime" and "race" are political concepts, which means they are *labels* imposed by those in positions of power on less powerful groups (hence the term "labeling" theory). Consequently, these perspectives argue that social structure has a direct impact on social control, since those in power are more likely to label as deviant those groups that are powerless, most notably the poor and minorities (Becker, 1963, pp. 156-161; Liska, 1994). Being poor and/ or minority also increases the probability of being sanctioned and the severity of the sanction (Quinney, 1970; Chambliss and Seidman, 1971).

Relative to other types of conflict theory, labeling theory stresses stereotyping, status or personal resources, and disadvantaged groups' skills in offsetting or resisting efforts of state control (Farnworth et al., 1991). The emphasis of labeling theory has been primarily at the level of the individual (e.g., labeling the offender) and on middle-level agents of social control (e.g., juvenile court officers). A criticism of the labeling perspective has been its neglect of explaining why differentials exist between the powerful and the powerless. In comparison, other conflict approaches address this shortcoming by placing a greater emphasis on macro-processes, most notably the use and structure of power in society, with a focus on the relationship between economic and political power and methods of punishing behavior defined as deviant or persons or groups perceived as a threat (Lynch and Michalowski, 2006).

Traditional conflict theorists view the poor, underclass, and minorities as a threat to the middle and upper class elite. Consequently, the former groups are more likely to be subjected to various forms of social control: for instance, arrest, formal processing in the juvenile and criminal justice systems, and increased incarceration (Turk, 1969). As a result of power differentials and the assumption that law and social control promote the interests of the powerful, the police, juvenile and criminal justice systems are seen by conflict theorists as biased against the poor and/or minorities. Thus, according to the conflict perspective, law and the "system" systematically work to the disadvantage of minorities. The conflict theory belief that the "system" systematically operates to the disadvantage of minorities has generated much debate with proponents of the "no discrimination thesis/ discrimination thesis" (see Wilbanks, 1987; MacLean and Milovanovic, 1990; Mann, 1993; Sampson and Lauritsen, 1997).

The No Discrimination Thesis/Discrimination Thesis

The first point of contention involves differences of opinion concerning what constitutes systemic discrimination. The issue centers on the concepts of overt and subtle racism and the extent to which these forms of discrimination should be incorporated into the concept of institutionalized racism. Wilbanks's book, *The Myth of a Racist Criminal Justice System* (1987), and a series of articles (Wilbanks, 1990a, 1990b), set the framework for the consensus theory position that discrimination toward minorities in the criminal justice system is not widespread and that the concept of institutional racism should therefore be abandoned. Instead, Wilbanks argues that we should define racism only in terms of conscious, intentional acts resulting from psychological attitudes. Following this logic, Wilbanks contends that we need to first establish that disparities in formal outcomes exist, and then attempt to discover through statistical analyses if the differences are the result of prejudicial attitudes. Many have criticized Wilbanks's prerequisites that institutionalized discrimination be reduced to malicious intent, that quantitative research methods be employed to discover institutionalized racism, and that the sole focus of attention be formal decision-making outcomes (Hagan, 1987; Lynch, 1990; Zatz, 1990).

Criticisms of Wilbanks's position on the study of formal decision-making outcomes center on the failure to consider informal behavior and practices that are discriminatory, such as: insults; rough or brutal treatment; unnecessary stops, frisks, and searches by police; and the acceptance by juries and courts of lower standards of evidence to convict minorities (Georges-Abeyie, 1990). The experience of being stopped by police for no apparent reason other than that one is "driving while black," for example, would not be viewed as discriminatory under Wilbanks's emphasis on formal outcomes (Harris, 1997; Warren et al., 2006). Wilbanks's position on quantitative methods has been criticized for failing to recognize the value that multiple research methodologies — including observational, ethnographic, and other techniques — can bring to the study of race and social control (Bridges and Steen, 1998; Conley, 1994; Georges-Abeyie, 1990).

Most definitions of institutionalized racism move the argument beyond the discriminator's intent, and focus instead on the discriminatory result and on indirect forms of discrimination (Georges-Abeyie, 1990). Institutionalized discrimination is often the legacy of codified laws, practices, and criteria that were overtly racist (e.g., the prevention of Blacks from voting or restrictions placed on Blacks from eating in restaurants with Whites, which can be traced to laws that permitted slavery). Institutionalized racism can also include the more subtle forms of discrimination — unintentional acts or procedures that have become part of the juvenile and criminal justice systems. According to this view, laws, procedures, and legal and extralegal criteria, such as age and employment status, may appear to be racially neutral but can enhance race disparities in arrests and incarceration (e.g., Leiber and Johnson, 2009; Spohn and Holleran, 2000). Inquiries into the neutrality of laws and procedures have examined determinate sentencing schemes, sentencing guidelines, crack-cocaine sentencing laws, transfer of youth to adult proceedings, and zero-tolerance policies (Chambliss, 1995; Beckett and Sasson, 2000; Fagan and Zimring, 2000; Miller, 1996; Tonry, 1995; Zatz, 1987b).

More specifically, in many instances racial disparities develop "because the system adopted procedures without analyzing their possible effects on different racial groups" (Petersilia, 1983, p. 112). One example is the effect of a defendant's prior record on a sentencing decision. Some argue that prior record is a racially tainted legal factor (i.e., the result of differential police deployment patterns, and false arrests) that operates to the disadvantage of African Americans not only in case processing (e.g., Farnworth and Horan, 1980; Farrell and Swigert, 1978; Hagan, 1974), but also in obtaining employment (e.g., Pager, 2003). In the juvenile justice system, racially biased assumptions concerning the ability of families to care for children have generated significant research (e.g., Frazier and Bishop, 1995; Leiber and Mack, 2003; Leiber, 2003). Historical and legal precedents allow juvenile probation officers to make assessments of the family's ability to provide a "good" home environment and to supervise the youth in arriving at juvenile court decisions (Feld, 1999). Research has shown that such family considerations have important implications for the juvenile court's handling of youth (e.g., Molgaard, Spoth, and Redmond 2000), especially females (e.g., Odem 1995) and racial minorities (e.g., Frazier and Bishop 1995). In regard to minority youth, Pope and Feyerherm (1993) found that youth from single-female households often faced more severe dispositions than youth from intact homes. Given that African-American youth were more likely to reside in such households, they were more likely than white youth to receive severe sanctions. Pope and Feyerherm argued that "family situation" might in fact be a proxy for "race" within juvenile justice proceedings. They suggested that this legally recognized criterion is racially tainted, and questioned whether it should be relied on by juvenile justice decision makers, given that assessments about the youth's family result in significant differences between the processing of white and minority youth (see also, Bishop, 2005).

Zatz (1987a) defines overt discrimination in statistical terms as a "main race effect" (i.e., statistically significant effects that remain after other relevant factors are statistically controlled, such as crime severity and crime type). Subtle forms of discrimination are evidenced by statistically significant indirect and interaction effects that operate through other variables and are closely associated with race (see above example of race and assessments about the family).

A related aspect of this debate has focused on the pervasiveness and the magnitude of racial discrimination that must exist to support the view that the system is discriminatory (Tracy, 2002). For some, proof of a discriminatory system is evident only when: (1) the poor and minorities receive more severe outcomes, and (2) such effects are present at every stage in the proceedings, in all jurisdictions, and under all circumstances (Wilbanks, 1987). Some scholars add a further condition that the direct effects of race must be stronger than legally relevant variables in predicting case processing and outcomes (e.g., Akers, 1994, pp. 26-27; Tittle, 1980).

Conflict theories, however, question these requirements for proving discrimination. The central hypothesis of conflict theories is that "the probability that criminal sanctions will be applied varies according to the extent to which the behaviors of the powerless conflict with the interests of the power segments" (Quinney, 1970, p. 18). Moreover, Georges-Abeyie (1990), Zatz (1990) and others (e.g., Hagan et al., 1979; Leiber and Jamieson, 1995) also point out that the criminal justice system and the juvenile justice system are not really unified "systems," but that each of these systems is in fact a series of interrelated processes that are loosely linked and tied together by the defendants moving from one to stage to the next. Thus, it is highly unlikely to expect race effects to be present at all stages, especially in the juvenile justice system, where there can be anywhere from three to five stages or more. As to whether proving discrimination requires that the effects of race must be a more influential predictor than legally relevant variables, Paternoster and Iovanni (1989) contend that only *some* statistically significant effect is sufficient to provide support for conflict theory.

Perhaps the most controversial aspect of the debate, and most damaging to the conflict perspective, is research that fails to find any evidence of racial discrimination (e.g., Cohen and Kluegel, 1978, 1979; Gorton and Boies, 1999; Hagan, 1974; Hagan and Bumiller, 1983; Tracy, 2002; Wilbanks, 1987). But other findings point to contradictory outcomes involving both harshness and leniency, or just leniency, for African Americans compared to whites in the adult and juvenile justice systems (Kleck, 1981; Leiber, 1994; Leiber and Stairs, 1999; Leiber and Fox, 2005; Myers and Talarico, 1987; Peterson and Hagan, 1984). For some, these anomalous findings cast doubt on the assumption that the system systematically discriminates against minorities (Petersilia, 1985; Myers and Talarico, 1987; Langan, 1994) and on the validity of labeling theory and conflict theory as explanations for understanding race and social control (Tittle and Curan, 1988). For others, these criticisms are misdirected and perhaps premature (see Mann, 1993; Zatz, 1990; 1987a).

Summary: Discrimination/No Discrimination Theses

Much of the debate concerning race and the purpose and objectives of the criminal and juvenile justice systems revolves around philosophical assumptions (Zatz, 1990). Sampson and Lauritsen summarize this point succinctly by stating:

> For some, *any* evidence of differential treatment, whether anecdotal or empirical, direct or indirect, or at the individual or jurisdictional level, is indicative of a discriminatory system. For those at the other end of the continuum, the term is reserved for widespread and consistent differentials in processing unaccounted for by relevant legal factors. Recognizing these differences in the use of terms implies that

the assessment of racial discrimination is not simply a matter of empirical debate. (1997, pp. 351-352)

Thus, we have on one end of the continuum the conflict orientation of Mann (1993, p. 160), who views the law and the legal system as perpetuating "an ingrained system of injustice for people of color." On the other, there is the consensus approach of Wilbanks (1987, pp. 5-6), who argues that the belief that the criminal justice system as racist is a "myth" and that, at most, discrimination should be viewed as a random occurrence.

THE CONTEXTS OF DECISION MAKING

Debate concerning the "no discrimination thesis/discrimination thesis" and related research paved the way for the development of "contextual" approaches to understanding race and social control. Perceived flaws within each of the perspectives also fostered the development of contextual explanations. Hawkins (1987), for example, pointed out that the orientation of certain conflict theories is economic, and as a result, these theories pay very little attention to race. That is, the unique effects of race are ignored since race becomes a proxy for class. In simplistic terms, underlying the emphasis on economic conditions is the belief that African Americans are more likely to be involved in the criminal justice system because they are disproportionately poor and they are more prone to commit crimes either because of impoverishment or powerlessness (Blalock, 1967). Consequently, a structural analysis that emphasizes economic contingencies is unable to make any predictions regarding differences in treatment of the African-American poor relative to the American-Indian poor, the Hispanic poor, and other low-status groups, including poor whites (Daly and Tonry, 1997; Leiber et al., 2007). In a similar line of thinking, others also suggested that the conventional interpretations of the consensus theories are inadequate to conceptualize the complexities of the structural and interactional processes that shape the relationships between race and decision making (Peterson and Hagan, 1984; Bridges et al., 1987; Hawkins, 1987; Tittle and Curran, 1988; Sampson and Lauritsen, 1997).

Contextual approaches to race and social control have been developed, in large part, in response to the perceived and actual shortcomings of traditional interpretations of both the consensus and conflict perspectives. For example, Dannefer and Schutt (1982) echo the need to view the effects of race on social control as a "variable" — meaning a factor whose impact changes depending on other aspects of the environment (or context) —

rather than as a constant under all circumstances in regard to the juvenile justice system:

> ... The theoretically important question is not whether there is bias in the juvenile justice system, but, rather, under what conditions it is more likely or less likely to occur. An answer to this question has been suggested ... in terms of the basic features of the social environment, ... and of an interaction between the two. (p. 1130)

Similarly, Myers and Talarico (1987) made a case for a contextual explanation to studying racial differences in outcomes in the (adult) criminal justice system:

> The most recent research ... underscores the need to change our focus of attention, and move away from an assessment of the relative importance of race and legally relevant factors toward an examination of the structural contexts where discrimination is likely to occur. In short, the question to pursue is not whether race affects treatment, but under what social and economic conditions and for which type of offenders and outcomes race makes a significant difference. (p. 4)

The contexts of decision making can be differentiated at the macro-level, mid-level or the organizational level (commonly referred to as the local community court perspective), and at the micro-level. Some perspectives incorporate all three levels or a combination of two levels. Although not meant to be exhaustive, a review of a number of these approaches from within each level is provided in the following pages.

Macro-Level Perspectives

Macro-level theories can be identified by a focus on structural factors in society, such as the rate of impoverishment in a community, the percentage of minorities in the community, the community's urban-rural composition, and more recently, the political orientation of a community (Republican versus Democrat). The macro-level theories discussed are: urbanism and formal rationality; minority group threat or racial threat theory; and a macro-level theory of inequality and social control.

Formal versus Substantive Rationality

The work of Max Weber (1969), a German sociologist of the early 20th century, emphasized the interrelationship between urbanization and bureaucratization and its influence on social control. Weber wanted to understand how people provide order to their world by relying on values and rules. The economy and the legal system, according to Weber, are two institutions that provide regularities and patterns of action and guide people in their everyday lives. The connecting link in the process is rationality, particularly formal rationality. Formal rationality legitimates means-end calculations and decisions by reference to universally applied standards, rules, or laws.

Weber argued that modern capitalist society rests primarily on the legal system, whose functioning can be rationally predicted by virtue of its fixed general norms, just like the expected performance of a "machine" (Weber, 1969). Thus a critical factor in formal rationality is the domination and legitimacy of law (Weber 1969, p. 336), which is carried out through a bureaucratic legal system. Bureaucracy produces a stable framework within which capitalist society is efficient at producing goods, including the dispensing of justice. All decision making in the formal rational legal system is grounded in the stated rules themselves. Thus, the law is applied to similarly situated individuals in an equal or like manner on the basis of legal criteria. Little room is left for discretion on the part of decision makers. In this setting, once differences in the severity of crime are considered, few differences should exist between whites and minorities in their likelihood of contact with and involvement in the criminal justice system.

In contrast to formal rationality, there is informal or "substantive" rationality, which is not based on a means-end calculation to resolve situations. Rather, substantive rationality refers to an entire cluster of external values such as notions of justice and respect. In this situation, legal systems are not organized bureaucratically: instead, decision making depends more on informal criteria and social tradition. As a result, decision makers' discretion is enhanced, and similar cases may receive different outcomes. Therefore, for example, in a more rural environment minorities should experience higher rates of criminal justice intervention than whites due to a reliance on stereotypes, racism and other subjective discretionary factors.

Other theorists, however, have argued just the opposite: that urban courts will evidence greater racial discrimination than rural courts. According to this view, adherence to a formal rationalized system may imprison individuals in an "iron cage": decision makers will not question the procedure and substance of the laws, but will accept them as binding and just and rely on factors (e.g., prior record, assessments about the family) that may be biased. In the act of following the rules, decision makers reinforce inequities in case processing (Zatz, 1987a) Some have also argued that because urban courts must contend with a large volume of cases, to increase efficiency decision makers must classify offenders into routine types. The routine types are often based on stereotypes reflecting assumptions about minorities and the poor, individual moral character, motivation, and behavior (Sudnow, 1965; Cicourel, 1968; Swigert and Farrell, 1976; Farrell and Holmes, 1991; Gaarder et al., 2004). Consequently, the influence of race and other extra-legal attributes on outcomes will be greater in urban than rural settings (Chambliss and Seidman, 1971; Bridges et al., 1987).

Some research has revealed that rural courts are less formal and more likely to discriminate against minorities in sentencing than urban courts (e.g., Pope, 1976; Austin, 1981). In contrast, research has also shown that urban courts are more punitive and discriminatory than rural courts (e.g., Miethe and Moore, 1986). In Pennsylvania, for example, urban courts demonstrated the greatest bias towards African Americans in the initial decision to incarcerate (Kempf and Austin, 1986; see also, Feld, 1991). Myers and Talarico (1986) analyzed data on felons convicted in Georgia for the period of 1976 through June of 1982 and found that urbanization was a contextual determinant of differential treatment of minorities. Rather than being impacted by the level of bureaucratization, the effects of urbanization, however, interacted with race, sex, age, and offense type, and the result was not always in the expected direction. While urbanization increased the likelihood of imprisonment for African Americans, it was associated with decreased length of imprisonment. Whites received longer lengths of sentences in urban courts than African Americans.

Minority Group Threat/Racial Threat Theory

Blalock's (1967) minority group power threat thesis is another theoretical strategy for understanding the contextual influence of place on race and social control. Recall that traditional interpretations of conflict theory have focused on the subordination and the powerlessness of minorities. This is in contrast to the minority group threat thesis, which is also a conflict theory approach, where the focus is on the perceived or actual threat such non-majority groups pose to the dominant group. Thus, the development and use of the interchangeable terms "racial threat" or "minority group threat" thesis. Two interrelated factors typically are contained within a "group threat" orientation: the size of the minority population and the economic situation of minorities compared to the advantaged group (Liska, 1992).

Blalock (1967) argues that the larger the proportion of the population made up by the minority group, the greater the competition over resources (i.e., money, property, prestige, voting rights) and the greater the perceived challenges to the dominant group's status. The second group-level factor linked to minority group threat is economic equality. The traditional interpretation of this concept is that increases in the income and wealth of minorities relative to whites should make the latter group feel more threatened. Prejudicial attitudes will develop and discriminatory practices will be employed by the dominant group to diffuse the minority group threat. The likelihood of the dominant group perceiving and acting upon a minority group threat is dependent on the existing political and economic relations between the groups.

Little research has been conducted that utilizes the minority group threat theory to explain the case processing decisions and outcomes of minorities relative to whites, especially in juvenile court settings. Most of the research that has been conducted based on the notion of the racial threat thesis has focused on the police and the use of deadly force (Chamlin, 1989), police force size and expenditures (Nalla et al., 1997; Stults and Baumer, 2007), arrest rates (Eitle et al., 2002), fear of crime (Liska et al., 1982), the lynching of African Americans in the South (Tolnay et al., 1989) and the desire to punish (King and Wheelock, 2007).

In the studies using the power threat thesis within the juvenile and criminal justice systems, the results have been inconsistent. Dannefer and Schutt (1982), for example, used the power threat thesis in their study of two counties and three police bureaus from each county in New Jersey. They discovered that in communities with a higher proportion of minorities, police responded in a biased manner toward minority youth (i.e., who were more likely to be arrested). But, the bias was corrected, to some extent, by the courts (i.e., who were more likely to release these youth).

Frazier et al. (1992) examined the case processing of youth in Florida with the specific objective of testing Hawkins's (1987) version of the power threat thesis. Hawkins (1987) called for a revised conflict approach that incorporates the historical contexts of race and punishment (Adamson, 1983; Peterson and Hagan, 1984) and the concept of Blalock's (1967) power threat thesis to account for the anomalous findings in the criminal justice system. Hawkins argued that as minority populations gain greater visibility through increased numbers and through gains in social, economic, and political domains, their threat to the advantage of majority groups becomes more intense, as does competition for resources. Under these conditions the criminal justice system will exert greater social control over minorities as a method of diffusing this perceived or actual threat. Thus, discriminatory treatment will be more evident in settings where minority presence and economic equality are greater.

Frazier and associates (1992) argued that Hawkins's thesis stands in direct opposition to several traditional conflict theories, which posit that a lower proportion of minorities in the population allows this relatively powerless group to be subjected to greater social control. To the contrary, Hawkins's thesis is that racial differences in social control will be evident in communities with greater numbers of minorities and greater economic equality between the racial groups. Frazier et al. (1992) tested this thesis by incorporating case-level variables and a number of social contextual variables (e.g., racial income inequality, percent white, white/black poverty, index crime rate, and juvenile arrest rate) to assess the case outcomes of blacks compared to whites at intake, court referral, and dispositions in juvenile court.

Although not always consistent, the contextual variables used in Frazier et al. (1992) were found to be significant determinants of case outcomes. Racial disparity was evident in each of the three stages of case processing (intake, court referral and court dispositions) and, to some degree, was conditioned by the percentage of whites living in a jurisdiction. However, the result was consistent with a traditional conflict theory interpretation rather than a power threat thesis. Frazier et al. (1992) found that as the size of the white majority increased in a jurisdiction, so did their ability to exert social control over minorities (see also Bridges and Crutchfield, 1988). Therefore, Frazier et al. (1992) concluded that the disadvantage of blacks in juvenile justice proceedings was better explained by the minority's powerlessness relative to the white majority than by the theory that blacks represented a "power threat" to the racial majority.

Bridges et al. (1995) also found mixed support for the effects of macrolevel contexts in their examination of the rates of confinement in juvenile correctional facilities for whites and minorities for all counties in the state of Washington for the years 1990 through 1991. The racial composition of a community and urban concentration did not have effects on the level of confinement for minority youth. Both of these structural factors, however, were discovered to have inverse statistically significant effects on the rate of confinement for white youth. Bridges et al. did find that youth in communities that experienced higher levels of violent crime were more likely to be confined, and the effect was strongest for minorities living in violent crime communities. The pattern held even after controlling for differences in white and minority rates of referral to the juvenile court.

Crawford and associates (1998) relied on Blalock's (1967) concept of minority group threat, and Sampson and Laub's (1993) emphasis on the white majority's perceptions of African Americans as racially threatening to "mainstream America," to examine African Americans' likelihood of being classified as habitual offenders, especially for crimes involving drugs and violence. They found race effects for drug offenses and property offenses. All significant race effects, however, were found in communities that were presumed to be low in terms of the racial threat (i.e., low in terms of the percentages of African-American residents, racial income inequality, drug arrest rates, and violent crime rates). The racial threat was greatest where the actual threat of crime itself was low.

A Macro-Level Theory of Inequality and Social Control

Sampson and Laub (1993) developed a conflict theory that incorporates the role of class and racial stereotyping, and the effects of the war on drugs, on the punishment of juvenile offenders. Sampson and Laub suggested that the poor, underclass, and minorities will be perceived by decision makers as threatening and in need of social control in communities ranking high on economic and racial inequality. Rather than perceiving youth as directly undermining positions of authority, as proposed by some versions of conflict theory, Sampson and Laub, similarly to Tittle and Curran (1988), emphasize that youth and minorities symbolize aggressiveness, sexuality, and a lack of discipline to juvenile justice decision makers. Thus, what is stressed is the interplay between the characteristics of youth, especially minorities, and the social psychological emotions of juvenile court officers. These emotions include fear and jealousy, and are thought to manifest in beliefs that youth — and in particular minority youth — pose symbolic threats to middle-class standards and public safety (Sampson and Laub, 1993, pp. 289-290).

Sampson and Laub (1993) further refined the symbolic threat concept by emphasizing decision makers' use of stereotyping within a larger context symbolized by the "war on drugs" and the characteristics of the social structure. Sampson and Laub discussed the evolving stereotype of the poor black male as a drug user and drug dealer. This stereotype became more pronounced as a consequence of two trends from the 1980s: (1) an increase in black males under correctional supervision, and (2) an increase in punitive responses toward drug offenders. Race, class, and drugs are seen as intertwined and difficult to disentangle (Sampson and Laub, 1993, p.

290). The overall effect is that the poor and African-American youths, especially those involved with drugs, will be subject to greater social control by the juvenile justice system.

In their examination of decision making in 200 counties across the United States, analyzing data from 1985, Sampson and Laub found that underclass poverty and racial inequality were significantly related to increased juvenile justice system processing for juvenile offenders, especially in decisions relating to secure predisposition detention and out-of-home placement. This macro-level variation was found to be more pronounced among African Americans and. to some degree, those involved in drug offenses.

Few studies have attempted to test Sampson and Laub's perspective. The exception is Leiber, who conducted three separate studies (1995; 1999; 2003). The commonality in this body of research is the identification not only of the structural factors associated with decision making, but also decision makers' beliefs in a punitive response to crime and delinquency, and in racial differences in involvement in crime, family structure and assessments about the family, and cooperation with justice proceedings. The overall findings lend support to many of the main propositions espoused in Sampson and Laub's perspective, while also suggesting refinements in this perspective. Some of the suggested refinements are: further elaborating the concept of "context" to include historical and organizational factors; taking into account socio-psychological processes of decision making (beyond a focus on punitiveness and drugs) to also include multiple orientations (i.e., toward rehabilitation, and the social welfare of the youth); and expanding the role of stereotyping to include the juvenile's family and his/her perceived respect for the court (Leiber, 2003).

A "Local Court Community" Perspective

Recent research on the courts has adopted a "local court community" approach to understanding case strategies and sentencing patterns. Although lacking in theoretical specificity, the concept of the "local court community" is a metaphor for community and the characteristics associated with a community, such as its legal culture and politics, its members' shared workplace behaviors and other organizational arrangements (Eisenstein et al., 1988). Eisenstein and colleagues (1988; 1977) have developed this concept by emphasizing the importace of "loose coupling" (see also Hagan et al., 1979) and the interdependent relations among court-related agencies (e.g., the prosecutor's office, the judges and the defense bar) and the other court system actors. The concept of "loose coupling" attempts to provide insights into how decision makers or other people try to make sense of their roles in organizational settings, especially in the contexts of rules and procedures and ambiguity and uncertainty. Consequently, the philosophies, norms, and traditions of the courtroom workgroup are seen as playing pivotal roles in the administration of justice on a day-to-day basis (Harris, 2007).

Because of the breadth of the "court community" framework, a variety of interrelated contexts external and internal to the court are seen as important determinants of court decision making. Examples of the contexts highlighted in this perspective are: (1) the size of the community, (2) court community stability and familiarity, (3) local party politics, (4) the character (morale) of the sponsoring agencies and the balance of power among them, (5) the attitudes of court personnel toward punishment, rehabilitation, and due process, (6) organizational type and leadership style, and (7) informal sentencing norms (Eisenstein et al., 1988; Ulmer, 1997; Helms and Jacobs, 2002).

Most of the studies that utilize a community court framework focus primarily on plea negotiations, unilateral decision making, adversarial strategies such as trials, and sentencing norms (e.g., Eisenstein and Jacob, 1977). Research has shown that variations in work group behavior patterns influence organizational arrangements, routine case processing, and sentencing strategies. However, the effects of defendants' race on case processing have been inconclusive. For example, Eisenstein and Jacob (1977) studied three large metropolitan courts and found weak evidence of race effects in all three cities. Likewise, Pruitt and Wilson's (1983) examination of court decision making in Milwaukee revealed that over time the effects of defendants' race declined due to changes in the composition of the judiciary, a more bureaucratic prosecutorial and defense bar, and the use of rules and procedures to reduce the effect of judicial ideology. Dixon (1995) found no evidence of race effects in her study of decision making in 73 counties in Minnesota. Legal variables were important determinants of sentencing irrespective of organizational context, while the degree of bureaucratization in courts influenced guilty pleas and sentence reductions. Cohen and Kluegel (1978) also failed to find support for their expectation of race effects in a juvenile court in the south (Memphis) where a pro-rehabilitation philosophy and informality were prevalent, compared to a court in the western region of the country (Denver) where a due process model and formality were adhered to. Defendants' prior record and the type of offense strongly influenced case dispositions for whites and nonwhites in both jurisdictions.

Conversely, in a series of articles, Ulmer (1995), Ulmer and Kramer (1996), and Steffensmeier et al. (1998) found that county court differences in personal relationships among the courtroom work groups and sponsoring agencies interacted with ideologies about case processing and sentencing to result in racial differences in case outcomes. In comparison to the other two county courts, the "Rich County" (pseudo name) court community shared personal, professional, and political relationships that lasted many years. In addition to the personal and working relationships, the Rich County court community shared a common ideological "get tough" orientation to sentencing that emphasized punishment and deterrence. African Americans were more likely to be incarcerated in Rich County relative to the other two county courts. Women defendants were less likely to be imprisoned in Rich County. These findings were evident despite the presence of sentencing guidelines (Ulmer and Kramer, 1998).

Through interviews, Ulmer and Kramer (1996) found that court actors in Rich County, who were mostly white and in a county whose population was predominately white, were strongly influenced by fear and the social attributes of the defendants, especially African Americans. African Americans were seen as poor, unemployed, on welfare, less educated, dangerous and poor risks for rehabilitation. Young male African-American defendants in particular were typecast as even more "dangerous, committed to street life, and less reformable" (Steffensmeier et al., 1998).

Micro-Level Perspectives

Micro-level perspectives of race/ethnic bias emphasize most often the social-psychological aspects of decision makers and the roles that discretion and stereotypes play in this process. The micro-level perspectives covered are: inter-group contact theory, stereotyping integrated with cognitive bias or attribution theory, the liberation hypothesis, the focal concerns perspective, and the symbolic threat thesis.

Inter-Group Contact Theory. Earlier, we discussed the minority group threat theory, which is sometimes also referred to as racial threat theory. This perspective suggests that the presence of a large minority population living near whites fosters a perception of economic and/or political threat among whites (Blalock, 1967). Conversely, inter-group contact theory proposes that a greater presence of minority population living near whites may lead to greater contact or interaction which, in turn, will reduce prejudice (Allport, 1954; Pettigrew, 1998). Allport (1954) introduced the most influential statement of inter-group theory in *The Nature of Prejudice*. For Allport (1954), attitudes, beliefs, and behaviors are separate but interrelated components of prejudice. He argued that contact between groups under certain (optimal) conditions could reduce prejudice and that these conditions are: equal status between the groups in the situation; common goals; inter-group cooperation; and the support of authorities, law, or custom.

Although inter-group contact theory has not really been employed to understand race and social control in the juvenile and criminal justice systems, the perspective has received attention in social psychology and to some extent in sociology as a means to explain prejudice (for reviews, refer to Dixon, 2006; Pettigrew, 1998; Pettigrew and Tropp, 2006). Research has yielded many qualifiers to the base premises of the theory, but Pettigrew and Tropp (2006, p. 3) conclude that support for inter-group contact theory is evident. Having greater contact with minorities under optimal conditions can aid in reducing prejudice. Still, criticisms of inter-group theory abound, ranging from the contention that greater contact may reduce prejudice toward an individual but may not generalize to a group, to the assertion that inter-group contact under unfavorable conditions may actually increase prejudice (Amir, 1976), to the hypothesis that prejudiced people may simply avoid contact with those in the "other" group (Pettigrew, 1998).

Furthermore, some researchers contend that because the dominant group in society has been generally successful in keeping minority groups powerless, especially by using negative stereotypes (dangerous, lazy, immoral, lacking intelligence), that contact will do little to affect prejudice (Blauner, 1972; Blumer, 1958). Underlying this contention is the belief that even if movement is made on some levels to change prejudices (e.g., desegregation, affirmative action, etc.), that increased inter-group contact will not transcend the stereotypes because they are so deeply ingrained in history, culture and structure (Blumer, 1958; Omni and Winant, 1986; Winant, 2001). However, others disagree and portray race relations as a cycle. Park (1950) argued that competition follows initial racial/ethnic contact, accommodation follows competition, and assimilation follows accommodation. As this cycle repeats, prejudice decreases.

Cognitive Bias, Attribution Theory and Racial Stereotyping. With the exception of claims that may be made from consensus and conflict perspectives, as well as the focus by some studies on police organizational policies, theory development in the area of police decision making and, in particular, racial profiling is lacking (Engel and Calnon, 2004). Most recently, Warren and colleagues (2006) attempted to explore the role of cognitive bias and stereotyping in racial profiling (see also, Smith and Alpert, 2007).

Social cognition theory maintains that the primary method individuals use to simplify and manage complex information and situations is to reduce them into social categories that are recognizable and provide meaning (Allport, 1954; see also chapter by Patterson in this volume). This theory suggests that when information is lacking, people turn for guidance to attributes such as race, gender, or age, which in turn can allow for race, gender, age and even class stereotypes to enter into their decision-making processes. Minorities are often the symbol of dangerousness, and to a lesser extent so too are males, younger people, and the poor (Smith and Allpert, 2007; Sampson, 1986; Steffensmeier et al., 1998).

Warren et al. (2006) contend that this integration of cognitive schemas with stereotyping can help provide a clearer understanding of racial profiling:

> When patrolling, police officers often must quickly process large amounts of information with few unique descriptors. They observe people doing many things in a variety of dynamic settings. Assuming police officers process information the same way other people do, racial categorization and the associated stereotypes of dangerousness and criminality may influence their determination of who seems suspicious or otherwise worthy of special attention. Therefore, when an officer is making discretionary decisions about who to pull over and who to cite, cognitive bias processes may make the misbehavior observed seem slightly more suspicious or dangerous when a car is driven by a minority citizen. (p. 715)

These processes are assumed to be heightened when information is lacking and when officers work in a police organization that tolerates acting on prejudices (Warren et al., 2006, p. 717).

The reliance on racial stereotypes by decision makers, and an explanation of how these subjective assessments shape case outcomes, was also highlighted in research by Bridges and Steen (1998). Underlying their study was the integration and use of theory and prior research on race stereotyping and attribution theory to explain race and juvenile justice outcomes. According to attribution theory, attributions provide individuals with meaningful explanations for their experiences and criteria for evaluating one's own behavior and others' actions and attitudes (Carroll, 1978).

Although attribution reasoning may use both dispositional or internal and situational or external explanations, people tend to overemphasize the former. Furthermore, prior research has shown that individuals who are more likely to blame the person are more likely to be punitive or retributive in their treatment philosophies (Leiber et al., 1995). Bridges and Steen (1998) used attribution theory together with findings from prior research showing that minorities are racially stereotyped, along with elements from Albonetti's (1991) contention that decision makers develop and rely on patterned responses based on past experiences and prior cases to reduce uncertainty and influence case outcomes.

Bridges and Steen (1998) discovered that probation officers used different causal attributions to assess the delinquent behavior of African Americans and whites. African-American youths' involvement in delinquency was viewed as related to internal or dispositional attributions (i.e., lack of individual responsibility), whereas delinquency among white youth was attributed to external causes (i.e., impoverished conditions). Because internal attributions resulted in perceptions that the youths were at a higher risk for reoffending, decision makers recommended longer sentences for African Americans than for whites (see also Steen et al., 2005). By exploring the subjective qualities that influenced the construction of a case, Bridges and Steen (1998) were able to determine how the values and beliefs of decision makers created a legally recognizable but racially stereotypic image of an offender that affected the decision making process.

More recently, Gaarder, Rodriguez, and Zatz (2004) discovered that attributions of delinquency and victimization assigned to females by court officials were often linked to racialized and gendered social constructions, leaving some females (i.e., Latinas) with minimal opportunities for addressing their histories of victimization and delinquency. Rodriguez (2007) extended the use of attributions to examine how juvenile court officials perceive environmental conditions (e.g., disadvantaged community) of juveniles and their relationship to juvenile court outcomes. By treating community characteristics as external attributes, Rodriguez found that Hispanic/Latinos from economically advantaged and disadvantaged communities were treated more severely than their white counterparts.

The Liberation Hypothesis. An underlying theme of a number of the micro-level perspectives up to this point has been the opening for bias to occur when individuals are faced with uncertainty and/or increased discretion. The liberation hypothesis operates from a similar premise. This hypothesis identifies conditions that are more and less likely to "liberate" decision makers from strict adherence to legal criteria and uniformity in decision making

Kalven and Zeisel (1966), for example, were among the first to suggest this in their study of jury decision making involving sexual assault cases. They found that jurors were more likely to exercise broad discretion when evidence against the defendant was weak and/or the crime was of a less serious nature. As stated by Kalven and Zeisel (1996, p. 165): "The closeness of the evidence makes it possible for the jury to respond to sentiment by liberating it from a discipline of the evidence" and under such circumstances, take a "very merciful view of the facts." When the circumstances indicated a more severe crime situation, jurors were less likely to feel liberated to follow their own sentiments and instead were constrained by the law in determining innocence or guilt.

The liberation hypothesis has been used to examine juror recommendations in sexual assault (Reskin and Visher, 1986) and capital cases (Baldus et al., 1985), and the behavior of judges involving sentencing of criminal felony defendants (Smith and Dammphousse, 1998) and misdemeanor offenders (Leiber and Blowers, 2003).

Spohn and Cederblom (1991), in particular, expanded the liberation hypothesis to specifically explain the effects of race on judges' decisions to imprison and impose the minimum length of incarceration. Case severity was differentiated by the seriousness of the charge, the defendant's prior record, whether the victim was a stranger and was injured, and whether a gun was used to commit the crime. Support was found for the liberation hypothesis as evidenced by race interactions with severity of the offense and decisions to incarcerate. Judges exercised little discretion in cases involving defendants convicted of murder, robbery, or rape. Factors such as prior felony convictions, victimization by a stranger, and the presence of a weapon also restricted judicial discretion. Legal factors, rather than the extralegal consideration of race, determined decisions to incarcerate. Conversely, in less serious cases, both legal and extralegal variables influenced decision making. For example, African Americans convicted of behavior involving less serious assaults had an increased likelihood of incarceration, whereas African Americans convicted of more serious assaults were no more likely than their white counterparts to receive a prison sentence.

An underlying premise of the liberation hypothesis, as interpreted by Spohn and Cederblom (1991), is that in circumstances indicating less severe situations, decision makers draw on their own sentiments, which in turn results in differential treatment for African Americans. Missing from this interpretation of the liberation hypothesis, however, is *why* African Americans are responded to differently from whites under these circumstances. That is, why does increased discretion result in greater punishment severity for minority offenders? The "focal concerns" perspective, discussed next, attempts to address this void.

A "Focal Concerns" Perspective. Steffensmeier and colleagues have developed and tested what they refer to as a "focal concerns" perspective to understand adult court processing decisions. At the heart of the perspective is the belief that judges typically have limited time and limited information about defendants, and therefore they may rely on three focal concerns and attributions involving racial and class stereotypes to make decisions. These focal concerns include the defendants' blameworthiness, protection of the community, and organizational considerations and constraints (Steffensmeier et al., 1998).

Blameworthiness involves assessments about the offender's culpability and the fit between the severity of the case and the punishment. According to Steffensmeier and Demuth (2001), "judges' views of blameworthiness are influenced mainly by offense severity, by offender's biographical factors such as criminal history," and "prior victimization," and "by the offender's role in the offense" (p. 151). Each of these factors, and the concept of blameworthiness in general, represent further clarification of the criteria relied on by decision makers when interpreting the severity of the case.

Protection of the community, the second focal concern, involves similar attributions as assessing blameworthiness, but deals more with concerns related to the need for incapacitation, the deterrence of other potential offenders, and future dangerousness and recidivism involving the offender. According to Steffensmeier et al. (1998), in determining the risk to the community judges rely on such factors as the nature of the offense, case information, criminal history, and ties to the community. The third focal concern, organizational constraints, includes assessments regarding the ability of the offender "to do time," available correctional resources, and the disruption of ties to family members, especially children.

The three focal concerns are interrelated, but judges often do not have complete information on each. Consequently, to reduce uncertainty, judges rely on attributions linked to the defendant, such as age, race and social class. For this aspect of the focal concerns perspective, Steffensmeier and his colleagues primarily draw upon the work of Albonetti (1991), who integrated assumptions from structural organizational theory with elements from attribution theory. Recall that Albonetti (1991) argued that decision makers, especially judges, rarely have complete information available, and that to manage uncertainty in the sentencing decision they rely on "patterned responses" or past experiences. These patterned responses are themselves a product of an attribution process influenced by stereotypes and prejudice (Albonetti, 1991).

Steffensmeier et al. (1998) incorporated Albonetti's ideas into their focal concerns perspective. In short, since judges do not always have enough information about a particular case, patterned responses are relied upon by judges when they are faced with uncertainty about the offender. This perceptual shorthand reduces uncertainty and allows such extralegal factors as sex, race, ethnicity, and age to influence decision making, thereby opening the door for possible discrimination.

Research by Steffensmeier et al. (1998; Steffensmeier and Demuth, 2000) and others (Hartley and Spohn, 2007; Spohn and Holleran, 2000) has offered support for a focal concerns approach and for the belief that African Americans and Hispanics will receive more severe outcomes than whites. For example, Steffensmeier et al. (1998) discovered through quantitative analyses that age, race, and gender had significant independent and interaction effects on adult felony sentencing. Young Black males received more severe sentences than any other age, race, or gender subgroup interaction. Steffensmeier and colleagues confirmed the contention that decision makers racially stereotyped young African American males as threatening, dangerous, and unsuitable for release into society (see also Ulmer and Kramer, 1996).

Despite some research testing the focal concerns concept, Hartley and colleagues rightly contend that what is provided is not a true theory but rather a perspective. For example, unlike a theory, there are no testable propositions, and furthermore many of the concepts are underdeveloped and some of the variables used to capture each of the focal concerns contain the same variables (Hartley and Spohn, 2007). While empirical results yield insights into criminal justice sentencing, the focal concerns approach is in need of further theoretical development.

Symbolic Threat Thesis. The symbolic threat thesis is one example of a theoretical perspective that attempts to identify the contingencies of juvenile justice decision making by focusing on the characteristics of youth, especially minorities, and the social psychological emotions of juvenile court officers. These emotions include a court officer's identification (or the lack of identification) with a youth and the youth's behavior, as well as fear and jealousy of the youth. Emotions such as these are thought to manifest themselves in beliefs that minority youth pose symbolic threats to middle-class standards and public safety. The symbolic threat is also fostered by negative perceptions of African Americans and corresponding stereotypes made by decision makers (Tittle and Curran, 1988). These stereotypical perceptions of minorities and youth are assumed to be "threatening" because justice officials are unable to identify with African Americans or experience a "youthful" lifestyle as adults.

As stated by Tittle (1994, p. 41), these "symbolically driven emotions rooted in identification and fear heavily influence the way individuals react to people and events. The less the identification and the greater the fear, the more likely is social control to be attempted." To my knowledge, no research exists that has *directly* assessed the extent that decision makers respond to youth due to a lack of identification that results in jealousy or perceptions of being threatening. Rather than tapping into the views of the decision makers themselves (cf. Bridges et al., 1995; Leiber, 2003), the limited research that exists has attempted to infer the threat from statistical evidence showing that minorities and minority youth involved with drugs are responded to differently in the juvenile justice system than are other youth (Leiber and Fox, 2005; Leiber and Johnson, 2009). Some research has incorporated the symbolic threat thesis within macro-level perspectives (Sampson and Laub, 1993; Leiber and Jamieson, 1995) and/or further refined the concept by focusing not on the perceived threat, but on the need for intervention for the social welfare of the youth (e.g., Bridges et al., 1995).

CONCLUSION

Traditional explanations of race/ethnic bias within the juvenile and criminal justice systems have been derived from the consensus and conflict perspectives. To account for minority groups' overrepresentation in these systems of social control, the consensus theory explanation emphasizes their differential involvement in crime, while the conflict approach focuses typically on the inability of minorities to influence law making as well as resist state intervention. Contextual approaches have emerged in response to the shortcomings of the consensus and conflict perspectives: they offer insights into the contextual conditions that are present when race/ethnicity matters. Within these contextual approaches, race/ethnic bias is more often subtle (unconscious) than overt (intentional), and it operates through justifiable criteria (such as defendant's prior record and family stability) that may be subject to racial/ethnic stereotypes. The conditions fostering race/ethnic bias can be linked to the characteristics of a community, to features of the police agency and the court, and/or to uncertainty related to a lack of information that produces a reliance by decision makers on stereotypes and patterned responses, all of which result in minorities having greater contact with and involvement in the juvenile and criminal justice systems than whites.

3. Racially Biased Policing: The Law Enforcement Response to the Implicit Black-Crime Association

Lorie A. Fridell

While some of the bias in policing is caused by intentional discrimination against people of color, there is a considerably body of research that points to another mechanism producing biased behavior. Social psychological research has shown that "implicit" or "unconscious" racial bias can impact what people perceive and do, even in subjects who consciously hold non-prejudiced attitudes. This chapter summarizes the research conducted on police officers and non-police subjects to gauge their implicit association between Blacks and crime, and it then discusses the law enforcement interventions implied by the findings. Agencies need to hire a diverse workforce composed of people who can police in a race-neutral fashion, use training to promote employees' controlled responses to override automatic associations, facilitate "unlearning" of the Black person/crime association in firearms simulations, set forth policy outlining the appropriate use of race/ethnicity for making law enforcement decisions, train first line supervisors so they can detect and respond effectively to biased behavior on the part of their supervisees, and implement a style of policing that promotes positive interactions between police and their diverse constituencies.

BACKGROUND

On February 4, 1999, four officers from the New York Police Department (NYPD) looking for a Black serial rapist saw Amadou Diallo, an African-American immigrant, on the sidewalk near a building. The plainclothes officers reported later that they identified themselves as police officers and ordered Diallo to stop and "show his hands." Diallo instead ran up the steps toward an apartment door and reached into his jacket. The officers perceived that Diallo was reaching for a gun and opened fire, killing him. Diallo was later found to be unarmed. He was on his own doorstep and had been reaching for his wallet (Cooper, 1999).

A number of factors likely influenced the officers' belief that Diallo's behavior was aggressive and dangerous. Among them might have been the level of violent crime in the neighborhood, the likelihood that Diallo was the suspect they sought and that he might resist apprehension, and the fact that Diallo did not respond to commands to stop and reached inside his jacket. In the controversy that followed this police-involved shooting, community members claimed that racial bias affected the police response. Did Diallo's race, in fact, impact the police officers' perception that he was a threat? If Diallo's race was a factor in what the officers perceived and how they responded to the situation, did this operate at a conscious level or did it occur subconsciously?

Racial bias has been an issue facing police arguably since the creation of the first police agencies in this country, and certainly since the civil rights movement (see Walker et al., 2000; Walker, 1998). During the 1950s and 1960s, a majority of the major urban riots were precipitated by perceptions that police had misused force against racial minorities (Walker, 1998; National Advisory Commission on Civil Disorders, 1968). Incidents of civil unrest in recent years — for instance, in Cincinnati, Los Angeles, Miami and other cities — were similarly precipitated by incidents identified as racially biased mistreatment of minorities by police.

When the issue reemerged in the late 1990s, it had a new label — "racial profiling." The particular focus was on police stops of drivers of color, and the blame was laid on U.S. Drug Enforcement Administration's (DEA) drug interdiction training. The problem manifested anew and somewhat differently following the terrorist attacks of September 11th, 2001. Prior to that time the salient issue was police bias against Blacks and Hispanics: after 9-11, people of Arab descent complained that police and other U.S. residents "saw crime" (specifically, they saw "terrorism") in them and treated them accordingly.

The longstanding nature of this issue is not proof of its insolubility. The law enforcement profession in the twenty-first century is much different than it was even 40 years ago. Local law enforcement leaders understand the importance of strong police-resident relationships for achieving their objectives. Additionally, the advances in the profession in the realms of hiring, training, policy directives, supervision and accountability all have potential applications for addressing the issue of racially biased policing. (In this chapter, the phrase "racially biased policing" will be used to reference the inappropriate consideration by law enforcement of race, ethnicity or nationality in deciding with whom and how to intervene in an enforcement or service capacity.)

How one characterizes or understands racially biased policing has significant ramifications for identifying the appropriate law enforcement agency responses to it. In this chapter, I focus on one particular "cause" of racially biased policing — arguably a major cause — and identify the agency interventions that are implied by this understanding of the nature of the problem. While many stakeholders have attributed the problem of police racial bias to overt and intentional discrimination on the part of police against people of color, there is a considerable body of research pointing in another direction. This literature tells us that even "good," well meaning individuals in our society have racial biases that lurk beneath our consciousness and impact our perceptions and behaviors. Interventions for preventing and responding to racial bias in policing that emanate from this source take a different form than efforts focused on intentional discriminatory behavior.

In the next section, I will review some of the seminal research on unconscious or "implicit" racial bias, including some recent studies involving police subjects. In the subsequent section I will identify the law enforcement agency interventions that are implied by this source of police bias.

IMPLICIT BIAS AND THE RACE-CRIME ASSOCIATION

In the national "discussion" on racially biased policing, stakeholders have charged that there are a lot of "bad apples" in policing who are intentionally practicing racial bias in the course of their work. There are certainly these types of people in law enforcement, as there are in all professions, and these folks are in part responsible for racially biased policing. A narrow focus on this source of police racial bias, however, can be detrimental to a considered agency response. These accusations reflect an overly narrow characterization of the problem.

Social psychological research reveals another likely source of racial bias in policing — one that likely manifests, not in the "bad apples" among police, but in the overwhelming number of well-meaning individuals who want to serve their constituencies fairly. Despite their good intentions, however, their behaviors may still manifest racially biased policing. It is likely that many of these officers, like humans in every profession, are not fully cognizant of the extent to which race/ethnicity impact on their perceptions and behaviors.

Supporting this view — that well-meaning people might be biased — is the considerable and growing literature on what is variously called "unconscious bias" or "implicit bias." Social psychologists working in this realm point to the "implicit system" of our brain that is designed to be "reactive rather than reasoned" (Gladwell, 2005). It was designed for, and indeed specializes in, quick generalizations, not subtle distinctions. It produces mental shortcuts that can be very valuable for facilitating human thinking and producing human reactions. Researchers have found that these associations or mental "shortcuts" include automatic associations between social groups and concepts, one of which is the automatic or implicit association between minorities, particularly Blacks, and crime. Considerable research has identified this implicit bias linking minorities and crime even in people who test as "non-prejudiced" and are otherwise "consciously tolerant." This association, as research over six decades has shown, impacts on both perceptions and behavior (see also chapters in this volume by Williams and Close, and by Leiber).

Implicit bias might influence the line officer who perceives crime in the making when s/he observes two young Hispanic males driving in an all-Caucasian neighborhood. It may manifest among agency command staff who decide (without crime-relevant evidence) that the forthcoming gathering of African-American college students bodes trouble, whereas the forthcoming gathering of white undergraduates does not.

In the sections that follow, I summarize the research literature that: (1) supports the existence of a widely-held stereotype linking minorities and crime, (2) distinguishes between explicit (conscious) and implicit (unconscious) biases, (3) indicates that implicit bias can affect *perceptions*, (4) indicates that implicit bias can impact on *behaviors*, (5) explores the mechanisms by which biased behavior can be prevented, and (6) tests these constructs and processes using police subjects. As will be seen below, this research has, for the most part, focused on the link between Blacks and crimes, not on the potential link between other people of color (e.g., Hispanics, people of Arab descent) and crime (see Dovidio et al., 2000).

The Race-Crime Stereotype

Social psychologists have long been interested in how various schemata impact how we interpret evidence, including our tendency to classify individuals and draw conclusions about them based on their racial or ethnic grouping (e.g., Duncan, 1976; Hilton and Von Hippel, 1990). These researchers have identified some widely shared cultural stereotypes, including the cultural stereotype that Blacks are violent and otherwise criminal (Allport and Postman, 1947; Correll et al., 2002; Devine, 1989; Devine and Elliot, 1995; Dovidio et al., 1986; Duncan, 1976; Greenwald et al., 2003; Payne, 2001; Sagar and Schofield, 1980).

Devine (1989) conducted one of the key studies in this long line of research. She asked subjects to list the content of cultural stereotypes "regardless of their personal beliefs." Both high-prejudiced and low-prejudiced subjects were knowledgeable of the cultural stereotype associating Blacks with aggressiveness, hostility and criminality. (The chapter by Williams and Close, in this volume, discusses the sources of these widely held stereotypes.)

Explicit and Implicit Bias

The widely held assumption concerning the Black-crime association can operate at the conscious and/or unconscious levels. Dovidio et al. (2000) distinguish between "the traditional form of prejudice that is blatant and conscious" and the "subtle, unintentional, and, possibly, unconscious forms of bias" (pp. 157-158). These researchers argue that because of societal changes in attitudes toward minority groups, as well as the corresponding reduced tolerance for overtly expressed racism, we now see less of the traditional form of prejudice and more of the unconscious form.

A person might have contrasting conscious and unconscious racial "attitudes." Dovidio et al. (2000) describe a conflict that occurs in people who, at a conscious level, proclaim and indeed hold egalitarian personal beliefs, but who unconsciously harbor the widespread implicit associations between race and crime. The research discussed below shows how these contrasting belief systems manifest in different circumstances and how people can actively promote their conscious beliefs to inhibit their unconscious biases.

Impact of Implicit Bias on Perceptions

Research has shown that this widely held Black-crime association influences what people perceive. Payne (2001) examined how the Black-crime association can impact how people process visual stimuli. In his study, Payne used the "racial priming" technique, whereby subjects were exposed to black or white faces to see if these stimuli would promote stereotype-consistent errors. Subjects sat before a computer screen and were told that they would see a picture flash that would be the cue to them that the "target picture" was about to appear. This target picture would be either a tool or a weapon, and they were to respond very quickly by hitting one key if it was a tool and another if it was a weapon. The flashing pictures that served as the cues were either white or black faces. That is, the first flashing picture was either a black or white face and it was followed by the "target picture" that was either a tool or weapon. In two separate but similar studies, Payne measured the speed at which the subjects identified the target object as well as the level and nature of the categorization errors.

The results supported the existence of an unconscious Black-crime association. With regard to speed of response, Payne found that subjects were quicker at identifying weapons following a black face prime; conversely, subjects were quicker to identify the tools when primed with a white face. The nature and level of the errors similarly supported a Black-crime association. Following a black face prime, subjects were more likely to classify a tool as a gun. Referencing this finding, Payne (2001, p. 188) reports, "the critical finding is that simply priming participants with a Black rather than a White face was sufficient to make them call a harmless item a gun."

Eberhardt et al. (2004) used black and white face primes to assess their impact on the subjects' ability to identify degraded images of crime-related objects. They argued that, if the Black-crime association exists, exposure to a black face will make crime concepts more accessible. A group of white, male college students were randomly assigned to one of three subliminal priming conditions. During the first part of the study, the subjects were primed with either all white faces, all black faces, or no faces (the latter group was primed with lines.) During the second part of the study, the subjects saw degraded objects on the screen that would become more and more clear in small increments (41 frames). The subjects were instructed to push a button when they could identify the object and then say what the object was. The objects were either crime-related objects (e.g., gun, knife) or neutral objects (e.g., camera, book). The speed of identification was recorded.

The results indicated a strong Black-crime association. The subjects who had been subliminally primed with black faces were much quicker than the subjects in the other two conditions to identify the crime-related objects. Conversely, the subjects who had been subliminally primed with white faces were slower than even the control group (no face prime) to detect crime-related objects. Further confirming the existence of the Black-crime link were the findings that: (1) the priming condition had no impact on the speed at which subjects identified the non-crime objects, and (2) subjects in the no face-prime condition identified the crime-related and neutral objects at equal speeds.

Researchers have found that the Black-crime association impacts a subject's memory of other related phenomenon: in a subway scene, identifying who held the deadly weapon (Allport and Postman, 1947), and how subjects interpret "ambiguously aggressive behavior" (Devine, 1989; Duncan, 1976; Sagar and Schofeld, 1980). Researchers have found that the implicit association between Blacks and crime affects perceptions in both high-and low-prejudiced subjects (see, e.g., Devine, 1989). That is, even people whose conscious or "explicit" attitudes are egalitarian, exhibit implicit associations between Blacks and crime.

Impact of Implicit Bias on Behavior

Researchers have shown that the implicit association between Blacks and crime influences not just visual processing, but also behavior even "without the knowledge or intent of the perceiver" (Payne, 2001, p. 181). Correll et al. (2002) conducted two studies using White undergraduate subjects. In both studies the subjects faced a computer screen that flashed pictures of males with objects in their hands. The pictures varied by the race of the person (white or black) and by the object (gun or neutral object). The subjects were instructed to push the "shoot" button if the person held a gun and the "don't shoot" button if he held a neutral object. In the first study, the subjects were instructed to act quickly, but were given a "sufficient response window" so that they almost always made the correct decision to shoot or not shoot. The researchers measured time to decision. In the second study, the response window was shortened to force the respondents to act quickly. This shorter time window increased the number of errors.

The results supported a Black-crime implicit association. In the study examining time to decision, the subjects shot an armed male more quickly if he was black than if he was white. Conversely, they more quickly decided not to shoot an unarmed White than an unarmed Black. The results of the second study that examined the nature of errors were consistent with the first in terms of confirming a Black-crime association. One type of error occurred when the subject shot a person holding a neutral object. When the male in the picture was unarmed, the subjects mistakenly shot him more often if he was black than if he was white. The other type of error was not shooting the person in the picture who held a gun. When the male in the picture was armed, the subjects mistakenly did not shoot him more often if he was white than if he was black. The researchers summarize their findings as follows: "Studies 1 and 2 provide evidence that the decision to shoot an armed target is made more quickly and more accurately if that target is African American than if he is White, whereas the decision not to shoot is made more quickly and more accurately if the target is White" (Correll et al., p. 1320).

Plant et al. (2005) found similar results using similar methods and subjects. College students were shown white or black faces with objects superimposed on them. The object was either a gun or neutral object, and the students were instructed to hit one key for "shoot" if the object was a gun and another key for "don't shoot" if the object was neutral. The subjects' responses were consistent with the Black-crime association.

Reducing the Race-Crime Association and/or its Impact on Behavior

The social psychologists conducting these studies have examined how to combat the automatic processes that reflect the Black-crime association. Some of these researchers have explored how to promote behavior that can override the implicit Black-crime association; other studies have tested whether the Black-crime association can be weakened or eradicated. Some of these studies have explored the impact of intergroup contact on the manifestation of implicit bias, producing implications for its reduction.

Dovidio et al. (2000) describe the individuals who have contrasting explicit egalitarian beliefs and *implicit* Black-crime associations. Indeed, a number of the researchers who have examined the impact of the Black-crime association on perceptions and behavior have determined that even people who test as non-prejudiced (i.e., they have egalitarian beliefs) exhibit the Black-crime implicit bias. As noted above, in the studies that test the subjects' *automatic* response to Black-crime stimuli, the non-prejudiced people produce prejudiced responses (e.g., Devine, 1989).

Some studies, however, have shown that these automatic responses can be overridden by "controlled responses" — producing non-prejudiced behaviors — in certain circumstances. Controlled processes are, by definition, intentional ones. They include non-prejudiced behaviors that people can exhibit in rejection of their implicit or automatic biases. According to Dovidio et al. (2000), making a non-prejudiced person aware of his/her automatic biased response produces the motivation and ability to consciously override the automatic response with a controlled response that reflects one's egalitarian beliefs. Devine (1989), too, reports that promoting awareness of the automatic response allows and motivates the non-prejudiced person to implement counteractive forces that reflects his/her personal (egalitarian) beliefs. As Devine explains (1989, p. 16): "Although stereotypes still exist and can influence the responses of both high-and low-prejudiced subjects, particularly when those responses are not subject to close conscious scrutiny, there are individuals who actively reject the negative stereotype and make efforts to respond in nonprejudiced ways."

Overriding the automatic implicit associations, however, requires active attention and thus *time* to recognize the implicit association and decide to act in a manner that reflects one's explicit, or conscious, egalitarian beliefs. The time-restricted shoot/don't shoot types of situations do not provide the time necessary to implement the controlled response (Greenwald et al., 2003). This fact highlights the importance of another line of research that tested whether the learned race-crime association can be unlearned.

In the study conducted by Plant et al. (2005), the researchers found support for the automatic association between Blacks and crime when they exposed college students to white and black faces upon which guns or neutral objects were superimposed. These researchers also wanted to see if they could eliminate the implicit bias through repeated exposures of the subjects to these pictures with the weapons *randomly* placed with the black and white faces. The researchers argued that unbiased responses might be produced if subjects — over repeated exposures — saw that group membership (white or black) did not improve their decision making. According to Plant et al. (2005, p. 143), "exposure to multiple decision trials where the race of the suspect is unrelated to the presence or absence of a gun could potentially eliminate biased responses for subsequent decisions."

To test this, the researchers looked at the error rates of the subjects, comparing the result to their early trials. Their expectations were confirmed by the finding that biased behavior was reduced during the second half of the trials. The researchers conducted two additional studies to assess: (1) whether the effect of reduced bias would persist for 24 hours, and (2) whether the reduced bias seemed to be due to experience with the task ("practice") or to the random pairing of faces and objects ("unlearning" of the association). Plant and her colleagues found that the reduced bias exhibited after repeated random exposure to faces and weapons persisted after 24 hours. To determine this, they had the subjects in the first study return 24 hours later to complete the shoot/ don't shoot task. They supplemented the experimental group with a control group of students who, at time 1, completed a similar computer exercise that involved different stimuli (flowers, birds and insects as opposed to humans) and, at time 2 (24-hours later), completed the shoot/don't shoot exercise.

The third study attempted to determine whether the reduced bias during time 2 trials could be attributed to "practice" with the computer exercise or was due to "unlearning" the Black-crime association. As above, the "unlearning" was thought to be produced by the *random* pairing of black and white faces with guns and neutral objects; this random pairing is contrary to the Black-crime association. For this study, they compared the time 1 and time 2 rates of error for two groups: one group saw random pairings of faces and objects, and the other group was exposed to pictures in which black faces were more frequently paired with guns and white faces were more frequently paired with neutral objects. The researchers found error reduction only in the first group. Plant et al. report (p. 150): "these findings indicate that it was not merely practice with the shoot/don't shoot program that eliminated the automatic race bias in the previous studies, but that it was likely the fact that race was unrelated to the presence of a gun."

Some of the studies examining how to control or reduce implicit biases have incorporated concepts from the intergroup contact hypothesis (see chapter by Leiber, this volume). According to this hypothesis, contact with groups other than your own can impact on levels of explicit and implicit bias (Allport, 1954; Pettigrew, 1997). Dovidio et al. (2000) describe the various mechanisms by which contact with other groups can influence attitudes toward those groups. Through the "decategorization" mechanism, contact with members of other groups transforms the members into individuals as opposed to "group members." The interactions produce "more individualized perceptions of outgroup members and more personalized relationships." Two other mechanisms involve "recategorization." In one version of recategorization, the group boundaries are maintained, but the group is ascribed more positive characteristics through interaction with its members. In the second version of recategorization, the group boundaries are broken down such that the separate groups become one. The character of the contact is an important determinant of its impact and, in this regard,

Sherif and Sherif (1969) report that "cooperative interaction" is the type most likely to reduce intergroup bias.

Research on Police

Several of the researchers conducting studies on implicit bias have commented on how the Black-crime association might manifest in police work. Peruche and Plant (2006) suggest that officers' implicit biases might increase the scrutiny of Blacks compared to others; it might lead to more searches of Blacks than others. Officers might interpret ambiguous behavior on the part of blacks as more threatening or aggressive and might, in turn, respond in a more aggressive fashion. Payne commented on the implications of the findings of his shoot/don't shoot study for the real world of policing (2001, pp. 190-191):

> If the officer is like the average participant in our experiments, he or she will experience some degree of automatic bias when interacting with a Black suspect. That is, the officer will be more prone to respond as if a Black suspect is armed, compared to a White suspect. In situations where a Black suspect is actually armed, this bias will facilitate performance. The officer will be faster to respond, and less likely to make an error, compared to the case in which a White suspect is armed. However, in situations where a Black suspect is unarmed, the automatic bias may tragically interfere with performance.

It is noteworthy that most of the shoot/don't shoot studies have been conducted on non-police subjects, despite the fact that, in reality, only police are legally authorized to make this decision in real life (Correll et al., 2002; Greenwald et al., 2003; Peruche and Plant, 2006; Plant and Peruche, 2005). Importantly, Plant and Peruche (2005) and Peruche and Plant (2006) have conducted shoot/don't-shoot studies using a sample of police officers as subjects. Forty-eight police officer subjects participated in a study using the methods described above involving black or white faces with guns or neutral objects superimposed on them. Officers were instructed to "shoot" or "not shoot" depending on whether a gun or neutral object appeared. The results of the police officers matched those of the lay subjects; they were consistent with stereotypes of Blacks as violent criminals. Officer subjects were more likely to erroneously shoot an unarmed suspect when he was Black and more likely not to shoot an armed suspect if he was White. Next, replicating their study referenced above (Plant et al., 2005) that used college students as subjects, Peruche and Plant determined that the officer subjects manifested reduced bias during the second half of the trials compared to the first. The officers completed several surveys that allowed the researchers to assess factors that were linked to the initial bias (first set of trials). The officers reported their years of experience and the number of hours of diversity training they had received, and they completed surveys measuring their attitudes toward Blacks (the instrument was developed by Brigham, 1993), their beliefs about race and criminality, and — reflecting the intergroup contact hypothesis — the level and quality (positive or negative) of their work and personal contacts with Blacks.

With regard to the relationships among the attitudinal and contact variables, the researchers found that officers with positive experiences with Black people in their personal lives had more positive attitudes toward Blacks and more "positive beliefs" about Blacks and crime (i.e., they did not think Black suspects were more dangerous). Conversely, more negative personal and work contacts were linked to negative attitudes about Blacks; the negative work contacts also correlated with negative attitudes about Blacks and crime. (The causal directions of these associations are unknown. The negative contacts might produce the negative attitudes or the negative attitudes might lead to negative interactions.)

In terms of the bias manifested in the initial trials, the results showed that the officers who had negative attitudes toward Blacks and the ones who thought Black suspects were more dangerous were more likely to shoot the Black suspects and not shoot the White suspects. Years of experience had a "marginally significant effect" in terms of predicting initial bias; more years of experience predicted less initial bias. The researchers found no relationship between hours of diversity training and either explicit attitudes or the level of bias manifested in the computer exercise.

THE LAW ENFORCEMENT RESPONSE TO UNCONSCIOUS RACIAL BIAS

An understanding that biased policing could be caused by implicit associations in well-meaning officers has implications for the incentive on the part of police leaders to implement change efforts, as well as the substance of those interventions. This conceptualization can *promote* change because conceiving of biased policing as caused in part by widespread human biases, not just intentional discrimination, can reduce police defensiveness. Police leaders are more likely to initiate change if both they and their constituencies understand that: (1) even the best police officers, because they *are* human, might engage in biased policing; and, (2) even the best police agencies, because they *hire* humans, will have biased decisions made by their personnel. Line personnel and supervisors are more likely to accept the fact that they have human biases that may lead to unintentional discrimination while they are less likely to accept that they intentionally discriminate.

The broader conceptualization of the cause of racially biased policing also guides the direction of change within agencies. A different package of remedies is implied depending on whether one focuses on ill-intentioned people practicing intentional discrimination or well-meaning humans with unintentional biases. The first group likely manifests other problem behaviors as well, and these employees are a great challenge to executives. Policy and training are not likely to impact on these officers; for the most part, their actions are already contrary to the existing policies of the agency and the training they have received. The greatest hopes for changing the behavior of these practitioners are close and effective supervision, an early warning system to identify problem officers, and accountability through discipline or dismissal (see below).

With a focus on the human biases of well-meaning people, an agency needs to: (1) hire a diverse workforce comprising people who can police in a race-neutral fashion; (2) use training to promote employees' controlled responses to override automatic associations and structure firearms simulations to facilitate "unlearning" of the Black-crime association; (3) set forth policy to ensure that personnel understand when it is and is not appropriate to use race/ethnicity to make law enforcement decisions; (4) train first-line supervisors so they can detect and respond effectively to biased behavior on the part of their supervisees; and, (5) implement a style of policing that promotes positive interactions between police officers and their diverse constituencies.

Hiring

Recruiting and hiring practices have the potential to reduce racially biased policing in two basic ways: (1) hiring to produce a police workforce that is diverse in terms of race/ethnicity, and (2) hiring officers who can police in an unbiased manner. There are a number of reasons an agency would want to hire a diverse workforce.

First, a diverse workforce can convey a sense of equity to the public, especially to minority communities. Second, it increases the probability that, as a whole, the agency will be able to understand the perspectives of its racial minorities and communicate effectively with them. Third, it increases the likelihood that officers will come to better understand and respect various racial and cultural perspectives through their daily interactions with one another (Fridell and Scott, 2005). This third reason for a diverse workforce reflects the intergroup contact hypothesis, reported above. It is consistent with findings that positive contact with people in other groups reduces bias against those groups.

Another aspect of hiring that pertains to racially biased policing is screening for people who can police in an unbiased manner. Although the race-crime implicit association is widespread, studies indicate that people who have explicit egalitarian beliefs can produce non-prejudiced behavior by overriding automatic associations with controlled responses. This would affirm the (obvious) desire to hire officers who do not have explicit prejudices against racial/ethnic groups. Findings that people who have had positive contacts with people in other groups exhibit less explicit and implicit bias are relevant here as well. Police agencies should consider in the screening process the extent to which each applicant has interacted positively — in social, employment, or other settings — with racial and ethnic groups not his/her own.

The background investigations can be used to help identify who among the applicants appears to be unprejudiced and has had positive experiences with diverse groups. Background investigators in all agencies interview numerous people who know the police applicants, asking many questions about the applicants' experiences, attitudes and behaviors. Questions should be (and often are) incorporated to find out whether the applicant has exhibited racial/ethnic prejudices. Additionally, background investigators should determine the extent to which the applicant has had experience interacting with members of other races/ethnicities and cultures (i.e., in work and social settings) and the quality of those interactions.

Training

Training, particularly academy training for new officers, can play a critical role in reducing racially biased policing. There are no national surveys regarding the content of academy training on this topic. Anecdotally, we find that many agencies across the country identify the following as the content associated with their academy or in-service "racial profiling" or "bias-based policing" training: (1) traditional diversity training (i.e., conveying to officers how to most effectively interact with people of varying races, ethnicities, traditions), (2) highlighting Fourth Amendment restrictions on police practices, and (3) professional traffic stop training.

The conceptualization of racially biased policing presented in this chapter and the research findings supporting it imply the need for training that goes beyond these necessary, but arguably insufficient, topics. A department that acknowledges the potential impact of implicit bias on police behavior would want training that promotes officers' use of controlled responses to override automatic ones and that facilitates the "unlearning" of the Black-crime association that might impact on split-second decisions.

To promote the use of controlled responses to override automatic ones, departments should provide training that makes academy trainees aware of their unconscious biases so that they are able and motivated to activate controlled responses to counteract them. For example, I observed the Chicago Police Department's innovative curriculum, which helps the recruits see how their biases and stereotypes (pertaining to gender, race/ethnicity, sexual orientation, and other characteristics) impact their perceptions and behavior and result in unjust, ineffective and unsafe policing. In compelling role-playing exercises, the recruits consistently respond to the calls for service based on their biases and stereotypes. Their stereotype-consistent behavior results in unsafe tactics, ineffective investigations and unjust arrests that include the following: the "woman with a gun" is not frisked, the sex crime committed by a female against a male is not uncovered, the law-abiding young men of color on the corner are arrested. In the debriefings the recruits realize, and are dismayed by, how their biases led them to faulty police decisions.

The Chicago Police Department exercises convey two messages: (a) well-meaning people (including the recruits themselves) have biases that impact what they perceive and do; and (b) action based on biases/stereotypes produces unsafe, ineffective, and unjust policing. The former message might be reinforced or supplemented with computer, role-play or other exercises that helps the recruit recognize his/her own implicit biases and provides the recruit with tools for counteracting those automatic responses with controlled ones.

The recruits should be challenged to identify the key police decisions that are at greatest risk of manifesting bias. In fact, while the key messages of this training might be included in a single session, the most effective curriculum would have these concepts infused throughout the academy curriculum. Officers should — in learning about traffic stops, consent searches, reasonable suspicion to frisk, and other procedures — reflect on the potential impact of implicit bias on their perceptions and behavior.

The training described above seeks, not to rid the recruits of their biases, but rather to make these future police officers conscious of their unconscious biases. The research reported above has shown, however, that overriding automatic biases with controlled responses requires time for this adjustment. The "split second decisions" to shoot or not shoot often do not provide for this moment of bias recognition and adjustment. While the research is still very preliminary, the work of Plant et al. (2005) using lay subjects and Peruche and Plant (2006) using police subjects is instructive. Their findings that random pairings of black and white faces with weapons and neutral objects can lead to a reduction in biased behavior could have implications for firearms training. State of the art training on firearms uses simulation exercises for purposes of training in decision making as well as marksmanship (Fridell, 2005). Computer simulators, "marking cartridges" exercises with human opponents (that is, using weapons loaded with, for instance, paint ball ammunition), and live exercises featuring pseudo-targets on the firing range are all popular teaching methods. These methods simulate as closely as possible the interactions officers can have with subjects. The preliminary research on reducing the Black-crime implicit association highlights the importance of *random* pairings of suspect race with degree of threat in these simulations (Plant et al., 2005).

Policy

Training officers to reduce the link between race and crime or to promote their recognition of biases so that they can inhibit them when they act, is critically important, but insufficient for promoting fair and impartial policing. The officers need to know under what circumstances the consideration of race/ethnicity in making a law enforcement decision is legally appropriate versus inappropriately discriminatory. Reasonable minds differ on this distinction.

Racially biased policing occurs when law enforcement officers are inappropriately influenced by race, ethnicity, or nationality in deciding with whom or how to intervene in an enforcement capacity (Fridell et al., 2001): agency executives need to articulate in agency policy what is "appropriate" and "inappropriate." Executives shouldn't assume that all of their personnel use race/ethnicity in the same way, and should be concerned that their use may be broader than the executive (and the agency's constituencies) believes is just. In focus groups held around the country (Fridell et al., 2001), it became clear that practitioners at all levels — line officers, command staff and executives — have very different perceptions regarding the circumstances in which officers can consider race/ethnicity. Participants discussed when officers can use race/ethnicity as one factor in the "totality of the circumstances" to establish reasonable suspicion or probable cause. There were many differences of opinion among line officers and command staff, *even within agencies*, on this point.

It is important that these policies reflect *meaningful definitions* of what constitutes racially biased policing. While empirical support is lacking, anecdotally it appears that one policy model that is arguably meaning*less* predominates nationwide. These policies are distinguished by the use of the words "sole" or "solely," such as in "the race or ethnicity of an individual shall not be the sole factor in determining the existence of probable cause . . . in or constituting a reasonable and articulable suspicion" (Connecticut Public Act No. 99-198). These policies come close to defining the problem out of existence by indicating that an officer has engaged in racial profiling *only* when the single factor race/ethnicity is used to make a police decision. Such policies do not encompass many uses of race/ethnicity that most police and stakeholders alike would consider inappropriate. For instance, this definition in a policy would not prohibit an officer from making decisions based on two factors like race/ethnicity and gender (e.g., pulling over male drivers of Arab descent *because* they are males of Arab descent) or race and place (e.g., pulling over Blacks in White neighborhoods *because* they are Blacks in White neighborhoods). These "solely" policies not only lack meaningful guidance, they are detrimental to efforts to promote fair and impartial policing because they define the problem so narrowly that officers can decide that they are not committing the prohibited act and thereby separate themselves from the issue altogether.

The policies that provide more meaningful guidance reflect some significant differences of opinion as to when it is and is not "appropriate" to consider race or ethnicity. Two models that have been adopted by agencies are the "suspect-specific" model and the one set forth in a 2001 report of the Police Executive Research Forum (PERF; see Fridell et al., 2001, hereafter the "PERF report policy").[1] Both of these policies attempt to distinguish between the appropriate, or legally relevant, use of race/ethnicity in making decisions and the inappropriate use of race/ethnicity–when that usage is based on stereotypes and/or biases.

The suspect-specific model is more restrictive than the PERF report model: that is, it sets forth fewer circumstances when race/ethnicity can be used. The suspect-specific policies generally read as follows: Officers may not consider the race or ethnicity of a person in the course of any law enforcement action unless the officer is seeking to detain, apprehend, or otherwise be on the lookout for a specific suspect sought in connection with a specific crime who has been identified or described in part by race or ethnicity. The key to this model is that the set of identifiers — which includes reference to race/ethnicity — must be linked to a particular suspect who is being sought for a particular crime. Thus, if reliable witnesses describe a suspect in an ATM robbery as 5'10", black, lean, short-haired and wearing a red sweatshirt, "black" can be used along with the other information and with other evidence in developing reasonable suspicion to detain or probable cause to arrest.

The PERF report policy encompasses the suspect-specific provision, but allows for additional uses of race/ethnicity beyond the circumstances involving a "specific suspect" and a "specific crime." It reads: "Officers shall not consider race/ethnicity to establish reasonable suspicion or probable cause except that officers may take into account the reported race/ethnicity of a potential suspect(s) based on trustworthy, locally-relevant information that links a person or persons of a specific race/ethnicity to a particular unlawful incident(s)" (Fridell et al., 2001, p. 52). This provision disallows the use of race/ethnicity as a general indicator for or predictor of criminal behavior; it disallows the use of racial or ethnic stereotypes in making law enforcement decisions. It allows for the use of race/ethnicity when trustworthy local intelligence transforms those demographics into legally relevant descriptors.

A meaningful policy in the standard operating procedures of an agency — such as the two models described above is a necessary, but, again, not sufficient, accomplishment. It is also critically important for the agency to ensure that its personnel know and act in accordance with its content. All policy models require effective dissemination: some of the models (because they are complicated) require training to ensure that officers understand how to implement them. All require appropriately selected, well-trained supervisors to promote adherence to them.

Supervision

Sergeants, lieutenants, and captains wield the most powerful influence over the day-to-day activities, attitudes, and behaviors of street personnel. These supervisors should be selected based on criteria that promote the likelihood that they are able to reflect on their own biases, strong role models, and effective managers of people. The first-line supervisor has the responsibility to spot-check officer performance in a variety of circumstances, observing the style of verbal communication and quality of discretionary decision making and enforcement action. The supervisor must be alert to any pattern or practice of possible discriminatory treatment by individual officers or squads (through observation, information from fellow officers, or close review of complaints) and be willing and able to take appropriate action in response to inappropriate behavior (Fridell and Scott, 2005).

Supervisors need to be trained in how to identify officers who may be acting in a racially biased manner — including those well-meaning officers whose biased behavior may not be consciously produced. Supervisors should be challenged to think about how the implicit Black-crime association might manifest in their supervisees. As above, implicit racial bias might impact on any number of police decisions, including who is stopped by the officer for a traffic violation, from whom he requests consent to search, on whose license plate he runs a record check, of whom he asks "do you own this car?"

Supervisors also need guidance in how they should respond to officers who exhibit biased policing behaviors. Not only is biased behavior very difficult to prove through the traditional complaint review system, but, for the officers whose biased behavior is not intentional/malicious, "disciplinary" action would be inappropriate. Since, in many instances, there will only be "indications" and not "proof," it will be important to determine when and how supervisors can intervene to stop/prevent what appears to be inappropriate conduct while keeping in mind the ambiguous nature of the evidence as well as the sensitive nature of the issue.

Style of Policing

The research that supports the intergroup contact hypothesis has implications for the style of policing used by an agency. Peruche and Plant (2006) identified an inverse relationship between manifestations of bias on the part of police in laboratory settings and positive work and social interactions with diverse groups of people. Community policing promotes interaction with residents beyond the enforcement functions of the agency. One important principle of community policing is the long-term assignment of police personnel to geographic areas so that they can develop a comprehensive knowledge of those areas. Knowing many citizens by face and name improves officers' abilities to differentiate between suspicious and non-suspicious people on a basis other than race; getting to know the community's law-abiding citizens helps police overcome stereotypes based on characteristics such as race. The finding that cooperative interaction is the most potent form of contact for purposes of reducing bias highlights the potential value of problem-oriented policing wherein police and residents join together to identify and solve problems that produce crime and disorder.

CONCLUSIONS

Chief John Timoney (2004) of the Miami Police Department acknowledges that, "race is a factor in policing." That statement prompts the question: *How* is race a factor in policing? What are the mechanisms at work and how do they manifest in police behavior? What are the implications of those mechanisms and manifestations for police reform efforts? While much of the attention has been focused on officers who might intentionally discriminate against people of color, arguably too little attention has been paid to another source of police racial bias: unconscious, automatic implicit associations between race and crime. The NYPD officers who killed Amadou Diallo proclaimed that race was not a factor that affected their perceptions and response. Maybe race wasn't a factor in this incident; or maybe it *was* a factor — one that impacted perceptions and behavior below consciousness during the split-second period that the police had to decide to shoot or not.

Social psychological research has consistently confirmed the existence of Black-crime stereotypes that can operate implicitly, even in people who explicitly hold egalitarian, non-prejudiced views. The good news is that, if people are made aware of these automatic responses, they can override them with controlled responses producing non-prejudiced behavior. Further, some preliminary research indicates that the learned Black-crime association can be "unlearned" through repeated random pairings of race and threat. This important information can and should guide how law enforcement agencies respond to the issue of racially biased policing. Agencies need to respond to their "bad apples" who overtly, intentionally discriminate against people of color in the course of their work. They need to respond as well to the well-meaning officers who, like humans in every profession, are vulnerable to perceptions and behaviors consistent with the Black-crime association. An understanding of this phenomenon can guide agencies in deciding whom to hire, in developing training for recruits and supervisors and for firearms simulations, in providing guidance through policy on the "appropriate" use of race/ethnicity in making law enforcement decisions, and in deciding how to police the community in a manner that can reduce stereotypes and biases on the part of both police and community.

While the studies conducted to date give constructive direction to police reform efforts, additional research is needed. Most of the social psychological research on the race-crime association has used white college students as subjects and black people as the stereotype-promoting stimuli. Future research should broaden the subject pool to include other people of color and individuals from outside the college setting. More research should use police as subjects. Research should go beyond the focus on the Black-crime association, to explore automatic associations between, for instance, Hispanics and crime and people of Arab descent and crime. Building upon the work described here, studies should continue to explore the mechanisms by which individuals can overcome or weaken the race-crime association.

The issue of racially biased policing is hardly new. It has a long history and has produced tensions between police and the diverse communities they serve; it has produced very destructive and violent civil unrest. The law enforcement profession has made tremendous advances in recent decades in many realms and the prospect for continued reform to address bias in policing is great. In fact, the research-guided efforts implemented by the police profession may ultimately serve as a model for the other professions who hire humans.

NOTES

1. The Police Executive Research Forum, or "PERF," is a non-profit agency dedicated to the improvement of U.S. law enforcement. See *www.policeforum.org* for more information.

4. Perceptions of Bias-Based Policing: Implications for Police Policy and Practice

Brian N. Williams
Billy R. Close

This chapter examines the perceptions of police bias among African-American police officers and community residents. Our research explores whether African-American community residents and police officers express similar or divergent perceptions of policing. This question was explored via a content analysis of transcripts from 10 focus group discussions with 9 African-American police officers and 43 residents from a large southern U.S. city. The information obtained from these interviews yields important implications for police policy and practice related to local law enforcement training and the evaluation of police practices that impact the quality of African-American life.

Assessing citizen satisfaction with the development, delivery, and distribution of local governmental services is useful for evaluating, restructuring and implementing governmental policies. With the emergence of what some have described as the post-bureaucratic era (Heckscher, 1994; Maravelias, 2003; Josserand, Teo and Clegg, 2006) and its emphasis on alternative strategies for producing and delivering public services (Brudney and England, 1983; Savas, 1986; Ruchelman, 1989; Castells, 1996; Goldsmith and Eggers, 2006), assessing citizen satisfaction has become a more pressing concern. Citizen evaluations provide public officials with important cues about public perceptions of the performance of local agencies and oftentimes highlight barriers that hinder community involvement, citizen participation, and integration and collaboration between residents and service providers (Williams, 1998; 1999) — all of which are necessary ingredients in the co-production of public services (Whitaker, 1980).

Community Policing — The Co-Production of Public Safety and Public Order

Citizen evaluations of police practice and performance are especially important in community policing. Community policing, or the co-production of public safety and public order by police and the communities they serve (Williams, 1998; 1999), has emerged as the dominant approach to order maintenance and law enforcement. Over 75% of law enforcement agencies have indicated that they have adopted or plan to implement this approach to policing (Annan, 1995).[1] Community policing is often characterized as a philosophical approach that embraces two complementary components: community partnership and problem solving. As such, it has been described as a full-service approach to policing.

Cordner (1999) has noted four dimensions that describe the breadth of community policing — the philosophical, the strategic, the tactical, and the organizational dimensions. These dimensions seek to: increase community involvement and input; expand the role of law enforcement beyond crime fighting to include a much broader social service role or function; reintroduce personal service policing in place of bureaucratic behavior; reorient operations and emphasize proactive or preventive policing, coupled with geographic focus (mini or sub-stations); foster positive police-resident interactions and experiences; establish active partnerships between the police and vital institutional/organizational members of the community (local media, businesses, educational institutions, faith-based and other human service organizations, etc.); and adopt a problem-solving orientation toward policing via restructuring police agencies.

In theory, this approach stresses a closer working relationship between police agencies and the communities they serve, and requires reforming decision-making processes and creating a new culture within law enforcement agencies. Consequently, the police role and function have evolved, resulting in the transformation from more traditional reactive (responding to calls for service) and proactive (police-initiated activities) functions into a more "co-active" function that facilitates the police-community collaboration in the co-production of public safety and order.

Community policing's emphasis on co-activity and collaboration provides a justification for exploring both police and community perceptions of factors such as perceived racial bias in policing because such perceptions can interfere with the goals of community-oriented policing. To explore this issue, we examined several research questions: (1) What are the perceptions of African-American officers and African-American residents on bias-based policing? (2) Are there convergent or divergent patterns in these perceptions among African-American community residents and police officers? and, (3) What are the implications of these perceptions for police policy and practice as they affect the quality of African-American life?

Bias-Based Policing and Racial Profiling

Bias-based policing (BBP) is a term that refers to any form of bias — whether it involves race, religion, gender, age or sexual preference — that one might encounter from law enforcement officers during the performance of their duties. Research on traffic stops and searches served as the primary means of assessing bias-based policing practices.

In the late 1980s and early 1990s, researchers began studying the racial distribution of traffic stops to gauge the rate at which blacks were being stopped compared to the percentage of blacks driving the same stretch of road (Lamberth, 1996). Since that time, numerous studies have discovered that blacks and Latinos are substantially more likely to be stopped, questioned and/or searched compared to whites (Close and Mason, 2006; 2007; Meehan and Ponder, 2003; Smith and Petrocelli, 2001; Rojek, Rosenfeld, and Decker, 2004; Cordner, Williams, and Zuniga, 2000). These and other findings, coupled with the anecdotal evidence of minority motorists, have reinforced the belief that police officers engage in racial profiling.

Racial profiling has been defined by Ramirez, McDevitt, and Farrell (2000) as

> . . . any police-initiated action that relies on the race, ethnicity, or national origin rather than the behavior of an individual or information that leads the police to a particular individual who has been identified as being, or having been, engaged in criminal activity. (p. 3)

This association of race and/or ethnicity as a proxy for an increased likelihood of criminal behavior reflects Skolnick's (1975) conception of America's "symbolic assailant" and is symptomatic of the much larger issue of bias-based policing.

Even though a plethora of evidence highlights racial and ethnic disparities in traffic stops and searches, methodological shortcomings have made it difficult to conclusively state that the disparities associated with traffic stops and searches are a result of police departments engaging in discriminatory practices. These methodological shortcomings include difficulty in empirically identifying or determining the members of the driving public, inadequate data collection due to officer disengagement or lack of interest, and questions related to the accuracy and reliability of the data (Meehan and Ponder, 2002, Engle and Calnon 2004, Engle, Calnon, and Bernard 2002, Ramirez, McDevitt, and Farrell 2000, Smith and Alpert 2002). Nonetheless, perception is reality in the eyes of the beholders: hence, the allegations of racial profiling, and the perception of the police it creates among citizens, lessen the likelihood of meaningful collaboration between minority citizens and police with respect to the co-production of public safety and order.

STUDY SITE

A large city in the southeastern United States served as the study site for this research. This city's metropolitan statistical area (MSA) has a population exceeding 1.2 million people, with African Americans making up approximately 15% of the population (United States Census Bureau, 2000). The primary local law enforcement agency employs over 1,200 sworn officers. The agency's policing philosophy emphasizes community and problem-oriented policing approaches to the co-production of public safety and order, with a particular focus on neighborhood-based partnerships.

Research Design and Methodology

A qualitative, non-experimental design using focus group interviewing was used to collect information about the perceptions and attitudes of African-American police officers and community residents on community policing in general, and bias-based policing, in particular. More specifically, a hybrid clinical-phenomenological approach to focus group research[2] (Calder, 1977) was used. This hybrid form is appropriate when the researcher is out of touch with the reality or lived experiences of targeted subjects, an assumption that holds in this study.

A sequenced set of open-ended questions concerning the issues of community problems, trust or satisfaction with police services, awareness of community policing principles and practices, and experiences with neighborhood officers were used with community residents and police officers alike. Table 4.1 lists the questions that were posed to each focus group cohort. This format served as a stimulus for respondents of both populations — officers and community residents. In particular, it allowed participants to clarify their statements and share anecdotal evidence, while also allowing the researcher to probe responses of the participants with follow-up questions.

Focus Group Interviewing

Focus group interviewing is an extension of the non-directive interviewing style. It is directed toward eliciting the concerns, needs and feelings that underlie people's opinions and preferences. Six fundamental assumptions provide the basis for focus groups: (1) people are a valuable source of information; (2) people can report on and about themselves; (3) the focus group facilitator can help people retrieve forgotten information; (4) people who share a common problem will be more willing to talk amid the security of others who face that same problem; (5) group dynamics can generate valid information rather than establish group think; and, (6) utilizing a group interviewing format is more efficient than interviewing an individual (Stewart and Shamdasani,1990; Krueger, 1988). Participants in in-depth group interviews are selected because they form a purposive, but not a representative sample of a specific population (Stewart and Shamdasani, 1990).

Focus group interviewing is rooted in market research, but it has been effective in educational and social scientific research efforts (Byars and Wilcox, 1991; Krueger, 1988). Studies that utilize this approach highlight its advantages. Of particular note is its ability to capture rich data in large amounts. This yield of information is associated with the lessening of the control and domination by the researcher in order to get in touch with the lived and perceived realities of participants (Krueger, 1988; Morgan 1988). This approach has proven fruitful in providing a holistic understanding of the perceptions, experiences and attitudes of African Americans and other minorities (D'Amico-Samuels, 1990; Jarrett, 1993; Jenkins, 1995; Williams, 1998) and groups including the elderly, children, and illiterate and marginalized populations (Morgan, 1988; Byars and Wilcox, 1991; Krueger, 1988; Williams, 1998; 1999).

Notwithstanding these advantages, several limitations are also associated with the focus group method: difficulty in assembling groups; limited ability to generalize findings to a larger population due to the small sample

Table 4.1. Bias-Based Policing Focus Group Questions

Issue	Questions to Groups	
	Community Residents	Police Offiers
Community Problems	Thinking back over the past three years, what are the major problems facing this community?	Thinking back over the past three years, what would you consider the major problems facing the community that you serve?
Levels of Trust and Satisfaction	How do you feel about police services in this community? What would you like to see the police do?	How do you think the residents feel about police services you provide? What do you perceive influences their viewpoint on police services?
Enlightenment or Awareness of Bias-Based Policing	There have been some allegations of bias-based policing by the department. What are your views on this matter?	There are some in the community who have alleged that they have been the targets of bias-based policing. What are your views on this matter?
Perceptions of Bias-Based Policing	What are the *behaviors* of police officers that have made you feel uncomfortable or made you feel you were the target of bias-based policing or racial profiling?	Have you ever witnessed, heard of, or participated in any police actions that might lead the public to perceive that action was bias-based? What *behaviors* of police officers might make citizens feel uncomfortable or feel they were the target of racial profiling?
Empowerment or Community Suggested Improvements	What can or should the police do to provide better police services to residents of your community and minimize the allegations of bias-based policing? Have you ever expressed these suggestions to the police?	How do you feel about the level of citizen/community involvement in combating the problems facing this community? If any, what suggestions have individuals or community groups offered to improve the police-community relationship?

size; biasing of the focus group discussion by the moderator or facilitator; and emergence of "group think" due to the interactions of the participants. In this study, the researcher attempted to decrease the likelihood of moderator-generated bias and domination by a single group participant by controlling body movements, facial expressions and voice inflections, as well as by ensuring that all participants had an opportunity to express their perceptions, attitudes, and experiences.

Focus Groups and Discussion Sites

This study included two groups of African Americans: police officers and community residents. All focus group discussants, both officers and community residents, volunteered to participate in this study. This project was supported by the local police department, which encouraged officers to participate, as well as by key individuals, organizations, and institutions within the community (e.g., the local affiliate of the National Urban League, community activists, elected representatives of public housing residential associations, pastors of neighborhood churches, etc.).

The African-American police officers were divided into two focus groups: male officers (n=5) and female officers (n=4). Eight focus groups of African-American community residents were formed: two groups of male adults (n=10), three groups of female adults (n=18), two groups of male youth (n=10), and one group of female youth (n=5). Adult focus groups consisted of residents 26 years-old and older, while youth focus groups consisted of residents between the ages of 18 and 25 years old. Seven of the eight different groups of African-American residents who participated in focus group discussions resided in or near public housing, and these participants considered themselves "working class." Members of the sole group of African-American male adults who didn't reside in or near public housing were college graduates and considered themselves "middle class."

All focus group discussions took place at locations or facilities that would facilitate the free disclosure of information (e.g., the conference rooms of neighborhood or community centers, at an apartment of a participant, at a local church). These locations were selected to provide an increased comfort level that would facilitate the disclosure of information.

Data Breakdown and Analysis

Group discussions were audiotaped and transcribed. In order to get a more intimate feel for the data, a manual approach to capturing the content and context of group discussions was used in lieu of a computer-assisted approach. In conjunction with this manual approach, an interpretive process (Knodel, 1993; Morgan, 1988) was utilized to determine the criteria for arranging the textual data into analytically useful subdivisions. This process facilitated the use of a two-step approach to data breakdown, which leveraged the cut-and-paste and scissor-and-sort technique described by Morgan (1988) and Stewart and Shamdasani (1990). First, this process yielded two major categories for each group discussion: (1) *major incidents and experiences* of participants, and (2) *prevailing perceptions* of participants. Second, from these incidents and experiences, emerging themes were then identified.

A combined ethnographic/content analysis approach was used to analyze the resulting data and leverage the strength associated with an ethnographic summary — the richness of using direct quotes from group discussions — and the more precise coding of information that is the strength of content analysis. This combination mirrored approaches to earlier research (Krippendorf, 1980; Morgan, 1988; Williams, 1998; 1999) and enabled the researcher to describe, in explicit detail, the focus group discussions by using direct quotations as well as counting and coding the frequency of words and phrases. This helped to identify group themes and perceptions. Those themes that surfaced and cut across all group discussions were then highlighted for additional analysis and interpretation.

RESULTS: THE EMERGENCE AND CONVERGENCE OF THEMES

Several themes emerged from the focus group discussions. Three themes cut across the African-American police officers and African-American resident groups. These themes included: (a) bias-based activities as a social construction that transcends the professional boundaries of policing; (b) lack of respect for poorer residents and neighborhoods; and, (c) impersonal, infrequent, and negative police-resident interactions and encounters. Each theme is elaborated upon below.

Bias-Based Perceptions and Actions as a Social Construction

Loury (2002) defines race as

> A cluster of inheritable bodily markings carried by a largely endogamous group of individuals, markings that can be observed by others

> with ease, that can be changed or misrepresented only with great difficulty, and that have come to be invested in a particular society at a given historical moment with social meaning. (p. 20)

This definition highlights the social construction of race reflected in: (1) the relative ease with which people identify members of the "other" races; (2) the relative immutability or unchanging quality of this construct of the different races; and (3) the very great social importance or consequence of these racial designations. Moreover, it underscores how physical traits within the American context are taken to signify something of import, oftentimes based upon an historical context. As such, Loury's concept of "race" connects with Goffman's (1963) definition of "stigma" as those "bodily signs designed to expose something unusual and bad about the moral status of the signifier" (p. 1) and that results in biased social cognition or

> politically consequential cognitive distortion to ascribe the disadvantage to be observed among a group of people to qualities thought to be intrinsic to that group when, in fact, that disadvantage is the product of a system of social interactions. (Loury, 2002, p. 26)

The first theme that emerged and converged across officer and resident focus groups was that bias-based perceptions and activities were a result of the social construction of race — the concept that race as we know is not a biological construction but a societal one that has been constructed and supported by the powerful members and institutions of American society or culture. Moreover, these perceptions and actions were not limited to the policing profession, a particular segment of the police department (e.g., male officers or female officers), or a particular segment of the population (e.g. members of one gender or socio-economic class). This theme surfaced in multiple ways, including that bias-based perceptions and actions were a result of exposure to the "media," popular culture and the policing profession, inclusive of its culture.

> *Male Officer #1*: Let's say [racial] profiling ... if you look at it, profiling has been done for a long time. It's not just only blacks that have been profiled ... other cultures have been profiled too ... there are certain points that may make profiling more susceptible to a particular culture or nationality. Just think about how some cultures, nationalities and races are portrayed on television, in the movies, in cartoons, on the news. I think that kind of shapes how we [society and cops] look at people, what we think about them ...
>
> *Male Officer #3*: As cops, sometimes you have to do some degree of it [profiling] because that's one of the instincts that we have, that

we [cops] pick up over the years if you stay in it [policing] long enough. Profiling will come to you [as a black officer] to a certain degree like anybody else . . .

Male Officer #2: Sometimes it's [profiling and bias-based actions] just what you've been exposed to . . . we get some officers on the department . . . who've been home with mom and dad, mostly white officers, because that's what the department mostly consists of, and they've never been exposed to anything, you know, diverse things . . . when they get out here, you know, they've probably been introduced to a lot of stereotypes that been indoctrinated into them and they go by them . . .

Older Male Resident #5: I think that there is a learned behavior [on the parts of police officers] that comes along with more than one African-American in the car . . . because of the way many of those individuals [blacks] are portrayed in movies and TV programs . . . many times, unfortunately, when we see individuals that have the so-to-speak "gold grill," we tend to subjectively associate those individuals with the drug environment or the gangster environment.

Older Male Resident #3: When you look at stuff on TV and most of the folks that are stopped, you know a lot of times on the news, a lot of blacks are being stopped or talked about in connection with crimes, drug crimes in particular. I think they [the police officer] look at that, you know you look at the news and it gives you that profile . . . it might support the profiling behavior.

Older Male Resident #2: With my job, I encounter kids that now are enrolled in college . . . Some of them [black males] that I see . . . when you look at them, your first inclination is, "Do you really belong here? Are you out of place?" But then you have to bring yourself back to, you know, who am I to really tell you how to dress, what to wear, how to look? Why do I look and think about them [black males] that way?

Older Male Resident #1: I saw a pamphlet that had something to do with gangs. When I opened that up, I saw things "like wear baggy pants," "have skull caps with their favorite team logos on their skull caps." I saw terminology that they use amongst each other, you know, some slang and that sort of stuff. When I read it, I thought "Wow, man, that could be 40-50% of African-American males in the city. . . . " It's like if you are black and dress I guess by the hip-hop standard, the police might look at you like you are a gangster. My question is: how come the police think that about black guys who dress that way? How come we think that about black guys who dress that way?

Male Youth #7: You're judged off the top around in this community. The police is already programmed in their head a certain way. If you're over in the projects, you're doing something wrong. If you're driving a nice vehicle, you're doing something wrong. It already is programmed in them . . . It's like when they see us they think the worst. I don't know if it's because if they only work in the black neighborhood and arrest black people, they begin thinking that all black people are like that. Or, when you look at the 10 o'clock news, you see a lot of stuff about us. Now we all know that there are other folks [races] doing the same if not worse things . . . but somehow, when one of us do it, we all get associated with it . . . you know, drugs is a black problem, gambling is a black problem, shootings is a black problem . . .

Older Female Resident #12: My oldest son was coming home from work. They stopped him and told him to put his hands up and everything. And right at the back door . . . they searched him and everything . . . they was going to put him in handcuffs until I came to the door and said, "He's a resident here. He don't sell drugs. He just came home from work. Can you not smell them hamburgers and onions?" You know, he just had ketchup all over his shirt. He had a uniform on and they was just harassing him on the back porch . . . He's not a drug dealer . . . I don't know why they would think he was. It's almost like every young black boy who lives here is caught up in the drug game. There are a lot of nice kids who live in this neighborhood . . .

Female Officer #2: It [profiling] is not only white officers. It's black officers too. Because you hear them say, "Well, he must be doing something to drive that vehicle." The assumption is there that we can't have African-American males with affluent parents, whose car they're driving. Or, they can't be an entrepreneur or hard working person and actually own that vehicle or be purchasing that vehicle. It's like if you're driving this, then you must be involved in something illegal. And the unfortunate thing about it is it is not only the thoughts. Those thoughts don't only come from people other than African-Americans, people other than whites but black people think that about black people too. That's what really concerns me. I think we bought into the thoughts processes of other people about our own people. We kind of let society change our own views about us . . .

Lack of Respect for Poorer Residents and Neighborhoods

A perceived lack of respect reflected in the tactics of patrol officers and policies of police departments toward marginalized or stigmatized populations has been a dominant theme in the annals of scholarly research on police. Previous studies have concluded that poor, disadvantaged, black residents perceive a lack of respect by police officers and, as a result, black residents rate policing service quality far lower than their white counterparts (Fogelson, 1968; Bordua and Tifft, 1971; Hahn, 1971; Jacob, 1971; Rossi, Beck and Eidson, 1974; Cooper, 1980; Webb and Marshall, 1995; Williams, 1998; 1999; Weitzer and Tuch, 1999).

In both the officer and resident focus group discussions in our study, this perceived lack of respect was articulated in reference both to black people in general, and poorer black communities in particular. Even though this theme traversed the officer and resident boundary, the perception of lack of respect was more pronounced in African-American younger and older male resident focus groups.

Female Officer #4: We've [local police department] got some educated idiots out there. You know, they don't know anything about someone other than themselves ... and half of them don't know anything about themselves ... I know one of my [white] training officers when I first came out, she used the "N" word like it was nothing. I was shocked. I was shocked that she said that to a guy [suspect] ... I'll never forget it. And when she said that, I just looked at her ... I think they ended up letting the guy go. But all I remember is when we went back to the station I told them that I couldn't ride with her. And her thing was, "Well, I'm from so and so. I've never been around black people."

Older Male Resident #10: If you lived in —[exclusive neighborhoods] you wouldn't get harassed like you do in [public] housing. Even if you got stopped out there, it would be a more respect thing than if you got stopped in these projects. They're [the police] going to talk to you more about it. "Sir, I stopped you for" so and so, such and such. So you know, "Could I see you license, your insurance" ... But if you got stopped in this community over here, a whole lot more things is going to go on. And it ain't going to be no "Sir, let me see your license" but "Get out of that car!!! Get out of the car!!! Put you hands behind your back!! Spread your legs!!"

Male Officer #5: Before I left the streets, I worked in an area where there was a housing project ... and there was a big deal about the stats [number of arrests], and I was watching all the other boys making them stats, but they were making them illegal stats. No probable cause ... mighty trumped up charges just to say, "Hey Sarge, I've got this paperwork over here." And I remember one day at roll call I'd just had enough about the stats. I confronted the Sarge in front of everybody. And I said, "Sarge, you know the reason these guys got these stats is because they're going around the corner getting them in the wrong kind of way." I'm not going to go out of the way to get no stats ...

Older Female Resident #7: Sometimes you just need to watch them [patrol officers]. Just look at them . . . . I mean look at their attitudes. Their attitudes say, "This is the projects. You've got to be drug dealers." It's not true! That's not true! You don't have to be a drug dealer if you live in the projects . . .

Young Male Resident #8: It's [profiling] bad. It's real bad. Especially in the projects . . . you're treated totally different. And if you was in the suburbs or living somewhere better, it would be totally different . . . You know when you're in the projects and your being stopped or whatever, you must be doing something wrong. This is just their [patrol officers] thinking, especially if you are a black man . . .

Female Officer #3: My mom had a nice vehicle. I've only driven her vehicle probably a handful of times in town, but I remember one incident. We [the officer and her friends] were going to —[local black college] for a parade and for no apparent reason, we were pulled over. And of course when the officer came, I had to show him my badge . . . Once I came to a scene and they [police officers] had two cars stopped in the middle of the road and a wrecker was loading this nice BMW on top of it. There was a black officer and a white officer. The white one said, "The dope business must be good." I said, "Oh, yeah?" He said, "Yeah. You see that car he's driving. You see how he looks . . . " And I said, "Oh yeah. Is he a dope dealer?" He said, "I don't know." I said, "Do you know him?" He said, "No.." I said, "Well how do you know he's a dope dealer?" He just looked at me. I said, "Put that car down. You can't give me any reason why you're towing the man's car? You've got him in the back of your car and handcuffed, but you don't know why?"

Young Male Resident #3: From day one, you're getting harassed. You might have been coming to visit someone. Before you can get out of your car, them folk [the cops] probably will snatch you up walking to someone's house. Now, you're stretched out just for visiting a person because they live in the projects. . . .

Young Male Resident #6: Everybody who lives here got to suffer. Everybody suffers because really they're getting to the point that if you live in [public] housing you really don't have no rights. They can just walk in your house like you don't even live there. They've got more power in your house than you do . . . just because I'm living in the projects, it's still my home.

Male Officer #1: I think profiling is good, but I think where the problem comes in is where officers . . . take advantage of the situation. Where I work, I profile. I work in the projects. We get a white person coming in . . . a white female or male black and they have out of county tags, you know something's going down. They're getting ready to buy

... probably some narcotics. But I just can't stop them because of that. I have to find a reason to stop them. But I think officers should use profiling as a tool but not to take advantage of people. And that's the sad part about it. They take advantage of people by using a profile.

Young Male Resident #4: The community is really becoming an inner-city jail. Really!! That's what it's coming down to around here ... because as you can see, they're putting bars up everywhere [fencing around public housing development]. How can you lock a person up in their own house? They [the police] are labeling this as a drug community, high crime area, however they want to put it. That is why it is becoming a jail ...

Older Male Resident #8: ... Man, I just want to be respected. I come to get my son every day off from work. I was getting stopped every day. And I told them the first time they stopped me ... I said, "I'll be out here every day at this time officer. You don't have to write anymore [tickets]. Everyday I have a son and everyday I have to come and get him" ... Almost every day I was being harassed. I just wish that they treat a man or woman just like they'd want to be treated. It's their job to protect and serve. It isn't their job to haze, to jump down our throats ...

Random, Infrequent and/or Negative Interactions

Murty, Roebuck and Smith (1990) suggested that positive images of the police are necessary for the police to function effectively and efficiently. Their findings are even more relevant to community and problem-oriented policing and community-oriented governance. In particular, these positive images can be created and reinforced or irreparably harmed and dismissed during police-citizen encounters and interactions. Hence, the quality of police-citizen contacts and interactions is of paramount importance and has been found to affect public attitudes toward the police (ATP) and citizen satisfaction with police officers and their departments (Williams, 1998; 1999; Brandl, Frank, Worden and Bynum, 1994; Scaglion and Condon, 1980; Cooper, 1980; Campbell and Schuman, 1972; Brunson and Miller, 2006).

In this study, the theme of random, impersonal and/or negative interactions surfaced in all group discussions, and while more pronounced in the residents' focus group discussions, its emergence within the officer discussions signifies it importance.

Female Officer #2: Sometimes it is difficult to serve as "Officer Friendly" when you have to arrest people. It's sad but true that oftentimes that may be the only time you interact with the people, you know, when you make an arrest or come to a home because of some kind of disturbance. I mean, I often think of the damage we do in terms of police and community relations when we have to do the order maintenance or law enforcement part of our jobs. I am not sure if some family members, say, like children, can understand that part of our jobs. One of the strategies I have used [when kids are present] is I try not to talk bad about mommy or daddy or big brother or uncle. I just tell the kid that mommy or daddy or whoever made a bad decision and we have to take them downtown to talk to them about the decision they made . . .

Male Officer #1: One of the reasons . . . people might look at us in a negative way is because we may not take the needed time to get to know the people that we are working for . . . you know the people we are trying to serve and protect. We have talked a little bit about the pressure to get the stats or get the job done and I think that that pressure impacts how much time you can put into getting to know the community and the community getting to know you. As a result, the contact that we do have with the community is what I call negative contact and not positive contact. You know, we are trained to think about officer safety during these interactions so we may not be putting our happy faces on. Your adrenaline is flowing, you are on guard and I think that can be kind of intimidating to the people. . . .

Female Officer #3: I used to work in ——-on bike patrol. Every morning we would get over there and by having the bikes we were able to interact with the residents of that housing project a little more. We were able to say hello, you know, do some small talk with the adults and the kids. You know the patrol car can serve as a barrier. It can put distance between us and them . . . After a while those people . . . well they really cared. They'd start having us coffee, grits, and eggs. And you know, it made us feel like they really believed that we're working for them, which we were . . . I think the more we can get that type of interaction going, the better things will be. I really think it would make our jobs easier . . .

Female Officer #1: . . . I think they [the community] really like the community-oriented policing concept. They like to know that the police have a little substation nearby where the community can come and converse with the people and discuss whatever problems or concerns they may have . . . they [community residents] like to be able to speak with them, have a good rapport with them . . . They want the officers . . . instead of riding by, to get out and talk with them. That's what they [community residents] tell me.

Residents, however, expressed views that could promote discord between the police and communities they serve:

Young Male Resident #10: You know, sometimes I hate to see a cop because I am always wondering what does he see me as . . . one of the guys has already said that he thinks they [the police] are already programmed against us and I agree with him. You know what you are going to get when you get stopped by them. I just wish that that they could just get to know us . . . Tell them to take their badges off. Tell them to come to the community and take their badges off. Why don't they come and get to know us as people? You know, get to know us as folk . . .

Young Male Resident #7: The problem I have is the only time they interact with you is when you might fit a description or they might have some questions. I don't like that. Man, don't treat me like no criminal, treat me like a man . . . I try to do the best I can, you know to treat people right because I want to be treated right, but every time you interact with them, they look at you like you some kind of criminal. . . .

Young Female Resident #3: I can recall a couple of times where they [the police] haven't been, I guess, on the job . . . you know when they weren't stopping to check you out, or to ask you questions, but were just stopping to say hello and try to get to know you. One time one gave me a card with his name on it and just said if there was any time that we needed him just to pick up the phone and call him . . . I liked that, you know, I felt good to have a cop like that who worked over here . . . I guess he was transferred or something because I haven't seen him in years, but we need more cops who say hello, who try to get to know people, and let people try to get to know them too. . . .

Thematic Summary — The Power and Pervasiveness of Stigma

As previously noted, focus group interviewing is not designed to reach consensus but to examine the diverse perceptions, attitudes, and opinions of participants regarding a particular topic of discussion. However, in this study, consensus was reached by the emergence of three themes that cut across and connected the different groups of African-American police officers and residents regarding their perceptions of community policing, in general, and bias-based policing, in particular.

Figure 4-1 provides a schematic depiction of the interaction of these themes. During the analysis of transcript data, the impact of popular culture, particularly its effect on the local media (i.e., images that popular culture projects of African-American people and the communities in which some

Figure 4-1: The Power and Pervasiveness of Stigma

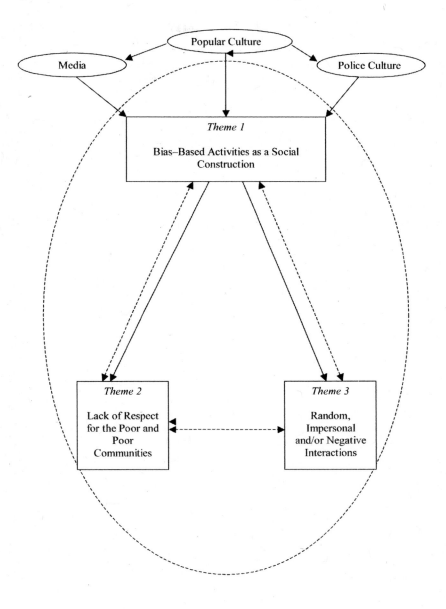

may reside), and its influence and impression on police or departmental culture, became obvious. Popular culture appeared to impact the shared perceptions held by officers and residents of Theme 1: bias-based policing activities being a result of the social construction of race. Theme 1 influences (signified by the single-arrows) seem to become manifest in two ways: through Themes 2 (lack of respect for the poor and poor communities) and 3 (impersonal and/or negative interactions between the police and community residents).

These three themes also seem to reinforce each other, as symbolized by the segmented lines with arrows in both directions. In particular, Theme 1 reinforces Themes 2 and 3, which in turn reinforce Theme 1, as well as each other. In essence, this interplay and connection of themes across the various focus groups speaks to the power and pervasiveness of stigma. These findings provide the context for some additional discussion related to important implications for police policy and police practice. These implications for police policy and police practice can and do impact the quality of African-American life.

IMPLICATIONS

This study employed focus group interviewing to explore the perceptions of African-American residents and police officers concerning community policing in general, and bias-based policing, in particular. Strikingly, what emerged from the focus group analysis was a consensus and convergence of three themes that spanned the police-resident divide. These themes speak to the power and pervasiveness of stigma. Moreover these shared, cross-group perceptions carry important implications related to the policies and practices of the police organization. These implications, if properly addressed, can impact and improve the quality of African-American life within this city.

Police and Community Training: Since the onset of community policing and its emphasis on the co-production of public safety and public order, a clarion call for more extensive training for both police officers and community members has been continuous (Brown, 1992; Miller and Hess, 1994; McLaughlin and Donahue, 1995, Williams, 1998; 1999). The findings from this study — in particular, the random, impersonal, and often negative interactions and the perceived lack of respect for poor residents and poor communities — highlight the need for additional training of officers and community residents.

As discussed earlier, contemporary policing is collaborative in nature. As such, there has been an emphasis on partnering with communities to better understand and problem-solve community issues and concerns. Facilitating this "ends" approach to the co-production of public safety and public order requires a collaborative "means" approach to training. This collaborative "means" approach to training must leverage strategies that can dispel the negative myths and misperceptions of residents and officers alike, open channels of communications across the multifarious divides (professional, social economic, racial, gender, etc.), and foster a greater understanding and appreciation between the two principals in this co-productive arrangement — police and residents. Consequently, more emphasis should be placed on generating graduates, in general, and African-American graduates, in particular, of Citizen Police Academies. Citizen Police Academies involve programmatic activities sponsored by local police departments designed to produce informed citizens through a limited immersion into the professional lives of police officers. Citizens are exposed to the rules, regulations, and policies that police officers must follow. The intent of these programs is to open the lines of communication between the police and the community (see, *www.nationalcpaa.org*).

Equally important are Police Citizen Academies, or community-based training arrangements where residents can facilitate the learning process for officers who are assigned to their communities and neighborhoods. By leveraging Citizen Police Academies and Police Citizen Academies alike, a greater understanding of the lived experience of the "other" can emerge and provide some insight on how the actions and inactions of officers and residents alike can be perceived and misinterpreted by each other.

An added value that accompanies the emphasis placed on facilitating a greater understanding of the "other" via these academies is the newfound knowledge that can be generated from these experiences. The infusion of this new knowledge within the training curriculum of pre-and in-service officers could be extremely beneficial to the officers, the department, and the community. This coupling of professionally or institutionally-oriented and based skills and values presently contained within the training efforts of the department, with community-oriented and -based skills and values that emerge from the Police Citizen Academy experiences and interactions, could begin the process of deconstructing the very pronounced social construction that accompanies race and social economic status found within this study.

Evaluation of Performance. The findings from this study also have implications for the evaluation of police performance. As noted in Figure 4-1, popular culture impacts bias-based activities as a consequence of the social construction of race. In turn, Theme 1 supports Themes 2 and 3 (e.g., perceived lack of respect for poorer residents and neighborhoods and random, impersonal and/or negative interactions). Yet, what also seems evident from this analysis is the relevance of the officer's pressure to perform, or as described by one participant, to "get them stats," on all three themes. This pressure may be the catalyst that fuels the perception of lack of respect, encourages the frequency and perceived randomness of impersonal and negative interactions, which, in turn supports and reinforces the perception of bias-based activities as a consequence of the social construction of race.

An approach to negate this pressure to perform requires a revision in the evaluation of officer performance. Selected quotes from the transcripts of focus group discussions describe this pressure from the officers' perspective, but also the impact of this pressure from the perspectives of residents. To address this issue and its adverse impact on the perceptions of officers and residents who participated in this study and ultimately the effective co-production of public safety and public order brings into focus the need for an integrated approach to the appraisal or evaluation of officer performance. Outcome-based performance measures need to be identified, incorporated and included with the more traditional output-based approach to evaluating officer performance currently used by the department. The development of outcome-based performance measures (e.g., the results, accomplishments, and impact of police action) and the reevaluation of output-based measures (e.g., the number of products and services produced by police action) as well, should reflect the collaborative framework (i.e., community and police) that is part and parcel of the community policing philosophy (Schalock and Bonham, 2003; Schalock, 2001; Ottemeir and Wycoff, 1988; 1997).

CONCLUSION

Irving Goffman (1963) described three different types of stigma: physical deformities, blemishes of individual character, and the tribal stigma associated with race, religion and nation of origin. The findings from this study are solely concerned with the latter: the "undesired differentness" of the tribal stigma of race. This "undesired differentness" impacts the stigmatized person (or community) as well as the attitudes and behaviors of "normals" (or those governmental agents) who interact with the stigmatized person or community. As Goffman (1963, p. 5) noted:

> We believe the person with a stigma is not quite human. On this assumption we exercise varieties of discrimination, through which we effectively, if often unthinkingly, reduce his life chances. We construct a stigma-theory, an ideology to explain his inferiority and account for the danger he represents, sometimes rationalizing an animosity based on other differences, such as those of social class.

The "normals" in the context of this study are African-American police officers and the stigmatized population is African-American residents. Nonetheless, both groups share perceptions which coalesce and highlight the power and pervasiveness of stigma.

Like Loury's *Anatomy of Racial Inequality* (2002), the findings of this study speak to the impact of the social signification and consequence of race. The resulting analysis of the perceptions shared by officers and residents alike elucidates the power, pervasiveness and impact of stigma, even when the stigma of race is shared by the agents of government. These findings offer important implications for police policy and practice in hopes of negating the adverse impact on collaborative efforts between the police department and African-American residents of the community in question. A revision of this sort will require political will on the parts of elected officials, as well as effective departmental leadership and management. The impact of such revisions can enhance the co-production of public safety and public order and improve the quality of life, both personally and professionally.

NOTES

1. A Bureau of Justice Statistics Special Report by Hickman and Reaves (2001) noted that as of 1999 an overwhelming majority of police agencies had invested heavily in community policing. In particular, 87% of all local police officers were employed by departments that provided community policing training for some or all new recruits, and the number of community policing officers at the local level had increased from 16,000 in 1997 to 91,000 in 1999.
2. The hybrid, clinical-phenomenological approach to focus group research allows the researcher to examine participants who are not amenable to personal surveys or direct observations.

5. Race, Ethnicity and Sentencing

Amy Farrell
Donna M. Bishop

Over the past century, significant efforts have been made to understand the effects of race on criminal justice processing and sentencing. As a result of this research, sentencing policies have undergone numerous periods of reform. Yet, racial disparities in sentence outcomes and incarceration rates continue to give rise to serious questions about how and through what processes race continues to affect sentencing outcomes. This chapter reviews the scholarly research on race and sentencing, and discusses a number of important sentencing reforms that have taken place in the U.S. over the past three decades in response to evidence of disparate racial treatment and to pressure from advocates for reform.

Following widespread sentencing reforms, such as the adoption of federal and state sentencing guidelines, researchers have continued to examine the complex role of race in the sentencing process. In addition to reviewing empirical research, this chapter also explores theoretical frameworks that can be used to understand differences in sentence outcomes by race or ethnicity and examines the interaction of defendant race with other important micro-and macro-level characteristics. Finally, we discuss a number of the implications of racially and ethnically disparate sentencing outcomes for research and policy.

The potential for racial bias to influence sentencing and imprisonment threatens core principles of fairness and equality under the law. As a result, researchers, policy makers and legal advocates have devoted significant attention to questions about what role race plays in the sentencing process and to policies that might reduce racial bias in sentencing. Despite significant efforts to understand and address this vexing problem, new evidence suggests that rising incarceration rates over the past few decades have exacerbated racial disparities in imprisonment. Black inmates now constitute roughly 38% of the nearly 2.2 million people incarcerated in U.S.

prisons and jails (Bureau of Justice Statistics [BJS], 2007), where they are overrepresented relative to other populations. For instance, there are 3,042 black male inmates per 100,000 black males in the United States, compared to 1,261 Hispanic male inmates per 100,000 Hispanic males, and 487 white male inmates per 100,000 white males (BJS, 2007). Today, black defendants serve as much time in federal prison for drug offenses as white defendants serve for violent offenses — a result largely attributable to biases in federal statutory penalties for offenses involving crack versus powder cocaine (Mauer and King, 2007a). Understanding why, how, and under what contexts defendant race affects sentencing decisions is crucial to addressing such disparate outcomes.

EARLY RESEARCH ON RACE AND SENTENCING

Since the early 20th century, scholars have grappled with questions about the existence of racially discriminatory case processing practices and the potential for differential criminal sentences being imposed on racial and ethnic minorities. Early research on the role of race and ethnicity in criminal sentencing was more descriptive than theoretical. The methodologies involved in early studies were weak, and when theoretical explanations were offered, they often entailed unsophisticated notions of individual prejudice and racial discrimination. For example, Thorsten Sellin (1935) conducted simple comparisons of the average length of sentences given to black, native-born and foreign-born white male prisoners within very broad offense categories. Sellin claimed that the data revealed "the marked influence of race and nationality prejudice in the administration of justice" (p. 212). He concluded that, in light of the prejudice against blacks and the foreign born within the society at large, "it would be denying to the judge the ordinary attributes of human nature to assume that he could render justice free from all preconceptions" (ibid.).

Early studies such as Sellin's were seriously flawed. They analyzed sentencing data within broad offense categories and did not control adequately for the seriousness of the offense or the offender's prior record. Further, they drew sweeping inferences from the data that have not been supported by empirical research. In recent years, significant advances have been made both in the methodological sophistication of research designs, and in the development of more complex theoretical frameworks that enhance our understanding of the factors that contribute to racially disparate sentencing outcomes and the manner in which they operate. Yet, understanding the effect of race on sentence outcomes is a complex undertaking. Bias is one of several potential explanations of racial differences in sentence outcomes or rates of imprisonment. Racial differences in sentence outcomes may be explained by legitimate legal differences, such as differences in the type or severity of crimes committed by different groups. As statistical designs have become more sophisticated over time, researchers have begun to account for some of these racially disparate, but legally relevant, causes of disparity. Despite these advances in our ability to study the phenomena of race and sentencing, researchers remain divided about how race — and the interaction of race and other factors — influence sentence outcomes.

Since researchers developed the ability to control for the independent effects of legal factors (e.g. criminal history, severity of offense) and extra-legal factors (e.g., defendant race, gender, class, education) on sentencing outcomes, findings about the role of race in sentencing have been mixed. Some research suggests that racial or ethnic minorities are sentenced more harshly than whites, even after controlling for legally relevant factors (Albonetti, 1997; Kramer and Steffensmeier, 1993; Klein, Turner et al., 1988). Conversely, other research has concluded that racial differences in sentence outcomes can be explained by legally relevant factors (Myers and Talarico, 1986; Wilbanks, 1987). Attempts to summarize the large body of scholarship on race and sentencing (both before and after sentencing reforms) indicate that inconsistent findings are largely attributable to differences among studies in methodology, types of data, sampling and regional variation (Chiricos and Crawford, 1995; Hagan and Bumiller, 1983; Kleck, 1981; Spohn, 2000; Tonry, 1995).

In 2004, Mitchell and McKenzie conducted a formal meta-analysis of 85 different studies on race and sentencing. They concluded, after taking into account legally relevant variables such as defendant criminal history and offense seriousness, that Black and Hispanic defendants were generally sentenced more harshly than white defendants. While they found that legal factors were the strongest predictors of sentencing outcomes, race continued to have a modest, but statistically significant effect. That is, racial differences persisted, and this persistence is difficult to understand especially once legally relevant sources of variation are addressed.

These findings are complicated further by research evidence that race influences sentence outcomes not only directly, but indirectly, through interaction with other extra-legal factors such as ethnicity, gender, class and age (see Zatz, 2000, for a comprehensive review), and by legally relevant factors such as prior criminal record, charging decisions and bail status (Spohn et al., 1981).

Advances in research design and methodology have not put to rest nagging concerns about racial inequality in criminal justice processing. Instead, they have suggested that the connections between race and sentencing outcomes are exceedingly complex, conditioned by a diverse set of variables, including characteristics of the defendant, the victim, the crime itself and the geographical area where it took place, as well as the bureaucratic organization of local courts, the culture of courtroom workgroups, and even broader features of the social and political environments in which case processing takes place.

THE SENTENCING REFORM MOVEMENT AND THE ADVENT OF STRUCTURED SENTENCING SYSTEMS

Numerous reforms to sentencing policy, such as the development of sentencing guidelines and "structured sentencing" models (see section on "The Sentencing Reform Movement" below), were introduced between the late 1970s and early 1990s to neutralize the perceived effect of defendant characteristics on sentence outcomes, which were most often attributed to the enormous discretion accorded judges under indeterminate sentencing schemes (Tonry, 1995). In reaction to perceived inequalities in the federal and state sentencing systems, social and legal scholars pressed for legislation that would replace indeterminate sentencing with a system that offered greater predictability in determining proper sentence dispositions and lengths of imprisonment (Frankel, 1973; von Hirsch, 1976; Kennedy 1979).

During the 1970s and early 1980s, a number of scholarly studies were published that revealed a lack of uniformity in judicial sentencing and parole practices in both federal and state courts. One of the most interesting and illuminating of these studies was conducted in the federal Second Circuit courts in the mid-1970s (Partridge and Eldridge, 1974). In this study, 50 district court judges from the second circuit, which includes the federal districts in New York and Connecticut, were given a set of identical criminal files and instructed to indicate a sentence for each case. The "hypothetical" sentences imposed by the 50 judges varied dramatically for each test case. For example, the "hypothetical" sentences given in a bank robbery case ranged from five years' imprisonment to eighteen years' imprisonment.

In addition to exposing stark disparities in sentencing practices among individual judges, a number of studies concluded that sentencing disparities were highly correlated with individual characteristics of defendants, such as race, gender, education, and income (Hagan, 1974; Tiffany, 1975; Lortz and Hewitt, 1977; Farrell and Swigert, 1978; Sutton, 1978). These studies suggested that judicial discretion produced wide variations in sentence outcomes across different judges, which often resulted in race, class, and gender disparities in sentencing.

The Sentencing Reform Movement

Sentencing reformers advocated for structured systems that limited judicial discretion with the expectation that these would create certainty in sentencing outcomes and increase the transparency and legitimacy of sentencing processes (Stith and Cabranes, 1998). This movement was part of a broader shift toward formalism and rationalization in American criminal law. Substantive criminal law and criminal procedure underwent major revisions during the 1960s, setting the stage for broad-based sentencing reform. In 1965, the American Law Institute drafted the Model Penal Code (MPC) in an attempt to standardize criminal law. The MPC provided a template of definitions of crimes and their elements for states to adopt. Simultaneously, the United States Supreme Court began placing stringent rules on police investigation and interrogation practices, and expanded the procedural rights of criminal suspects, in an attempt to insure minimum standards of fairness in the treatment of suspects, which had historically varied from state to state.

Until the late 1980s, federal and state judges had relatively unrestricted power to sentence defendants. While sentences could be reviewed by appellate courts, appellate courts generally showed great deference to the "fact sensitive" process of sentencing in the trial courts. Appellate courts could not be counted on to correct for biases that emanated from the extraordinary discretionary latitude afforded to sentencing judges.

In response to external pressure from scholars and legal advocates, governmental pressure to develop standardized models of sentencing led the United States Board of Parole to become the first agency to experiment with a guidelines model. The federal parole guidelines, initially developed in the late 1960s, allowed parole hearing examiners to set the length of incarceration within a narrow range specified in a chart (or grid) based on a) offense severity and b) the offender's past criminal record. Deviations from the parole guideline ranges were granted by written request (Bureau of Justice Assistance, 1996). This guidelines model, which appeared to be racially neutral, was later applied to sentencing in experiments in four local jurisdictions (Essex County, New Jersey; Polk Country, Iowa; Denver, Colorado; and the State of Vermont) from 1974 to 1976. By the late 1970s and early 1980s, nearly all states were experimenting with or adopting variations of these standardized sentencing models.

Responding to public demand for harsher and more certain punishment, the United States Congress passed the 1984 Sentencing Reform Act, a comprehensive structured sentencing system designed to reform and equalize sentencing in the federal courts. The Sentencing Reform Act created the United States Sentencing Commission, abolished federal parole, and narrowed judicial discretion at sentencing through the use of standardized sentencing ranges.

In response to the federal trend, numerous state legislatures began adopting stringent structured-sentencing systems. Notable among the first state sentencing guideline models were Minnesota's (1980), Washington State's (1981), Pennsylvania's (1982), and Florida's (1983). State guideline systems are similar to the federal guidelines, although federal guidelines tend to be more rigid and allow less judicial discretion (Stith and Cabranes, 1998). In all guidelines systems, defendant race is a prohibited factor in decisions to sentence above or below the guidelines. Under the federal system, the Sentencing Commission explicitly instructed that sex, race and class were factors that should never be relevant to sentencing (USSC Manual, 5H1.10).

In addition to adopting sentencing guidelines to limit judicial discretion, numerous states and the federal government adopted mandatory minimum sentencing laws that prescribe a mandatory penalty for particular types of crimes, mainly drug-related offenses. These laws were largely enacted following widespread public concern about drug-related crime in the early 1990s. Unlike sentencing guidelines, which were adopted to bring equity and uniformity to the sentencing process, mandatory minimum penalties were adopted largely in response to public demands for more certain and severe punishments; as a result their proponents were generally less concerned about their potential to produce racially disproportionate sentence outcomes. A variant of mandatory minimums are "Three-Strikes" laws, which require lengthy minimum sentences and in some cases a mandatory life sentence for offenders with multiple felony convictions. "Three-Strikes" laws have been strongly criticized for their disproportionate impact on Black and Hispanic defendants (Free, 1997).

A number of recent efforts to control judicial discretion within guideline systems have revitalized debate about the role of discretion in the sentencing process. In 2003, the U.S. Congress narrowed the range of options judges have for granting departures from the federal guidelines through passage of the Feeney Amendment (Title IV of S. 151, Public Law 108-21). However, strict rules of adherence to the sentencing guidelines based in the Feeney Amendment were weakened a few years later when the U.S. Supreme Court held that judicial decisions to enhance sentences through upward departures under the Washington state guideline system violated the Sixth Amendment (*Blakely v. Washington, 542 U.S. 296, 2004*). The court subsequently followed suit with the federal guidelines, ultimately ruling that the guidelines should be advisory rather than mandatory (*United States v. Booker, 543 U.S. 220, 2005*).

Research on Race and Sentencing under Guideline Systems

While sentencing reforms have dramatically altered the way criminal defendants are sentenced, it is not clear whether they have reduced racial disparities in sentences. Some researchers suggest that racial disparities in sentence outcomes have been reduced or eliminated through structured-sentencing models, while others suggest that strict structured-sentencing policies have actually exacerbated racial disparities.

Since the adoption of sentencing guidelines, scholars have used various methods to examine whether defendant characteristics or offense-related variables better explain the existence of sentencing disparity under sentencing guidelines systems (Miethe and Moore, 1985; Dixon 1995; Albonetti, 1997; Ulmer, 1997; Albonetti, 1998; Kautt and Spohn, 2002). Although findings about the existence of racial disparities in sentencing outcomes under the guidelines systems have been mixed, numerous studies have concluded that non-white defendants receive longer sentences than white defendants, especially because of a) the operation of the downward departure system, which allows the judge to sentence below the guidelines for one of a set of allowable reasons; and b) the advent of mandatory minimum sentencing (Engen et al., 2003; Everett and Wojkiewicz, 2002; Kautt and Spohn, 2002; Kramer and Ulmer, 1996; Mauer, 2007; Nagel and Schulhofer, 1992; Steffensmeier and Demuth, 2000). Though research confirms that legally relevant variables account for much of the variation in sentence outcomes, variation in the application of sentencing guidelines across courts, particularly with regard to departures from the guidelines, is believed to explain much of the persistent disparity in sentence severity based on defendant characteristics (Kautt, 2002; Johnson, 2005; for legally relevant rulings see: *U.S. v. Booker* [2005]; *Blakely v. Washington* [2005]).

Over a decade of research on federal sentencing guidelines illustrates the complexity of studying race and sentencing. Clearly, guidelines have effectively limited judicial discretion and reduced the direct effect of race on sentence outcomes. Despite these changes, defendants' race continues to interact in important ways with legally relevant and extra-legal variables, thereby resulting in continued racial disparities in sentence outcomes. These findings suggest the need to better understand the processes and context through which race continues to affect sentencing.

THEORETICAL APPROACHES TO UNDERSTANDING THE ROLE OF RACE/ETHNICITY IN SENTENCING

In addition to empirical research examining the effect of defendant race on sentence outcomes, a number of important theoretical approaches have been developed to understand the various mechanisms through which race may affect sentencing. We discuss the main theoretical developments of the "racial-threat" hypothesis, uncertainty avoidance and focal concerns below.

The "Racial-Threat" Hypothesis

One of the earliest theoretical approaches to understanding the impact of race on sentencing is conflict theory, initially developed by Quinney (1970) and Chambliss and Seidman (1971) to explain the effect of social class on the making and enforcement of law. Conflict theorists argued that powerful elites were largely responsible for shaping the law to support their class interests (e.g., by criminalizing the harms committed by the poor, and immunizing corporate harms from criminal liability), and for enforcing the law selectively against poor and powerless segments of society. These ideas were later applied to race, suggesting that blacks and other disadvantaged minorities were more likely to be arrested, prosecuted, convicted and sentenced more harshly than similarly situated whites because they had fewer resources with which to resist the imposition of criminal sanctions (Hawkins, 1987). This hypothesis — which claims that racial and ethnic minorities are discriminated against because they lack the power to ensure equal treatment — led some to predict that minority disadvantage would apply to all offenses and under all circumstances. Empirical research has not supported that expectation. Instead, empirical studies show that sometimes minorities are disadvantaged, while at other times they are treated the same as, and sometimes more leniently than, legally-similar whites.

In order to make sense of this inconsistent pattern of results, some have proposed a revision of conflict theory that focuses not on the power-lessness of racial and ethnic minorities but, instead, on the "threat" that they pose to white authority structures and to middle-class and working-class white Americans who make up the dominant majority, and who view themselves as the protectors of mainstream American values (Hawkins, 1987; Tittle and Curran, 1988; Sampson and Laub, 1993; see also chapter by Leiber, this volume). In this view, minorities may commit some crimes under some circumstances that are not perceived as particularly threatening, while other crimes under other circumstances may be viewed as especially threatening to the majority. The "racial-threat" hypothesis predicts that minorities will be treated more harshly than whites only when they are perceived as a threat. Theorists and researchers then set out to determine what crimes, under what circumstances, are viewed as particularly threatening.

Those who espouse a "racial-threat" hypothesis have suggested that minorities are perceived to be most threatening, and are therefore most likely to be disadvantaged at sentencing, when they: (1) commit violent crimes and other crimes that provoke fear among whites (Tittle and Curran, 1988); (2) victimize whites (Peterson and Hagan, 1984; Alvarez and Bachman, 1996); and, (3) reside in areas where minorities make up a substantial portion of the population (Sampson and Laub, 1993).

Support for the first of these hypotheses has been mixed. Some studies have found that whites and minorities are sentenced quite similarly when they commit very serious crimes for which there is strong evidence of the defendant's guilt. In such cases, the sentence is greatly influenced by the seriousness of the crime and the defendant's prior record, and judges have little discretion to attend to personal characteristics of the defendant (Walker et al., 2007). In contrast, judges and juries may have the greatest discretion in less serious cases and in serious cases where the evidence against the defendant is not so strong. According to the "liberation hypothesis" (Kalven and Zeisel, 1966), it is in less serious cases, where judges have greater discretion, that minorities are more likely to be disadvantaged. There is some support for this view. One study of defendants convicted of violent felonies found that minorities were more likely than whites to receive harsher sentences in cases: a) that did not involve a gun; b) where the defendant did not have a record of prior felony convictions; and c) in cases of assault, but not in the more serious cases of murder, rape, or robbery (Spohn and Cederblum, 1991).

Support for the second hypothesis — that the effect of race on sentencing is affected by the race of the victim — has generated a fairly consistent pattern of empirical support. When blacks murder other blacks, for example, they tend to receive more lenient sentences than in cases where blacks murder whites. This is precisely what one would expect based on the "racial-threat" perspective. The idea is that a greater value is placed on white lives than on the lives of minorities, so that the victimization of a white by a minority group member presents a more significant threat. The finding that cases involving white victims and minority offenders are dealt with most harshly at sentencing has also been replicated for the crimes of rape, robbery, and even some property offenses.

There has also been considerable support for the third hypothesis mentioned above — i.e., that minorities receive harsher sentences in communities where minorities make up a larger proportion of the population, the idea being that in such communities minorities are perceived as more threatening to the white establishment. For example, in their analysis of juvenile court dispositions across 31 Florida counties, Tittle and Curran (1988) found that dispositional severity was predicted by the relative size of the nonwhite and youth populations. Irrespective of crime rates, significant racial disparities occurred only in communities with large percentages of nonwhites and young people, and especially for drug and sex offenses (see also Bridges et al., 1993; Dannefer and Schutt, 1982). Tittle and Curran interpreted these results as suggesting that it is not the objective level of threat posed by minority groups that impels efforts to control them but, rather, "symbolic" aspects of threat. In counties and regions with substantial populations of young nonwhites, "nonwhites and youths symbolize to white adults resentment-provoking or fear-provoking qualities like aggressiveness, sexuality, and absence of personal discipline" (Tittle and Curran, 1988, p. 52). When whites perceive that there are concentrated populations of minorities who are believed to be engaging in behaviors that provoke fear, anger, and other negative emotions, they subject them to intensified social control.

We would be remiss if we did not mention the federal "War on Drugs" in conjunction with the racial-threat hypothesis. The war on drugs reached its peak in the 1980s and early 1990s. Although self-report studies showed little change in drug use from earlier time periods, legislatures nevertheless targeted drug offenders for stepped-up enforcement and harsher punishments (Blumstein 1993, 1995; Tonry, 1995). Arrest rates for drug offenses among whites were higher than among African Americans throughout the 1970s. However, after the initiation of the war on drugs, white drug-arrest rates declined, while arrests of African Americans skyrocketed, even though drug use patterns across these groups remained unchanged (National Institutes of Health, 1995). By the early 1990s, arrest rates for drug offenses among African Americans were four to five times greater than the arrest rates for whites (Miller, 1996). The National Criminal Justice Commission concluded that racial disparities in drug arrests were attributable largely to enforcement strategies that focused almost exclusively on low-level dealers in minority neighborhoods: "Police found more drugs in minority communities because that is where they looked for them" (Donziger, 1996, p. 115). The war on drugs has been waged differentially against young minority offenders, and was undoubtedly influenced by the media, which exaggerated the dangers associated with drugs, promulgated the view that drug crime was exclusively an urban African-American male phenomenon, and linked black males both to dangerous drugs and drug-related gun violence (Mauer and King, 2007b). As a consequence, legislated penalties for possession and sale of crack cocaine were made many times greater than those for its powder equivalent, which was more often found in the white community. The race-linked differentials in criminal penalties virtually guaranteed that minorities would be sentenced to prison in much greater numbers, and for much longer terms, than whites arrested for possession and sale of equally harmful drugs.

Uncertainty Avoidance

Celesta Albonetti (1991) has proposed a variant on the racial-threat hypothesis that focuses on what she calls "uncertainty avoidance." According to this view, judges at sentencing try to make rational decisions that will achieve the goal of protecting the community. However, these decisions are fraught with uncertainty because judges typically possess only limited information about each defendant and because predictions about a defendant's future behavior are notoriously difficult even when a decision maker has all the information that s/he could possibly want. Lacking complete information, the judge tries to reduce the uncertainty in achieving the sentencing objective by relying upon a rationality that attributes meaning to the defendant's current and future behavior consistent with stereotypes associated with membership in certain social categories (Albonetti, 1991).

Albonetti argues that judges develop patterned responses to certain kinds of cases and defendants, and respond to cues tied to past experience, stereotypes and prejudices. Cues believed to increase the likelihood of future criminal behavior increase the severity of the sentence, while stereotypical cues believed to decrease the likelihood of reoffending decrease the severity of the sentence. For example, a judge may believe that a violent offender is inherently aggressive and likely to reoffend, or s/he may believe that situational factors that can be altered or that are unlikely to recur precipitated the violent act. These attributions about the causes of a defendant's behavior lead to conclusions regarding the offender's rehabilitative potential, the threat posed to society, and the type of criminal sanction that should be imposed.

The key is that attributions about offender traits and the causes of an offender's behavior are linked to social categories, such as race and gender. Imposing a sentence, then, is the result of making causal assumptions in an effort to reduce uncertainty and achieve rationality. Understood in this way, racial and ethnic disparities in sentencing are the products of judicial attempts to make rational sentencing decisions by relying on stereotypical images concerning which defendants pose the greatest threat of reoffending. Minorities receive more severe sentences because of stereotypes that they are more dangerous than whites, and these effects are exacerbated when they also possess other attributes stereotypical of more dangerous offenders, such as being male and unemployed. Empirical evidence consistent with these hypotheses has been regularly reported. For example, in their research on felony sentencing outcomes in multiple cities, Spohn and Holleran (2000) described a "punishment penalty" that is applied to young and unemployed males who belong to racial minorities. Similarly, in research on drug offenders, Steen, Engen and Gainey (2005) interviewed criminal justice officials and found that they constructed stereotypes of dangerous drug offenders into which African Americans were more likely to fit. Furthermore, Steen et al. (2005) found that whites who matched the stereotype tended to be seen as "atypical," and that among offenders who matched the stereotype, African Americans were more likely than whites to be incarcerated.

Albonetti's perspective helps us to understand how and why racial stereotypes can unwittingly shape sentencing decisions. When judges attribute stable, enduring causes of crime to black offenders, the sentence is likely to be enhanced (see Bridges and Steen, 1998). It is the attribution link between race and the stability of the defendant's disposition to commit future criminal behavior, coupled with the judge's desire to reduce uncertainty, that together explain race differentials in sentence severity.

Focal Concerns Theory

Another prominent framework for understanding sentencing decisions is "focal concerns" theory, initially presented by Darrell Steffensmeier (1980; see also Spohn and Holleran, 2000; Steffensmeier and Demuth, 2001; Steffensmeier, Ulmer, and Kramer, 1998; Ulmer, 1997). This theory is consistent with Albonetti's uncertainty-avoidance perspective, but is more complex, suggesting that court officials make attributions about a defendant's character, the causes of his/her crime, and predictions of future behavior relative to three focal concerns. The first is blameworthiness, which has to do with the seriousness of the offense and the defendant's role in the crime. All other things equal, judges want to sentence defendants in ways that are proportionate to the harm done by the offense. Fulfilling this goal requires a backward-looking assessment of "just desert." The second concern stems from the social defense perspective, which seeks to protect the community through incapacitation (i.e., incarceration) of the potentially dangerous offender. Fulfilling the goal of community protection requires that the judge be forward-looking, to make an assessment or prediction about the offender's risk of recidivism. The final focal concern is a practical rather than a philosophical one, and has to do with the various consequences associated with sentencing alternatives for the criminal justice system (e.g., effects of the sentence on jail/prison overcrowding), the offender (e.g., family disruption), and the court (e.g., negative public reaction to the sentence).

Included in this perspective is the notion that judges have limited time and information about defendants when making sentencing decisions. To supplement legally relevant factors (offense seriousness, prior record), judges will also rely on attributions relevant to focal concerns that include extra-legal characteristics such as race, gender, and socioeconomic status. In this view, minorities are often more likely to be sentenced more harshly than their legally equivalent white counterparts because racial stereotypes that abound in our culture suggest that minorities are somehow more morally blameworthy for their crimes than whites. Offending among whites is more often attributed to external pressures, such as delinquent peers or dysfunctional families that can be said to mitigate culpability, while offending among nonwhites is more often attributed to enduring character traits (see Bridges and Steen, 1998). Largely due to the influence of the media, which provide extended and often sensationalized coverage of violent offenses committed by young black males, minority offenders are more often viewed as both dangerous and more likely to reoffend than their white counterparts. Finally, and related to the last of the focal concerns, judges are more likely to err on the side of harshness in sentencing minorities out of practical considerations. For example, judges may believe that minorities can handle imprisonment better than whites, that imprisonment is more disruptive to white than to black families, or that negative public reactions will result if they sentence minorities too leniently (e.g., that the public will view them as "soft on crime"; see Bridges and Steen, 1998).

The focal concerns perspective also incorporates the idea that members of courtroom workgroups (prosecutors, judges, defense attorneys) develop shared concerns, ideologies and biases regarding these focal concerns and regarding desired sentencing outcomes, that these concerns reflect local culture and can therefore be expected to vary from one court community to another. Hence, variations in racial disparities can only be understood by appreciating the organizational, legal, and political cultures within which decision making takes place.

Locating Sentencing on the Case Processing Continuum

Racial disparities in sentencing cannot be fully understood exclusively in relation to what takes place during the sentencing phase of a criminal proceeding. For too long, researchers have studied sentencing decisions in isolation, as if they were unaffected by what has taken place at earlier stages in the criminal justice process. But even if judges' sentencing decisions are wholly unaffected by race, racial inequities in sentencing outcomes can occur by virtue of biases that were introduced at earlier stages in processing and that reverberate through subsequent stages. Judges can only make sentencing decisions in the cases that they receive. They have no control over earlier decisions made by police (e.g., decisions to arrest versus release with a warning) or by prosecutors (e.g., charging decisions, charge reduction decisions, and plea agreements), which may have introduced selection biases that will inevitably produce differential final outcomes for whites and minorities who may be legally equivalent.

Studies that examine the sequence of events leading up to the sentencing decision provide strong support for the assertion that extra-legal defendant characteristics influences sentence outcomes indirectly, because these characteristics affect earlier processing outcomes such as pretrial release status, type of counsel, and mode of conviction (Hagan, 1975; Swigert and Farrell, 1977). For example, the practice of conditioning pretrial release decisions on defendants' financial ability to make bail has an effect that consistently works to the detriment of minority defendants (Albonetti, 1991; Dermody Leonard, 2002; Hagan 1975; Lizotte, 1978; Swigert and Farrell 1977; Willison, 1984). Because minorities are less likely to be able to make bail than their more affluent white counterparts, and because being held in jail awaiting trial is related to more punitive sentencing outcomes, minorities are systematically disadvantaged at sentencing. The effect of race on sentencing is obscured because it is mediated by bail outcomes (Patterson and Lynch, 1991). At sentencing, judges penalize those who were earlier perceived to pose a risk of flight or a danger to the community if released, which redounds to the disadvantage of poor (disproportionately minority) defendants.

There is also considerable evidence that sentencing outcomes are affected by mode of conviction. Those who plead guilty generally do so in exchange for prosecutorial concessions to drop or reduce charges, and some prosecutors may not be inclined to make equal concessions to minorities and whites. Defendants who plead guilty are likely to receive more favorable sentences than those who exercise their constitutional right to a trial (Clarke and Kurtz, 1983; Kramer and Ulmer 2002; LaFree 1985; Nardulli, Eisenstein, and Flemming, 1988; McCoy and Cohen, 2003; Uhlman and Walker, 1980). Consistent with these findings, minorities are less likely to plead guilty than whites (Albonetti, 1990). This may reflect a greater distrust of their attorneys, whose advice to accept a plea in return for a reduced or dropped charges is more often rejected by minority clients. Attorney-client relations are more often strained for minority defendants. Minority defendants are more likely to be represented by an attorney of a different race and by court-appointed rather than privately retained counsel (Albonetti, 1990). This helps explain why appointed counsel have more difficulty gaining the trust and confidence of their clients than attorneys who are privately retained, and hence find it more difficult to convince their clients that pleading guilty is in their best interest.

UNDERSTANDING THE INTERACTION OF RACE, GENDER AND CLASS ON SENTENCING

While empirical research devoted to understanding the effect of race on sentencing is substantial, less attention has been paid to the multiple ways in which race interacts with other characteristics such as ethnicity, gender and class. Since the late 1970s, researchers have documented lenient treatment toward women in the sentencing process (see Daly and Bordt, 1995, for a review). This literature suggests that judges see women in general as less blameworthy than men and are concerned about the implications of sentencing women with families to prison (Steffensmeier, Kramer and Steifel, 1993). Even under sentencing guidelines systems, women appear to continue to receive more lenient sentences than men for comparable offenses, in large part because they have disproportionately benefited from the downward departure processes that were built into most guideline systems (Patterson and Lynch, 1991; Kramer and Ulmer, 1996; Albonetti, 1998). Despite the general finding that women as a group are treated more leniently at sentencing than similarly situated men, race and gender interact in important ways to condition sentence outcomes. Judicial concern about the protection of women and families appears to be tied to stereotypical notions of "good women" or "good mothers" that are shaped by race and class.

Race is not a single factor among many for women of color, but rather, one that intensifies the significance of other disadvantages faced during sentencing (Hill-Collins, 1991). Historically, white women have benefited from judicial chivalry, while women of color have not been so advantaged. These biases often resulted in women of color being sentenced to prison while white women were placed in less harsh reformatory systems (Feinman, 1986; Rafter, 1990). Today, black women are still overrepresented in the prison population and, on average, serve longer prison terms than white women. Black women constitute over 30% of the female inmates in state and federal prisons and Hispanic women constitute 16% — both far greater than their representation in the overall population (Bureau of Justice Statistics, 2005, Table 10). Black women are more than three times as likely as white women to be incarcerated in prison or jail, and Hispanic women are 69% more likely (Bureau of Justice Statistics, 2005, Table 11). These aggregate counts, while illuminating the potential problem of racial disparity among women, are limited because they do not control for important variables such as the offenders' prior criminal history or type of crime.

More systematic studies suggest that race mediates other key factors, such as the offender's family ties and her estimated likelihood of recidivism, that have been found to influence sentence outcomes for women. For example, research suggests that judges sentence women with children more leniently than men in an attempt to preserve the family unit (Daly, 1994). But even these effects may be conditioned by race. Bickle and Peterson (1991), for instance, found that having dependent children did not automatically lead to lenient sentencing outcomes for black women compared to white women. They suggested that while judges assume white women are "good mothers," black women, like black men, must prove that they play significant emotionally supportive roles in the family to receive leniency at sentencing to sustain family ties (p. 391). Historical patterns of extended kinship ties among black women may also work to their detriment at sentencing. Because white women less often rely on intergenerational female support networks, a judge may view a white mother as more essential to her family than her black counterpart (Bishop and Frazier, 1990).

Race and gender also interact in important ways in the sentencing of male offenders. Black men are disproportionately likely to be arrested, convicted and sentenced to longer prison terms than white men (see Daly and Tonry, 1997, for a review of this literature). Black men make up 38% of incarcerated males in the U.S.; white men make up 34%; and Hispanic men, 21% (Bureau of Justice Statistics, 2007).[1] One in six black men in America has been incarcerated during his lifetime, and, if current trends continue, one in three black males born today will serve time in prison (Bonczar, 2003). Numerous studies confirm that young men of color are disadvantaged at sentencing compared to other groups (see, Mitchell, 2005). Race appears to have the strongest effect in explaining sentencing disparities for young black men. Steffensmeier et al. (1998) found that older black and older white males received similar sentences, while young black males were sentenced more harshly than young white males. They suggested that stereotypes about age, race and gender interact, leading young black males to be viewed by court officials as a greater threat to the community, with less likelihood for reform and rehabilitation. This research affirms the importance of examining the convergences of race, gender and age — as opposed to looking at group characteristics separately in sentencing research — and lends support to racial threat perspectives described earlier in this chapter.

THE IMPORTANCE OF CONTEXT TO STUDIES OF RACE AND SENTENCING

While the majority of research on sentencing has focused on the relationship between defendant characteristics and the sentence, the context in which sentencing occurs also affects sentencing outcomes. The type of crime, victim-offender relationships, and social and community contexts in which sentencing occurs all affect the relationship between race and sentence outcomes.

Though less scholarly attention has been devoted to the role of the victim's race or the interaction of victim and defendant race in the sentencing process generally, a rich body of research about the death penalty suggests that the race of the victim is a primary factor in determining whether or not someone will be sentenced to death (Baldus et al., 1983; Paternoster 1984; Radelet, 1981). In 1983, Baldus and his colleagues found that prosecutors sought the death penalty in Georgia in over 70% of cases involving a black defendant and a white victim, compared to only 34% of cases involving a black defendant and a black victim. Over all, defendants of any race charged with killing a white victim were over four times more likely to receive a death sentence than those charged with killing a black victim. These findings were used by attorneys in the landmark case McCleskey v. Kemp (481 U.S. 279, 1987) to allege that administration of the death penalty in the state of Georgia was unconstitutional. While the Supreme Court rejected that argument, the Baldus et al. research illustrates the interactive effect of victim and defendant race on the sentencing process. Research on the effect of victim race in rape cases similarly suggests that prosecutors are more likely to pursue charges and achieve convictions when the victim is white than when the victim is black (Frohman, 1987; LaFree, 1980, 1989).

In addition to research exploring the effect of victim race on sentence decision making, the place and social context in which sentencing occurs also have been found to interact with defendant race in sentencing decisions. The severity of legal sanctions may well be expected to vary across communities. Different crimes and types of offenders have been perceived to be more dangerous at particular times or in particular places. For example, Austin and Irwin (2001) suggest that variations in local enforcement of California's "Three-Strikes" laws were caused, in part, by differences in fear of crime and sentiment about the criminal justice system across communities. Research by Kautt (2002) and Ulmer and Johnson (2004) confirmed that variation in the effect of race on sentence outcomes is attributable, in part, to differences in the characteristics of the federal court district in which a defendant was sentenced.

Researchers examining the effect of community-level variables on sentencing severity have further suggested that, "what occurs inside the courtroom may be potentially more important, at least with regard to specific sentencing options, than factors outside the courtroom" (Fearn, 2005, p. 482). This is particularly relevant to questions of race and sentencing because local legal and organizational cultures of specific courts can influence outlooks and decision-making routines of court workers, in turn affecting case processing and altering the potential for racial disparity in sentence outcomes (Eisenstein and Jacobs, 1977; Stapleton, Aday and Ito, 1982; Ulmer and Kramer, 1996, 1998; Ulmer, 1997; Ulmer and Johnson, 2004; Dixon, 1995).

One area of court organizations that has been explored in some depth is the racial backgrounds of judges. Conclusions about the effect of the decision maker's race on case outcomes have been mixed. In one of the earliest studies, Uhlman (1978) concluded that Black trial court judges were not as a group notably distinct in their sanctioning patterns, but failure to control for relevant case and contextual characteristics rendered these results inconclusive. Subsequent studies introducing controls for case and contextual factors have yielded conflicting results. Some found that minority judges do not treat defendants differently from white judges (Spohn, 1990b; Walker and Barrow, 1985), while others reported that minority and white judges *both* sentenced minority defendants more severely than white defendants (Spohn, 1990b). Others have found race-related judicial decision-making differences, including evidence that non-white judges: (1) sentenced non-white defendants more leniently than white defendants (Welch et al., 1988) or more harshly than white defendants (Steffensmeier and Britt, 2001); (2) favored the defense at higher rates than white judges (Gottschall, 1983); and (3) were distinctively sensitive to specific defendant claims of procedural impropriety, such as police misconduct (Scherer, 2004). Still others have found that non-white judges sentence all defendants more consistently than white judges (Holmes et al., 1993).

LOOKING FORWARD: NEW AND REMAINING QUESTIONS ABOUT RACE, ETHNICITY AND SENTENCING

We conclude this chapter with a discussion of some issues and prospects for change that have recently come to the fore, as well as some challenges to understanding race and sentencing that have not been satisfactorily addressed in the existing literature.

The prosecutorial role in sentencing. Structured sentencing has not been as effective as its advocates had hoped in producing equality under the law. Reforms have not eliminated racial and ethnic disparities in sentencing, and some researchers question whether they have reduced disparities at all (Tonry, 1995) While it seems that the most overt forms of racial and ethnic discrimination have been reduced — for example, instances when minority and white defendants with similar criminal histories receive vastly different sentences for the same crime — there can be little doubt that biases continue to influence sentencing outcomes in less obvious ways. For example, the advent of "fixed" sentencing (requiring sentences of a fixed number of years, rather than sentencing offenders to a maximum/minimum range of years of imprisonment), mandatory minimum sentences (statutes specifying that offenders serve at least a minimum number of years for a given crime), habitual offender laws (which require enhanced punishments for offenders with specified numbers and types of prior convictions), and sentencing guidelines — all of which limit and sometimes altogether eliminate the judge's ability to choose a sentence — have made the prosecutor's role in sentencing much more important. Today, sentences are determined largely by the type and severity of the conviction offense, which is largely a function of the charge(s) filed by prosecutors, together with whatever concessions may be made be during plea negotiations. Since responsibility for determining the initial charges, and for plea negotiations, is vested in the prosecutor, sentencing discretion has shifted from judges to prosecutors (Miethe, 1987).

Assessing the influence of race and ethnicity on prosecutorial charging decisions is notoriously difficult. Prosecutorial charging is a "backstage" decision, largely invisible and not subject to judicial review. It is difficult for researchers to determine the extent to which prosecutors treat similar cases alike when they are not privy to the information on which prosecutors base their decisions. For example, it is almost impossible for researchers to control for evidentiary strength, willingness of victims or witnesses to testify, or the credibility of witnesses, all of which are legally relevant factors about which prosecutors must make judgments when deciding whether to file charges and what charges to file. Although there is reason for concern that minorities may be subject to differential "overcharging" — especially in cases that are stereotypically linked to minority offenders (e.g., cases involving drugs, gangs, and violence) — there is little research on the subject because the measurement problems are so formidable. In many cases prosecutors are unwilling to share information about their charging or bargaining decisions publicly because such information has the potential to jeopardize an ongoing or future investigation.

In some contexts, it is possible to identify a pool of cases that are eligible for a particular charge, and to assess whether race is systematically linked to prosecutorial decision making without needing controls for evidentiary considerations. The application of habitual offender statutes is a case in point. Habitual offender eligibility is determined by the number and type of convictions that a defendant has accumulated, and prosecutorial decisions to seek habitual offender status should be unaffected by prosecutorial assessments of evidentiary strength, or witness cooperation and credibility, which influence most prosecutorial charging decisions. Thus, research into the effects of race/ethnicity on decisions to seek habitual offender status constitutes a very fruitful avenue for future research.

Effect of new policy changes on racial disparities in sentence outcomes: Earlier we discussed the fact that some criminal behaviors are stereotypically linked to race. This is true of crimes involving gangs and violence, and it has been especially true of serious drug crimes, which have become almost synonymous with poor people of color. For example, federal law provides that persons convicted of selling crack — which is more often found in impoverished minority areas — face mandatory minimum sentences that are 100 times greater than those applied to the sale of equivalent amounts of the chemically-identical powdered version of the drug, which is more often found in affluent, predominantly white communities.

Recently, the federal sentencing commission has taken steps to reduce disparities in the penalties for crack versus powdered cocaine. Immediately following the Supreme Court's decision to uphold a lower court decision to sentence below the guideline range based on the unfairness of the crack cocaine sentencing disparity (*Kimbrough v. U.S.*, No. 06-6330, 2007), the United States Sentencing Commission voted to make retroactive a recent guideline amendment on crack cocaine offenses. The decision will make an estimated 19,500 prisoners eligible for a sentence reduction averaging more than two years (Stout, 2007). The new guidelines will reduce the average sentence for crack possession to 8 years/10 months from its current 10 years/1 month. Since nearly 85% of defendants convicted of crack offenses are Black, the retroactive changes could have a significant impact on reducing racial disparities in federal sentences. Currently, 53% of the nation's 175,000 federal prisoners are serving time for drug offenses.

Though U.S. Attorney General, Michael Mukasey tried to block the retroactive application of the reductions proposed by the commission, contending that "1,600 convicted crack dealers, many of them violent gang members, will be eligible for immediate release into communities nation-wide" (New York Times, February 8, 2008), reductions in crack sentences have already been awarded. To date more than 7,000 crack offenders have received reduced sentences since the Sentencing Commission's policy went into effect in March, 2008 (Fears, 2008).

The federal sentencing commission's attempt to correct disparities in the application of drug laws is echoed on the state level by efforts to repeal laws that have had a disproportionately negative effect on minority offenders. Motivated primarily by a desire to reduce prison overcrowding in the states, efforts have been undertaken to repeal mandatory minimum penalties, to restore "good time" provisions — which reward inmates' good behavior with reductions in the proportion of the sentence that they must serve in prison — and to bring back early release programs, which were largely abandoned in the 1980s and 1990s after some inmates who received early release committed violent crimes that generated significant publicity, and criticism of justice officials. Research indicates that early release pro-grams can be quite effective. Inmates enrolled in them remain supervised following release, and pose a risk of committing new crimes that is less than or equal to the risk posed by inmates who are released after "maxing out" (Austin, 1986; Pearson and Harper, 1990). While it is too early to know if these reforms will be successful, there is growing support among state and federal policy makers to develop new approaches to sentencing. In June, 2008 a bipartisan group of senators introduced the Justice Integrity Act, which would establish pilot programs in 10 federal districts "collecting and analyzing data on charging, plea negotiations, sentencing recommen-dations and other factors" to enhance fairness and equality in sentencing" (Mauer, 2008)

Overcoming weaknesses in criminal justice processing data: Most studies of race/ethnicity and sentencing are limited to comparisons of either whites and Blacks, or whites and non-whites. The "non-white" category is especially problematic because it is unclear which racial groups it includes or how they are distributed. Separate data for Native Americans, Asians and Pacific Islanders are frequently unavailable. More problematic still, most datasets fail to disaggregate race from ethnicity. Hispanic individuals are most often coded as "white." As a result, the extent of racial disparity in sentence outcomes, as well as the effect of race/ethnicity on sentencing decisions, is almost surely underestimated.

Moving forward, what is needed is research that includes breakdowns of groups by both race and ethnicity, so that Hispanic whites and non-Hispanic whites can be compared to each other and to other groups. We also need the capacity to explore disparities in the processing of subgroups within race. It is frequently averred, for example, that Asians are dealt with more leniently than whites. But there are many Asian populations, and the differences among them in sentencing outcomes may be substantial. When we group together Chinese, Vietnamese, Laotian, and Cambodian populations, we may be masking important differences in criminal justice handling across Asian subgroups. Large numbers of Chinese immigrants have been in this country for more than a century, while the other subgroups mentioned are much more recent arrivals. Stereotypical perceptions of the involvement of these Asian subgroups in gangs, drugs, and crime have already developed, and there is reason to suspect that they may be responded to by the courts in different ways than their Chinese counterparts. Similarly, research is needed on subgroups of the Black population (e.g., Haitians, Jamaicans, Cape Verdeans) and on Hispanic subgroups (e.g., Puerto Ricans, Mexicans). Finally, in light of controversy surrounding recently proposed U.S. policies to decrease illegal immigration — such as establishing a new "guest worker" program and the construction of a fence at the southwest border with Mexico — there is a pressing need for research on the criminal justice system's treatment of native-born versus immigrant populations (Martinez and Lee, 2000). Future research must attend to the possibility that court officials and court communities — depending on the racial and ethnic composition of the larger communities in which they are located — may perceive and respond to minority subgroups in quite different ways.

Future research also needs to disentangle the effects of race/ethnicity and social class. Unfortunately, most court data do not include measures of socioeconomic status, so the effects of race and class are confounded. Without measures of social class, it is impossible for researchers to determine whether white and minority defendants from the same socioeconomic backgrounds are treated similarly or differently. There is reason to suspect that class differences in access to resources (e.g., privately retained versus appointed counsel, and in the ability to make bail) may help to explain racial disparities in sentencing. Moreover, just as we have seen that qualities are attributed to defendants based on racial stereotypes — which, in turn, affect sentencing outcomes (e.g., Albonetti, 1991; Spohn, Gruhl and Welch 1981) — it is possible that class-linked stereotypes are also operative (e.g., stereotypes of the unemployed as lazy and irresponsible; stereotypes that link offending in the middle-class to situational factors, rather than to more enduring deficits of character), and that they interact with race to produce more severe outcomes for poor minority defendants.

The benefits of qualitative research: To date, the majority of the research on race and sentencing has focused on refining our measurement of disparities in sentencing practices. More research is needed to understand why and through what processes racial disparities exist, and the role played by racial stereotyping. Qualitative research, such as studies based on interviews with decision makers in the criminal justice system and on researcher observation of charging and sentencing negotiations, may be especially useful in this regard, although these kinds of studies need to be more systematic than they have been in the past. (Many qualitative studies present anecdotal accounts which, while frequently insightful, are of limited scientific utility.) An important unanswered question is whether court officials differentially minimize or ignore problems like drug abuse, which might result in less punitive and more treatment-oriented sentences for minority defendants, when assessing the backgrounds and life circumstances of minority defendants. There is an enormous need for research aimed at identifying how decision making produces differential judgments about similar white and minority offenders, and whether and how these are related to typifications linked to gender and social class. Although testing for evidence and effects of subtle forms of discrimination is difficult, it needs to become a major research priority.

Qualitative research is also needed to gain insight into the dynamics of decision making at all stages in criminal justice processing. Though time consuming, systematic observational studies can be especially valuable in providing insight into the qualities and circumstances to which justice officials attend; the processes and criteria involved in the formation of evaluative judgments about defendants' culpability and risk, and the link between these and official processing decisions.

Need for a more holistic understanding of differential sentencing mechanism and outcomes: Sentencing research has come a long way since the days when researchers tested overly simplified conflict models and looked only for direct, main effects of race on sentencing outcomes. We now know that racial disparities in sentencing are contingent upon the interaction of race with legal variables (such as offense type, prior record, and pretrial release status) and with other sociodemographic factors (e.g., gender, victim race). We understand that disparities are related to characteristics of decision makers and the court and community contexts in which they work, and to legal and social policies that, although appearing to be race-neutral, have a greater impact on some groups than others (institutional racism). Future research on the role of race and ethnicity in sentencing, and future policies and programmatic attempts to achieve greater equality under the law, need to be informed by models that examine sentencing as one stage in a criminal justice process, taking account of the complexity and interrelationship of decisions at multiple stages of the system. It also seems especially important that we continue to move beyond narrow questions relating to the organization and operation of criminal justice agencies to explore connections between macro-level community factors, especially those related to social and economic inequality, and justice system responses. Ultimately, racial disparities in sentencing outcomes are the cumulative result of decisions made in local communities and influenced by local cultures, a process that must be better understood if we are to develop sound policies to remedy disparity.

NOTES

1. These statistics are for state and federal prisons, and do not include jails or juvenile facility populations.

6. Race, Drugs and Juvenile Court Processing[1]

E. Britt Patterson

In 2002, the U.S. Delinquency Prevention and Control Act of 1974 was modified in an effort to direct states to conduct more comprehensive investigations into the disproportionate number of minority youths having contact with the juvenile justice system. This directive had strong empirical support from the scientific community. Pope et al. (2002), for example, had concluded from their literature review on disproportionate minority confinement (DMC) that the "issue of race is central to the administration of juvenile justice in this country" (p. 10).

The present study examines the role of race in the processing of juveniles referred for drug offenses — an area which many believe is at least partially responsible for DMC. Using both national and individual data from one state, the results from this study consistently indicated that racial differences affected how White, Black and "Other" youths were treated by the juvenile justice system during the period of study. A multivariate analysis of the decision to file a petition for charges of drug use/possession indicated that Black youths were treated more formally than White and "Other" youths. It is suggested that the association between crime and being Black may be a function of an automatic response of individuals in a culture where the stereotype of Black citizens as violent and unconstrained is deeply engrained.

Background: Thinking About the Importance of Race

> "There is nothing more painful to me at this stage in my life than to walk down the street and hear footsteps and start thinking about robbery — then look around and see somebody white and feel relieved."
>
> (Rev. Jesse Jackson, quoted in Cohen, 1993, p. A23)

In order to understand racial differences in the treatment of youths in the juvenile justice system, it is necessary to come to grips with the contexts in which racially based differential treatment emerges. These differences are represented in a few real-life scenarios described below.

1) Picture your average small town of approximately 2,900 people. The median income of the 720 families residing in the town reflects closely the state median. Twelve percent of the town's population is Black. The local high school, composed of 499 eighth to twelfth graders, is 81% White. A tree known as the "white tree" grows next to the school. It provides desired shade on hot days for the students — but as the name implies, not for all students. It is a "whites-only" tree. Three nooses appear tied to the tree shortly after a male Black student defies tradition and sits under the tree. This "act of defiance" results in an escalation of racial tension within the small community. Several Black students get into a fight with a White student. The Black students are initially charged with attempted 2nd degree murder — a charge that is later reduced to 2nd degree battery. One of the Black students (age 16) is charged as an adult. The jury is all White. He is convicted and faces a possible 15 years in prison, though a higher court later remands the case to the juvenile court (Jones, 2007).

2) Picture a juvenile correctional facility whose mission is to help change the lives of young offenders. The facility houses primarily African-American males. Guards and staff are predominately White. Routinely, the African-American youths are physically and emotionally abused. Racist language is common (e.g., "monkeys"). With little provocation, guards punch and pepper spray youths. In one instance, a youth who has a colostomy bag (due to surgery for a gunshot wound) is forced to lie face down on the concrete floor while a guard restrains him with a knee on his back. As a result, the youth's intestines are forced into the colostomy bag (Butterfield, 2000; U.S. Department of Justice, 2000).

3) A 14-year-old Black female shoves a 58-year-old teacher's aide in a small town high school. Although the youth had no prior arrest record and the aide was not seriously injured, the juvenile was sentenced to spend up to seven years in a juvenile facility if she failed to "adjust" to the requirements ("steps"/"phases") of the

program in the juvenile correctional complex. Indeterminate sentencing is used in about 90% of the cases in this state's juvenile justice system (Witt, 2007). These sentences may play an important role in explaining sentence length differences across racial groups. Indeterminate sentencing allows for juvenile justice personnel to formulate requirements for release. If the personnel determine that the youth has not "adequately completed" the requirements, then s/he will not be released. In this case, the youth was penalized because she was found with "contraband" in her cell (an extra pair of socks), which was deemed in violation of the previously determined requirements for her release. (After considerable public uproar, she was released after being confined for one year.)

4) County juvenile facility personnel kick, knee and punch a-14-year-old African-American boy. He later dies. The all-white jury, after 90 minutes of deliberation, finds seven former guards not responsible for the 14-year-old boy's death. The attorney for the boy's parents remarks, "You kill a dog and go to jail, you kill a little black boy and nothing happens" (Price, 2007).

For many readers, these situations may represent examples of a distant tragic era in American history — the hundred-year time period between the end of the Civil War in the mid-1860s and the civil rights movement of the 1960s. To others, these may be considered as anomalies in a generally color-blind juvenile justice system. In reality, these incidents are just a few of the incidents of racial discrimination that occur systematically throughout the juvenile justice system in the 21st century, where members of minority groups represent 68% of the detained juvenile population. This percentage is even more striking given that 25 years ago 56% of the juvenile population detained was white (Bell, 2005). As Patterson (2007) questioned: "How after decades of undeniable racial progress, did we end up with this virtual gulag of racial incarceration?" (The term "gulag" typically refers to a prison characterized by hardship and misery, originally a harsh and isolated facility in the Soviet Union.)

This chapter will present an overview of the issue of race and ethnicity in the juvenile justice system, as well as an original analysis of drug cases, a type of case which has been especially linked to this disproportionate representation of minorities (Feyerherm, 1995; Sampson and Laub, 1993; Patterson, 2007) in the juvenile justice system.

Government Recognition and Involvement

In 1974, the federal Juvenile Justice and Delinquency Prevention Act (JJDPA) was enacted. This act represented an attempt by the federal government to formalize prevention and control efforts in regard to juvenile delinquency. It replaced the Juvenile Delinquency Prevention and Control Act of 1968, which required the Department of Health, Education and Welfare to develop a national approach to the problem of delinquency. The 1974 act contained several requirements, among them the creation of several administrative agencies, including the Office of Juvenile Justice and Delinquency Prevention (OJJDP) within the Law Enforcement Assistance Administration the National Advisory Committee on Juvenile Justice and Delinquency Prevention, the Federal Coordinating Council on Juvenile Justice and Delinquency prevention, and the National Institute for Juvenile Justice and Delinquency Prevention to sponsor research. Despite its reauthorization in 1977, 1980, and 1984, the Juvenile Justice and Delinquency Prevention Act gave little attention to issues of race and ethnicity.

Concern over the overrepresentation of minorities in the juvenile justice system was not formally recognized until the act was reauthorized in 1988. In 1988, the act required the development of yearly plans to "reduce the proportion of juveniles *detained or confined* in secure detention facilities, secure correctional facilities, jails, and lockups who are members of minority groups if such proportion exceeds the proportion such groups represent in the general population" (Hsia, 2006; emphasis added). Even so, the new provision was narrow in scope: it addressed only the issue of confinement. The act also targeted programs for one specific minority group, by requiring a study of Native American justice systems. Interestingly, at this time a provision was made to establish programs to provide prevention and treatment for drug abuse.

With the act's next reauthorization in 1992 came a more "forceful hand" by the federal government. A new amendment made the issue of disproportionate minority confinement a core concern, and enforced this focus by authorizing a potential 25% funding reduction for states that did not comply with the law's four core requirements: deinstitutionalization of status offenders (youths adjudicated for behavior such as truancy or running away from home that would not be criminal for adults); sight and sound separation between incarcerated juveniles and adults; removal of juveniles from adult jails; and reduction of disproportionate minority confinement.

In 2002, the act was again modified. The new requirements broadened the scope of concern in regard to minorities in the juvenile justice system.

Specifically, the act stated that plans must "address juvenile delinquency prevention efforts and system improvement efforts designed to reduce, without establishing or requiring numerical standards or quotas, the disproportionate number of juvenile members of minority groups who come into *contact* with the juvenile justice system" (Hsia, 2006, p. 4; emphasis added). The act's new language conveyed a belief that the disproportionate number of minorities in confinement may only be the "tip of the iceberg." Issues from differential enforcement to differential adjudication practices were now recognized as potential areas for concern.

In June 2008, Sen. Patrick Leahy (D-VT) introduced S. 3155: Juvenile Justice and Delinquency Prevention Reauthorization Act of 2008. The bill was referred to the Senate Committee on the Judiciary — the first stage of the legislative process — and the legislation may go through several iterations before final reauthorization. It is anticipated that the act will continue to impose on the states a requirement for reducing racial disproportionality in the juvenile justice systems.

EMPIRICAL FOUNDATION

Several studies have been sponsored by the OJJDP to examine the extent of disproportionate minority representation in the juvenile justice system (Pope and Feyerherm, 1993; Roscoe and Morton, 1994; Hamparian and Leiber, 1997: Pope et al., 2002). These studies have typically examined research that explores the sources and solutions to the disproportionate representation of minority youths in the juvenile justice systems around the country.

Pope, Lovell, and Hsia (2002) wrote the most recent review of published research in regard to the disproportionate minority confinement. Using studies published in academic journals and in scholarly texts from March 1989 through December 2001, they concentrated on 34 publications (see the original report for a more detailed discussion of the methodology). Their review of this research led them to conclude:

> Considering the evidence from this and the previous DMC literature review, it is clear that the issue of race is central to the administration of juvenile justice in this country. The majority of the empirical studies over the past three decades report race effects — direct, indirect, or, more often, mixed. The number of studies reporting mixed results highlights the complexity of the problem. (p. 10)

Pope et al. (2002) reiterated recommendations for future research made earlier by Pope and Feyerherm (1990). These recommendations included the following: (1) *disaggregation* should be done whenever possible (i.e., research should look at individual jurisdictions within states rather than whole states since higher levels of aggregation at the state level may mask effects at lower levels); (2) both qualitative and quantitative methods should be used; (3) interaction of race with attitudes, background and other social characteristics should be explored; and (4) bias against minority groups other than African Americans should be more thoroughly examined. Other researchers have stressed the importance of context (i.e., the characteristics of the community and the characteristics of the criminal justice organization) in understanding the disproportionate representation of minority youths in the system (Feld, 1999; Sampson and Laub, 1993).

Recently, Leiber et al. (2007) analyzed 3,777 cases from two jurisdictions in a northwestern state from July 1, 2002 to June 30, 2003. Studying both legal factors (prior record, number of charges, and offense type) and extralegal factors (race, age, gender), bias was examined at four decision making points: dismissal at intake; diversion at intake (i.e., referral to other agencies); petition at intake; and adjudication. In regard to race, adequate information was available to go beyond the typical "White/Nonwhite" or "Black/White" dichotomy of race. Responding to the recommendations of Pope et al. (2002), five "races" were used: Black, Native American, Asian, White, and "Other" (multiracial)

With regard to dismissal at intake, Leiber et al. (2007) found that Blacks were significantly more likely to have charges dismissed at intake relative to Whites. Asian-American youths, however, were significantly less likely to be dismissed relative to Whites. Other evidence of racial differences in treatment was discovered at later processing stages. When it came to diversion at intake, Leiber et al. (2007) found that Blacks and older Native Americans were significantly less likely to be diverted relative to Whites. The effects of race and its interaction with other variables were also quite evident at the petition decision, which is the filing of a petition in juvenile court alleging that a juvenile is a delinquent. Being Black or multiracial, in combination with multiple charges, resulted in a significantly higher probability of a petition being filed than was the case with White offenders. In addition, being an older Native American made a petition significantly more likely. Finally, the adjudication decision indicated that race also had an effect. Specifically, Asian and multiracial youths were more likely to be adjudicated compared to Whites.

Thus, more recent data seem to support the conclusion that race remains an important determinant in juvenile justice decision making.

Leiber et al.'s (2007) research affirms that race continues to play an influential role in the processing of juvenile offenders, and suggests the need for more research to advance our understanding of this important and complicated issue.

THEORETICAL EXPLANATIONS

Various theoretical perspectives explain the reasons behind the observed lack of proportionality in regard to race and juvenile justice processing.

Among theories in criminology, Tittle and Curran's (1988) "symbolic threat theory," points to the perceived threat to the *status quo* experienced by criminal justice decision makers in their interactions with youths, particularly minority youths:

> According to the logic of the threat hypothesis, members of threatening groups should be more severely sanctioned than others. . . . However, it is reasonable to imagine that when adults are most threatened they will differentially react against those who most clearly embody the fear-provoking aspects of youthfulness. We maintain that adults fear, or perhaps resent, youthful aggressiveness, sexuality, and carefreeness — all qualities stereotypically associated with nonwhiteness, particularly blackness. (Tittle and Curran, 1988, pp. 48-49)

Leiber et al. (2007) maintain that the main thesis of symbolic threat theory today (after some reformulation by Sampson and Laub in 1983) is essentially that Black juveniles are seen stereotypically as "dangerous" and likely "drug offenders" (see also the chapter by Leiber in this volume). As a result, Blacks are perceived as requiring differential treatment because of stereotypes attached to notions of their "dangerousness" as violent and as drug-prone offenders. These perceptions, in turn, tend to enhance the likelihood that they will be processed more formally than White juveniles.

Research based on social psychological theories has investigated the role of stereotypes on visual processing and behavior (Correll et al., 2002). Some researchers have concluded that the stereotypic association between Blacks and crime can be characterized as "automatic" (Payne, 2001):

> The paradigmatic understanding of the automatic stereotyping process . . . is that the mere presence of a person can lead one to think about the concepts with which that person's social group has been associated. The mere presence of a Black man, for instance, can trigger thoughts that he is violent and criminal. . . . Merely thinking about Blacks can lead people to evaluate ambiguous behavior as

aggressive, to miscategorize harmless objects as weapons, or to shoot quickly, and, at times, inappropriately. (Eberhardt et al., 2004, p. 876)

The implication for the processing of juveniles, therefore, is that juvenile justice personnel and police more readily see Black youths as guilty of the alleged behavior. Thus, processing of the juvenile is more normalized or routine since the "determination" of guilt has already been perceptually established as a foregone conclusion (i.e., the youth is Black, therefore he or she is criminal).

Eberhardt et al. (2004) suggested that not only can social groups activate stereotypical attributes, but also that stereotypical attributes can activate social groups. They state that, "In a crime-obsessed culture, for example, simply thinking about crime can lead perceivers to conjure up images of Black Americans that 'ready' these perceivers to register and selectively attend to Black people who may be present in the actual physical environment" (p. 877). Thus, the relationship is ultimately reciprocal. Being Black can activate certain stereotypical concepts/attributes, and certain stereotypical concepts/attributes can activate the thought of being Black (Kawakami and Dovidio, 2001). This bidirectional association produces selective perception — which filters the kind of information that is and is not important for decision making. Eberhardt et al. (2004) thus concluded: "Not only are blacks thought of as criminal, but also crime is thought of as black" (p. 883).

In support of this association, Eberhardt et al. (2004) conducted several experiments. The conclusions with regard to the race/crime link were:

1. "The results ... demonstrate that stereotypic associations have the power to alter the threshold at which real-world objects are detected. In comparison with white faces, black faces triggered a form of racialized seeing that facilitated the processing of crime-relevant objects, regardless of individual differences in racial attitudes" (p. 881). Interestingly, they found that white faces generally "inhibited the detection of crime-relevant objects" (p. 880). The participants in this study were 39 white male students from the University of California, Berkeley and Stanford University.

2. "The concept of crime affected selective attention such that participants were over 350ms (milliseconds) faster to direct their attention to the location of the black face when the concept of crime was activated than when it was not" (p. 883). The participants in this study were 50 white male Stanford University students.

3. "We now have some initial evidence that exposure to a concept can lead to the triggering of a social category image that is strongly representative of the social category. Indeed, thinking about the concept of crime not only brought black faces to mind but brought stereotypically black faces to mind" (p. 888). Interestingly . . . these findings were obtained from a sample of 57 police officers from an urban area (population over 100,000).

4. "When officers were given no information other than a face and when they were explicitly directed to make judgments of criminality, race played a significant role in how those judgments were made. Black faces looked more criminal to police officers; the more black, the more criminal" (p. 889). These conclusions were based on a sample of 166 police officers from an urban area (over 100,000 population).

Others have also pointed to the effect of stereotypic attributes on decision makers. For example, Leiber and Mack (2003) concluded that African American males are often perceived as dangerous, violent and lacking constraint. Bridges and Steen (1998) found that probation officers were more inclined to attribute delinquent behavior to dispositional (internal) factors when the juvenile was African American. In contrast, when the offender was a White juvenile, the source of the problem was seen as situational (external to the juvenile). These perceptions may explain why police officers, teachers, and others in the public may be more likely to refer "suspicious" behavior by Blacks to juvenile justice authorities.

Ultimately, even minor offenses lead public officials and some members of the White majority to a presumption of guilt and the perceived higher possibility of future crime and violence on the part of the Black youth. Moreover, less information on relevant social and legal factors is deemed necessary for decision making depending on the race of the youth (Bridges and Steen, 1998; Tomkins et al., 1996). Given less and lower standards of information, intake officers, probation officers, prosecutors, and judges will tend to interpret Black youths as more potentially dangerous than White youths.

Studies also indicate that, throughout the system, personnel will choose a more formal course of action for Black youths. Once a disproportionate number of Black youths become enmeshed in the system, the stereotype of Black youths as offenders is reinforced. In effect, the results become a self-fulfilling prophecy where the results, though biased, justify the initial assumption. Common racial stereotypes are not only reinforced by outcomes, they are "also reinforced by the media, who often inspire fear about

African-American youths. The public then responds by electing judges and prosecutors who favor more harsh interventions and consequences" (Drakeford and Staples, 2006, p. 56).

PRESENT RESEARCH

The present study examines racial disparity among drug-related referrals and processing decisions for juvenile offenders. Many authors have suggested that drugs laws and their enforcement have long been and continue to be a mechanism used by a fearful White majority to control minorities (e.g., Glasser, 2006; Cuomo, 2005; Nunn, 2002; Jones, 2001; Small, 2001; Manderson, 1999; Helmer, 1975; Musto, 1973). Under such conditions, and in light of the theories reviewed above, we would expect overrepresentation of minority youths in drug referrals and processing outcomes.

The first part of the analysis examines four decision-making points and the effect of race of the juvenile at the national level. The four decision points are: (1) whether to formally file a petition or for court personnel to informally process a drug referral; (2) whether to detain or not to detain the juvenile prior to the adjudication hearing; (3) whether to adjudicate the juvenile as delinquent for the drug offense or to find the youth not guilty; and, (4) which disposition to select for the drug offense. Only those 10-17 years old are examined for each decision point.

The second part of the analysis examines the same decisions at the individual level among youths in Pennsylvania. In this research in Pennsylvania, the data cover variation in juvenile justice processing of individual youths. This stage represents a significant decision — the beginning of the process of labeling a child as delinquent. Given the broad nature of drug offenses, this analysis concentrates only on those cases where the referral charges were for possession/use of drugs. A multivariate analysis examines racial effects on whether a petition is filed or not, while controlling for other relevant factors.

Data and General Trends

Two datasets are used in the present analysis. The source of information on the processing decisions at the national level is the National Center of Juvenile Justice (2007). In these data, drug law violations represent the most serious offense for which the youths were referred to juvenile court.

Table 6.1. Formal Handling of Drug Referrals by Race — National Data

Year	White	Black	Other	N
2002	54.7%	77.1%	51.4%	185,482
2003	53.3%	76.8%	53.2%	183,390
2004	52.5%	75.8%	52.1%	187,812

These violations include "unlawful sale, distribution, manufacture, cultivation, transport, possession, or use of a controlled or prohibited substance or drug, or drug paraphernalia, or attempt to commit these acts. Sniffing of glue, paint, gasoline, and other inhalants are also included; hence, the term is broader than the UCR category drug abuse violations" (see the glossary in Stahl et al., 2007). Race is operationalized as White, Black and "Other" (Native Americans, Asian, Indian, Pacific islands), and was self-identified or court-determined (Stahl et al., 2007; see Knepper 2000 for discussion of official usage of race). Data from 2002 were used for the majority of the descriptive analyses (N=185,482).

The second dataset was obtained from the Pennsylvania Juvenile Justice Judges Commission, Information and Technology Division, and it represents cases disposed by juvenile probation departments across Pennsylvania. Race has been operationalized to be comparable to the national data. Drug cases examined were limited to possession/use as the most serious charge, in order to control for the extreme variation in possible drug offenses (see operationalization for the national data above). A total of 2,059 cases from 2002 were used for this analysis.

National Trends in the Handling of Drug Referrals

Table 6.1 presents the national breakdown of the formal handling of all drug referrals for the years 2002-2004. Formally handled cases refer to petitioned cases (Stahl et al., 2007). Approximately 59% (2002) and 58% (2003/2004) of referrals for drug offenses were formally processed. In all three years, the percentage of Black youths formally handled exceeded the percentage of Whites. In general, those in the "Other" category of race (Native Americans, Asian, Indian, Pacific islands) were handled similarly to Whites: a little over half of youths in the White and "Other" groups were petitioned into court, as compared to about three-quarters of the Black youths.

Table 6.2. Detention of Drug Referrals by Race 2002 (N=185,482)

	White	Black	Other	N
Detained	17.2%	32.2%	18.2%	37,900
Not Detained	82.8%	67.8%	81.8%	147,582

Table 6.3. Adjudication of Drug Referrals by Race 2002 (N=185,482)

	White	Black	Other	N
Adjudicated	39.1%	46.6%	35.9%	75,378
Not adjudicated	60.9%	53.4%	64.1%	110,104

Detention. Detention typically takes place between referral (when an offense is brought to court intake) and court intake (the court's decision to informally or formally handle the case) and case disposition (the action taken by the court after adjudication) (Stahl et al., 2007). In 2002, only 20.4% of drug referrals resulted in detention. Here again, Black youths were more likely to be detained relative to the White and "Other" youths (see Table 6.2). Thirty-two percent of Black youths were detained in a restrictive facility compared to approximately 17% of Whites and 18% of others.

Adjudication. Of the 185,482 drug referrals in 2002, approximately 41% resulted in a delinquency adjudication. Black youths (47%) were significantly more likely to be adjudicated delinquent than White (39%) and "Other" (36%) youths (see Table 6.3).

Dispositions. Once adjudicated, Black youths referred for drug violations were more likely to be placed in residential facilities (see Table 6.4). White and "Other" adjudicated drug offenders were more likely to receive probation or other services (e.g., fines, restitution, community service, referrals).

The "disposition" of non-adjudicated drug referral cases was also examined. As Table 6.5 indicates, Blacks were more likely to have their cases waived to an adult court. Though not adjudicated, White youths and "Other" youths received probation or other miscellaneous actions, while Black youths were more likely to be released without further treatment or

Table 6.4. Disposition of Adjudicated Drug Referrals by Race 2002 (*N*=75,379)

	White	Black	Other	*N*
Placed in residential facility	15.4%	31.9%	16.5%	14,690
Probation	67.6%	58.0%	68.6%	49,212
Other	16.9%	10.1%	14.8%	11,477

Table 6.5. Disposition of Non-adjudicated Drug Referrals by Race 2002 (*N* = 110,103)

	White	Black	Other	*N*
Waived	0.7%	3.3%	0.5%	1,330
Probation	25.4%	14.9%	22.6%	25,688
Released	41.3%	62.2%	48.2%	50,096
Other	32.6%	19.5%	28.6%	32,989

supervision. This may suggest that Black youths are seen differently than White youths. Waiving a youth to adult court is usually done when the offense is serious and/or the youth is deemed beyond rehabilitation. Thus, Black youths may be perceived as more serious and less receptive to rehabilitative efforts than are White youths. On the other hand, Black youths who commit less serious offenses may be brought into the system without adequate evidence to support adjudication, which ultimately leads to their release. The Black youths may again be seen as potentially more criminally inclined, and thus juvenile justice personnel pursue cases where the evidence is less than sufficient for adjudication.

In sum, bivariate analyses of the processing of drug offenses at the national level support a race-decision point association. But, as mentioned earlier, because of the wide range of offenses included in the drug law violations (e.g., ranging downward from distribution to possession), as well as other case processing factors, the associations between race and these four decision points may be spurious. Further analysis is required to determine if other factors override the race-decision associations noted above.

Table 6.6 Formal Handling of Drug Referrals by Race, Pennsylvania Sample (*N*=2,059)

Petitioned	White	Black	Other	*N*
No	44.6%	20.7%	55.2%	831
Yes	55.4%	79.3%	44.8%	1228

Table 6.7. Detention of Drug Referrals by Race 2002, Pennsylvania Sample (*N*=2,059)

Detained	White	Black	Other	*N*
No	94.3%	85.9%	96.6%	1911
Yes	5.7%	14.1%	3.4%	148

Pennsylvania Trends in the Handling of Drug Referrals in 2002

Table 6.6 presents the breakdown of the formal handling of juvenile possession/use cases for the year 2002 in Pennsylvania. Approximately 60% of the referrals for drug possession/use were formally handled through the filing of a petition, which is about the same proportion as appeared in the national data (Table 6.1). Blacks were significantly more likely to have a petition filed when referred for possession or use of drugs.

Detention. As indicated at the national level (see Table 6.2), the use of pre-adjudication detention is an infrequent occurrence for drug referrals. In Pennsylvania, only 148 (7.2%) of drug case juveniles were held in secure detention. Even so, Black youths fared worse (see Table 6.7): they were significantly more likely to be detained relative to White and "Other" youths. (See Patterson and Patterson, 1996, for a further discussion of detention decisions as they involve race and drug offenses.)

Adjudication. Of the 2,059 cases originally referred to the juvenile court, 36% (773) resulted in a delinquency adjudication (see Table 6.8). Fifty-five percent of Black youths were adjudicated, while the percentages of White and "Other" youths adjudicated were significantly lower.

Dispositions. Once adjudicated, most Pennsylvania youths received a disposition of probation (62.4%). However, as Table 6.9 indicates, White youths were most likely to receive this disposition. Black and "Other" youths

Table 6.8. Adjudication of Drug Referrals by Race 2002, Pennsylvania Sample (*N*=2,059)

Adjudicated	White	Black	Other	*N*
No	68.3%	45.5%	69.0%	1318
Yes	31.7%	54.5%	31.0%	741

Table 6.9. Disposition of Adjudicated Drug Referrals by Race 2002, Pennsylvania Sample (*N* = 741)

	White	Black	Other	*N*
Placed in residential facility	25.5%	34.7%	38.9%	211
Probation	71.0%	51.2%	61.1%	482
Other	1.2%	2.3%	0.0%	11
Released	2.4%	11.7%	0.0%	37

were more likely to receive a placement relative to White youths. Curiously, Black youths were more likely to be released (warned, dismissed, or complaint withdrawn), suggesting the possibility of referral to court without sufficient evidence for Black youths.

Alternatives to adjudication are often employed to provide services to youths. Two frequently used alternatives are informal adjustments and consent decrees. An informal adjustment typically involves either no finding of guilt or an adjudication of not guilty in exchange for some sort of specific requirements to be fulfilled by the juvenile. If, after six months, the juvenile has complied with stipulated conditions, the charges are then withdrawn. In these Pennsylvania data, Black youths were less likely to receive this option relative to White and "Other" youths (see Table 6.10). Similarly, a consent decree is an agreement whereby the juvenile is kept under supervision in his or her own home under the terms and conditions negotiated with the probation officer. As in an informal adjustment, if the terms of a consent decree are satisfied, there is no juvenile court record of the incident. As Table 6.10 indicates, White and "Other" youths were slightly more likely to receive this disposition than Black youths. Finally, again, as was the case in the national data, Black youths in Pennsylvania were more likely to be released with no further action than were Whites and "Other" youths.

Table 6.10. Disposition of Non-adjudicated Drug Referrals by Race 2002 (N = 1,318)

	White	Black	Other	N
Informal adjustment	52.5%	30.3%	50.0%	651
Consent decree	30.6%	32.0%	25.0%	404
Other	5.1%	7.3%	5.0%	71
Released	11.8%	30.3%	20.0%	192

This outcome may indicate the tendency to detain Black youths more often that White youths when legal evidence needed for further processing is lacking.

Bivariate Analysis of Petition for Delinquency Decisions

Referral is the gateway to the juvenile justice system. Once a petition is filed (typically by juvenile court personnel at intake), the process of determining guilt begins. Approximately 40% of the drug use and possession referrals were handled informally without filing a petition, for example by dismissal, referral to other agencies, and etc). Table 6.11 presents bivariate associations of various legal, individual and contextual variables associated with the filing and non-filing of a petition.

Legal Factors. Legal variables examined included whether the possession/use was for marijuana (approximately 60% of the cases) or another drug. Table 6.11 shows that those referred for a "harder" drug than marijuana were more likely to have a petition filed.

A distinction was made as to whether the charges were filed as a felony or misdemeanor. Not surprisingly, the data indicated that those charged with a misdemeanor drug charge were less likely to be formally processed. The vast majority were misdemeanor charges (approximately 98%; cases with no information on the charge were placed in the "misdemeanor" category).

The source of the referral, whether police or others (e.g., parents, school officials), was also examined. Ninety-six percent of referrals were made by the police. Here, the data suggest that non-police referrals by school, family or other agencies were just as likely to result in formal processing. An important limitation of our data was the lack of information on the prior record of the youth.

Table 6.11. Bivariate Associations for Formal/Informal Decision for Drug Use/Possession Referrals, Pennsylvania Sample (2002)

	N	No petition	Petition
All cases	2059	40.4%	59.6%
RACE (.000)[a]			
White	1610	44.6%	55.4%
Black	391	20.7%	79.3%
Other	58	55.2%	44.8%
AGE (.024)[a]	97	51.5%	48.5%
10-13			
14-15	574	42.3%	57.7%
16-17	1388	38.8%	61.2%
GENDER (.000)[a]			
Female	337	50.7%	49.3%
Male	1722	38.3%	61.7%
Marijuana (.000)[a]			
No (other drug)	819	29.3%	70.7%
Yes	1240	47.7%	52.3%
SINGLE PARENT (.044)[a]			
No	1159	42.3%	57.7%
Yes	900	37.9%	62.1%
IN SCHOOL(.017)[a]	464	35.6%	64.4%
No**			
Yes	1595	41.8%	58.2%
REFERRAL (.056)	91	30.8%	69.2%
Other			
Police	1968	40.8%	59.2%
CHARGE (.007)[a]	50	22.0%	78.0%
Felony			
Misdemeanor	2009	40.8%	59.2%
COUNTY (.001)[a]	1613	42.3%	57.7%
Other			
Allegheny	446	33.4%	66.6%

a. Probability for chi-square test.

Individual Factors. In addition to the race of the youth, the gender, family status, school status, and age of the child were also examined. The family situation was dichotomized into single-parent households and other types of households (e.g., including step parents and both biological parents). Findings imply that youths from single-parent households were more likely to have a petition filed. Also, whether the youth was in school was examined (cases with no information on school affiliation were placed in the "out" category). Those youths not in school were more likely to be formally processed. Females made up about 16% of the cases and were less likely to have a petition filed. Over all, older youths more likely to have a petition filed. Dummy variables were used for race, with "White" serving as the suppressed reference (comparison) group (for the variable Black: being Black is coded "1" and being White or "Other" is coded "0"; for the variable White: being White is coded "1" and being Black or "Other" is coded "0";. for the variable "Other": being "Other" is coded "1" and being Black or White is coded "0"). Black youths were more likely to be formally petitioned relative to White and "Other" youths.

Contextual Factors. The counties were dichotomized into Allegheny County (Pittsburgh) and other counties. Allegheny County (categorized as a Class 2 county) has approximately 1,270,000 residents, with a juvenile population (age 10-17) of approximately 131,700. The only larger county in Pennsylvania is Philadelphia (Class 1), which was not examined. The other counties ranged in populations between 610,400 (Class 2A) to approximately 18,220 (Class 8) . Youths from these smaller counties made up 78% of the youths examined. Over all, youths from Allegheny County were more likely to be petitioned.

Multivariate Analysis of Petition for Delinquency Decisions in the Pennsylvania Sample

Table 6.12 presents logistic regression estimates (appropriate for dichotomous dependent variables) for drug referrals and the decision to file a delinquency petition. Model 1 includes only the race variables, with the White youths serving as the reference group. While Whites and "Other" youths had about the same likelihood of having a petition filed against them, Black youths were three times more likely to be formally processed.

Model 2 introduces the available legal variables. Controlling for the effects of legal variables, Black youths remained significantly more likely to be processed formally. Also, youths charged with felony drug use/possession (rather than misdemeanor use/possession) were more likely to be petitioned. Youths charged with possession of marijuana (relative to a "harder" drug) and those referred by police (rather than by school or family member) were significantly less likely to be petitioned.

In Model 3 the individual variables of age, gender, family and school status are included. Once again, the effect of being Black significantly

Table 6.12. Logistic Regression Estimates of Formal/Informal Decisions for Drug Use/Possession Referrals, Pennsylvania Sample (2002) (*N*=2,059)

	Model 1 Coefficient	S.E.	Model 2 Coefficient	S.E.	Model 3 Coefficient	S.E.	Model 4 Coefficient	S.E.
Black	1.125[a]	.134	1.091[a]	.136	1.064[a]	.139	1.040[a]	.143
Other	-.425	.269	-.445	.273	-.482	.277	-.470	.278
Marijuana			-.745[a]	.098	-.728[a]	.098	-.727[a]	.098
Police referral			-.527[a]	.238	-.663[a]	.243	-.673[a]	.244
Felony			.739[a]	.356	.714[a]	.358	.725[a]	.358
Male					.490[a]	.126	.490[a]	.126
In school					-.229	.117	-.228	.117
Single parent					.062	.096	.058	.097
Age					.149	.083	.147	.083
Allegheny							.088	.123
Constant	.217		1.177		.655		-.659	
-2 log likelihood	2691.83		2619.95		2595.98		2595.47	

a. Significant $p <0.5$.

increased the probability that a youth will be petitioned. Being male also significantly increased the likelihood of a petition. The other "individual factors" were insignificant, while the legal factors remained significant.

Finally, the contextual variable was included in Model 4. Cases from Allegheny County (Pittsburgh) were not significantly different from those in less populated counties in relation to petitioning decisions. Black youths, males, those charged with felony non-marijuana charges and those referred by non-law enforcement agencies remained significantly more likely to have their behavior deemed serious enough for formal entry into the juvenile justice system.

CONCLUSIONS

As stated earlier, the lack of a prior record variable is of concern in regard to the findings. It is quite possible that if a youth's prior record were taken into account, the observed relationship between being Black and being petitioned would prove to be spurious. In order to partially take this limitation into account, the outcomes for the youngest (10-13) of these youths were examined (n=97) on the assumption that these individuals lacked a prior record. At the bivariate level, Black youths remained significantly more likely to be formally petitioned relative to White youths (there were no 10-13 year old "Other" youths). When a multivariate analysis was performed (including all remaining legal, individual and contextual variables), the only significant factor was whether the youth was Black (results are available upon request). Black youths, ages 10-13, referred for drug possession/use were approximately three times more likely to be petitioned for formal penetration into the juvenile justice system.

Over all, the examination of these data at both the national level and in Pennsylvania suggests that race is an important consideration in the decision making of juvenile justice practitioners. As suggested earlier, this does not imply conscious intent to discriminate by these decision makers, but rather an automatic response not subject to intentional control (Payne, 2001). Black faces, even young Black faces, activate stereotypical attributes (Eberhardt et al., 2004). Juvenile justice personnel, by definition, think of crime and criminality on a daily, if not hourly, basis. Consequently, when a Black youth is referred, "a form of racialized seeing" occurs (Eberhardt et al., 2004). Blacks are seen as predisposed to crime (Bridges and Steen, 1998). Black faces equal criminal faces, and thus must be treated as criminal — that is, punished. This is not a condition limited to those working in the field of juvenile justice, but applies to all of us (Eberhardt et al., 2004). It is incumbent among all of us to increase awareness of this stereotypical association between being Black and being criminally predisposed — the "rhetorical wink" (Miller, 2000) — and to continue researching the role of race in official decision making and in our day-to-day lives.

NOTES

1. Special thanks to Linda Bender and the Pennsylvania Juvenile Court Judges' Commission Juvenile Court for the use and management of the data, and to Laura Patterson for her helpful comments and support.

7. The Racial Divide in U.S. Prisons: An Examination of Racial and Ethnic Disparity in Imprisonment

Michael J. Lynch

Beginning in the early 1970s, the U.S. correctional system began a period of expansion during which the rate of imprisonment increased every year for more than 30 years (1972-2006). In 1972, there were slightly more than 196,000 inmates in U.S. prisons, and the rate of imprisonment stood at 93 inmates per 100,000 citizens (Sourcebook, 2005). By the end of 2006, U.S. prisons housed more than 1.5 million inmates (Sabol, Couture, and Harrison, 2007) — 1.3 million more inmates than in 1972. During 2006, the rate of imprisonment topped 500 inmates per 100,000 citizens.

Why begin a discussion of race, ethnicity and imprisonment with facts concerning the growth of the American prison system during the last 35 years? Because during this period — a period identified as the "imprisonment binge" due to the consistent rise in incarceration (Austin and Irwin, 2001; Lynch, 2007) — there is evidence of a persistent racial and ethnic disparity in incarceration. For some (Lynch and Sabol, 2000; Human Rights Watch, 2000; Tonry, 1995) the chief concern during this period was the effect of the U.S. government's "war on drugs" on racial disparity in prison populations. Whatever the cause of these disparities, the percentage of the prison population composed by minorities rose dramatically.

This chapter explores the issue of minority overrepresentation in the U.S. prison system. Data on the racial and ethnic composition of the U.S. prison system are examined along with studies of the lifetime probability of incarceration by race and ethnicity. Attention is also focused on the persistence of minority overrepresentation in prisons across time and place, the effect of imprisonment on minority communities, and the disproportionate impact of imprisonment on felony voter disenfranchisement.

By the Numbers: Evidence of Minority Overrepresentation in Prisons

At the end of 2006, there were 1,570,861 inmates in state and federal prisons in the U.S. Approximately 96% of these inmates were serving sentences longer than one year (Sabol et al., 2007). Black, Hispanic/Latinos, and White Americans composed 37.5%, 20.5% and 35.1% of this latter group[1]. Using these figures, the U.S. Department of Justice estimated that 4.8% of the Black, 1.9% of the Hispanic/Latino and 0.7% of the White American populations were incarcerated in U.S. prisons (Sabol, Minton and Harrison, 2006).

While Black Americans have been overrepresented in prison compared to White Americans for some time, 1991 marked the first year in which there were numerically more Black than White Americans in prisons (Snell, 1995). Indeed, historical trend data indicate that the U.S. prison population was composed primarily (majority) of White offenders until the mid-1980s (Cahalan, 1986, p. 85). For example, in 1933, 74% of the U.S. prison population was White. The racial composition of U.S. prisons began to slowly shift toward larger proportions of Blacks over the next few decades. A half century later, prisons were predominantly inhabited by minorities.

Available historical data for the U.S. also indicate that sentence differentials, which contribute to inequities in the racial and ethnic composition of prisons, have long favored White offenders. Cahalan (1986) reported that in 1890, average sentences for prison and jail inmates varied by race. Whites had the shortest average sentences (3.66 years), followed by Blacks (5.01), Native Americans (5.64) and Chinese (6.58).

The overrepresentation of Blacks in prison (data on Hispanics in prison are historically limited, and must be omitted here) can also be examined using race-specific rates of imprisonment, which describe the number of people in each racial group in prison for every 100,000 citizens in the nation. In 1980, for instance, the Black rate of incarceration was 1,156 per 100,000 residents, while the White rate of incarceration was 174 per 100,000 (Snell, 1995), or 6.6 times higher for Blacks than Whites. In 2006, these rates had reached 3,190 per 100,000 for Blacks and 535 for Whites, or 6 times higher for Blacks. Thus, while the incarceration rate expanded for both Black and White Americans from 1980 through 2006, there was a modest reduction in racial disparity measured by race specific incarceration rates. Despite this small decline, Black Americans continue to be significantly overrepresented in prison populations compared to White Americans.

Table 7.1. Incarceration Rates per 100,000 by Race, Ethnicity and Age, Males, 2005[a]

	White[b]	Black[b]	Hispanic	B/W[c]	H/W[c]
Age					
18-19	274	1920	791	7.0	2.9
20-24	948	6345	2493	6.7	2.7
25-29	1098	8082	2618	7.4	2.4
30-34	1172	7726	2450	6.6	2.1
35-39	1067	6630	2255	6.2	2.1
40-44	923	5472	1975	5.9	2.2
45-54	493	3136	1327	6.4	2.7
55+	135	697	416	5.2	3.1

a. Adapted from Harrison and Beck, 2006.
b. Excludes Hispanics.
c. Ratio of Black (B/W) or Hispanic (H/W) inmates in each age group rounded to nearest 0.1.

Discrepancies in racial and ethnic rates of incarceration are evident when we decompose prison population by categories. For example, these disparities are evident across age groups and states. At every age group, Blacks and Hispanics are overrepresented in the U.S. prison population compared to Whites (Table 7.1). These data indicate that either there is a fairly persistent form of discrimination in criminal justice processes that produces these results, or that, at every age, minorities are significantly more likely to engage in crimes that result in incarceration. To address this question, a further discussion of racial differences in crime will be presented later in this chapter.

The *extensive* racial differences in incarceration described above do not apply to the imprisonment of women. This observation does not mean, however, that biases are not evident among the female inmate population. In 2006, females composed 6.9% of sentenced offenders (Sabol et al., 2007). White females made up 47.6% of female inmates, while Black and Hispanic/Latino females comprised 27.7% and 20% of female inmates, respectively. Minority females, while not overrepresented to the same extent as minority males, are still overrepresented in prison relative to their proportions in the general U.S. population. Two factors could explain the differences noted in the racial and ethnic composition of male versus female prison populations.

First, it is possible that minority males and females have dramatically different rates of offending, which could explain why they are incarcerated at different proportions within their sex groups. For this explanation to be considered plausible, it would also indicate that, relative to other women, White females have higher rates of offending than White males have in comparison to minority males. On these grounds, this explanation appears questionable — White females do not have higher within-gender crime probabilities than White males. Second, the difference between minority male and female imprisonment concentrations could have a relationship to stereotypes or expectations concerning crime that are both gender- and race-linked. Crime stereotypes, for example, depict minority males, especially Black males, as the average or typical offender. These stereotypes do not need to be true to impact racial representation in imprisonment, nor must they be true to explain minority male-female differences in imprisonment. Rather, they simply need to be acted upon as if they were true (see chapter by Patterson, this volume).

Cross-Sectional Racial Disparities in Imprisonment

In his role as director of The Sentencing Project (TSP), Marc Mauer has examined issues related to racial disparity in the criminal justice system for 25 years. A 2007 report from TSP (Mauer and King, 2007a) examines racial and ethnic disparities in incarceration across U.S. states (see also, Lynch, 2007). While there are significant variations in the rate at which minorities and Whites are incarcerated across states, Mauer and King (2007, p. 4) noted that, "The American prison and jail system is marked by entrenched racial disparity in the population of incarcerated people." This claim is illustrated in Table 7.2.

In Table 7.2, the national averages for the Black/White and Hispanic/White incarceration rate ratios for each state are 5.56 and 1.8, respectively. Clearly, these figures illustrate that, on average, Black Americans are much more likely than Hispanics to experience disproportionate rates of incarceration compared to Whites. In 24 states and the District of Columbia, the Black/White incarceration ratio exceeds the national average. Among these locations, the District of Columbia (18.86), Iowa (13.59), Vermont (12.49), New Jersey (12.38), Connecticut (12.0), Wisconsin (10.64), North Dakota (10.05), South Dakota (10.02), have extraordinarily high B/W imprisonment ratios.

For Hispanics, 15 of the 42 locations providing information that allows separate calculations for Hispanics have higher than average H/W incarceration ratios. In no location is the high H/W ratio close to the highest B/

Table 7.2. Ratio of Black to White (B/W) and Hispanic to White (H/W) Incarceration Rates per 100,000 by State for 2005[a]

State	B/W	H/W	State	B/W	H/W
Alabama	3.54	——[b]	Missouri	5.25	1.18
Alaska	4.33	0.76	Montana	8.24	1.95
Arizona	5.58	1.82	**NATIONAL**	**5.56**	**1.80**
Arkansas	3.86	0.60	Nebraska	8.34	2.55
California	6.50	1.70	Nevada	4.65	0.99
Connecticut	12.00	6.54	New Jersey	12.38	3.32
Delaware	6.36	2.35	New York	9.31	4.47
DOC[c]	18.86	4.77	N. Carolina	5.40	——
Florida	4.45	0.65	N. Dakota	10.05	3.18
Georgia	3.32	0.93	Ohio	6.38	1.78
Hawaii	1.83	0.41	Oklahoma	4.40	1.12
Idaho	4.25	2.45	Oregon	5.84	1.14
Illinois	9.06	1.86	Pennsylvania	9.05	5.62
Indiana	5.46	1.25	Rhode Island	9.62	3.30
Iowa	13.59	2.47	S. Carolina	4.47	1.15
Kansas	6.99	——	S. Dakota	10.02	——
Kentucky	4.98	1.35	Tennessee	4.12	1.15
Louisiana	4.69	0.47	Texas	4.74	1.24
Maine	7.60	——	Utah	9.15	2.14
Maryland	5.48	——	Vermont	12.49	——
Mass.	8.13	6.11	Virginia	5.89	1.23
Michigan	5.49	0.96	Washington	6.42	1.34
Minnesota	9.14	——	W. Virginia	5.58	0.54
Mississippi	3.46	1.21	Wisconsin	10.64	——

a. Adapted from Mauer and King (2007, p. 6). Ratios above 1.0 indicate overrepresentation.
b. Data on Hispanics are missing for some states.
c. DOC is the District of Columbia.

W imprisonment rate ratios. In contrast to the B/W imprisonment ratios in Table7.2, the H/W imprisonment ratio sometimes is less than one (for 9 of the 42 locations for which these data are available). When this ratio is less than one, it indicates that the White rate of imprisonment exceeds the Hispanic rate. Note that such a result never occurs for the B/W imprisonment rate. This finding indicates that B/W imprisonment rate differentials are persistent across states, though more or less exaggerated in some locations, while there is much more extensive variation in the Hispanic/White ratio to the extent that this bias is not evident in all locations.

Imprisonment and the Life Course and Lifetime Estimate of the Probability of Incarceration

The data reviewed above indicate a fairly persistent racial difference in the prevalence of incarceration across time, place, and even age groups. On the basis of similar observations, Pettit and Western (2004) argued that the effect of incarceration on Black populations has become so pervasive that it can now be considered part of the *life course of African American males*. Indeed, Pettit and Western argue that, "In the historic context of the prison boom, incarceration may collectively reshape adulthood for a whole cohort" (p. 155) of African-American males.

In an earlier study, Bonczar and Beck (1997) estimated the lifetime likelihood of incarceration for various populations. Based on incarceration and population trends, they estimated that 5.1% of all Americans would spend some time in a state or federal prison during their lifetimes (1997:2). The likelihood of incarceration, however, varied by race and gender. For example, while 9% of all men could be expected to spend some time in prison during their lifetimes, 28.5% of Black men and 16.0% of Hispanic males, but only 4.4% of White males, were expected to serve some time in prison during their lifetimes (1997). Lifetime chances of incarceration were much lower for females, and showed much less variation. For White, Black and Hispanic females, the cumulative lifetime chances of incarceration were: 0.1%, 0.4% and 0.2%, respectively.

Combining Pettit and Western's (2004) views with Bonczar and Beck's (1997) analyses, one could clearly conclude that imprisonment is not a normal part of the life course of White Americans, while it certainly appears to be part of the life course for more than one-quarter of the African American male population, and for approximately one in six Hispanic males. Bonczar's later analysis (2003) confirmed these results for men born in 2001, among whom 5.9% of White, 17% of Hispanic, and 32% of African-American men were expected to be incarcerated during their lifetimes.

Pettit and Western (2004) also examined race-linked, cohort-specific incarceration probabilities for men born between 1945-1949, and 1965-1969. Their analyses revealed several relevant findings.

First, significant racial differences in imprisonment persisted across age groups within each cohort. For example, for 15 to 19 year olds in the first cohort, African American men were 6.15 times more likely to go to prison than young White men. Among older men (30-34), African-American men were 7.54 times more likely to have been in prison compared to White men.

Second, Pettit and Western hypothesized that the probability of incarceration should increase for men in the second cohort since imprisonment had expanded rapidly as these men reached adulthood. They found that the likelihood of imprisonment for young White (+ 0.07%) and young African-American (+0.11%) males had not changed dramatically. In contrast, for older White and African-American males a doubling in the likelihood of incarceration was evident. For older Whites the doubling effect was numerically small, from 1.4% to 2.9%. For African-Americans, however, the doubling effect was numerically large, and jumped from 8.6% to 15.07% for those age 25-29, and from 10.56% to 20.50% for those aged 30-34. Moreover, the doubling effect maintained the large discrepancy in the rate of incarceration between Whites and African-Americans.

Racial Differences Among Female Inmates. Earlier, it was noted that Black women composed approximately 28% of the female prison population. To be sure, Black females make up a much smaller percentage of the incarcerated female population than Black males do of the incarcerated male prison population. This comparison suggests that Black females do not experience the same level of racial disparity in imprisonment as Black males. Yet, this comparison still leaves open the question of addressing racial disparity among females.

The extent of racial and ethnic disparity among female prison populations can also be examined using race-specific incarceration rates and lifetime likelihoods of incarceration, as was illustrated above for males. With respect to incarceration rates, Harrison and Beck (2006) estimated that 359 of every 100,000 Black females in the U.S. were in prison or jail in 2004, a rate that was about one-fourth the combined incarceration rate for African-American males and females. For Hispanic females, the incarceration rate was 143 per 100,000, while for White females the rate was 81 per 100,000. In terms of race-specific incarceration ratios, the Black female to White female ratio of 4.5 was significantly lower than the Black to White male incarceration ratio. Though lower, this ratio is still high and troubling, perhaps indicating extensive processing biases that lead to the overrepresentation of Black females in prison.

In his analysis of lifetime probabilities of incarceration, Bonczar (2003) also calculated race-and gender-specific incarceration probabilities. He found that the percentage of Black females ever incarcerated was 1.7% of the Black female population. This likelihood of incarceration was nearly six times higher than the percentage of White females ever incarcerated (0.3%).

Taken together, these studies indicate that the life course of Black females is much less likely than the life course of Black males to include a term of incarceration. Indeed, since only 1.7% of Black females were estimated to experience incarceration, it would be difficult to conclude, as Pettit and Western did for Black males, that incarceration is part of the life course for Black women in America. Nevertheless, relative to White females, incarceration is six times more likely for Black females. Thus, relative to White females, a Black female's life course is much more likely to include incarceration.

Life Course Effects

The previous section described differences in the probability of incarceration that have effects that vary over the life course of individuals from different racial and ethnic groups. It is clear from this review that imprisonment has greater impacts on minorities than Whites, and especially on African-American males. To illustrate this point, Pettit and Western (2004) suggest that the likelihood of imprisonment is so high for African-American males that it can be considered part of the life course of a significant portion of that population. This section examines some of the ways in which this high probability of imprisonment affects other aspects of the life course for African Americans.

In a 1998 study, Rose and Clear suggested that high rates of incarceration could disrupt communities, increasing rather than decreasing the level of crime (see also, Clear, 2007). Drawing on social disorganization theory, they argued that communities where a large number of residents were incarcerated might experience a disruption in informal networks of social control within families, local economies and political networks. In effect, high rates of incarceration could reduce the "collective efficacy" of neighborhoods (on collective efficacy see, Sampson et al., 1997) or the community's ability to control crime through informal mechanisms. Rose and Clear also noted that this effect is not necessarily continuous, but probably works in a "tipping point" fashion — that is, there is a threshold, that when crossed, impairs a community's collective efficacy.

Social mobility has long been examined as one of the factors that influences informal community social control. Social mobility is often perceived as a "voluntary" outcome produced by the upward and downward social mobility of residents, which, in turn, affects residential movement into and out of communities. Rose and Clear added the idea that in some communities, the level of social mobility is influenced by involuntary movement or mobility, such as removal from the community through incarceration. Thus, imprisonment may be an important source of involuntary mobility and community disruption, especially in African-American communities, because of the high lifetime probability of incarceration experienced by African-American males. To place this explanation in context, Clear et al. (2003) provided an example of a community in the Brownsville section of Brooklyn, New York, where the incarceration rate for residents was 150 times greater (3% of residents were imprisoned) than for some nearby Brooklyn neighborhoods.

Clear et al. (2003) provided a modified test of the assertion that communities with high incarceration rates would experience community disruption associated with involuntary mobility, and hence an increase in crime. They found that "after a certain concentration of residents is removed from the community through incarceration, the effect of additional admissions to prison is to increase, not decrease, crime," thereby supporting the contention that there is a tipping point where "removing a high concentration of offenders from a community has a destabilizing effect on the community's level of social disorganization" (p. 55).

Interpreted through the framework of the life course perspective, Clear and Rose's research speaks to the contention that life courses can be treated as reflections of social structures (Lynch, 1996). In this view, the average life course of an individual can be related to the conditions of life and opportunities that attach to structural locations in society, such as being male or female, wealthy or poor, White or Black, and so on. Moreover, these structural locations intersect, so that being a poor, Black male presents different opportunities and life course patterns from being a poor, Black female, or a poor White male. In effect, structural locations shape the kinds of opportunities and choices individuals can easily or normally access (Lynch and Michalowski, 2006), which can be used to explain patterns or similarities in life courses across individuals in similar structural locations, including, for example, the likelihood of incarceration. The structural antecedents of an individual's life course could, therefore, also be used to explain the impact of imprisonment on community mobility, disruption, and crime as suggested by Rose and Clear.

Rose and Clear's (1998) findings are also important to the deterrence debate — that is, the question of whether raising the rate of incarceration necessarily results in a diminished rate of criminal offending (see Lynch, 2007, for further analysis of prisons and deterrence). Rose and Clear's results suggest that once incarceration passes a tipping point, it begins to drive up the rate of offending by removing individuals who, despite their criminal involvement, in some way contribute to community stability. Because these effects are concentrated in minority communities, the policy of expanding incarceration that has characterized American imprisonment trends since 1972 is likely to have a differential impact on minority and White communities. Given the extensive nature of the problem for minority communities, escalating rates of incarceration, especially because they impact minorities to a greater extent, are likely to generate a rise rather than a reduction in crime.

Finally, to place the idea of life course effects into greater context, consider the findings of Schiraldi and Ziendenberg (2002) in their study *Cellblocks or Classrooms?*. Schiraldi and Ziendenberg pointed out that the life course of African-Americans males is much more likely to include time spent incarcerated than at an institution of higher education. In the year 2000, for example, there were 791,600 African-American men in state and federal prisons and jails. That same year, there were 603,032 African-American males enrolled in institutions of higher education — or 188,568 more African-American men incarcerated than in college. According to this study, there were 13 states (Alaska, Connecticut, Delaware, Indiana, Louisiana, Michigan, Missouri, New Jersey, Ohio, Oklahoma, Pennsylvania, Texas, Wisconsin) where there were more Black males in prison than in college, three states with less than a 5% difference (Arkansas, Florida and Kentucky), and four states where the difference was less than 10% (Georgia, Mississippi, Nevada, South Carolina). Among the states with the worst records were Texas and Wisconsin. In Texas, 66,300 African-American men were in prison compared to 40,872 in higher education — or 62% more African-Americans in prison. Wisconsin faired slightly worse with 71% more African-American males in prison than in higher education (9,100 versus 5,291). Schiraldi and Ziedenberg estimated that nationally, African-American men in their earlier 30s were nearly twice as likely to have a prison record (22%) compared to a Bachelor's degree (12%). The difference between the size of the African-American male prison and college population is likely a product of other life course structures such as the likelihood of being born into poverty or urban areas with poor educational opportunities and job markets, and the extensive forms of geographic racial segregation that continue to characterize American society (Massey and Denton, 1994).

Felony Disenfranchisement

One of the compounding effects of incarceration is its impact on life after imprisonment. In theory, imprisonment is a severe penalty handed out to violators of the criminal law, which is calculated in proportion to the severity of the offense. In this view, the offender has "paid" his or her debt to society by serving a term of incarceration, and no additional punishment is justified. In practice, however, ex-inmates suffer additional penalties after their release, facing, for instance, the stigma of possessing a criminal record and the restricted life chances and life course that accompany the ex-inmate label. One of the post-incarceration impacts faced by ex-inmates relates to their right to vote, which is restricted in numerous jurisdictions and through a variety of procedures.

The loss of voting rights has become part of incarceration in the 48 states that restrict the right to vote while in prison (only Maine and Vermont permit inmates to vote). Thirty-five states prohibit felons from voting while on parole, and 30 extend this rule to felons on probation (Mauer and King, 2007a). Several states ban ex-felons from voting permanently under certain conditions (e.g., second felony conviction, or certain types of offense), and some restrict voting rights for a period of 2 or 5 years after release (The Sentencing Project, 2007).

As Fellner and Mauer (1998) point out, because felony disenfranchisement rules tend to be complex and reinstatement of voting rights is not necessarily automatic, many ex-inmates remain disenfranchised for life or long after their terms of incarceration end. This not only affects the ability of ex-inmates to participate in democratic government, but there is also a concern that the racial disparity noted in incarceration is reflected in felony disenfranchisement.

The Sentencing Project (2007) estimated that 5.3 million American citizens, or 1 in 40 adults, had lost their right to vote in any given year due to permanent or temporary felony voting restrictions. Of these individuals, 1.4 million were African-American men, which translated into approximately 13% of the African-American male population 18 and older. The Sentencing Project indicated that this rate of disenfranchisement was seven times higher than the national average rate of felony disenfranchisement — a ratio that is even greater than the Black to White incarceration ratio. The Sentencing Project also estimated that the effects of felony disenfranchisement on Black males were greatest in the five states that denied ex-offenders voting rights. In those states, one quarter of African-American men were permanently barred from voting. According to the Sentencing Project, given current incarcerative practices in states that disenfranchise ex-offenders, 40% of African-American men may experience permanent disenfranchisement during their lifetimes.

In short, the practice of felony disenfranchisement has been critiqued on several grounds (Fellner and Mauer, 1998). For African Americans, and in particular for African-American men, an additional concern is that the processing biases that produce differential incarceration rates by race have a prolonged impact on their lives after prison, including their right to air their democratic rights through the process of voting.

OVERREPRESENTATION AND CRIME

One criticism often levied against the type of discussion of racial and ethnic bias in imprisonment presented above is that it fails to take account of the fact that minorities may be over-represented in prison because of the amount and type of crime they commit relative to Whites. Given the purpose of this chapter, an extensive analysis of this claim cannot be undertaken here (for a discussion, see Lynch, 2002, 2007). Instead, the following discussion focuses on known drug use patterns across racial and ethnic groups, and the prevalence of racial and ethnic groups in prison serving time for drug convictions.

One reason for focusing on drug use difference is that the federal government's "war on drugs" is often cited as an important cause of racial and ethnic disparity in incarceration (Tonry, 1995). Researchers have noted that racially- and ethnically-biased enforcement practices, along with differences in punishments focusing on certain drugs, contribute to minority overrepresentation in prison (Mauer, 1999). For example, in 2004 the federal Drug Enforcement Administration arrested 4,648 Whites, 2,273 Blacks and 3,943 Hispanics for crimes involving powdered cocaine, but 695 Whites and 3,161 Blacks for crack cocaine offenses (Office of National Drug Control Policy, 2006). As these data indicate, combined cocaine arrests are much higher for Blacks than for Whites. These data are, in themselves, misleading to the extent that they do not take into account differences in drug user patterns across racial and ethnic groups. Data on the distribution of drug use across racial and ethnic groups can help address whether such biases exist, and whether they contribute to disproportionate racial and ethnic representation within prisons. Though data on drug use and drug incarceration cannot be generalized to other offense types, the analysis of drug use and incarceration patterns provides a useful illustration of potential racial and ethnic biases observed for other offenses.

Periodically, the U.S. Department of Health and Human Services estimates racial and ethnic differences in drug use among the U.S. population for ten drug categories (crack and powdered cocaine, inhalants, hallucinogens, psychotherapeutics, stimulants, tranquillizers, PCP, LSD and heroin; see, National Institute on Drug Abuse [NIDA], 2003). Numerous studies indicate that differential enforcement and codified sentencing distinctions for different forms of cocaine (e.g., penalties for powdered versus crack cocaine) contribute to racial disparities in imprisonment (U.S. Sentencing Commission, 2007). Thus, while the use of each drug type named above is greater among Whites than among other racial and ethnic groups, with the exception of small differences for heroin, we concentrate on cocaine for the present analysis.

NIDA reports the following cocaine use patterns by race and ethnicity for males: White, non-Hispanic 0.9%; Black, non-Hispanic, 1.7%; and Hispanic, 1.8%. Some additional context is needed to make sense of these figures which appear, on their surface, to indicate higher cocaine use among minority groups compared to Whites. That context requires adjusting these figures to represent the population proportions of each racial and ethnic group. Whites comprise approximately 72% of the U.S. population, while Blacks and Hispanics comprise about 13% and 9% of the U.S. population, respectively. Omitting other racial and ethnic groups, we can calculate the number of expected cocaine users by treating the population percentages as the number of persons in a racial and ethnic category for every 1,000 Americans (e.g., 720 Whites per 1,000 Americans, 130 Blacks per 1,000 Americans, 90 Hispanics per 1,000 Americans) and multiplying by NIDA's racial and ethnic use estimates. In doing so, we can determine that there are 6.48 White (720 x 0.9%), 2.21 Black (130 x 1.7%) and 1.62 (90 x 1.8%) Hispanic cocaine users for every 1,000 Americans. When we place NIDA use estimates in the context of racial and ethnic representation in the U.S. population, we see that there are nearly three White cocaine users for every Black cocaine user, and four White cocaine users for every Hispanic cocaine user.

We can now compare these adjusted use patterns to the estimated distribution of persons sentenced for cocaine offenses in the U.S. prison population. This comparison does not correct for offense severity, so some of the racial differences may be a consequence of offense severity. Nevertheless, offense severity charges may themselves be the result of prior biases in charging, plea bargaining, etc. (see, chapter by Patterson in this volume; and see Mauer and King, 2007b, for extensive discussion), and this issue is beyond the scope of the present comparison. In addition, this estimate is based on racial differences in incarceration for all drug types. As noted, previous research provides a reason to believe that this procedure will underestimate racial and ethnic differences in incarceration for cocaine offenses.

Using drug incarceration data provided by Harrison and Beck (2003), we can estimate that for every 1,000 inmates sentenced to prison, 570 were African American, 230 were White and 190 were Hispanic. We can determine if these figures are unbiased by returning to the population-adjusted NIDA figures presented earlier, which indicated that, out of a population of 1,000 Americans, there were 6.48 White cocaine users, 2.21 Black cocaine users and 1.62 Hispanic cocaine users. These figures indicate that to discover 230 White cocaine users, we would need a population of *35,500* Whites (230/6.48 * 1000), *257,920* African Americans (570/2.21 * 1000), and *117,280* Hispanics (190/1.62 * 1000) — or a population that is 8.6% White, 62.8% African American, and 28.6% Hispanic; that is, a population that is vastly different from the racial and ethnic composition of the U.S. population.

For minorities, the disparities described above are seen across use, arrest, and incarceration data for drugs more generally (Mauer and King, 2007b, p. 20). As Mauer and King note, among African Americans monthly drug use is reported by 14%, while African Americans make up 37% of drug arrests and 56% of those incarcerated for drug offenses. In effect, biases at the arrest, charging, and sentencing stages may all contribute to the racial and ethnic differences in drug arrest incarceration noted here.

It is plausible that these same decision-making biases operate for other offense categories, and that estimates of racial biases that fail to account for racial and ethnic representation of the U.S. population will underestimate the level of bias in the criminal justice system (see Lynch, 2002). Prior research, for example, makes standardized comparisons across racial and ethnic groups employing a standard population adjustment procedure that measures crimes per 100,000 population. These estimates, however, are biased when it comes to race and ethnicity since they create racial and ethnic population groups that are equivalent (e.g., 100,000 Whites, 100,000

African Americans, etc.). Since Whites comprise 72% of the U.S. population, the ordinary form of standardized population estimates employed by many criminologists will underestimate racial bias.

CONCLUSION

Racial and ethnic biases have long been a part of American culture. Studies too numerous to review here indicate the broad kinds of impacts that cultural and institutional racial and ethnic biases have on minority groups (e.g., Massey and Denton, 1994; Hacker, 1995). It should come as no surprise that broader institutionalized and cultural biases also play themselves out in the criminal justice process. Legal rules, as the U.S. Sentencing Commission's research has illustrated, cannot necessarily remove the effect of racial and ethnic biases (e.g., see: *http://www.ussc.gov/hearings/11_15_06/McCurdy-testimony.pdf*). Nor can we rely on the fact that even rules that appear racially and ethnically neutral on their face will be enforced equally.

As this chapter has illustrated, racial and ethnic biases have become an entrenched problem in the American criminal justice system. These biases are pervasive to the extent that they are evident across time periods, cohorts of those subjected to incarceration, and even across states. One of two conclusions is possible from revelation of these extensive biases: either African Americans and Hispanics are, across time and place in America, much more criminally inclined than Whites, or the time and place independence of these racial and ethnic differences is evidence of the persistence and extent of institutional and cultural bias in America that acts to the detriment of minorities.

Even if we accept the first conclusion, we must address why the pattern of difference in criminal involvement across racial and ethnic groups persists. This question also cannot be addressed without examining the role that institutional and cultural biases play in the different life chances and structures various racial and ethnic groups can access, or the life courses commonly traveled by different racial and ethnic groups.

It is unfortunate that in the 21st century, with its myriad of serious problems, the problem of racial and ethnic bias has not been solved. Moreover, during the past three decades, many indicators of racial and ethnic bias — measures of income and wealth inequality, housing market opportunities, racial segregation, and occupational access — suggest that these biases persist, and in some cases have expanded. The extent and continuation of these biases in the criminal justice system, which is based on a presumption of equal treatment, require continued research. But, more than research is needed: concrete plans of action that alleviate these problems should remain at the forefront of criminological investigations. Without such plans and policies, the continued efforts of criminologists to research and expose these problems become a futile effort.

NOTES

1. Readers should be cautioned concerning conclusions about trends in the racial and ethnic composition of the U.S. prison population due to changes in counting racial and ethnic groups that have occurred in recent years and in the long term. Sabol et al. (2006, p. 7) summarized the problems associated with racial and ethnic prison composition trend data from recent years after the Bureau of Justice Statistics changed the procedures for counting and classifying race and ethnicity in 2005. This change included an effort to count persons with one race (97%) and multiple races separately. This procedural change in recording race reduced the number and percentage of inmates counted in non-White categories. In addition, some states do not report persons of Hispanic origin, or those with multiple racial identities, which Sabol et al. concluded underestimates the size of the Hispanic prison population while overestimating the proportion of White Americans in prison.

   In the long term, the racial and ethnic proportion of the prison population is difficult to measure due to changes in classifying the racial and ethnic composition of the U.S. prison population. In 1980, for example, 7.7% of the U.S. prison population was estimated to be Hispanic (Beck and Gilliard, 1995), while in 2006 this group accounted for 20.5% of the U.S. prison population. It is unlikely that the percentage of Hispanics in U.S. prisons tripled between 1980 and 2006. Rather, the dramatic increase in the proportion of the population that was Hispanic reflects increased efforts to identify and count persons of Hispanic origins. As the counts for Hispanic inmates became more accurate. by forcing Hispanics to be counted separately, a larger number of states recorded these data, and Hispanic ethnicity became a routine category in data reporting systems, this tended to reduce the number of inmates reported as White when race/ethnicity was reported as tri-categorical (i.e., White-non-Hispanic, Black-non-Hispanic, Hispanic).

   To be sure, some of the increase in the prevalence of Hispanics in prison stems from the growing proportion of the U.S. population composed of Hispanic populations over time. However, because Hispanic ethnicity was not officially or effectively recorded in the U.S. Census until 1970 (Hispanic origins were recorded indirectly in the 1950 and 1960 Censuses for five Southwestern states, but these data are considered unreliable because of the collection technique; the 1940 Census recorded persons who claimed Spanish as their "mother tongue"; in the 1930 Census, Mexican was included as a racial subcategory; see Guzman, 2001), it is difficult to estimate the precise impact of changes in the proportion of the general Hispanic population on imprisonment in the long term. Nevertheless, according to Census data, the percentage of the U.S. population that was Hispanic (any race) grew from 4.7% in 1970 to 12.5% by 2000 (Gibson and Jung, 2002; Guzman, 2001), while the African-American population expanded at a much slower rate, from 11.1% in 1970 to 12.9% in 2000 (McKinnon, 2001).

8. Racial Bias and the Death Penalty

Judith Kavanaugh-Earl
John K. Cochran
M. Dwayne Smith
Sondra J. Fogel
Beth Bjerregaard

In 2005, blacks constituted 12.8% of the U.S. population but 48.6% of persons arrested for criminal homicide, 53% of those convicted of criminal homicide, 42% of those currently under a sentence of death, and 34% of persons executed since 1976 (Death Penalty Information Center, 2007). In addition, while blacks and whites are victims of criminal homicides in almost equal numbers, approximately 80% of the persons executed since 1976 were convicted of killing white victims compared to 13% for killing blacks (Amnesty International, 2003). About half of this country's executions since 1976 have involved whites convicted of killing whites and about one-tenth involved blacks convicted of killing blacks (Amnesty International, 2003). More telling than these intra-racial execution data is the fact that only about one out of every fifty executions involved whites convicted of killing blacks (Amnesty International, 2003) — there is an approximate tenfold difference in execution outcomes for inter-racial killings involving black offenders compared to whites.

These figures make it relevant to ask if the current capital punishment process in the U.S. is free from racial bias. After all, similar racial disparities are evident throughout the criminal justice system in this country. For example, while blacks comprise about 13% of the population, they account for approximately 48% of all inmates under local, state, or federal authority (see chapter by Lynch, this volume), and the Bureau of Justice Statistics (2007) has estimated that more than one in every four black men will be sent to jail or prison during their lives. Past patterns of racial disparity in death sentencing played a significant role in the U.S. Supreme Court's holding in *Furman v. Georgia* (1972) that discretionary death sentencing statutes violated the Eighth Amendment ban on cruel and unusual punishment due to the arbitrary and capricious manner in which capital sentences were produced. Does such a problem continue to plague the capital punishment process today?

Defining Racial Disparity and Discrimination

Before addressing this issue, we must first distinguish between racial differences, racial disparities, and racial discrimination. A *racial difference* is, for us, a simple, absolute mathematical difference between the probability of a death sentence for a black defendant versus a white defendant (or the odds of execution). For instance, blacks comprise 42% of those currently under a sentence of death, while whites comprise approximately 56%; the racial difference is thus 14 percentage points. Such a value suggests that any racial difference in capital sentencing *appears* to indicate bias against white defendants.

However, there are many reasons not to accept this definition of racial differences as evidence of a race problem with capital punishment. Hence, social scientists and jurists both elect, instead, to examine evidence of *racial disparity*. In its most simplified form, a racial disparity compares the odds of a death sentence for each race by the percentage of the general population that is from each race. For instance, if 42% of those under a sentence of death are black, but blacks comprise about 13% of the U. S. population, then blacks *appear* to be overrepresented on death row by a function of 3.2 times their representation in the general population (3.2 = 42 / 13). Conversely, while whites constitute a majority of those under a sentence of death (56%), they constitute an even larger share of the general population (80%). Thus, whites *appear* to be underrepresented on death row by a factor of 0.7 times their composition of the general population (0.7 = 56 / 80). Evidence of a *racial disparity* in capital sentencing *appears* to be more in line with conventional wisdom. However, it is, once again, a simplified form of such evidence.

These measures do not correct for potential differences in offending across racial groups. Thus, instead of comparing the proportions of blacks and whites sentenced to death against their proportions in the general population, the comparison should involve the proportions of blacks and whites sentenced to death against their proportions in the population of capital offenders. Unfortunately, such comparisons are not as easy to make because the "true" racial composition of the population of capital offenders is unknown: this is because prosecutors' decisions to charge homicide offenders with capital murder are discretionary and possibly tainted by racial disparity/discrimination.

With this in mind, this "next best" evidence of racial disparity in capital sentencing examines the proportion of those currently under a sentence of death who are black (42%) against the proportion of those charged with murder or non-negligent manslaughter who are black (approximately 49%; the data for whites are 56% and 49%, respectively). This evidence *appears* to suggest that death sentences are less likely for black homicide defendants, and more likely for white homicide defendants, convicted of murder. But not all, or even most, criminal homicides are eligible for the death penalty ("death-eligible"). So, even this corrected measure of racial disparity in capital sentencing is based on the wrong subpopulations of blacks and whites. Again, instead of comparing the proportion of those under a sentence of death who are black to the proportion of homicide offenders who are black, the appropriate population for comparison is the proportion of capital offenders who are black. But, this population is not known. Moreover, there are many other factors across which whites and blacks differ that could account for any observed differences in the likelihood of a capital sentence and which, in turn, would need to be examined, adjusted, and controlled before we could arrive at a reliable figure of the degree of racial disparity, if any, in capital sentencing. Criminologists and social scientists have gone to great lengths to employ the best statistical techniques and data to examine racial disparity. Below, we review this body of literature and the evidence produced, and present some additional evidence as well. But before we can do so, there are still some unresolved conceptual matters to be addressed; these have to do with the concept of *racial discrimination.*

Legal Issues in Racial Discrimination

The Fourteenth Amendment to the U.S. Constitution guarantees citizens equal protection under the law. The arbitrary, unequal or capricious application of the death penalty violates the Eighth Amendment's ban of cruel and unusual punishment. As such, criminal penalties should not be unequally applied to black offenders relative to white offenders; blacks should not be punished more harshly than equally blameworthy and morally culpable white offenders. As applied to capital punishment, both the Fourteenth and Eighth Amendments would appear to protect against racial disparity in the application of the death penalty. However, the courts, particularly the United States Supreme Court, have been very conservative in interpreting these amendments, and have made an important distinction between the legal and the social scientific definition of racial discrimination (see *Maxwell v. Bishop, 1970* and *McCleskey v. Kemp, 1987*).

The legal definition of racial discrimination applied to the death penalty under the Equal Protection Clause is limited to intentional or purposeful imposition of a sentence of death to a particular defendant based upon his/her or the victim's race. Arbitrariness, amounting to cruel and unusual punishment within the meaning of the Eighth Amendment, has not been defined in legal terms beyond stating that only "stark" patterns of race-based differences in imposition of the death penalty would suffice (*McCleskey*, 1987). However, for social scientists, the definition of racial discrimination is much broader: it is equal to the "best" measure of racial disparity. This social scientific definition is not restricted to a specific case in which *particularized discrimination* is evident, but is applied more generally to a body of "death-eligible" cases within a common legal jurisdiction over a period of time and for which there is evidence of a significant, statistical pattern of racial disparity in capital sentencing (after adjusting for the influence of other legally relevant factors). This social scientific version of *generalized discrimination* has also been subsumed under other conceptual tags, including unconscious bias, systemic discrimination, structural racism, institutional racism, reasonable discrimination, and rational racism. The Supreme Court has held, however, that generalized, statistical patterns of racial disparity can be tolerated (reasonable discrimination or rational racism) provided they can be justified by legally relevant factors, such as, at a minimum, the presence of one or more of the statutory aggravating circumstances necessary under the *Furman* and *Gregg* decisions to make a murder so extraordinary as to be eligible for imposition of a death sentence. So the Court has, to date, found tolerable what the social scientist questions.

SYSTEMIC RACIAL DISCRIMINATION IN CAPITAL PUNISHMENT: THE EVIDENCE

The Legal Context for the Research: *McCleskey v. Kemp* (1987)

While *Furman v. Georgia* (1972) established the legal principles under which the death penalty must be administered, *McCleskey v. Kemp* (1987) focused on the degree to which race influences the application of the *Furman* principles to death sentencing. The *McCleskey* case established the evidentiary standard, type and weight of statistical evidence needed to sustain either an equal protection claim under the Fourteenth Amendment or arbitrariness claim in violation of the Eighth Amendment:

> This case presents the question whether a complex statistical study that indicates a risk that racial considerations enter into capital sentencing decisions proves that petitioner *McCleskey's* capital sentence is unconstitutional under the Eighth or Fourteenth Amendments. (*McCleskey v. Kemp,* Powell, J., p. 283)

For purposes of an equal protection claim of disparate impact, the *McCleskey* decision required proof of intentional or purposeful discrimination, applying the test established in *Washington v. Davis* (1976). As to the Eighth Amendment, the *McCleskey* court indicated that where the sole proof of discrimination lies in a statistical analysis, an unquantified "stark" level of evidence of race-based disparity would be necessary to demonstrate actionable arbitrariness. The Court accepted the comprehensive and sophisticated statistical study by Baldus and his colleagues of the Georgia capital justice system (for discussion see, Baldus, Woodworth and Pulaski, 1990) as valid for admissibility purposes, but found it lacked the necessary evidentiary weight to support the claims of denied equal protection and race-based arbitrariness.

The *McCleskey* majority cited several methodological issues that in its estimation reduced the evidentiary weight of the Baldus study for Georgia (see *McCleskey v. Zant,* 580 F. Supp. 338, 379 [N.D. Ga. 1984]): (1) gaps in the database relating to cases and variable information rendered it "untrustworthy" and susceptible to sample bias; (2) the lack of statistical significance in how the death penalty was imposed across racial groups made the results insufficient; and, (3) the instability and low explanatory value of the models made them unreliable, noting the low R^2 values — less than .50 — even in the most complex model incorporating more than 200 variables (*McCleskey,* footnote 6; *Zant v. Kemp,* pp. 353-361). These criticisms, the Court held, combined to reduce the evidentiary weight of the Baldus et al. study, supporting at best a conclusion of a "risk," an "association" or a "mere correlation" of race and death sentencing, which did not rise to constitutional significance under the Fourteenth or Eighth Amendments, particularly when weighed against the overall importance of jury discretion in our justice system and the damage that could be done to the jury system if sentencing decisions could be challenged on less than the strongest proof (*McCleskey,* pp. 313-314).

Regardless of the scientific correctness of the Court's interpretation of the Baldus et al. Georgia study in *McCleskey*, the case had an important influence on empirical research on the death penalty. First, it discouraged the subsequent use of statistical proof to challenge state capital sentencing procedures. Some commentators see *McCleskey* as effectively foreclosing the use of statistical evidence for race-based claims of disparate impact in a capital sentencing context, or at best setting the evidentiary bar impossibly high by accepting the inevitability and "ineradicability" of some level of racial bias in death sentencing (*McCleskey*, Powell, J. at footnote 6; see, Kennedy, 1988; Bohm, 1994; Ogletree, 2002; Howe, 2004). Others argue that *McCleskey* may be read more narrowly, so that it may be possible to present empirical evidence that would support additional procedures to minimize racial disparity (Blume et al., 1998; Baldus and Woodworth, 2004). This approach begs the unanswered legal question as to whether *any* race-based discrimination is tolerable under the Unites States Constitution.

State responses to the *McCleskey* holding have varied. Kentucky passed a Racial Justice Act providing a mechanism to challenge the prosecutorial capital charging decision. Several other states have attempted to pass such statutes, but failed. New Jersey and New York abolished the death penalty in their states, by legislative and judicial acts, respectively (for a discussion of post-*McCleskey* state actions, see Lesman, 2005). The courts of New Jersey, New York and Connecticut have also indicated that their state constitutions may not tolerate any level of disparity in how the death penalty is imposed, in assessing whether arbitrariness in death sentencing violated state equal protection principles, regardless of the *McCleskey* holding. New Jersey's abolition of the death penalty was based in part on the earlier legal conclusion that the administration of the death penalty was unequally applied across the state in a way that could not be cured and that was unacceptable under the New Jersey Constitution (Lesman, 2005). In Connecticut, a state trial court recently allowed submittal of a statistical study of racial disparity in death sentencing as support for death row inmate claims of race-based arbitrariness in the imposition of the death sentence, again based in the state's, not the federal constitution (*In re: Claims of Racial Disparity v. Commissioner of Corrections*, Docket No. CVO-4000632S, State of Connecticut, Tolland Judicial District Court, 2008). Thus, not all jurisdictions agree with the idea that some level of racial disparity in the imposition of the death penalty is acceptable.

One important result of *McCleskey* is the majority's affirmation that there may be some level of racial bias that reaches "constitutional significance" and cannot be tolerated, particularly in black defendant/white victim interracial cases, as expressly acknowledged in *Turner v. Murray*, 1986 (for analysis of Justice Scalia's contrasting view in *McCleskey*, see Dorin, 1994). The *McCleskey* result must be taken into account in research designs, particularly with respect to sample selections and control variables when examining race and application of the death penalty (Baldus et al., 1998; Baldus and Woodworth, 2003a, 2003b, 2004). As discussed below, recent research has produced evidence of both a white race-of-victim effect and an apparent interaction of race-of-defendant and race-of-victim bias that greatly increase the likelihood of a death sentence in black-on-white cases versus other racial combinations Despite the setback that *McCleskey* represents to those seeking to assess racial differences in how the *Furman* sentencing principles have been applied, research continues and the empirical evidence of racial inequity in the capital justice system continues to grow.

Scope of the Discussion

Both *Furman* and *McCleskey* were directed at systemic racial bias at the *sentencing* stage of the capital justice process; therefore, this chapter addresses the empirical research seeking to detect and quantify racial variance at the sentencing stage of the capital process. However, numerous studies also examine the effect of race at the capital charging stage because prosecutorial decisions filter the cases that are tried and eventually reach the death sentencing stage, producing sample selection bias if racial bias at the charging stage is not taken into account.[1] Some argue, however, that when examining racial disparity at the sentencing stage, it may not be necessary to take into account earlier sources of bias (Berk et al., 2005). Again, this chapter focuses on the empirical evidence of racial disparity, if any, in capital sentencing, while acknowledging that racial bias at other stages of the capital process may also be involved (e.g., geographic disparities in charging and sentencing patterns across intra-state jurisdictions may result in racial disparities: see Paternoster and Brame, 2003; Blume et al., 2004; Poveda, 2006; Barnes et al., 2008).

Space precludes discussion of all post-*Furman* race and the death penalty studies. Nor is this necessary since several excellent overviews of post-*Furman* studies exist (Baldus et al., 1998; Baldus and Woodworth, 2003a).

For that reason, attention is directed to studies published since 2003 (see also Appendix A).[2]

Numerous studies have also addressed issues relevant to the imposition of the death penalty that do not specifically involve racial disparity in sentencing outcomes. These are not discussed here, but they include: processual factors such as the apparent advantage, in terms of a life sentence versus a death sentence, of using private defense counsel instead of public counsel (Beck and Shumsky, 1997); differences across states based on the differences among their various capital statutes (Holowinski, 2002); and the high rate of errors and resultant appellate reversals of death sentences nationwide (Liebman et al., 2000). The role and effect of culture-based, unconscious racial stereotyping by jurors, and juror attitudes as the source of variance in death sentencing, have also generated much research and discussion (Eberhardt et al., 2006; Hime, 2005; Baldus and Woodworth, 2004; Bowers et al., 2004; Haney, 2004; Lenhardt, 2004; Sommers and Ellsworth, 2003; Howe, 2004; Ogletree, 2002.). These studies offer insight into the sources of the systemic racial disparities in capital justice beyond the scope of this discussion (see other chapters in this volume for discussion).

The Pre-*Furman* Research

Studies of capital sentencing prior to *Furman* (1972) showed a clear bias against black defendants, particularly in the South (see, generally, Hagan, 1974). For example, Johnson (1941) conducted a seminal study of a cohort of cases from Richmond, Virginia between 1930 and 1939, and from five North Carolina counties between 1930 and 1940 (see also, Mangum, 1940). Johnson documented a bias in death sentencing and execution where the victim was white, regardless of the race of the defendant, with the greatest bias seen in black defendant-white victim cases. These patterns were also seen in a subsequent study of ten North Carolina counties between 1930 and 1940 (Garfinkel, 1949), and a study of black-on-white interracial effects for North Carolina from 1909 to 1953 (Johnson, 1957), which was among the first to take crime seriousness into account. Other studies published before 1972, although unsophisticated and often based on incomplete data and/or small samples, continued to search for racial differences in sentencing and executions (e.g., Wolfgang et al., 1962 [Pennsylvania, 1914-1958]; Bedau, 1964 [New Jersey, 1907-1960]; Bedau, 1965 [Oregon, 1903-1964]; Wolf, 1964 [New Jersey, 1937-1961]; Zimring et al., 1976 [Philadelphia, 1914-1958]).

The racial effects seemed strongest in the South (Wolfgang and Reidel, 1973). Bohm's (1991) analysis of executions between 1910 and the late 1950s showed that nearly two-thirds of those executed in the South were black men (see also, Schneider and Smykla, 1991). Rape appeared to be a key factor in whether the death sentence was imposed or carried out (Wolfgang and Riedel, 1973; Johnson, E., 1957; Johnson, O., 1951, 1970; Partington, 1965). As to northern states, the research was more limited and mixed. For example, statewide race effects in Ohio executions (Bridge and Mosure, 1961) were not evident in Cleveland (Bensing and Schroeder, 1960). No race effect was found for sentencing or execution/commutation rates in New Jersey (Bedau, 1964; Wolf, 1964). In Pennsylvania, racial patterns were evident in execution/commutation rates (Wolfgang et al., 1962) and felony cases (Wolfgang and Riedel 1973). Zimring et al. (1976) found that in 1970, blacks who killed whites were by far the most likely to get death sentences than other racial groupings. For western states, no significant effects were seen in a study of first-degree murder sentencing in California (Judson et al., 1969) or in Bedau's (1965) analysis of executions in Oregon (1903-1964). Although the studies varied in complexity, the body of research led to the conclusion that race had a significant influence on who received a sentence of death and would be executed in the United States. These studies played a key role in the *Furman* decision in 1972.

The Empirical Research 1972-1990

After *Furman* was implemented by the capital punishment states in 1976, the thrust of the empirical research shifted to evaluating whether the *Furman* principles altered the racial distribution of death sentencing to more equitable patterns than those demonstrated in earlier studies. Riedel's (1976) study comparing the racial composition of death rows in 1972 and 1975 showed a proportionally larger death sentencing rate for nonwhite defendants whose victims were white. Although there was no statistically significant victim-race effect, a disproportionately larger number of white victim cases resulted in a death sentence. This indicated that the guided discretion standards imposed under *Furman* had not eliminated racial bias from the capital justice system. While overt racism against black defendants had been reduced under the new standards, a more subtle form of racism continued in that there was a higher rate of death sentences for those who killed whites, with the highest rate of death sentencing among black defendants whose victims were white. This appeared to reflect a societal devaluation of black citizens that had not been cured by *Furman*. Similar patterns were seen in studies in Florida (Lewis et al., 1979; Arkin, 1980; Zeisel, 1981; Radelet, 1981) Georgia, Ohio and Texas (Bowers and Pierce, 1980), Louisiana (Smith, 1987) and South Carolina (Paternoster, 1983, 1984). Gross and Mauro's (1985) study of all homicides reported to police in Arkansas, Florida, Georgia, Illinois, Mississippi, North Carolina, Oklahoma and Virginia between 1976 and 1980 documented a clear race-of-victim bias in capital sentencing, which was stronger where the defendant was black.

Despite these results, it was not until 1987, in *McCleskey v. Kemp,* that a case reached the Supreme Court challenging a *Furman*-compliant capital justice system using statistical analysis as sole evidence of racial inequity. As noted earlier, the result was seen as a setback to those seeking to challenge the racial neutrality of the death penalty post-*Furman*.

The U.S. GAO Study (1990)

At least partly in response to the *McCleskey* holding (Baldus et al., 1998), in 1989 the United States Senate authorized the U.S. General Accounting Office (GAO) to examine the question of whether race was still an influence in death sentencing despite implementation of *Furman*-mandated procedures. Rather than conducting a time-consuming and expensive new analysis, the GAO synthesized existing research from 53 published and unpublished post-*Furman* capital sentencing pattern studies (GAO, 1990, p. 2). After eliminating those that did not include empirical data or were duplicative, 28 studies remained.[3]

The GAO assessed and rated the selected studies as low, medium or high in overall quality and design, sampling, selection and measurement of variables, data collection and completion and statistical methodology. Studies published after 1985 were of higher quality, with the Baldus study of the Georgia capital justice system (the basis of the claim in *McCleskey*) representing the most comprehensive, highest quality study to date (Berk, 1996). Three methodological limitations were identified that related to compiling accurate and complete data: sample selection bias, small sample sizes and the problem of omitted variables to account for legitimate case characteristics that may also contribute causally to a death sentence outcome (GAO Report, 1990, p. 3). For example, failure to control for factors indicative of case seriousness, such as the level of aggravation the jury accepts, would result in comparing less aggravated cases for which the death penalty might be less appropriate, with the most heinous of murders. It would be impossible to know whether any racial differences were due to racial bias or to legitimate differences in the case seriousness (Baldus et al. 2003). These same limitations were noted by the Court in *McCleskey*, and these same problems continue to frustrate researchers today (see Hoeffel, 2005; Pierce and Radelet, 2005; ABA State Death Penalty Moratorium Implementation Project, 2007).

The GAO Report found "a pattern of evidence indicating racial disparities in the charging, sentencing, and imposition of the death penalty after the *Furman* decision" (GAO Report, 1990, p. 5), including: (1) a race-of-victim effect was seen in 82% of the studies, at all stages of the capital justice process, although it was stronger at the prosecutorial charging stage; and, (2) there was "equivocal" evidence as to a race-of-defendant effect. The race-of-defendant effects seen were apparently the result of interaction with other factors, such as geographic jurisdiction. There appeared to be a higher likelihood of a death sentence for black defendants in rural versus urban jurisdictions (Paternoster and Kazyaka, 1988) and in black defendant-white victim interracial cases (Baldus, Woodworth et al., 1990). The GAO report did not result in any change in government policy, but the research effort has continued undiminished to date. However, no case has again been presented to the Court offering statistical proof of racial disparity in death sentencing, despite increasing sophistication of the research since 1990.

THE RESEARCH 1990-2008

Since the release of the GAO study, research has continued unabated, fueled in large part by the conclusions of the GAO study and unsuccessful efforts to pass "Racial Justice" legislation in Congress (see Baldus and Woodworth, 2000b, pp. 331-332). The purpose of this type of legislation is to afford a capital defendant a viable means to challenge a death sentence on the grounds that it was sought and/or obtained as a result of racial bias, and to allow use of statistical evidence to support this claim. Only Kentucky has passed such a statute, limited to the capital charging decision, in 1998 (Powell, 2001). More recently, the North Carolina legislature failed to adopt a similar law in its 2007-2008 session ("Another push for racial justice law," 2008). These efforts are supported by the compelling weight of the empirical evidence leading to the conclusion that there is race/

ethnicity-based discrimination in death sentencing in this country that must be addressed (see evidence above and Mitchell and McKenzie, 2004; Spohn, 2000; Pratt, 1999 for overviews of race and sentencing post-*Furman*).

Baldus and Woodworth (1998, 2003a, 2003b, 2004) identified four primary conclusions which may be drawn from the modern post-*Furman* research:

- The race of the defendant, by itself, is no longer a significant source of systemic bias in how state death sentencing statues are applied;

- The race of the victim remains a significant source of systemic bias in how state death sentencing statutes are applied, with an increased likelihood of a death sentence where the victim is white, regardless of the race of the defendant;

- There continues to be an interactive effect between race of the defendant and race of the victim which makes black defendants who kill white victims significantly more likely to receive a death sentence than any other racial combination, despite the fact that most capital cases are intra-racial; and

- There appears to be a racial difference in charging and sentencing decisions between urban and rural jurisdictions where a capital crime is processed, with black defendant cases less likely to result in areas where the black population is high and more likely where the population of white victims is high.

There are two other points made by Baldus and Woodworth with which the literature generally agrees. First, to avoid sample bias when examining penalty stage data, the effect of racial bias in prosecutorial selection of death penalty cases to be tried must be considered. Secondly, the greatest racial disparity is seen in cases involving mid-level aggravation as determined by measures of culpability, such as the number of aggravators accepted by a capital sentencing jury, or a high score on an index of culpability (Baldus et al., 1990). For example, one or two accepted aggravators is generally considered low, and is less likely to produce a death sentence. Four or more aggravators accepted is much more likely to produce a death sentence. At these two ends of the culpability spectrum, jury discretion is less flexible: with only one or two aggravators accepted, a life sentence may seem fairer; at the other end, in cases of highly aggravated murder, a death sentence may seem to be the only fair sentence. It has been suggested that capital jurors may feel more liberated to exercise their own discretion to impose or not impose death in a case where the facts are more equivocal in terms of whether death is the just penalty, and it is here where extra-legal factors such as race might affect the sentencing decision (Baldus et al., 1990). The empirical research supports this "liberation theory," and it is in the mid-range of aggravation that the most racial difference in death sentencing has been seen (Baldus et al., 1998a; 2003b).

Most of the research since 2003 has been generally consistent with these conclusions as to the presence of race/ethnicity-based arbitrariness in the capital justice process, particularly with respect to role of prosecutorial bias and the race-of-victim effect.[4] Research since 2003, using more complete databases and different analytical techniques, indicates that the race-of-victim effect evident in earlier studies may be weaker than originally concluded, or part of a complex interaction of other factors, including victim gender and intrastate regional disparities across racial/ethnic groups (Phillips, in press [Harris County, TX]; Kremling et al., 2007 [North Carolina], Poveda, 2006 [Virginia]; and Stauffer et al., 2006 [North Carolina]).

Death Penalty Research Centers

Although there are many independent researchers examining the issue of race and the death penalty, several important research groups have conducted much of the death penalty research since 1990. Baldus and Woodworth and their research colleagues based at the University of Iowa have continued to lead the empirical research, using increasingly sophisticated regression techniques to examine racial variance in capital justice (Baldus et al., 1990; Baldus et al., 1998; Baldus and Woodworth, 2001; Baldus et al., 2002; Baldus et al., 2006). The Capital Jury Project, initiated in 1991 by a consortium of university-based researchers with support from the National Science Foundation, has conducted over a thousand in-depth interviews of capital jurors across 14 states to develop a better understanding of factors that affect decision making (Bowers et al., 2004; Bowers, 1995). The Cornell Death Penalty Project, based in the Cornell Law School, has conducted extensive research on the influence of race on the criminal justice process (Blume et al., 2004).

In 1997, the American Bar Association (ABA) adopted a resolution calling for a nationwide moratorium on the death penalty pending an appropriate, comprehensive scientific evaluation of the fairness and impartiality of the capital justice process. In 2001, the ABA's Death Penalty Moratorium Implementation Project was established. Since then the Project has assessed the operation of capital justice in eight states, assessed the available data and empirical research, and funded new empirical studies (available at www.abanet.org/moratorium).

The American Civil Liberties Union (ACLU) has also reviewed the application of the death penalty in Virginia (ACLU, 2003) and Alabama (ACLU, 2005). The biases evident in rates of death sentencing involving black defendant/white victim race combinations are consistent with prior studies.

Finally, although not a death penalty bias research group, no discussion of race and the death penalty can ignore the efforts of the Innocence Project and other case/evidentiary review projects on public and legal opinion (Dieter, 2004). These projects have used both DNA evidence and close examination of capital case records for legal and investigatory errors to obtain appellate reopening of cases. These efforts have given new impetus to the death penalty abolition/moratorium effort. Since 1973, 129 death row inmates, the majority black, have been exonerated and freed from death row using such evidence and procedures (Scheck, 2007).

Although there is no absolute proof that any innocent person has been executed, studies have demonstrated the high likelihood that this has occurred not once, but multiple times (Gross, 1998). Those proved innocent have been disproportionately black (Taslitz, 2006; Scheck, 2007), thereby renewing interest in a death penalty moratoria at a state level (Dieter, 204; Lanier and Acker, 2004) and nationally through the efforts of the American Bar Association, which has also called for the abolition of the death penalty (Sarat, 2003).

Types of Sentencing Studies Post-*Furman*

As in all empirical research, data availability dictates the methodology for examining racial neutrality in application of death sentencing statutes. Data are a constant problem. Most jurisdictions do not keep complete and readily available records of the capital justice process, much less the capital sentencing decision or the evidence and deliberation which produced it (Hoeffel, 2005; Kremling et al., 2007; Pierce and Radelet, 2005; ABA Death Penalty Moratorium Implementation Project, 2007).

Post-*Furman* studies have used a variety of methods, with regression modeling[5] as developed and refined by Baldus and Woodworth and their colleagues generally accepted as the "gold standard." In addition to data availability, expense is another issue impacting death penalty studies because data compilation can be both costly and time consuming (Baldus et al., 1998). Nevertheless, more than 70 studies have examined capital sentencing and race since the *Furman* standards were implemented. These studies can be categorized methodologically as: regression analyses of racial disparities in the capital justice process (Baldus and Woodworth, 1998; Paternoster and Brame, 2003); descriptive sentencing rate analyses of the frequency of death sentencing among black and white defendant cases with comparable case characteristics (ABA Death Penalty Moratorium Implementation Project, 2007; Barnes et al., 2008); jury studies, particularly by the Capital Jury Project, using quantitative and qualitative methods to assess juror factors that affect sentencing outcomes (Bowers, 1995); and studies related to the legal process for death sentencing (Kremling et al., 2007). Although regression analysis has been the favored method, other methods, such as CART analysis and classification trees (see end note 7), have been used to assess the influence of race on the capital justice system, but these latter techniques have generally failed to produce the same racial effects seen in regression analyses (Klein and Rolph, 1991; Berk et al., 2005; Klein et al., 2006). This does not mean there were no race-based differences seen, or that such differences do not exist. What seems to be demonstrated is that the differences produced using regression modeling are fragile and could not be replicated using other methodologies (Klein and Rolph, 1991; Berk et al., 2005; Klein et al., 2006). Thus, regression results may still be susceptible to the Supreme Court's *McCleskey* criticisms as to their evidentiary value in proving systemic racial bias in the capital justice system.

Baldus and Woodworth Overview of Studies 1990-2003

In 2003, Baldus and Woodworth published an overview of the empirical research since 1990. As was done in the U.S. General Accounting Office study (1990) discussed above, Baldus and his colleagues selected studies that met the following key criteria relating to analysis of both defendant and victim race: (1) the choice of the unit of analysis as appropriate to the research goal and limited by the data available (i.e., "death-eligible cases" — those cases for which the death penalty may be sought versus cases that have reached a specified discrete stage of the capital proceeding including charging, guilt trial, sentencing trial, death row, executions); (2) the completeness of the database used to represent the capital justice system or stage under study in order to test for disparate impact (systemic bias); and (3) whether the analysis is appropriately controlled to allow "apples-to-apples" comparison across racial groups based on case seriousness and defendant culpability (Baldus and Woodworth, 2003a).

As to the first issue, most post-1990 studies examined both race-of-defendant and race–of-victim effects to the extent the data allowed (Baldus and Woodworth, 2003a; ABA Death Penalty Moratorium Implementation Project Final Report, 2007). Because of the difficulty of obtaining complete data and the limited nature of the data available in some jurisdictions, the unit of analysis has varied widely in post-1990 studies, and has included: homicides that resulted in a death sentence (Radelet and Pierce, 1991), indicted first degree murder cases (Bortner and Hall, 2002); first-degree murder convictions (Pierce and Radelet, 2002; Ziemba-Davis and Meyers, 2002); "death-noticed" or capitally-charged cases (Baldus and Woodworth, 2001; Lenza et al., 2005); first-and second-degree murder cases (Unah and Boger, 2001; Brock et al., 2000); and jury recommendations in capital murder trials (Kremling et al., 2007; Stauffer et al., 2007).

As to the second and third criteria used by the GAO study and Baldus et al. (2003) in identifying reliable studies assessing racial bias in death sentencing, the unavailability of complete data was and continues to be a problem for researchers (Pierce and Radelet, 2004) and is a weakness in the capital justice system on which the American Bar Association has now focused in its Death Penalty Moratorium Implementation Project (ABA Report, 2007). The lack of valid or complete data in turn affects the selection of variables, including the ability to control for the degree of culpability and crime seriousness in order to ensure true comparability among cases necessary to isolate the race effects. As a result, there has been a wide range of methods to incorporate culpability and case seriousness into the analyses.[6]

The Capital Jury Project Studies *Post*-1990

The Capital Jury Project (CJP) has followed capital trials since 1988 in 14 states (Alabama, California, Florida, Georgia, Indiana, Kentucky, Louisiana, Missouri, North Carolina, Pennsylvania, South Carolina, Tennessee, Texas, and Virginia), selecting in each state half of the cases resulting in life sentences, and half of the cases resulting in death sentences. Data were obtained from exhaustive interviews with more than 100 jurors from each jurisdiction, with a minimum of four from each trial selected (Bowers, 1995; Bowers et al., 2004). The CJP research has produced nearly 50 published studies on all aspects of capital juries including: their selection and impartiality (Sandys and McClellan, 2003; Sandys, 1995); empathy, feelings and attitudes towards the defendant and the victim at the guilt and sentencing stages (Antonio, 2006; Bowers et al., 1998; Sundby, 1998, 2003); and understanding of or confusion about their duties and responsibilities (Eisenberg and Wells, 1993; Eisenberg et al., 1996; Garvey et al., 2000; Bowers et al., 2003; Bowers and Steiner, 1999; Foglia, 2001). The role of race-based jury arbitrariness is one of the foci of current research (Bowers et al., 2001, 2004; Bowers and Foglia, 2003; Bowers and Steiner, 1998; Brewer, 2004; Eisenberg et al., 2003; Foglia, 2001; Foglia and Schenker, 2001). One purpose of the research has been to provide a possible basis for developing alternative jury selection criteria to address the racial bias that appears in interracial murders, addressed by the Supreme Court 20 years ago in *Turner v. Murray*, 1986 (Bowers et al., 2004), and reaffirmed in *McCleskey v. Kemp*, 1987. (A complete list of the CJP research may be found at www.albany.edu/scj/CPRIjuryproj.htm.)

Because CJP research involves explaining capital sentencing outcomes in terms of jury racial composition and attitudes, and in relation to the jury decision-making process, the CJP research was not included in Baldus and Woodworth's 2003 overview. However, the CJP research between 1990 and 2003 is consistent with the overall findings of race-based influences on death sentencing. For example, Bowers et al. (2001) published a comprehensive study of the racial and gender composition of capital juries and the attitudes and outcomes associated with them, using all completed jury interviews conducted by CJP interviewers, a total of 1,155 jurors from 341 trials. They examined three defendant-victim racial combinations — white-white, black-black and black-white cases — to examine whether the racial and gender composition of the jury affect sentencing outcomes, and to better understand jurors' thinking during the sentencing process, with particular focus on the black-white interracial cases (Bowers et al., 2001, 2004). The primary findings were that juries with white male dominance were more likely to produce a death sentence in black-white cases, while the presence of black male jurors reduced the likelihood of a death sentence. This effect was not seen in the intra-racial cases, leading to the conclusion that black-on-white murders carry the greatest race-based emotional baggage, which can skew jury neutrality. These patterns are consistent with other empirical studies using regression and other hypothesis test-based methodologies (Baldus and Woodworth, 2003a, 2003b, 2004). The CJP research thus dovetails with empirical research supporting the conclusion of a racial skew to capital sentencing.

The American Bar Association Death Penalty Implementation Project

In 1997, the American Bar Association (1997) adopted a resolution calling for a moratorium on state executions pending adequate scientific proof that capital justice is administered fairly, including race neutrally, and that the risk of the execution of the innocent can be minimized. The Individual Rights and Responsibility Section (IRRS) of the ABA was assigned the responsibility for moving the moratorium forward, and in 2001 the ABA established within the IRRS the ABA Death Moratorium Implementation Project to support state moratorium efforts. As discussed below, the ABA Death Moratorium Implementation Project has completed eight State Death Penalty Assessment Reports, which present information as to racial patterns in the administration of capital justice to the extent available data permitted in each state.

AN OVERVIEW OF THE RESEARCH IN 2003–2008

Appendix A summarizes the findings of studies published from 1990 through 2008, organized by jurisdiction. The research since 2003 generally confirms the hierarchy of race-based disparity the earlier body of research had shown: (1) there is no main systemic race-of-defendant influence; (2) there is an overall race-of-victim bias that enhances the likelihood of a death sentence where the victim is white, regardless of defendant race, but (3) race-of-defendant effects are masked by the larger proportion of intra- to inter-racial cases (black-on-white murders are most likely to result in death penalties, followed by white-on-white murders, with the lowest likelihood of a death sentence occurring in black–black murders; see Baldus and Woodworth, 2004; Howe, 2004; Baldus et al., 2006).

State-Level Research

There have been several studies of varying quality since 2003 that have looked at race and the death penalty as administered in specific state jurisdictions. Some have focused more on race and the capital charging decision by prosecutors within and across intrastate jurisdictions (e.g., Phillips, in press [Texas]; Barnes et al., 2008 [Missouri]; Songer and Unah, 2006 [South Carolina]; Poveda, 2006 [Virginia]). For example, a recent

Harris County, TX study by Phillips (in press) supported the previously discussed themes of racial disparity in death sentencing, but found an offsetting difference in effect at the prosecution and sentencing stages. Prosecutors there were much more likely to charge black defendants and cases involving white victims capitally, but sentencing jurors were slightly more likely to approve death sentences in cases with white defendants and black victims. The "net effect" was a small but discernible attenuation effect at the sentencing stage, which reduced the racial disparities seen at the prosecutorial stage. This may indicate that jurors deal with white defendants slightly more harshly when considering a death sentence than prosecutors do at the charging stage. It should be noted, however, that the black defendant-white victim and overall white-victim effects remained, but the black defendant-white victim and overall white-victim effects remained (Phillips, in press).

There have also been controlled studies which examined both the charging and sentencing stages for racial effects, and measured whether these effects varied across regions (Donohue, 2007 [Connecticut]; Lee,2007 [San Joaquin County, CA, race and ethnicity]; Hindson et al., 2006 [Colorado, race and gender]; and Pierce and Radelet [California]). In Connecticut, Donohue (2007) reported finding significant evidence of capriciousness in capital justice between 1973 and 2007. Black defendants had a likelihood of a death sentence three times the rate of white defendants in similar cases involving white victims; non-white defendants whose victims were white had a statistically higher rate of being capitally charged and sentenced to death; non-white defendants had statistically significant higher rates of capital-charging and receipt of death sentences than white-on-white murderers. A similar white-victim effect was seen in Lee's (2007) study of disparities based on Hispanic and white death-eligible case in San Joaquin County, CA. Cases involving Hispanic victims had a lower likelihood of being processed capitally than cases involving white victims, regardless of the ethnicity of the defendant.

Hindson, Potter, and Radelet (2006) published a comparative analysis of the probability of a death sentence across various case groups, based on race, region, and gender in Colorado in 1980-1999. In addition to regional effects, the study found an overall higher probability of a death sentence if the victim was white (4.2 higher rate than for black victims, 3.8 times higher rate than for Hispanic victims). Female victim cases were nearly twice as likely to result in a death sentence than male victim cases —

although this study did not attempt to parse out the possible interaction of race and gender in capital sentencing (see, Stauffer et al., 2006; Williams and Holcomb, 2004).

Pierce and Radelet's (2004) study of the influence of race on charging decisions and death sentencing in California in 1990-1997 produced results consistent with the racial hierarchy of death sentencing likelihood evident in other studies. Using the descriptive and logistic regression methods employed in their work for the ABA Death Penalty Moratorium Implementation Project (discussed below), the California study showed both regional disparities and an overall white-victim effect. Compared to cases involving white victims, black victim cases were 59% less likely to result in a death sentence and Hispanic victim cases 67% less likely, controlling for comparable levels of aggravation and other relevant factors.

American Bar Association Studies

As noted earlier, the ABA has called for states to enact moratoria on executions pending sound empirical studies into the fairness of their capital justice systems. The ABA Death Penalty Implementation Project (2007) has released eight state assessment studies, which describe the current status of capital justice within each state in 12 areas, including the collection and analysis of complete and accurate data on the capital process and the role of race and ethnicity. Four new regression analyses of data from Arizona, Georgia, Ohio and Tennessee are included.

All of the reports support the literature indicating the importance of white race-of-victim effects, the highest likelihood of a death sentence for black defendants who kill white victims, and the lowest effect where both defendant and victim are white (ABA Death Penalty Moratorium Implementation Project, 2007). Regression studies for Georgia, Indiana, Ohio and Tennessee, controlling for defendant and victim race, level of aggravation present, and region (Pierce et al., 2006; 2007a; 2007b; 2007c), discovered significant white race-of-victim effects in each location. In Indiana, for example, white victim cases were more than five times more likely to result in a death sentence than if the victim was black (Pierce et al., 2007a). In Ohio and Tennessee, white victim cases were about four times more likely to end in a death sentence (Pierce et al., 2007b;2007c), and in Georgia almost nine times more likely in low-aggravation cases (Pierce et al., 2006). Black-on-black murders universally had the lowest likelihood of death. The black defendant-white victim effect was less important, although a strong effect was seen in Ohio.

American Civil Liberties Union Studies

The ACLU has published several descriptive analyses of racial disparities in state death penalty administration. For example, 81% of those executed in Alabama since 1976 were convicted of killing whites, yet only 35% of all murders in the state involved white victims (ACLU, 2007). The Virginia study also showed a higher death rate for white-victim cases and the lowest rate in black-victim cases. While these studies are not well-controlled or methodologically sophisticated, they support the racial hierarchy of death generally seen in more complex and comprehensive studies.

Different Methodological Approaches

Three studies that apply a different methodological approach to the question of racial variance in capital justice have important implications to future research. The Capital Jury Project (Blume et al., 2004), supports the body of regression results, while two others (Berk et al. and Klein et al., see below) raise questions about the accuracy and inferential weight to be afforded regression studies. The significance of these last two studies on the future of death penalty research has not yet been addressed in the literature, but must be if the credibility of the body of regression-based research is to be maintained.

Blume, Eisenberg and Wells, 2004

In 2004, Blume, Eisenberg and Wells published a study of 31 capital jurisdictions, assessing racial disparity in death sentencing, and a detailed study of eight states (Arizona, Georgia, Indiana, Maryland, Nevada, Pennsylvania, South Carolina, Virginia) to examine the "conventional wisdom" about the death penalty, including the widely held belief that African Americans are at a higher risk of a death sentence than whites, particularly in the South. The study included descriptive analysis and logistic regression, but the units of analysis were death row defendants compared to the number of homicides in a jurisdiction, and controlled for defendant and victim race and to the extent possible for a jurisdiction's legal, political, social/demographic environments, and the death selecting factors used. Comparing death row populations to the number of murders in each jurisdiction generally and by racial composition, the authors sought to explain why, despite the empirical evidence, racial bias disadvantageous to black defendants was not reflected in the racial composition on death rows, where there were proportionally more white defendants.

The study results indicate that the proportion of black defendants in death row populations was lower than in the population of murder offenders because most black murders involved black victims, and these cases were the least likely to end in a death sentence. This represents a manifestation of the offsetting white and black race-of-victim effects at either end of the death sentence scale of likelihood, with the effect being stronger in the South. For example, in South Carolina only 2.9 per 1,000 black-black cases resulted in death sentences, compared to 67.8 per 1,000 black-white cases. These effects are different at a statistically significantly level from the rate of 27.1 per 1,000 for white-white cases. These same differences were seen in Virginia, Maryland, Georgia and Indiana (Blume et al., 2004, p. 199).

Berk et al. Reanalysis of Maryland Data and Study of Federal Prosecutions

Two important studies by Berk and his colleagues have diverged from the typical regression analysis used to study racial bias in capital cases. The first study (Berk et al., 2005) involved a reanalysis of the Maryland data used by Paternoster and Brame (2003). Berk et al.'s regression results replicated the Paternoster and Brame findings (showing strong racial effects, especially a white race-of-victim effect). However, no race-based effects were produced by propensity or CART analyses of the same data.[7] Berk et al. stated that the results do not imply that there were no race effects evident, only that with the data used it was not possible to tell "whether meaningful racial effects exist or not."

In 2006, Klein, Berk and Hickman published a new study of race and prosecutorial decision making in application of the federal death penalty. Like earlier studies commissioned by the U.S. Department of Justice (2000a, 2000b), the focus was race effects at the prosecutorial charging stage. Also at issue was the methodology: that is, whether multiple studies, independently designed by different teams of researchers, produced consistent results. The earlier studies consisted of unadjusted descriptive analysis and qualitative analysis of charging practices.[8] As re-assessed by Baldus and Woodworth (2003a), unadjusted race-of-defendant and race-of-victim effects were detected. Klein et al. used slightly different data and a novel test design. They recruited three teams of scientists and allowed each group to design and conduct an independent study of the data, then regrouped the data to assess and draw conclusions from the collective results. Three issues were addressed: race-based arbitrariness, capriciousness and geographic disparity.

All three teams concluded that the race effects disappeared if the data were adjusted to reflect case seriousness, and that other factors (e.g., jurisdiction, case characteristics) played a greater role than race in the prosecutors' decision to seek the death penalty. The authors did not speculate as to why these results differed from prior state-level studies, except to note that the varying results may stem from methodological differences that may limit the generalizability of their conclusions beyond federal prosecutorial decisions (Klein et al., 2006).

Although some scholars have questioned the validity of the Klein et al. studies (Hindson et al., 2006), these alternative approaches raise methodological questions which, in light of *McCleskey* and the precedent it established as to the value of statistical evidence in establishing racial disparity in death sentencing, must be resolved to strengthen the credibility and evidentiary value of the empirical research on racial bias in death sentencing.

Research: North Carolina Capital Sentencing Project

A data compilation by three of the authors of this chapter (Smith, Bjerregaard, and Fogel) provides the unique opportunity to assess the effects of race on jury recommendations in an entire population of post-*Gregg* capital murder trials. Termed the North Carolina Capital Sentencing Project, this effort has yielded a dataset that includes all known murder trials having a capital sentencing phase that were conducted from the reinstatement of North Carolina's capital punishment statutes in June 1977 through December 2005. The dataset contains 1,272 jury decisions emanating from both original capital trials and retrials that involved a penalty phase hearing. The jury sentencing decisions, which require a unanimous vote, include those directly issued by the jury and those occurring by default (a deadlock on the sentencing decision, which by statute results in a life sentence).

The comprehensiveness of the North Carolina dataset facilitates the comparative use of alternative analytical approaches, as suggested by Berk et al. (2005) and others. This allows researchers to confirm consistent results and diagnose problems with model design in order to achieve a complete understanding of the factors — legal and illegal, conscious and unconscious — that affect death sentencing. While the degree to which these findings could be generalized beyond North Carolina is open to debate, the significance of the dataset is that it enables assessment of a *Furman*-based capital sentencing procedure in action over the total history of its operation within a single jurisdiction.

Table 8.1. Patterns of Death Sentencing in North Carolina, 1977-2005, by Race of Defendant and Victim

Defendant Race	# of Cases	Number (Percent) of Death Sentences
All Defendants	1,272	559 (43.9)
White Victim	792	375 (47.3)
Black Victim	407	164 (40.3)
Other Victim	73	20 (27.4)
White	544	249 (45.8)
White Victim	484	226 (46.7)
Black Victim	45	15 (33.3)
Other Victim	15	8 (53.5)
Black	653	277 (42.4)
White Victim	270	126 (46.7)
Black Victim	357	148 (41.5)
Other Victim	26	3 (11.5)
Other	75	33 (44.0)
White Victim	38	23 (60.5)
Black Victim	5	1 (20.0)
Other Victim	32	9 (28.1)

There is no centralized listing in North Carolina regarding trials for which the state seeks the death penalty, and the researchers had to create this list by reviewing all first-degree murder convictions to determine which ones were capitally tried. More difficult was discovering subsequent legal actions resulting in a retrial of a capital case. While the study involves all "known" capital murder trials, there remains a small possibility that some cases resulting in a life sentence (those proving the most elusive to identify) may not have been discovered. Nevertheless, the dataset is so close to complete that, despite a few missing cases, it constitutes a *de facto* population of capital jury decisions in North Carolina over the past three decades (for discussion, see Kremling et al., 2007; Stauffer et al., 2006).

An overview of capital sentencing by defendant and victim race in North Carolina is displayed in Table 8.1. While the racial category of "Other" is included, this category contains a mixture of self-identified groups (Native Americans, Hispanics, Asians, and Unknowns) who, for purposes of analyses, are not easily included in either of the two dominant categories. Consequently, the ensuing summary of findings focuses on differences between blacks and whites:

- The majority of jury decisions resulted in a life sentence; 43.9% specified a death sentence.

- White defendants (45.8%) were more likely to receive a death sentence than blacks (42.4%).

- Defendants who killed white victims were more likely to receive a death sentence than those who kill black victims (47.3% vs. 40.3%).

- Perhaps unexpectedly, white and black defendants who killed white victims were sentenced to death in exactly the same proportions (46.7%).

- Both black and white defendants who killed black victims were less likely to be sentenced to death than those who killed white victims (41.5% and 33.3% respectively).

Published Studies Using the North Carolina Dataset: Findings Regarding Racial Patterns of Sentencing

Although the North Carolina data seem to bear out the thrust of the death penalty/race literature, studies published with these data reveal the complexities of the relationship. Stauffer et al. (2006) sought to replicate the findings of Williams and Holcomb (2004) regarding a reported inter-active effect between two extra-legal factors, victim race and gender, for sentencing outcomes in Ohio. Williams and Holcomb's work suggested that the much-reported white race-of-victim effect was actually a product of more likely death penalty sentencing in cases involving white *female* victims. Approximating the Ohio analysis, Stauffer et al.'s North Carolina study found no statistically significant racial effects of defendant or victim race when controlling for a variety of legal and extra-legal factors. This finding held when specific controls were included for white and black female victim cases. Further, they found that neither the defendant nor the victim's race, whether or not in concert with victim gender, proved to be a predictor of death sentencing. In contrast, a legal factor, the number of aggravating circumstances accepted, was, by far, the strongest indicator for defendants sentenced to death.

Kremling et al. (2007) examined the effect of the U.S. Supreme Court ruling in *McKoy v. North Carolina* (1990) on the operation of the North Carolina death sentencing statute. The *McKoy* decision struck North Carolina's initial *Furman*-compliant capital statute because it required jurors to be unanimous in accepting the validity of a mitigating circumstance. As a result, individual jurors were thereafter (and remain today) free to consider the impact of any mitigating factor in determining their vote for a life or death sentence, even if all other jurors find that factor to be unconvincing. Kremling and her colleagues tested the intuitive hypothesis that opening the mitigation evidence so broadly would enhance the effect of mitigation on death sentencing, and most likely would serve to decrease the number of death sentences meted out by North Carolina capital juries. Surprisingly, their findings did not support this expectation. Comparing trials conducted before and after the *McKoy* ruling, an actual weakening of the influence of mitigators in the post-*McKoy* era was found, accompanied by an increase in the effect of aggravators. However, they also noted that neither defendant race nor victim race was found to be a statistically significant predictor of death sentencing, suggesting that the effects shown in Table 8.1 do not hold when the influences of other factors — most notably, aggravation and mitigation — are taken into account. For purposes of this chapter, it is notable that neither defendant race nor victim race were statistically significant predictors of death sentencing, suggesting that the effects shown in Table 8.1 do not hold when the influences of other factors — most notably, aggravation and mitigation — are taken into account.

Current Research

Current work in progress as of this writing takes a more specific and detailed look at the influence of race in North Carolina's death sentencing patterns. Among these is a study of models of sentencing that are specific to defendant and victim racial combinations. While a main effect for race is not statistically significant in the general models, some racial variance does appear in other models. Most notably, the threshold for death sentences seemed particularly low for black defendants when the victim was white. Said another way, the overall proportions of whites and blacks receiving death sentences were similar, but the deconstructed model suggests that aggravation seemed to weigh more heavily for black defendants when their victims were white, especially when compared to other defendant race/victim race models.

Although these findings are preliminary, their potential implications are of considerable legal significance. First, if substantiated, such results may provide further empirical evidence of systemic race-based arbitrariness in death sentencing under the *Furman* principles as applied in one state, which may be more credible in a judicial challenge than those subject to the *McCleskey* criticisms.

The second important potential implication of these results, if confirmed, would be support for a conclusion that race — an illegal and extra-statutory factor which cannot be cured by further procedural fixes — is producing a racially inequitable application of facially neutral, *Furman*-compliant, death sentencing procedures (*see* Section 15A-2000, N.C. Gen. Stats. 2005). Such a challenge would be particularly powerful if this pattern can be shown to hold in the contemporary (i.e., past 10 years) practice of capital punishment in North Carolina.

Studies on Race and Death Penalty Capriciousness

Another basis for Eighth Amendment challenges to state death sentencing statutes that has been largely ignored is the question of capriciousness concerning who gets a death sentence. *Furman* prohibits "freakish," random death sentences as well as "wanton," arbitrary ones. Few studies have examined this issue, and none using regression techniques. Berk, Weiss and Boger's (1993) study of charging decisions in cases in San Francisco used a probabilistic "*as if* lottery" approach, controlling for various factors suggested by the regression literature. They found large white race-of-defendant effects, with white defendants being five times more likely to be charged capitally than nonwhite offenders, all else being equal. Weiss (1995) used Bayesian techniques[9] on the same cohort of cases to test the influence of variable selection in analyzing the race effects on capital charging. Weiss found conflicting results that supported the overall conclusion that there were no race effects. Weiss et al. (1996), again using the San Francisco capital charging data, analyzed the level of capriciousness in prosecutorial charging decisions — that is whether "differences between offenders and their crimes translate *consistently* into the charges leveled" (Weiss et al., 1996, p. 611). Measures of capriciousness were developed using the Shannon Information Index to assess diversity within the sample or population, as well as probabilistic techniques such as CART (see end note 6). The capital charging and sentencing standards in place were found to eliminate two-thirds of the potential capriciousness in charging, although they note that these findings are highly dependent on the variables included in the model. While Weiss and his colleagues (1996) were more concerned with the methods through which capriciousness can be quantified, they noted that the level of capriciousness seen — one third of the cases examined — was still high, and that ultimately the question is how much capriciousness, if any, the Eighth Amendment will tolerate in imposition of the death penalty.

Recently, Keil and Vito (2006) used a similar methodology to test for capriciousness in prosecutorial charging decisions in Kentucky. They found race-based differences in capriciousness at the prosecutorial charging stage to be inherent in the process, although the level of randomness in charging decisions was reduced as case seriousness factors were introduced. The degree of capriciousness varied with the race of the defendant and was higher in white defendant cases, with the strongest degrees of capriciousness occurring in white-victim cases. These findings are consistent with the arbitrariness studies in that they indicate a more consistent application of capital justice to black defendants, most of whose victims are also black, than to white defendants, most of whose victims are white. Further study is warranted because, while one may debate the merits of these studies for drawing conclusions regarding race-based arbitrariness in administration of the death penalty, their value is in their demonstration of capriciousness in the administration of the death penalty and racial disparities in its effect. Moreover, the use and comparison of results from analytical approaches to the same data, if consistent, strengthens the body of regression research indicating racial disparity in capital justice, and also operate as a diagnostic tool to refine regression studies for more reliable results (Berk et al., 2005).

LEGAL IMPLICATIONS OF DEMONSTRABLE RACIAL BIAS IN DEATH SENTENCING

The question remains whether "inevitable" and "ineradicable" racial bias continues to taint the death sentencing process established under *Furman*, and whether this is constitutionally acceptable. Under *McCleskey*, unless the disparate impact of a death sentencing statute on different racial groups reaches levels sufficiently stark to support an inference of purposefulness, it is probably not actionable under the Equal Protection Clause or the Eighth Amendment. Does this mean that some level of racial inequity in death sentencing is tolerable under the Constitution? Only one state, New Jersey, has rejected the *McCleskey* concept of "inevitable" inequity in capital sentencing (*State v. Loftin*, 1999), holding that systemic disparity unrelated to the seriousness of the crime violates the New Jersey state constitutional guarantee of Equal Protection. At the federal level, *McCleskey* controls.

Issues of Denial of Substantive Due Process

Assuming, as the Supreme Court did in *McCleskey*, that some level of racial bias exists as an inevitable and incurable part of the capital justice process, two questions remain: (1) is there any constitutional remedy for racial bias in death sentencing? and, (2) is abolition of capital punishment the only remedy? As to the first question, the underlying concept of fundamental fairness inherent in the Constitution arises when a death sentence is based in any way on race. As to the second question, abolition may not be the only option, but no resolution of the dilemma is possible without fully understanding the extent to which race does or does not impact capital justice. Extant evidence suggests that race plays a role in determining death sentence outcomes despite the facially neutral, due process involved. Surely the idea that race influences whom the state kills "offends some principle of justice so rooted in the traditions and consciousness of our people as to be ranked as fundamental" (*Washington v. Glucksberg*, 521 U.S. 702, 720-21, 1997). Demonstrated systemic racial inequity in death sentences produced by a state law, even if it does not rise to the stark levels actionable under the *McCleskey* analysis, amounts to a denial of substantive due process.

It is unlikely that any statute or procedure will filter all unconscious racial attitudes out of the death sentencing process. Where a human life is at stake, it would seem fundamentally unfair to subject a defendant to a state capital justice procedure infected with inevitable and incurable racial influences without strict scrutiny and a showing by the state as to the public necessity to take the defendant's life. *Furman* has reduced, but did not and cannot eliminate, culture-based racial bias at this point in our history.

Application of a substantive due process analysis to the issue of racial discrimination in death sentencing does not inevitably lead to abolition or to irreparable damage to the jury system as feared by the Supreme Court in *McCleskey*. While abolition is not the only option, thus far there has been no government-sponsored national effort to assess racial disparity in death penalty processes. One option that the Supreme Court has rejected in the past, which could be revisited, is a mandatory death penalty implemented through uniform death penalty procedures.

Reassessing a Mandatory Death Penalty

The premise for the Court's refusal to accept mandatory death penalty statutes is a consideration for the dignity of man, which requires individualized sentencing (Woodson, 1976; *Lockett v. Ohio*, 1978). Were death sentences completely fact-dependent and limited to a few specific, clearly defined crimes, the likelihood of racial bias might be reduced. All other aggravated murders would be subject to life without parole. Mitigatory factors could also be defined factually by statute, treated as an affirmative defense, established in a separate hearing and subject to a more stringent burden of proof (a "preponderance of the evidence" standard), and perhaps subject to a less than unanimous jury voting standard. State legislatures could redefine available defenses (e.g., raise the death-eligible age for defendants or their minimum IQ levels) and add additional absolute defenses such as mental illness, lack of criminal capacity, and so on. Provided the elements of the capital crimes and capital defenses were adequately defined by statute, this would substantially reduce jury discretion and the potential for racial bias. The current system of mandatory death eligibility crimes coupled with the wide-open defenses allowed in individual cases may actually incorporate the worst of both approaches (Kirschmeier, 1998).

A second step that would make the capital justice system fairer, although insufficient by itself, would be the establishment of minimum, uniform procedural standards. Among the 36 states with death penalty statutes, there are scores of substantive differences concerning which crimes are eligible for the death penalty and how death sentences are produced and decided. The lack of both substantive and procedural uniformity related to the implementation of *Furman* across states has produced arbitrary and capricious application of the death sentence, which cannot be said to have fulfilled the mandate for neutral, consistent capital justice (Holowinski, 1998).

CONCLUSION: A NATIONAL EFFORT IS NEEDED

The bulk of the empirical research since *Furman* indicates significant racial disparity in applying the death penalty. Recent use of different methodological approaches raises new questions concerning the significance of the race effect, but does not deny its presence (Berk et al., 2005). The time is ripe for a national examination of this issue — to either lay to rest or substantiate claims of race-based disparity in death sentencing. Part of this examination should include addressing moral and legal issues related to evidence that innocent persons have been sentenced to death and executed (Unnever et al., 2005). Outside of race issues, the ultimate question is: Can the death penalty be fundamentally fair if it results in the death of even one innocent person?

The weight of the empirical evidence unfortunately indicates the existence of racial disparity in death penalty processes. While the evidence may not meet legal criteria (i.e., intentionality), it meets social scientific standards. Thus, it is unlikely that the Supreme Court will impose a national moratorium or direct a conclusive scientific study on the role of race in death sentencing because existing evidence does not meet the standard of systemic racial bias set forth in *McCleskey*. Despite the convincing empirical evidence of latent racism in our society, it has received little judicial or legislative attention (Ware, 2007). To deny that racism continues to haunt American society and pervade group and individual consciousness, seems contrary to various studies of this issue (see chapter 1). At the same time, racial biases in death penalty processes violate fundamental American values of fairness and equal justice for all — ideals particularly important where a death is the consequence.

In the current climate, research will continue on a sample-by-sample, jurisdiction-by-jurisdiction basis, exploring the continued influence of race in the capital justice process. New studies and research methods and more complete databases, such as the North Carolina dataset, may produce results more credible to the courts (i.e., sufficient to demonstrate the existence of racial disparity the application of *Furman's* objective of neutrality in death sentencing). Only then will the Supreme Court and the nation be in the position, armed with scientific fact, to address fully the legal, social and moral issues the death penalty presents to a modern democracy.

NOTES

1. See: Baldus et al., 1998; Baldus and Woodworth, 2003b; Garfinkel, 1949; Bowers and Pierce, 1980; Baldus et al., 1990; Radelet and Pierce, 1985; Lugginbuhl and Burkhead, 1994; for studies on prosecutorial charging decisions, see Keil and Vito, 2007; Klein et al., 2006; Songer and Unah, 2006; Weiss et al.,1996; Berk et al., 1993.

2. The Appendix is not intended to encompass all valid studies of racial disparity in the capital justice system since 2003, nor does it include all data from the studies described. Its purpose is to summarize representative studies that were moderately well-controlled (Baldus and Woodworth, 2003). Additionally, although the focus of the chapter is racial disparity in capital sentencing, and

sentencing studies are the primary focus of the appendix, also included are important studies looking at the prosecutorial charging decision (e.g., United States Department of Justice, 2000a, 2000b; Klein et al., 2006).

3. See: Gross and Mauro, 1984; Kleck, 1981; Nakell and Hardy, 1987; Riedel, 1976; Berk and Lowery, 1985; Bowers, 1983; Bowers and Pierce, 1980; Foley and Powell, 1982; Keil and Vito, 1989; Klein et al., 1989; Radelet and Vandiver, 1983; Radelet and Pierce, 1985; Radelet, 1981; Baldus et al., 1990; Barnett, 1986; Eckland-Olson, 1988; Klemm, 1986; Smith, 1987; Arkin, 1980; Foley, 1987; Lewis et al., 1979; Zeisel, 1981; Klein, 1989; Paternoster and Kazyaka, 1988; Vito and Keil, 1988; Keil and Vito, 1990, Beinin et al., 1988; Murphy, 1984.

4. See: ACLU , 2007 (federal death penalty); Donohue, 2007 (Connecticut); Lee, 2007 (San Joaquin County, CA); Pierce, et al., 2006 (Georgia), 2007a (Tênnessee), 2007b (Indiana), 2007c (Ohio); Baldus, et al., 2006 (U.S. Military Justice System); Hindsman et al., 2006 (Colorado); Songer and Unah, 2006 (South Carolina); Eisenberg, 2005 (multi-state); Lenza, et al., 2005 (Missouri); Pierce and Radelet, 2004 (California); Blume et al., 2004 (multi-state); Holcomb et al., 2004, and Williams and Holcomb, 2004 (Ohio).

5. One of the main advantages of regression modeling is the ability to control for all factors which might affect an outcome in order to tease out the actual effect of the target factor: in this case, race. Baldus and his colleagues combine key elements in their approach in order to strengthen the inferential value of the results. A Baldus-type regression model will at a minimum include maximization of data completeness and accuracy; adjustment for legitimate case characteristics other than race which affect the perceived seriousness of the case to ensure maximum "apples to apples" comparisons; and analyses of race of defendant, race of victim and defendant-victim combinations to detect interactive racial patterns of difference (Baldus et al., 2003).

6. There were a wide range of "adjustment" methods used in the 1990-2003 studies to control for the degree of culpability and crime seriousness. Some studies have used jury acceptance of aggravating and mitigating circumstances either as bare counts of the number of aggravating and mitigating circumstances accepted or using individual aggravating and mitigating factors as dummy variables (Baldus et al., 1998, 2002, 2004; Brock et al., 2000; Keil and Vito, 1995; Klein and Rolph, 1991; Lenza et al., 2003; Paternoster and Brame, 2003; Pierce and Radelet, 2002; Unah and Boger, 2001). Indices of culpability have also been used to measure the overall level of aggravation in a case to account for the possibly different weights individual aggravators might carry with jurors (for example, the difference between a heinous, atrocious and cruel murder and a "record" aggravator such as a prior violent felony (e.g., Baime, 2001; Baldus et al., 1983, 1985, 1990, 1998, 2002; Brock et al., 2000).

7. Analytic methods, such as Bayesian analysis, CART analysis and propensity scoring, are non-parametric and do not rely on assumptions about the population under examination, but deal with the actual data, "as is" and as informed by new information. Regression analysis is a parametric method which assumes certain characteristics of the population, such as normal distribution and data measured at least at the interval/ratio level. Regression analyses sets up hypotheses about changes in the *likelihood* of an event occurring within the population

under specified conditions. Probabilistic methods, such as Bayesian or CART analysis, ask whether the event occurred given specified conditions, or not, and the probability (odds) of each outcome is determined to a mathematical certainty (Berk, Western and Weiss, 1995). For example, in regression analysis the question might be whether the *likelihood* of a death sentence outcome from application of the capital sentencing statute in North Carolina between 1978 and 2004 differs based on race. Probabilistic analysis asks what the odds of a death sentence (or not) resulting from application of the capital sentencing statute in North Carolina between 1978 and 2004 were for black defendants and for white defendants, then the odds are compared for difference. These odds can be calculated for each category of defendant and compared as other conditions, such as level of aggravation or race of victim are added.

8. Descriptive analysis involves computing descriptive measurements of the data, such as mean, variance, standard deviation, and so on. The frequencies of subsets of cases reflective of the presence of specified conditions/variables thought to affect the life-death outcome can be used to calculate rates and ratios of decisions such as capital charging and sentencing, for comparison between defendant and victim racial combinations. Qualitative studies, such as those conducted by the Capital Jury Project, include information obtained through observation and interviews of those involved to assess racial attitudes and charging practices within a given jurisdiction.

9. Bayesian techniques produce definitive probabilities of an outcome under specified known conditions versus the likelihoods of an outcome based on the effect of selected variables produced in a regression analysis (Berk et al., 1995).

APPENDIX 8A. RACE AND THE DEATH PENALTY: EMPIRICAL STUDIES, 1990-2008

Study by Jurisdiction	Time Frame	Unit of Analysis	Sample Size	Methodology	Controls	Significant Race Effects at Sentencing		
						Black Defendant	White Victim	Black Defendant/ White Victim
ARIZONA								
Bortner and Hall (2002)	1995–1999	First degree murder cases	921 total; 143 capital; 31 death	Unadjusted rates analysis of all cases	Death noticed	Not substantively analyzed	Not substantively analyzed	Not substantively analyzed
Baldus & Woodworth additional analysis by Bortner and Hall data (2003)	1995–1999	1995–1999	921 total; 143 capital; 31 death	Unadjusted rates analysis of death-noticed cases tried and reaching penalty stage	Death noticed	No	Yes	N/A

APPENDIX 8A. *(continued)*

Study by Jurisdiction	Time Frame	Unit of Analysis	Sample Size	Methodology	Controls	Significant Race Effects at Sentencing		
						Black Defendant	White Victim	Black Defendant/ White Victim
CALIFORNIA								
Klein and Rolph (1991)	1977–1981	Penalty trials	496	Unadjusted descriptive analysis; adjusted CART analysis	15 case characteristics; race of defendant, race of victim	No	Yes	N/A
Pierce and Radelet (2005)	1990–1999	Death sentence cases	263	Descriptive analysis; logistic regression	Race of victim and defendant; level of aggravation; regional demographics	N/A	Yes	N/A
COLORADO								
Hindson et al. (2006)	1980–1999	Death sentence sought	110	Descriptive analysis of rates, proportions, probabilities	Defendant and victim race, gender	No	Yes	Yes

APPENDIX 8A. *(continued)*

Study by Jurisdiction	Time Frame	Unit of Analysis	Sample Size	Methodology	Controls	Significant Race Effects at Sentencing		
						Black Defendant	White Victim	Black Defendant/ White Victim
CONNECTICUT								
State v. Cobb 1995	1973–1994	Capital murder convictions	66	Unadjusted descriptive analysis	Race of defendant and victim	Yes	Yes	No information
Donohue (2007) [Executive Summary only]	1973–2007	Homicides	4,600	Descriptive analysis; evaluation of probability of death sentence	Race of defendant and victim; level of "egregiousness"	Unknown	Yes	Yes
FLORIDA								
Radelet and Pierce (1991)	1976–1987	Homicides	10,142 (415 death cases)	Descriptive analysis; regression analysis	Race of defendant (D) and victim (V); D-V relationship, V gender; weapon used; region	No	Yes	No

APPENDIX 8A. *(continued)*

Study by Jurisdiction	Time Frame	Unit of Analysis	Sample Size	Methodology	Controls	Significant Race Effects at Sentencing		
						Black Defendant	White Victim	Black Defendant/ White Victim
GEORGIA								
Pierce et al. (2006)	1989–1998	Homicide cases; D age 18+ yrs.	3,658 (59 death cases)	SHR and state death case data used; descriptive and regression analyses	Defendant race, victim race, level of aggravation	No	Yes	No
ILLINOIS								
Pierce and Radelet (2002)	1988–1997	First degree murder sentencing events	4,182 (76 death cases)	SHR and state data; descriptive and regression analyses	28 legal and extra-legal variables relating to the crime and victim; level of aggravation; region	No	Yes	No

APPENDIX 8A. (*continued*)

Study by Jurisdiction	Time Frame	Unit of Analysis	Sample Size	Methodology	Controls	Significant Race Effects at Sentencing		
						Black Defendant	White Victim	Black Defendant/ White Victim
INDIANA								
Ziemba-Davies & Myers (2002)	May 1993–July 2001	Murder convictions	224	Descriptive analysis of sentencing outcomes	None other than race of defendant and victim	No	Yes	No analysis
Pierce et al. (2007b)	1981–2000	Homicide cases, D age 18+	7,622 (238 death cases)	Used SHR and state death case data; descriptive and regression analyses	Defendant race; victim race; level of aggravation; region	No	Yes	No
KENTUCKY								
Keil and Vito (1995)	1976–1991	Death eligible cases	577	Regression analysis of capital charging and sentencing	Defendant and victim race; 6 case characteristics	No	Yes	Yes

APPENDIX 8A. *(continued)*

Study by Jurisdiction	Time Frame	Unit of Analysis	Sample Size	Methodology	Controls	Significant Race Effects at Sentencing		
						Black Defendant	White Victim	Black Defendant/ White Victim
MARYLAND								
Baldus & Woodworth (2001)	1978–1999	Death eligible, death noticed cases	346	Descriptive analyses, unadjusted and adjusted analysis of charging and sentencing	Race of defendant and victim; number of aggravators	No	Yes	Yes
Paternoster & Brame (2003)	July, 1978– 1999	Death eligible cases	1,311 (353 death noticed, 180 sentencing, 76 death cases)	Unadjusted descriptive and adjusted regression analyses of data; also county-by-county analyses	Race of defendant and victim; region; 12+ legal and extra-legal case characteristics	No	Yes	Yes

APPENDIX 8A. *(continued)*

Study by Jurisdiction	Time Frame	Unit of Analysis	Sample Size	Methodology	Controls	Significant Race Effects at Sentencing		
						Black Defendant	White Victim	Black Defendant/ White Victim
Berk et al. (2003)	July, 1978–1999	Death eligible cases	1,311 (353 death noticed, 180 sentencing, 76 death cases)	Replicated Paternoster/ Brame unadjusted descriptive and adjusted regression analyses; county-by-county analyses; Re-analysis using CART, random forests	Race of defendant and victim; sentence outcome; 12 case characteristics; region	No	No	No
MISSOURI								
Lenza et al. (2003)	1978–1996	Capital homicides	574 (152 death sentence cases)	Regression analysis	Race of defendant and victim, 8 controls	No	Yes	Yes

– 186 –

APPENDIX 8A. *(continued)*

Study by Jurisdiction	Time Frame	Unit of Analysis	Sample Size	Methodology	Controls	Significant Race Effects at Sentencing		
						Black Defendant	White Victim	Black Defendant/ White Victim
NEBRASKA								
Baldus et al. (2002)	1973–1999	Death eligible cases	185 capitally charged; 89 sentencing cases; 29 death cases	Unadjusted descriptive and adjusted regression analyses	Race of defendant and victim; culpability factors	No	No	No
NEW JERSEY								
Baime (2001) and Weisburd & Naus (2001)	1983–2000	Death eligible cases	penalty trials, 46 death cases	Unadjusted descriptive analysis; unadjusted and adjusted regression study; case sorting	Case characteristics/ culpability; region	No	Yes	No

APPENDIX 8A. (*continued*)

Study by Jurisdiction	Time Frame	Unit of Analysis	Sample Size	Methodology	Controls	Significant Race Effects at Sentencing		
						Black Defendant	White Victim	Black Defendant/ White Victim
NORTH CAROLINA								
Unah and Boger (2001a)	1993–1997	1st and 2nd degree murder convictions	502 (stratified by region from 3,592 cases)	Unadjusted descriptive analysis; adjusted regression analysis	10 statutory aggravators, 7 mitigators, 15 case characteristics	No	Yes	Yes
Stauffer et al. (2006)	1979–2002	Capital sentencing cases	953	Descriptive analysis; regression analysis	20 racial, case characteristic variables; gender	No	Yes	No
Kremling et al. (2007)	1979–2002	Capital sentencing cases	966	Descriptive analysis; regression analysis	Level of statutory aggravation and mitigation; other case factors	No	Yes	No

APPENDIX 8A. (*continued*)

Study by Jurisdiction	Time Frame	Unit of Analysis	Sample Size	Methodology	Controls	Significant Race Effects at Sentencing		
						Black Defendant	White Victim	Black Defendant/ White Victim
OHIO								
Williams and Holcomb (2001)	1981–1994	Homicides [SHR], death sentence cases	5,319 and 271	Descriptive analysis; regression analysis	Race of defendant and victim; case characteristics	No	Yes	Yes
Williams and Holcomb (2004)	1981–1994	Homicides [SHR], death penalty cases	5,319 and 271	Descriptive analysis; regression analysis	Race of defendant and victim; victim gender; case characteristics	No	Yes	No
Pierce et al. (2007c)	1981–2000	Homicide cases, defendant age 18+	7,622 (238 death cases)	Used SHR and state death case data; descriptive and regression analyses	Defendant race; victim race; level of aggravation; region	No	Yes	No

APPENDIX 8A. *(continued)*

Study by Jurisdiction	Time Frame	Unit of Analysis	Sample Size	Methodology	Controls	Significant Race Effects at Sentencing		
						Black Defendant	White Victim	Black Defendant/ White Victim
PENNSYLVANIA								
Baldus et al. (1998)	1983–1993 (Phila-delphia)	Death-eligible cases	384 (from 707 prosecutions analyzed, 114 death cases)	Unadjusted descriptive analysis; regression; multi-measure analyses	Multiple controls for case characteristics; murder severity; number of aggravators and mitigators; defendant and victim characteristics; socioeconomic status	Yes	Yes	No information

APPENDIX 8A. *(continued)*

Study by Jurisdiction	Time Frame	Unit of Analysis	Sample Size	Methodology	Controls	Significant Race Effects at Sentencing		
						Black Defendant	White Victim	Black Defendant/ White Victim
SOUTH CAROLINA								
McCord (2002)	1998	Aggravated murder cases	11 (20 defendants and 19 victims)	Unadjusted analysis of death sentence rates	Case selection based on comparable "depravity points"; defendant and victim race	No	Yes	No information
TENNESSEE								
Pierce et al. (2007)	1981–2000	Homicide cases; defendant age 18+ yrs.	3,567 (88 death cases)	SHR and state death case data used; descriptive and regression analyses	Defendant race; victim race; level of aggravation; region	No	Yes	No

APPENDIX 8A. *(continued)*

Study by Jurisdiction	Time Frame	Unit of Analysis	Sample Size	Methodology	Controls	Significant Race Effects at Sentencing		
						Black Defendant	White Victim	Black Defendant/ White Victim
TEXAS								
Brock et al. (2000)	1980–1986	Intentional homicide cases, age of defendants 17+	28,286 (543 death sentence cases)	SHR and state data; descriptive analysis	5-level scale of culpability/ deathworthiness with 4 case characteristics; region	No	Yes	Yes
Phillips (2008), in press	1992–1999	Death sentence cases, Harris County, TX	504	Logistic regression; calculated conditional probabilities	Race of defendant and victim; legal factors; SEC factors of defendant and victim; culpability and case seriousness factors	Yes	Yes	Yes

APPENDIX 8A. *(continued)*

Study by Jurisdiction	Time Frame	Unit of Analysis	Sample Size	Methodology	Controls	Significant Race Effects at Sentencing		
						Black Defendant	White Victim	Black Defendant/ White Victim
VIRGINIA								
JLARC (2001)	1995–1999	Death eligible cases	160 (regionally stratified from larger sample of 215 cases)	Unadjusted descriptive and adjusted regression analyses	Race of defendant and victim; other victim and case characteristics; region	No	Yes (unadjusted only)	No
ACLU (2003)	1978–2001	Potentially capital and death sentence cases	1,331 and 181	Adjusted descriptive analysis	Race of defendant and victim, "qualifying" case characteristics; county	Yes	Yes	Yes

APPENDIX 8A. *(continued)*

Study by Jurisdiction	Time Frame	Unit of Analysis	Sample Size	Methodology	Controls	Significant Race Effects at Sentencing		
						Black Defendant	White Victim	Black Defendant/ White Victim
MULTI-STATE								
Blume et al. (2004)	1977–1999	Homicides, death row populations in 31 states	5,593	Descriptive analysis; regression analysis [binomial, Logit OLS]	Race of defendant and victim; state legal and social factors; capital case standards; state SEC and demographics	No	Yes	Yes
FEDERAL DEPARTMENT OF JUSTICE								
DOJ (2000a) and DOJ (Supp. 2001b)	1995–2000	Death eligible cases	682	Unadjusted rates analysis of prosecutorial decisions	Race of defendant and victim; case characteristics	No (prosecutorial decisions)	No (prosecutorial decisions)	No (prosecutorial decisions)

APPENDIX 8A. *(continued)*

Study by Jurisdiction	Time Frame	Unit of Analysis	Sample Size	Methodology	Controls	Significant Race Effects at Sentencing		
						Black Defendant	White Victim	Black Defendant/ White Victim
Klein et al. (2006)	1995–2000	Death-eligible cases	312	Multiple methodologies including logistic regression, propensity scoring, CART	Race of defendant and victim; case characteristics	No (prosecutorial decisions)	No (prosecutorial decisions)	No (prosecutorial decisions)
FEDERAL MILITARY								
Baldus et al. (2006)	1984–2004	Death eligible cases under military code	99	Descriptive rates analysis; regression analysis at various stages of process	Race of accused and victim; culpability factors	No	No	No

9. Profiling White Americans: A Research Note on "Shopping While White"[1]

Shaun L. Gabbidon
George E. Higgins

Within the last decade, racial profiling has become a substantive research concern for researchers, policy analysts and policy makers, but it has been especially salient in the field of policing research (see chapter by Fridell, this volume). During this period, numerous studies have appeared that focus on a variety of aspects related to racial profiling (for an excellent summary, see Withrow, 2006). One of the more widely used definitions of racial profiling has been offered by Ramirez et al. (2000, p. 3), who state that:

> racial profiling is defined as any police-initiated action that relies on the race, ethnicity, or national origin rather than the behavior of an individual or information that leads the police to a particular individual who has been identified as being, or having been, engaged in criminal activity. (p. 3)

In general, two points are worth noting regarding this definition. First, it excludes the possibility that racial profiling occurs outside the context of police activity. This is clearly not the case because the use of racial stereotypes that result in outcomes such as racial profiling has historically been found in other aspects of American society that intersect with criminal justice, such as retail settings.

Second, this definition is not race-specific: that is, it does not eliminate the possibility that Whites may, in some circumstances, be racially profiled. However, most scholars have rightly focused their attention on racial profiling as it relates to American racial and ethnic minorities. In doing so, research on the racial profiling of White Americans has been neglected.

Whites have not been the subject of racial profiling research because many scholars may take the position that profiling is something that can only be perpetrated against racial and ethnic minorities. The standard argument is that racial and ethnic minorities cannot be racists or discriminate against Whites because the former groups lack the type of power required to engage in and enforce anti-White forms of discrimination. However, in recent years, some scholars have noted that a) Whites can also be the victims of profiling (Kennedy, 1999), and b) that Blacks, though to a lesser extent than Whites, also support and engage in the practice of racial profiling (Barlow and Barlow, 2002; Kennedy, 1999; MacDonald, 2003).

Although we know that racial profiling exists, the demographics and profiles of White individuals who perceived themselves as being the victims of racial profiling have not been examined in the empirical literature. The present study seeks to fill this gap by focusing on the characteristics of White individuals who perceived themselves as having been racially profiled by retail establishments, or by what we refer to as Consumer Racial Profiling (CRP). To fill this gap in the literature, the present study uses data from a representative sample of the general population of Philadelphia, PA, who participated in a phone survey to determine the nature and scope of their perceived profiling by retail establishments.

LITERATURE REVIEW

The late 1990s produced some of the first scholarly research devoted to racial profiling. Much of this research was concerned with racial minorities, particularly Black Americans, who complained about being excessively stopped on American roadways (e.g., Harris, 1999). It was during this period that the term "Driving While Black" was created to describe what is now known as racial profiling (Gates, 1997). The early literature in this area found that Black drivers were disproportionately stopped by police on interstate highways (Harris, 1999). Many of these early studies were the product of lawsuits in which minority drivers alleged that they had been racially profiled in violation of constitutional protections (Gabbidon et al., 2007). The litigation, especially class action suits in New Jersey and Maryland, clearly showed that Blacks were being targeted for traffic stops (Russell, 1998).

Following initial revelations that racial profiling existed, social scientists began to conduct studies that examined the intricacies of traffic stops. Such studies focused on who was getting stopped, why they were getting stopped, and the outcomes of the stops (see Withrow, 2006, for a cogent review of the literature). During this period, though, minorities were also complaining about another form of profiling — "Shopping While Black." However, this form of profiling has been overlooked in the literature in favor of studies related to "Driving While Black." Nevertheless, some social scientists focused on what was happening in retail settings. This limited research is reviewed below.

Consumer Racial Profiling (CRP): An Overview of the Literature

Some of the earliest literature on CRP was based on the blatant discrimination being experienced by Black shoppers in retail settings (Feagin, 1991; Fifield, 2001, Henderson, 2001; Lee, 2000; Williams et al., 2001). In particular, this literature was primarily concerned with the poor service received by Blacks of all socioeconomic levels in retail environments. In the early part of this millennium, the literature started to diversify. For example, Asquith and Bristow (2000) conducted a pre-experimental study that examined the perceptions of students regarding which racial and ethnic groups were most likely to shoplift. Their study clearly showed that students' views were not in line with the shoplifting arrest data in the state where the study was conducted. To address their false perceptions, the researchers showed the students a video correcting their perceptions. But even after using this approach, the students still did not accurately identify the demographics of shoplifters. The respondents continued to overestimate the participation of racial and ethnic minorities as perpetrators of shoplifting.

Gabbidon (2003) provided an empirical analysis of civil litigation involving allegations of CRP. In all, he located 29 cases, dating from the early 1970s, in which litigants sought compensation for their discriminatory and often demeaning treatment at the hands of representatives from retail establishments. He found that most of the cases involved Black plaintiffs who were falsely arrested based on "unsubstantiated hunches." This study found that store clerks were most likely to initiate the CRP incident. In addition, the research identified several ways in which shoppers were profiled. These included mistaken identity, extra scrutiny while shopping, requiring additional identification for purchases, undue use of force, and the enactment of blanket policies of how to treat minorities (Gabbidon, 2003). The research also revealed that plaintiffs were victorious in 58% of the cases.

Following the publication of these two studies, additional research appeared in the literature that examined the specific experiences of Black men in retail settings (Crockett et al., 2003). Dabney and his colleagues, for example, published two articles based on the results of their experimental study of shoplifting (see Dabney et al., 2004; Dabney et al., 2006). Their methodologically sophisticated study involved observing customers in an Atlanta drug store to determine "who actually steals." Based on their observations using closed-circuit television, it was found that about 8.5% of customers actually stole. This figure was higher than anticipated considering the data available from the FBI's annual *Uniform Crime Reports*. Moreover, while the study was initially designed to randomly observe every third shopper who entered the store, the researchers later modified to allow the observers discretion in choosing whom to observe. When given this added discretion, the trained observers exhibited a tendency to engage in racial profiling. Describing this serendipitous finding, the authors wrote: " . . . by allowing our trained observers some personal discretion on the selection of shoppers to video tape, the researchers apparently introduced a small, but detectable, level of racial bias into the selection of shoppers. This bias had the effect of artificially increasing the number of African American shoppers who were observed" (Dabney et al., 2004, p. 707). Of particular significance was the finding that racial and ethnic minorities did not shoplift at rates higher than Whites.

Additional research has examined legal cases to determine the nature and scope of CRP, how the courts respond to such cases (Harris, 2003; Harris, Henderson and Williams, 2005; Williams et al., 2006), and the nature of racial profiling as it relates to investigating employee theft cases (Patrick and Gabbidon, 2006). In this paper we diverge from the past and more recent research in focusing on perceived CRP victimization among a sample of White respondents. In addition to discussing the nature and scope of their CRP victimization, the paper examines whether there are any substantive differences between those Whites who have been profiled and those who have not been a victim of CRP.

METHODOLOGY

This paper is based on a subset of a larger dataset that examined whether Philadelphia-area residents felt they were victims of CRP. Conducted from November 30, 2006 to December 13, 2006, these data are based on phone interviews carried out by the Pennsylvania State University's Harrisburg's Center for Survey Research. The Center uses VOXCO computer-assisted telephone interviewing (CATI) software, which employs random digit dialing to ensure that a representative sample was selected from all Philadelphia-area telephone exchanges. To make certain that each member of a sampled household had an equal probability of being interviewed, the last-birthday method of respondent selection was utilized. This method was used to eliminate biases that arise from interviewing the person who answers the phone. During the data collection procedure, the CATI system accommodated 11 concurrent interviewers and quality control supervisors assisted by VOXCO's monitoring and productivity tools.

In an effort to maximize the cooperation rate, on average, the Center made 4.79 callbacks to respondents. This procedure yielded 500 completed and 16 partially completed interviews. Of these, five completed interviews were eliminated from the study because the respondents' self-reported zip code fell outside of Philadelphia. Over all, the cooperation rate, which is the total number of completed calls minus the refusals, was 40.2%. In order to ensure that the results from the CRP survey were not biased toward any single demographic group or geographic region, the results were checked against the demographic characteristics and the geographic distribution of Philadelphia's population using census data (Pennsylvania State Data Center, 2006). Weighting was used so that the sample's demographic profile accurately reflected the population's known properties.

The questionnaire was separated into several parts. To begin, the respondents were provided with the following definition and statement regarding CRP:

> CRP is the act of discriminating against customers, by retailers, based upon their race or ethnicity. This study is specifically concerned with CRP as it relates to your experience as a shopper being racially profiled by retail clerks, managers, and security personnel. ALL races and ethnicities can experience this type of discrimination.

If the respondents indicated they had been victims of CRP, the interviewer proceeded to ask them a variety of questions that solicited the frequency with which they encountered CRP, where it occurred, who was involved, what type of profiling occurred, what they did about it, how it made them feel, what they think should happen to the person who was involved in the encounter, and demographic questions on race/ethnicity of the victim and the offender, and the gender of the victim. If the person indicated that s/

Table 9.1. Education Level of White CRP Victims

Educational Level	Frequency	%
Less than high school	3	6.7
High school diploma	12	26.7
Some college	11	24.4
Two-year technical degree	6	13.3
Four-year college degree	6	13.3
Graduate work	7	15.6
Total	45	100.0

he had not been a victim of CRP, s/he was simply asked to respond to demographic questions for the researchers to later use as a point of comparison with those who felt they had experienced CRP.

RESULTS

Two-hundred and seven of the 500 respondents to the phone survey reported their race as White. These respondents form the basis of this analysis. Of the 207 White respondents, 45 or 21.7% reported that they had been a victim of CRP. Given the small sample size, we only present descriptive statistics in the analysis. In particular, we outline the demographics of those profiled, the nature of those perceived to be profiled, the emotional impact of CRP on victimization, and the best approaches to handling CRP incidents.

Demographics of Those Profiled

The 45 persons who reported being profiled were mostly males (55.5%) from urban (72%) or suburban (22%) areas. The average age of the 45 self-reported White profilees was 46.63 years (SD=14.2), nearly 90% of whom resided in homes with two or more persons. These 45 respondents were also well educated, with more than 60% having attended or graduated from college (see Table 9.1).

Table 9.2 shows that slightly more than half of the respondents had incomes of $60,000 a year or less. Two additional questions we asked to further provide background on respondents: (1) whether or not they had stolen from a retail establishment, and (2) whether they had ever been

Table 9.2. Total Household Income of White CRP Victims

Income Range	Frequency	%
Less than $10,000/year	2	5.3
$10,000-$20,000/year	1	1.3
$20,001-$40,000/year	9	20.0
$40,001-$60,000/year	11	25.3
$60,001-$80,000/year	3	6.6
$80,001-$100,000/year	4	8.4
$100,001-$125,000/year	4	9.9
$125,001-$150,000/year	1	3.3
More than $150,000/year	1	1.3
Refused	8	18.5
Total	44[a]	100.0

a. Does not equal 45 due to missing data.

caught doing so. On the first part of the question, 14.6% admitted to having previously stolen from a retail establishment. Only one of the respondents reported having been arrested for such activity.

Nature and Scope of Profiling

In general, very few of the respondents indicated that they were profiled with any significant frequency. In fact, 71% of them indicated they were occasionally profiled and 20% reported they had only been profiled once. All of the reported incidents occurred when the victims were adults. As to where the incident was most likely to occur, 32% experienced CRP in department stores, 21% in clothing retailers, and 18% in grocery stores. Approximately, 90% of the offending establishments were located less than ten miles from the respondents' homes, and 64% occurred in an urban area. Sales clerks, acting alone, were most likely to be identified as engaging in profiling (71%). As for the race of the person perpetrating CRP, the White respondents identified Blacks as being the main offenders (58%), with Whites (22%) and Asians (9%) comprising the second and third largest ethnicities of the persons alleged to have carried out the profiling.

Speaking to the nature of the incidents, the CRP victims in our study also reported that, in 27% of the situations, they felt they were being watched, with 13% reporting they were subjected to verbal abuse. In the other instances, the CRP victims were subjected to being followed around

Table 9.3. Reasons for Not Reporting CRP Incident

Reason for not reporting	Frequency	%
Not a big deal	18	48.6
Avoid inconvenience	7	18.9
Fear of not being believed	3	8.1
Fear of reprisal	1	2.7
Too embarrassed	1	2.7
Don't know/not sure	5	13.5
Refused	2	5.4
Total	37[a]	99.9

a. This total represents only those respondents who did not report the CRP incident.

the store, asked to leave, accused of theft, approached repeatedly, and were also targeted by racial slurs.

However, after having had such a negative experience, 64% of the respondents reported that they still made a purchase at the offending establishment, and 51% stated that they patronized the establishment again at a later date. Only 18% of the victims in our study reported the incident to store management or any company officials. When asked why they failed to report these incidents, the most frequent response (49%) was that the incident was "not a big deal." Another 19% said that they failed to report the incident because they did not want to be inconvenienced (see Table 9.3). Some additional considerations noted by the respondents for not reporting the incident included: "daughter worked at the store"; "just thought she might have been having a bad day"; "time and effort"; "nothing would have been done anyway"; and, "it didn't bother me since I'm law enforcement." For those who pursued a complaint of some sort, an apology or denial from the retailer were the most frequent responses.

Respondents were also asked whether the victims shared the incident with family and friends. In approximately two-third of the cases, they reported doing so. Interestingly, when queried about whether the persons they shared the incident with had also been a victim of CRP, 60% indicated they had. And not surprisingly, many of them had not reported the incident either (67%).

Emotional Impact of CRP Victimization

An often neglected area of racial profiling research is the emotional impact of such incidents on victims. Given the paucity of studies that query

Table 9.4. Emotional Impact of CRP*

The CRP incident was stressful.		
	Frequency	Percent
Strongly Agree	7	15.6
Agree	24	53.3
Disagree	11	24.4
Strongly Disagree	3	6.7
Total	45	100.0

The CRP incident made me angry.		
	Frequency	Percent
Strongly Agree	13	28.9
Agree	28	62.2
Disagree	3	6.7
Strongly Disagree	1	2.2
Total	45	100.0

I was shocked when I realized I was a victim of CRP.		
	Frequency	Percent
Strongly Agree	11	24.4
Agree	15	33.3
Disagree	13	28.9
Strongly Disagree	6	133
Total	45	100.0

The CRP Incident made me sad.		
	Frequency	Percent
Strongly Agree	12	26.7
Agree	14	31.1
Disagree	15	33.3
Strongly Disagree	4	8.9
Total	45	100.0

*Table 9.4 continues on next page.

respondents about this, we asked a series of questions to gauge the level of negative emotions evoked by the CRP incident. When asked about the emotions surrounding their CRP experience, respondents reported the following (see Table 9.4 for full results): 69% agreed or strongly agreed

Table 9.4. *(continued)*

The CRP incident embarrassed me.

	Frequency	Percent
Strongly Agree	10	22.7
Agree	9	20.5
Disagree	21	47.7
Strongly Disagree	4	9.1
Total	44*	100.0

My self-worth was negatively impacted as a result of the CRP incident.

	Frequency	Percent
Strongly Agree	5	11.4
Agree	8	18.2
Disagree	19	43.2
Strongly Disagree	12	27.3
Total	44*	100.0

The incident had a negative impact on me.

	Frequency	Percent
Strongly Agree	11	24.4
Agree	18	40.0
Disagree	13	28.8
Strongly Disagree	3	6.7
Total	45	100.0

* Total does not equal 45 due to missing data.

that it was stressful; 91% agreed or strongly agreed that they were angry about the incident; nearly 60% agreed or strongly agreed they were shocked by the incident; 58% agreed or strongly disagreed that the incident made them sad; 43% agreed or strongly agreed that they were embarrassed by the incident; 64% agreed or strongly agreed that the incident had a negative impact on them, and; nearly 30% agreed or strongly agreed that their self-worth was negatively affected by the incident.

Best Approaches to Handling CRP Incidents

The questionnaire was also designed to determine how respondents felt retailers should address CRP. More than half of the respondents suggested that "training employees on the perils of profiling" was the best way to handle the problem (56%). Another 29% suggested "diversifying the workforce" as the best option. The remainder of the respondents took a tougher stance by calling for the firing of employees who engaged in CRP. In line with this belief, one respondent noted: "A person should be fired if they can't deal with the public, if they can't be rehabilitated after many attempts." Other diverse suggestions/comments included: "Go to church and look into the soul of Jesus," "Education," "Culture change," "Everybody is racist in a way," and "Everyone should be treated equally."

DISCUSSION

The focus of this paper was to explore CRP as it relates to White Americans. Based on the results, it appears that CRP is not an experience that is exclusive to American racial and ethnic minorities. However, among White Americans who admitted to experiencing some degree of CRP, CRP appeared to happen relatively infrequently. It was interesting to find that nearly 60% of the CRP victims indicated that Blacks were the perpetrators of CRP. It could be that, given the large population of Blacks in the Philadelphia area, in some settings Whites stand out as the suspected shoplifters. Or, it could be that reverse discrimination is at play here. It is also plausible that, as some scholars believe, racial and/or ethnic minorities can also be racist and discriminate against non-race members (Sowell, 2005). As such, minorities may express discriminatory belief systems and take actions that can be considered racist and discriminatory. Unfortunately, the data collected in this study could not speak more directly to this possibility.

Turning to the context of the CRP experience, it was interesting to find that even after being profiled in a variety of ways, the CRP victims in this study continued to conclude their purchases in the "offending" retail establishment and, at a later date, returned to the store where the CRP incident took place. Perhaps this outcome reflects the reduced saliency CRP has for White victims of this practice. Indeed, the saliency of these incidents for White victims of CRP may be reflected in their reporting practices: a large percentage of White respondents did not report the incident because "it wasn't a big deal." These feelings were, perhaps, not restricted to the survey population alone. Respondents also indicated that a larger proportion of the family members and friends with whom they shared the incident also did not report their CRP incident.

Contrary to expectation, among the group of respondents who felt that the incident "wasn't a big deal" or it would have been an "inconvenience" to report it, those who perceived themselves to have been CRP victims clearly felt the "sting" of being profiled. And while the abundance of racial profiling literature has captured some of the anecdotal aspects of being a victim of the practice (see, Harris, 2002), our study uncovered an array of emotions felt by Whites who perceived themselves to have been victims of CRP. It was notable, though, that while this group expressed serious emotional aftereffects from the CRP incident, they did not believe that their self-worth was affected in any significant way. This could have resulted from the fact that they did not experience CRP very often, or because, as Whites, they didn't often encounter racism or discrimination in their lives. As such, they didn't see this experience as severely impacting their self-worth — another indicator that as members of the racial majority group, CRP has little saliency for Whites. It is also possible that the concept of "White-privilege" might be of some use in explaining this outcome (see McIntosh, 2006). Thus, Whites, because of their skin color and position in society, do not typically have to "put up" with this treatment — so, while they may be upset when they do encounter it, they know their privilege and status excludes them from encountering such behavior with any appreciable frequency. Given this reality, why would their self-worth suffer?

Another intriguing finding relates to participants' views regarding how to handle employees who engage in CRP. For respondents, training employees was high on the list of corrective actions. Since some scholars have argued that training has been effective in terms of reducing the racial and ethnic minority disproportionality in traffic stops (Gaines, 2006, p. 230), it is likely that a similar approach in the private sector might prove fruitful. On the flip side, training could promote more evasive forms of profiling. Diversifying the workforce was also a frequent response to the question concerning corrective actions that ought to be taken. In this case, though, considering that many of the Whites felt Blacks were the ones who profiled them, it is likely that "diversifying the workforce," at least for this unique sample, means hiring more *White* employees.

CONCLUSION

This paper explored the understudied area of White profiling. The findings revealed that some Whites do perceive themselves to have been victims of CRP. As a result, this opens up an avenue for a new body of racial profiling research, especially as it relates to retail settings. It seems as though scholars have neglected this line of research for two key reasons. First, the data needed to study CRP are extremely limited. Therefore, studying CRP requires scholars to produce dataset useful for this purpose. Given the heavy reliance on secondary data analysis in social science research, scholars are not likely to be enthusiastic about this requirement. Even so, we urge scholars to make the effort. To expand the racial profiling canon, additional data collection needs to take place. Future research might also attempt to locate and interview White profiling victims, to gain more in-depth information on their CRP experiences. Since this project was limited to one metropolitan area, future research should also be more national in scope.

Second, major governmental and private funding sources have already made serious monetary investments in traffic-stop research or other research that examines what one might call "mainstream" research on racial profiling. These funding agencies must be made aware that other forms of racial profiling also warrant consideration for their funds.

Future research on CRP is likely to yield additional information on White victims of CRP. If this supposition holds true, we believe it might hold the key to significantly curtailing, or in the best case scenario, ending racial profiling. Why? As strange as it might sound, making it more widely known that Whites are also victimized and "scarred," to some extent, by profiling, might spur more immediate action from the people most likely to hold the power to stop the practice — powerful White Americans (mostly males) in key governmental and justice system positions.

NOTES

1. This project was jointly funded by Penn State's Africana Research Center and Penn State Harrisburg's School of Public Affairs. The authors thank Auden Thomas, Stephanie Hintz, and the interviewers from Penn State Harrisburg's Center for Survey Research who assisted in the completion of this project.

10. The Things that Pass for Knowledge: Racial Identity in Forensics

Tom Mieczkowski

"The things that pass for knowledge, I can't understand ..."

Steely Dan, *Reeling in the Years*

The controversies associated with racial identification are so commonplace there seems nothing further to say: All that can be argued has been argued, and all that can be decided by consensus has been decided. What remains are the relatively hardened positions on the reality or illusion of racial categories as "true" biological typologies. A major activity of forensic science has been utilizing techniques to characterize individuals by gender or race (or both) for the evidentiary purposes of including or excluding individuals from suspected criminal involvement. In forensics these attributes are called "class characteristics." An example of a class characteristic is blood typing, where a persons can be assigned to one of four groups (A, B, AB, O), which allows the exclusion or inclusion of persons for forensic purposes. The assignment of the class characteristic is dependent on two things: a correct determination of the blood type by a physical test, and the assumption that these characteristics are *exclusive* and *exhaustive*. A person cannot be in two or more categories, nor are there any persons who cannot be assigned to one of these categories. In this chapter we consider the use of racial — and to some extent gender identity — as class characteristics in forensic identification.

No one denies the reality of race in a sociological or psychological context — although the amount of weight it deserves in different contexts has been debated. However, there is no denial by most that the classic sociological observation of Chicago's W.I. Thomas — that if a situation is perceived as real, it is real in its consequences — is amply illustrated by racial identity and the concept of race itself. Thus, race *is* a reality by definition and its consequences are profound and far-reaching.

The concept of race and racial identity ranks as one of the most important ascribed social attributes in an individual's life — a so-called "master status," a status generally ascribed at birth — and for most persons (but not all) immutable over the course of their lives. The effect of racial ascription is life-determining, and encompasses the most fundamental parameters in situating an individual in contemporary American society (Lieberman and Reynolds, 1978). The degree to which a person has a sense of "race identity" as a part of his or her self-concept, and the degree to which others perceive him or her to be a member of a race group and respond to the person in light of that perception, are the foremost critical dynamics of race identity. Yet for all the weight and dynamics associated with ascribed race, there remains at its heart an essential ambiguity.

Consider the words of Jean Toomer (1923), an American poet and novelist and an important figure of the Harlem Renaissance of the 1920s: "Racially, I seem to have (who knows for sure?) seven blood mixtures: French, Dutch, Welsh, Negro, German, Jewish, and Indian. Because of these my position in America has been a curious one. I have lived equally amid two race groups. Now white, now colored." Exactly what constitutes a "race"? In Toomer's personal reflection, the biological idea of race — even in an era of overt and rapacious racism — was ambiguous and indefinite, even as it was emotionally and politically powerful.

In this chapter I argue that biological race has no *commonly* agreed-upon definitive structure or scientific meaning — a position taken by many in the literature on racial identification (Nelson and Jurmain, 1991). When it comes to racial classification, it is indeed, as Toomer noted long ago, a question of "who knows for sure?" Two aspects of this question about race will be considered in this chapter. One is the concept of race as a biological versus a sociological entity and where current thinking leads us — what might be called the biological question. This is especially critical with the emergence of various attempts to use DNA to identify racial categories. The second is the *de facto* reification of race as it is used in the forensic sciences as the basis for scientific analysis of empirical data and as a system of classification and identification in establishing evidence in criminal investigations.

The Reification of Race: Racialism

Race continues to be used and reified as a biological variable in many contemporary research contexts, especially in forensics. A race-based identity is considered an innate characteristic of each individual. Among the cluster of traits used to describe individuals in crime contexts, race is generally a critical and ubiquitously used identifying feature. For example, "Suspect is a black male, 6"2," estimated age 20-30 years, has prominent scarring of the forehead" is a descriptor that anyone can imagine as the beginning of a police investigation. There is, in this paradigm, no "raceless" person. Everyone without exception is assigned a race — although not always without disagreement or with consistency. This is the essence of the reification of race. Race may be known or unknown in a particular person, but those are the only two states of racial knowledge. It then follows that the concept of race is exhaustive — every human being can be placed into a race. I term this paradigm one of "racialism," to distinguish this view from the term and paradigm of racism. Racism is attached to a set of ideological beliefs about the putative attributes associated with a racial group. Historically we have thought of these attributes mostly negatively (i.e., lazy, cunning, child-like, slow-witted, etc.), although in racism it is also quite possible that certain racial groups are seen as superior (intelligent, visionary, ambitious, etc.). Racialism precedes racism. Racism cannot arise until a prior belief structure is in place, the belief in the reality of race itself. This construction of race and its conversion into a "reality" is what constitutes race reification.

In my view, forensics has a firmly established racialism, but not in an intrinsically racist way. Forensic racialism results from accepting sociologically defined views of races, and their spillover into the physical sciences, effectively creating a process of reifying race into a physical reality. This occurs, as we noted above, by reflecting the exhaustive (there are no "raceless" beings) and exclusive views of race. This "exclusivity", results in the treatment of specific racial categories as if no person can be in more than one race category at a time. This represents one of the major problematic issues confronting "racial realists" and proponents of the biological reality of race, and presents a great difficulty in the utilization of racial data in statistical analysis.

Racialism and racism as social processes do not proceed in a singular and inevitable fashion, nor are they limited to "modern" life. Racial consciousness, and in some places racial animosity, have ancient anteced-ents (Gossett, 1963).

Historic Ideas of Racial Types

The ideologies behind racial consciousness, as they survive from ancient times, are varied. Aristotle, for example, believed racial distinctions were caused by environmental differences. Frequently racial distinctions are viewed as emerging from mythical feats and the actions of gods and other deistic myths in accounts of human ontology. Some have arisen out of tales of conquest or invasion. There is no necessary association between particular phenotypic expressions of shape or color or other physical attri-butes that are inevitably linked to racial identity, nor are there inevitable links to some behavioral attributes or capacities (Hannaford, 1996).

A substantive review of materials written on the origins and history of race is beyond the scope of this chapter. However, the idea of race as conceived in the 17th century is so influential that a brief review of these ideas helps place the remaining discussion in a broader historical context.

Racial typologies originated in the work of several 17th and 18th cen-tury writers, travelers, and observers of humankind. In 1684, French physi-cian, Francois Bernier, suggested a fourfold racial classification: Europeans, Asians, Africans, and Lapps (Gossett, 1963). The individual most frequently credited with developing the contemporary fourfold racial classification is the Swedish taxonomist and botanist, Carolus Linnaeus (Sauer, 1993), whose categorization was based primarily on skin pigmentation: Europeans (white), Americans (red), Asians (dark or yellow), and Africans (black). Other important figures include Georges Buffon, Georges Cuvier, Charles Lyle, Johan Blumenbach, and Alexander von Humboldt. A number of these researchers believed that races were hierarchical, and that the white race was the most advanced, and the black race the most degenerate (Gould, 1993). Some objected to this characterization, not so much as inaccurate, but rather because they believed that racial differentiation arose from differential environmental conditions. If the environment changed, then racial characteristics, in time, changed. The size and permanency of racial gaps was therefore in some dispute, but the reality and existence of racial types was not.

There is much more to this history than can be told here — the rise of monogenic and polygenic ideas about race (races as divisions from a common root or races as distinct creations of the deity), the convoluting of these ideas into a rabid racism, the service of the so-called "scientists" of race — like Nott — in rationalizing the institutions of slavery and racial suppression (Shipman, 1994). Race also became a component in 20th century eugenics, where both inter-and intra-racial categorization were marked by a premise that races could be manipulated by selective breeding practices (Gossett, 1963; Barkan, 1992; Shipman, 1994; Harding, 1993; Gould, 1993; Marshall, 1993). The thrust of these histories establishes the following general aspects of race and racialism:

1. While consciousness of racial difference is relatively ancient, it takes on major social significance in modern Western societies, emerging in social thought during the middle ages.

2. Racist ideas can be found rather universally, and include virtually all continents. Explicitly racial ideas are everywhere tied to an evaluative dimension of superiority and inferiority. Race, in this sense, includes characterizations of intelligence, aptitudes, propensities, and personae in addition to physical characteristics.

3. Racial identity has most often included skin color as a major physical marker, but has included many other markers as well — e.g., shapes of facial features, nose and eye characteristics, hair texture and color, skull size, body measurements and body shapes as important racial identifiers.

4. The historic utilization of race as a classificatory schema inevitably treated racial categories as exhaustive and exclusive properties, and race-based analysis is premised on those assumptions.

5. While often treated as an ascribed and unchangeable biological characteristic, racial differentiation was believed by some to be the result of environmental factors, and was therefore a mutable entity.

6. Ideological justification for discrimination and racial categorization inevitably accompanies racial thinking. In some circumstances the ideological characterizations were fanciful but not intrinsically malevolent, but mostly they incorporated negative, aggressive, and hostile attitudes towards those identified as members of a particular (and always inferior) racial group. Religion has often been a source for the ideological justification of racial thinking, but "scientists" have also lent their hand to supporting various racist ideologies.

7. Much racial thinking emerged as colonialism developed, with justifications for colonial expansion premised on either the racial inferiority

of native people, or the outright denial of the humanity of indigenous people who were deemed to be beasts or near-beasts.

While the crudest forms of these ideas on race have to some measure dissipated, the fundamental treatment of racial identity reflects this historic record. Furthermore, with the development of knowledge on the mechanics of genetic transmission, aspects of the biological "reality" of race have re-emerged.

Race in Science

Race, even within the past quarter century, has been dramatically transformed as a biological concept in modern science. However, it persists as a widely used descriptive variable in scientific research and is frequently included in data analysis. In addition to the traditional gross morphological racial markers (physical appearance, e.g., skin color) — historically used to determine racial identity — race identification has, to some degree, shifted towards genetic markers where a racial typology is now allegedly associated with particular STP (spanning tree protocol) segments culled from DNA samples (Ossorio and Duster, 2005).

Intrinsic Data Problems

One problem with race as a scientific variable is that the ambiguity and meaning of race remain unresolved, and its treatment as an analytic variable violates underlying assumptions about categorical data. Sunderland (1975) commented that on the basis of biological components "no classification of races as discrete categories seems possible." Sunderland's comment goes to the heart of a profound problem in the analysis of race — the underlying assumption of the properties of *exclusiveness* and *exhaustiveness* in the statistical treatment of categorical data. Biologically race exists in degrees or clines (see discussion below). Moreover, persons can choose to socially identify with one race or another — although they may in fact be the product of a heterogeneous "racial" parentage. In addition, persons may be assigned to different races as they are the object of the perception of an "other." This "other's perception" of race can of course vary. This in turn results in ambiguous and inconsistent racial assignment. The host of factors that impact the "other" and their view of racial identity may have nothing to do with biological facts. In fact, in contemporary racial typing, language has sometimes replaced biomarkers. Hence "Hispanic" has become a commonly designated "racial" category in which the spoken language determines the master race status.

A second problem with racial distinction is the problem of typology. Young (1971) characterized racial typologizing in the physical and social sciences as "naive" and "scientifically impossible and socially dangerous." While it is possible to understand the concept of race as the basis of sociological identity and the product of culture, it does not follow that race forms either a taxonomic or typological basis for bio-identification. Lacking a precise definition, race has no readily identifiable utility as a biological variable. It does not link together persons by a ubiquitous set of biological attributes. To quote Leach (1975), in real social life we use the concept of race "to discriminate a variety of sorts of a previously existing social collectivity, but we are able to do so only because the isolate concept *a race* has no explicit 'objective' meaning whatsoever." In this regard race is a part of cultural vernacular, and forms what Leach called a "folk taxonomy." Indeed, the number of "races" that exist is indefinite and unable to be scientifically specified. "Folk taxonomy" has seized upon visible traits such as skin pigmentation, hair color, and other physical features of the body as the "signs" or markers of race identity. However, through the thorough intermixing of racial types, the human population has an ambiguous and heterogeneous distribution of the identifying biomarkers of race.

A third problem is that the various "racial" traits are often distributed independently of one another. Thus, by shifting a single trait, a "race" disintegrates or alternately a new race is created. As C. Loring Brace (2000, p. 3) points out:

> ... there is a major but gradual change in skin color from what we euphemistically call white to black ... that ... is related to the latitudinal difference in the intensity of ultraviolet component of sunlight. What we do not see, however, is the myriad other traits that are distributed in a fashion quite unrelated to the intensity of ultraviolet radiation. Where skin color is concerned, all the northern populations of the Old World are lighter than the long-term inhabitants near the equator. Although Europeans and Chinese are obviously different, in skin color they are closer to each other then either is to equatorial Africans. But if we test the distribution of the widely known ABO blood-group system, then Europeans and Africans are closer to each other than either is to Chinese.

Thus the designation of any particular trait becomes a culturally arbitrary race marker — meaning the selection of racial traits rests on history, culture, sociological and psychological forces, not purely scientific factors. Thus race, is in this sense, is a socially constructed identity.

But problems with data analytics and race go beyond this issue. A fourth problem is the lack of knowledge of the distribution of the traits historically used as race markers. Even if we grant the arbitrary basis of racial traits and ignore the violation of the assumption of exhaustive and inclusive race categories, we are generally unable to specify the real distribution of the underlying traits utilized as race markers. The data sampling procedures and the scarcity of substantive and appropriate samples, as Bamshad et al. (2004, p. 601) have pointed out, offer "limited guidance," and "these studies highlight the deficits in our basic knowledge about the geographical distribution of human genetic variation." So, we know neither the unambiguous characteristics of the sample nor the relationship between the sample and the parametric values[1] we are seeking to identify. This situation places us in the curious position of relying on a subset of persons possessing some poorly measured trait of racial interest, which has an unknown distribution, and who *a priori* are identified as "members" of a particular race category, or are treated as "ideal types" (Weber, 1997).[2] These types are then projected on to others, who become included in the category. This is, in effect *circulus in probando* (circular reasoning).

How can we make sense of this idea of universal racial types? As Bamshad et al. (2004) noted, "gradations in distribution make it impossible to divide mankind into sharply distinct 'races.' " The most recent use of racial markers, called AIMS (Ancestry Informative Markers), involved the marketing of "race proportion markers." DNAPrint Genomics introduced a "genetic test for the deduction of the heritable component of race, called Biogeographical Ancestry (BGA) . . . This test provides not only the majority population affiliation (i.e., Indo European, Sub-Saharan African, East Asian or Native American), but the admixture as well (i.e., 82% East Asian and 18% Indo-European mix)" (Forensic Bioinformatics, 2007). However, in spite of the appeal of DNA as a "definitive technology" for racial identification, the ambiguity of racial identification is not substantially reduced using DNA studies. There are numerous problems that racial biomarkers and clusters fail to address. Foremost among these is the degree to which the database establishing these markers is itself a representation of the "races" with which they are associated. As Marks (2006, p. 4) has observed:

> The last issue of interest concerns the development of companies marketing a racial identity for their clients, based on the assumption

that a small sample of Nigerians represent "pure Africans," a small sample of Chinese represent "pure Asians," etc. — and examining the genetic residuals that remain when contrasted with pure Northern Europeans and Native Americans. These residuals have been isolated, patented and called "ancestry-informative" markers. Unfortunately while the work is technologically and statistically sophisticated, it is epistemologically very primitive.

One recognizes that in spite of these biological weaknesses, race possesses a very powerful sociocultural meaning (Lyman, 1994). Yet the clear distinction between races as a psycho-sociological idea and as a biological idea continues to be problematic for those who use race as an analytic variable. In many areas of medical/biological and psychological research, race is still widely treated analytically as a meaningful and identifiable *biological* category. This, of course, presents a serious challenge. There is a tendency, implicit or explicit, in the use of race as an analytic variable to treat it as a "self-evident" reality. This is especially so in the medical and biological research, so much so that I contend it has vested race with a pseudo-biological mantle that has delivered us dangerously close to the racialist views of the 19th century. Currently, for example, challenges to the "biological reality" of race are seen by some scientists as a sort of sophistry, or an assault on "common sense" (Brues, 1993).

Race as an Analytic Category in Forensics

A close examination of "race assignment" in contemporary forensics reveals problems that stem from the difficulties associated with the conception of race itself. Race is introduced into forensics in both direct and indirect ways.

First, race becomes an element in the attempt to characterize evidence, identify suspects, and establish particular persons as perpetrators of a crime. Second, race and its use contribute to reification, since the standards utilized become the basis for the field standards — this is the circular argument referred to earlier. In essence, the racial data collected at crime scenes becomes the standard by which further data is typified. In essence the logic is: "how do I know the suspect was African-American? I know this because his sample met the requirements defining the category 'African-American.' How do I know these standards are accurate? I know this because they were collected from people who are defined as 'African-American.' "

In forensic identification, evidence is typically sorted into two main categories — class characteristic and individual identification evidence.

Class characteristic evidence allows the inclusion or exclusion of an unknown into a particular class of objects, but cannot uniquely associate it with an object. A good example of a class characteristic is the caliber of a weapon from a surviving ballistic projectile. Information gleaned from the ballistic fragment identifies it as belonging to a particular class of objects — for example, a copper-jacketed, 9 mm caliber bullet. This level of evidence identification does not allow us to associate the object with a unique weapon, and the projectile could have come from any number of objects that constitute the class "9 mm guns." In contrast, examples of individual identification evidence include a sample of nuclear DNA or a useable fingerprint, both of which possess information that will allow us to associate it with one individual.

Racial identification in forensics is a *class characteristic.* Typically there are several motives in assigning racial identity to "evidence." One is that such identification may help clarify or solve a crime — it can provide investigative lead information. Another is that it may be introduced into a court of law in an effort to convict or exonerate a person facing a criminal charge. Forensic class evidence can allow only for the inclusion or exclusion of a person from a particular category. Hence it is often referred to as "exonerating evidence," since if one is excluded from a class essential to the criminal facts at hand, then one cannot be held under suspicion or if charged, convicted.

The converse is not true. If one is, in fact, a member of the class believed to have committed the crime, it does not prove guilt — since class evidence does *not* individuate. Any person belonging to the class has an equal chance of identification. A class that consists of a finite number of categories is useful only in so far as the categories are *exclusive* and *exhaustive.* As a forensic category, racial identification is useful in so far as: (1) a person's race can be inferred from the evidence with known accuracy, (2) a person can possess one and only one racial identity, and (3) all persons can be accounted for by the range of racial categories available to the classifier, who has a formal list of the characteristic criteria which apply to each category. By and large, the concept of "race" in forensics miserably fails this test.

The Problems of Racial Identity in Forensic Analysis

Why does the use of race in forensics fail so miserably and engender so much controversy? Because it is inadequately conceptualized, lacks any dynamics (see below), and lacks the exclusivity that categorical class characteristics require. Additionally it lacks a dependable underpinning of the actual distribution of the putative characteristics of the categories of each respective race, both internal to the category as well as externally across all racial groups.

A more accurate and dynamic definition of race can be developed by relying on two basic population genetics concepts, the "deme" and the "cline." The deme is a localized population with high rates of interbreeding. Because the occurrence of interbreeding is high, localized populations share many attributes that characterize their particular deme. Focusing on the physical appearance of a deme, which is the chief component of racializing, involves considering the phenotype or physical expression of the deme's genetic expression. Hence, a "race" is a historic deme referring to physical as well as cultural and linguistic attributes. Why particular attributes are chosen (e.g. complexion) and others ignored (colorblindness) appears to be an arbitrary decision — but historically it has consisted of both observables (skin color, eye shape, hair appearance) as well as cultural (cunning, lazy, volatile, etc.) and linguistic attributes.

The cline refers to the distribution of various phenotypic expressions and how they abut and join each other over a large physical domain, and it contains a gradient of phenotypic expression observed as one surveys a range of localized populations. Thus, population phenotypes merge into each other — the implication being that those members who exist near a phenotypic interface will exhibit the mixed characteristics of each adjoining deme. One sees the cline effect in cultural and linguistic phenomenon as well. So the cline describes the nature of the relationship of phenotypic characteristics associated with the deme. Conceptualizing race using concepts taken from population genetics allows us to deconstruct the implications of race as they are commonly used in forensics, and to avoid the great difficulties that such usage brings.

First, the deme provides a historic perspective that allows for a dynamic view of the race concept as the outcome of both physical and cultural circumstances. Demes arise from isolation (both physical remoteness and cultural isolation). Clines appear and take on increasing importance as remoteness lessens. Thus, the dynamic of "race" is one of constant change fueled by the loss of remoteness and the multi-layering of clines in physical space and time, as well as allowing for the impact of technology on cultural interaction and travel. In this sense race become a historic artifact; an imposition of a typology based on an historical past. Phenotypically, the attributes of race become, over time, more and more difficult to parse out. Hence Toomer's question of "What am I?" However, since race has not been a historically "neutral" concept in the sociological world, its social and psychological importance and realities do not track very well with its biological realities. And this is the crux of the problem — using race as a "scientific variable." It cannot be measured in an empirical fashion because it contains primarily cultural, sociological, and psychological content.

In forensics, comparative racial analysis reflects a biological reification of race that is extraordinary in its sweep, that exhibits a minimum consideration of the underlying assumptions of race or even if race is a sensible application to the issue at hand. The contemporary use of race in this fashion is a recapitulation and restatement (in subtler form) of the ideas of the 18th and 19th centuries.

Following a period where race was critiqued as a scientifically useful concept, racial identity recently regained more caché. This is due to political and social factors and is not based on scientific data reestablishing the validity of racial biomarkers (Sauer, 1993), resulting in renewed criticism of the "race variable" as an analytic construct. Goodman and Armelagos (1996), for example, criticize the attempted "resurrection of race" within anthropology and the resurfacing of the "ideal type" approach to racial identification: "The denial of race is not the denial of human diversity. Rather it is a stance that suggests human diversity is too complex to be explained by types . . . Racism is more real than race. To deny race does not deny the study of racism" (p. 183). In addition to criticisms from anthropologists, medical and psychological researchers have questioned the validity of race as an analytic construct. For example, a study examining the utility of race as a variable in health research concluded that race "has no clear definition" and "is not useful in public health surveillance" (Hahn et al., 1992, p. 262). The U.S. Department of Health and Human Services has also taken a critical position on race as an analytic variable, noting that "racial categories are too broad to be meaningful . . . distinctions between race and ethnicity are unclear . . . concepts of race and ethnicity may change over time" (Hahn et al., 1992, p. 269) and that "discrepancies exist between race and ethnicity as self-reported or observer-reported." Hahn et al. point out that data collection and coding for race and ethnicity is "remarkably inconsistent," even for relatively straightforward biological events such as the vital statistics measures of birth and death.

In their review of race in medical research, Osborne and Feit (1992, p. 275) noted that "the concept of race is, at best, elusive . . . there is no accepted scientific definition of race . . . the emphasis on racial categoriza-tion creates an illusion of mutual exclusiveness." Osborne and Feit con-cluded that due to problems associated with defining race, its use "seriously compromises the objectivity of scientific inquiry." The same critiques have been leveled at psychological research. For example Zuckerman (1990, p. 1297) stated that "the scientific premises for looking for statistical differ-ences between groups designated as races are questionable" and "the expla-nation of such differences in strictly biological-evolutionary terms is even more dubious." Yee et al. (1993, p. 1134) remarked that "the elusiveness of the race concept inhibits scientific research and theory in psychology," while Allan and Adams (1992) advocated abandoning race as an analytic variable in psychological and sociological research unless a consensual scientific definition can be established.

The Persistence of Racial Typing in Forensics

Given the arguments above, it seems the obvious question is why does racial typing persist, in science in general and in forensics in particular? Let us reserve that opinion until the end of this chapter. For now, let us consider several examples of how racial typing is used currently, and how these uses can demonstrate the frailties just described. Ultimately, the issue is the difficulty in specifying with precision the meaning and nature of race as a *physical* entity. To reiterate, this is not a "denial of race" argument — many recognize that the use of race variables as implicit biological categories has led to a dangerous obfuscation of the meaning of race, mixing its sociologi-cal and psychological dimensions with biological ones. The argument is not that research attributions of racial identity are *per se* illegitimate. Neither is there doubt about the power of the idea of race; nor are we calling into question the consequences (often tragic and terrible) of the application of the idea of race. What is criticized here is the treatment of race, although subtle (and often seen as for "good ends") as a definitive and explicit biological trait and the many problems to which it leads.

Race Markers

There have been a variety of "race markers" used over the centuries. Several major physical features and their application to racial typing in forensics are considered here: anthropomorphic measures of hair texture, bone structure, and skin color. While these hardly exhaust the list of race charac-teristics used over the centuries, they are the primary features associated with forensic identification.

Hair as a "Race Marker"

Hair as a "racial characteristic" was a centerpiece in 19th century "race science." At that time, race was essential considered as quintessentially in the "blood" and racial identity was determined by identifying an individual's "blood lines." In the U.S. Supreme Court's famous *Plessy* (1896) decision, the ultimate race determinant was the "proportion" of blood assignable to each race contained within an individual's circulatory system. Problematically, blood composition could not be directly observed, and isolated blood did not have any discernible physical racial differences. So, while blood was considered to contain the "essence" of race, race was manifest only in various observable characteristics of the body, such as, skull shape, hair type, etc. Interestingly, even in the 19th century, "mixed blood" determinations were problematic due to "race mixing." The essence of the *Plessy* case was a dispute over the legal basis and authority for enforcing race typologies. One of Mr. Plessy's eight great-grandparents was acknowledged to be "Negro." Under Louisiana law, Plessy was consequently "Negro" and was forced to use "Negro facilities" in public places, although based on descriptions of Mr. Plessy he did not, to the casual observer, "appear Negro." Plessy objected to his race classification as "Negro." Through the *Plessy* decision, the Supreme Court gave a free hand to the states to use any criteria they deemed appropriate to determine race identity — hence, "any admixture of Black blood" was legal and within state authority as a race marker.

Since race classifications used external manifestations of race in the form of body attributes, much early nineteenth century "race science" was based on variations of human anthropometrics. This "science" was devoted to uncovering and quantifying "indicators" of racial development and identity, such as volumetric displacement of the brain case, certain angular aspects of the face, and similar constructs. Haller (1971) noted that anthropometrists considered hair to be a definitive racial marker both in terms of its gross appearance and the "embedding" of hair in the scalp. The French anthropometrist Pruner-Bey (considered the first to scientifically study hair), divided hair into (1) "Negro" (flat or wooly), (2) Mongol/Chinese/Malay/American (coarse, cylindrical), and (3) "European" (intermediate and mixed in size and shape). The zenith of hair-based race classification was reached in Peter Browne's 1852 publication "The Classification of Mankind by the Hair and Wool of Their Heads," a notoriously and overtly racist tract. Browne was a favorite lecturer of slavery enthusiasts, especially the physician Josiah Nott and the anti-abolitionist crusader John Van Evrie. Hair typology was important to those who were anxious to establish the visible "racially distinct" characterizations of Negro slaves by reference to biological markers of "inferiority." It was taken as obvious that the "coarse hair" associated with Southern Europeans and non-Europeans (especially Negroid Africans) was considered to be of "lower developmental status" than "fine hair." While hair was never as enthusiastically embraced as the "cephalic index,[3] it played a role in the pseudo-science used to justify the oppression of slaves in America.

Karl Pearson, the eminent statistician and a champion of the eugenics movement in the early 20th century, rejected the "empirical work" of the race anthropometrists.[4] Pearson was not by any means a racial egalitarian, but he did recognize the dangers of non-scientific generalization based on flawed data. And this is precisely how he viewed the "hair typologists." He labeled their work "dilettantism," and said anthropometrics "was not a science." The two major criteria that Pearson used to attack anthropometrics are easy to apprehend, and both apply to current racial typologizing. First, race identification did not employ uniform criteria or operational definitions encompassing the phenomena it purported to measure. Second, it made no attempt to employ meaningful statistical techniques to determine the distribution of the "traits" which it alleged to be "characteristics" of a race. Problematically, as Pearson saw it, taxonomic theorists paid no attention to the distribution of *deviations* from these "types" and had no understanding of the variance within the populations of the putative "races" they were describing.

Race typologies, in Pearson's view, were devalued by the implication of racial types that ultimately implied a "pure race" with assignable physical attributes. The relatively long period of cross-cultural contact among the races had erased the original physical barriers which produced relatively isolated gene pools, creating "mixing and absorbing" which had gone on for centuries. Pearson's student, G. M. Morant (1939) produced a critique of typological racial views, especially as applied to Europeans in his work, *The Races of Central Europe*. Morant, as Stepan (1982) notes, showed that racial and language boundaries in central Europe did not coincide with "cephalic index, stature, hair and eye color" and that the racial traits typically used for racial classification "were in fact useless for dividing up the population" into various and sundry "races."

Contemporary Claims of Race Differences in Hair

Despite these difficulties, race terms have been used in scientific hair analysis research without much consideration of their potential problems. Furthermore these analyses move back and forth using "race" and "ethnic group" as equivalents.

Hair Type and Texture: Much has been made of hair as a race marker. Standard forensics texts, with an occasional caveat, maintain that "hair evidence found at a crime scene can be used to identify racial origin" (Lee, Palmbach and Miller, 2004). Saferstein (2004, p. 202) states that "in many instances the examiner can distinguish hair originating from members of different races," but adds the caution that these differences are "general in nature with many possible exceptions" and the "criminalist must approach the determination of race from hair with caution and a good deal of experience." Houck (2004, p. 131), who is quite thorough in analyzing the shortcomings of hair analysis in individual cases — states quite directly that "forensic hair comparisons have been involved in incorrect associations in actual criminal cases ... that resulted in convictions. In these cases the convictions were shown to have been wrong by subsequent DNA analysis." Houck notes a series of objections to the use of hair identification, including: the failure to do follow-up analysis on erroneous identifications; that crime laboratories often lack the funds and expertise to do such analysis competently; that the field has no standardizations of what constitute "expertise," including no ongoing and recognized training requirements, no performance monitoring of field challenges of laboratories to assess proficiency, no accepted criteria of what exactly is a "match."

Houck states that the racial typification used in assessing the gross morphology of hair is "simplistic." Contemporary forensic assignment of hair is largely limited to three categories; Caucasian, Negroid, and Mongoloid. Recently Ogle and Fox (1999) suggested that the geographic terms which these older names suggested be applied instead (European, African, and East Asian).

Frequently, Hispanics are assigned as a "racial category" in the hair analysis literature. Current writing on "race effects" of hair shows a general disregard for the differences between ethnic and racial groupings. This has been especially true in recent work examining hair as a matrix for toxicology testing. Cone and Joseph (1996) suggested that "there are differences in chemical and physical attributes of hair types together with considerable interethnic variation," a clear implication that "hair types" means "race types." But a reading of the sources they cited to support racial typologies reveals that research largely failed to support this contention. Indeed, the bulk of research attempting to isolate race-linked hair differences unequivocally states the opposite: that racial types *cannot* be consistently identified by morphological, histological, or biochemical analysis of hair. For example, Cone and Joseph (1996, p. 74) stated that "early observations of hair form prompted investigators to examine ultrastructural features of hair from different ethnic groups, and report differences between ethnic hair types." But almost all early researchers after 1920 reported just the opposite. Though Cone and Joseph cite Steggerda and Seibert (1941), as supporting systematic racial differences in hair, the latter clearly stated in their paper that "hair form" *differences between individuals of the same race are likely to be greater than the hair form differences across races.* Indeed, they suggest that the amount of variability is so great that one cannot determine by physical measure whether two strands of hair come from the same individual.

Cone and Joseph also cite Hausman (1925) as conducting "one of the earliest comparative ethnic studies of pigment in hair." But Hausman's article does not discuss this topic: there is neither a comparison of pigmentation of ethnic groups nor any other data on pigmentation in the article. Hausman, in fact, never uses the term "ethnic" in the article. Hausman's work is a comparison of "structural elements in head hair" compared across several races. Cone and Joseph go on to state that Hausman "reported that races could not be distinguished based on pigmentary structures of head hair and that hair color, but not race, reflected differences in hair pigmentation" (p. 77). Hausman never reported any such conclusions and never discussed pigmentation as a part of his analysis, but rather focused on both medullary and cuticular structures in the hair shaft. He concluded that the cuticle or scale structure of the head hair of humans is *"unrelated to race. It was found that the scales varied on contemporaneous hairs from the same head and on hairs from the same head at different periods of life, when the diameters of these hairs varied. Moreover, differences exist along the same hair, from base to tip"* (Hausman, 1925, p. 553, emphasis added).

Hausman's observations reflect one of the most frequent conclusions of hair morphologists — *that intra-race and even intra-individual hair form variations easily exceed inter-race and inter-individual variations.* Hausman concluded that this was true for both cuticle form and medulla and that "the medulla of human head hairs varied also, *not with race*, but with diameter of hair shaft" (1925, p. 534).

More extensive analysis has not been able to support a biochemical difference across racial types. Rook (1975), for example, states that "Negroid and Caucasoid hair" are "chemically indistinguishable." In reviewing a series of studies on hair collected from various racial populations and analyzed by a series of tests to determine amino acid composition, diffractive values for X-rays, stress-strain analysis, and electrophoretic studies, he noted that "identical results were obtained for all samples."

Forensic Identification of Race from Hair

In forensics, the use of hair as a determinant of racial identity clearly needs to be viewed with extreme caution. The alleged racial attributes of hair are so burdened with restrictions and qualifications that one can legitimately question whether or not the attempt to make such identification is worth the effort. In addition to the series of problems highlighted above, there remain very serious statistical questions regarding the utilization of "exemplars" as models of racial types, even if some kind of agreement could be reached regarding a definition of a racial group. We have discussed the issue related to the problems of exhaustivity and exclusivity in categorical analysis. Additionally, there is almost nothing known about the actual representation of the parametric values used in racial characterizations of hair. Let us consider one further example of the weakness of existing information for making racial distinctions.

Ogle and Fox (1999) published their *Atlas of Human Hair*, to provide a series of ideal types or ideal examples of particular micro and macro characteristics of hair for the purposes of training hair examiners, and to create a uniform terminology and a uniform "scoring system" so that identical data can be collected to assess such measures of hair characteristics as frequency of occurrence, covariation of characteristics, and etc. The authors acknowledge that "most hair characteristics have continuous variation over the entire range of variation exhibited. Continuous variation means that the difference between one variate and its closest neighbor in terms of similarity is virtually indiscernible" (p. 2). They also note that "in the microscopic examination of humans, individualization is rarely possible due to lack of a reference database for the assessment of uniqueness of the set of characteristic variates (the hair type) for a given hair" (p. 5). In essence, what Ogle and Fox are saying is that in theory we can imagine a set of characteristics, both microscopic and macroscopic, that when combined form a unique and thus individuating basis for associating a hair sample

Table 10.1. Hair Shaft Diameters by Race in Prior Research

Race	Bisbing & Girard	Shaft Diameter (îm) Ogle & Fox	Vernall
Negroid	60-90	< 40	58.5-98.2
Caucasoid	70-100	40-80	56.7-81.94
Mongoloid	90-120	> 80	76.8-94.3

with one and only one person. However, such a statement is nearly an idealization, because in reality we do not know what those characteristics might actually be, nor do we know the distribution of these characteristics in the general population. Lacking this knowledge it is impossible to construct a probability statement, and hence impossible to assign a probability of error. Thus, the use of hair samples as forensic evidence fails the Daubert requirement for known level of error,[5] as well as generally accepted validity.

Let's consider one example of the relative primitiveness of the knowledge base to which Ogle and Fox are referring. In 1982, Bisbing identified the shaft diameter of hair (measured in microns) from different races as follows: Negroid, 60-90; Caucasoid, 70-100; and Mongoloid, 90-120.

Bisbing's table is published without any attribution, so the source of these data is unknown. In 2008, this table was reproduced in *Criminalistics: Forensic Science and Crime* (Girard, 2008) without attribution, and is simply described as a table which "lists the characteristics human hair that are associated with particular racial groups" (p. 96).

In their study, Ogle and Fox define the smallest diameters of hair as "fine" (less than 40 microns in diameter), medium (40 to 80 microns), and coarse (greater than 80 microns). They state that "African ancestry hair is smaller than the other two groups ... the regional hair shaft diameter for East Asian ancestry individuals is thicker than those of the other two regional groups. They characterize European hair as "intermediate" but note that it has "considerable overlap with both of these groups."

The only other referenced research on hair shaft diameters by race comes from work done by Vernall (1961), who collected hair samples from 86 males (age 20 to 30 years) comprising: 20 Chinese; 21 Europeans (individuals who had been born, or whose parents had been born, in Great Britain, Germany, France, or Holland); 26 Asiatics (born in India); and 19 Negroids (9 born in Nigeria, 9 in the United States, and 1 in Jamaica). Verrnal's shaft diameter measures are shown in Table 10.1. He noted that as "much variability occurs among the hairs from each person, among the persons within each race, and among races" (p. 346). While he found that some (but not all) of his samples differed by racial group, he also found that there was great variation within groups. And to Vernall's credit he notes that it is not possible to generalize his findings because of the nature of his sample, which was "largely university students." Comparison of the size variations for hair shaft diameters by race for these authors is given in Table 10.1.

If we integrate the various measures claimed to be characteristic of a particular racial grouping, we are left with great confusion. The data in Table 10.1 represent a hypothetical sample of roughly 2,200 persons, each having one of the three racial identities. Assuming that the distribution of these samples was normal and the mean was the center or midpoint of Bisbing interval measure for each race, we could produce a series of hypothetical distributions or bar graphs labeled "Africoid," "Caucasoid" and "Mongoloid" illustrating the extensive overlap across the measures from each study. This chart is three dimensional and multicolored in order to discern each racial type and the measures in each study, and unfortunately cannot be reproduced here. Nevertheless, this chart illustrates the problems associated with assigning a race characteristic based on hair shaft diameter. We can reach the same conclusions by referring to Table 10.1. For example, the overlap between the Bisbing/Girard groups labeled as "Africoid" (Negroid) and "Caucasoid" is quite high, and much of the Afrocoid sample falls within the data range for Caucasoids. This overlap violates the condition of exclusivity in assigning group identities. The problem becomes more extensive as racial measures from other studies are included. For instance, Vernall's measure for Negroid hair almost completely overlaps all of Bisbing's "Caucasoid" class, while Vernall's "Asian" and "Chinese" designations excludes almost all of Bisbing's "Mongoloids." In addition, Vernall's "European" and "Negroid" categories almost completely overlap. Thus, the argument that this measure of hair morphology allows an independent examiner to assign a hair specimen to a specific racial category seems difficult to defend. Application of one or the other of these standards would result in dramatically different typologies being assigned to hair taken from the same individual.

Since no one has systematically documented the actual distribution of hair diameters, the real shape of the distribution is unknown. We do know two things. First, that comparative analysis of hair has repeatedly found that gross hair morphology variation within a group exceeds the variation across groups, and second that hair diameter variation within a single subject can be so extensive that it frustrates the effort to link hair samples to one subject. Consequentially, the amount of racial overlap would be so high as to render this measure essentially useless for purposes of racial differentiation.

An additional problem is that discussion of the Bisbing/Girard data lacks important information pertaining to its validity. Where did this data come from? What sort of sample was employed in calculating these values? What are the deviation measures (e.g., standard deviations, confidence intervals), associated with these data? What is the relationship between self-declared racial identity and assignment of racial identity by the researcher who compiled these data?

One of the arguments made in defense of hair characterization as a race marker is that an identification of race should not be made on any single measure, but rather on a composite of measures. However, without some expansion of the technique by which they incorporate these multiple measures, their utilization may actually reduce rather than enhance the probability of correct identification by multiple measure assignments to a specimen. Consider that probabilities for simultaneous criteria produce a new probability that is a product of the two discrete measures. Thus the probability of two measures, each with a probability of 0.8 being simultaneously correct is 0.64.

Bisbing and others readily admit that due to substantial "racial mixing" in the modern world the sampling methods by which these typologies are created is generally unknown, and the descriptive characteristics poorly operationalized or defined, which "may make it difficult if not impossible for the hair examiner to conclusively identify a hair's racial origin" (p. 407). The outcome of an attempt to utilize gross morphology can indeed result in absurdities. And we have seen this not only in the historic record during the 19th century use of rampant racialism, but even well into the 20th century under "Apartheid" in South Africa, where the "pencil test" became a "test" of race:

> A pencil would be placed in a person's hair, if it fell through they were classified as "White" (or "Coloured," depending on other subjective classification considerations); if the pencil did not fall through, they were classified differently ("Coloured" or "Black", also depending on other subjective classification considerations). Members of the same

family who had different hair textures would find themselves in different race groups as a result of this test. (Posel, 2001, p. 59)

Posel's work on South African attempts to reify and legal designate race identity is a very informative deliberation on the dangers involved in attempting to use various morphology criteria to establish putative "race."

Forensic Identification from Skin Color

It is of some interest that among the racial traits largely absent from forensic classification is the notion of skin color. In a way this is remarkable because historically the most prominent criteria for racial identification have been intimately bound up with skin color — the very terms "white" "black" "red," for example refer explicitly to complexion color. There are several possible reasons for the lack of skin color being an explicit criterion, although it is clearly an implicit criterion in most practical forensic racial characterizations.

Skin color is reacted to not as a "specimen" like hair, but rather as a holistic perception and characterization associated with a particular individual. The "skin" is an organ, and varies over different areas of the body. Its color varies as well, and its color varies in response to environmental stimuli, age, and physical health. There are no widely accepted technical "measures" of skin color normally employed in anthropometrics, such as there are in skeletal structure (although under certain circumstances bureaucracies have tried to develop complexion tests). Perhaps the idea of complexion color in relation to racial identity may be considered so obvious that, in effect, there is an appeal to "common sense" in characterizing the observed individual by race.

Characterizing race via complexion illustrates the intrinsic ambiguity of racial identity. The characterization of race by gross morphological observation of the whole person requires an assessment of multiple aspects of the person, some of which include physical characterizations (color of complexion, color or texture of hair) as well as linguistic and cultural cues (accent, clothing, stylizations of the hair, nails, ornamentation, etc.). For example, in sociology the concept of racial "passing" involves the ability of a person to manipulate these various characteristics so that an observer's impression of racial identity can be manipulated — the person can present himself or herself as a member of alternately different races. Additionally, at various times in the United States there have been officially adopted designations of non-binary characterizations of race by skin color. While the Plessy decision accepted the "one drop of [Negro] blood" standard or admixture rule, the U.S. government in both the late 19th and early 20th centuries designated intervening racial groups (octoroon, quadroon, mulatto) that were based on historic color distinctions or complexion types. What is not in dispute is that within any particular racial group there are variations in skin color that are often recognized within that group's identity culture (e.g., Frazier, 1957; Herring, 2002).

South Africa, under the Apartheid ideology, attempted to implement a major classificatory racial identification scheme that formalized skin color as part of the racial criteria. Like the United States, South Africa had within its boundaries many citizens representing all the classic Linnaean racial types — native Africans, Europeans, and Asians from the Indian subcontinent as well as from Indochina and China. The South African government created four racial groupings: Black, White, Indian, and Colored. Posel (2001) points out that the Apartheid classification of racial type in South Africa was capricious and arbitrary, and not based on any centralized standard. It was also extended beyond issues of physical appearance into the realm of history, behavior, occupation and other domains of activity. One of the ironic results was that different members of the same family could find themselves in different race groups. Posel states that "evidence for race was found most familiarly in skin color ... but this was not necessarily the overriding or conclusive factor, particularly when confronted with the ambiguities of an individual whose way of life seemed at odds with his or her skin color" (p. 58). Posel goes on to state that among the devices used to assess complexion were photographs (which were evaluated for race by an official examiner), the skin "pallor" or shininess, and the degree of pigmentation of the penis or scrotum of males and *mons* in females. Thus, even in an overtly racialist climate like South Africa's under Apartheid, the role of skin color was subsumed into a more complex amalgamation of traits and characteristics which were used to create a gestalt upon which a racial identity was founded.

Forensic Identification from Skeletal Measures

Perhaps the most persistent and hardiest survivor of the attempts to classify humans into racial groups has been various skeletal measures of both human crania and other bones. As Williams and his colleagues (2005, p. 341) stated: "forensic anthropology has been much more reluctant to divorce itself from the pre-modern partitioning of human biological variation into races, despite the fact that human biological variation in genetic markers and cranial morphology is quantitatively greater within than between major geographic regions or races." It is true that the most consistent utilization of racial identification within forensic anthropology focused almost exclusively on skeletal identification — primarily seeking answers to three questions — age, sex, and race. In contemporary terminology, the term "ancestry" is often a surrogate for race. A widely cited defender of skeletal race identification, George Gill (2000, p. 2), stated:

> I have found that forensic anthropologists attain a high degree of accuracy in determining geographic racial affinities (white, black, American Indian, etc.) by utilizing both new and traditional methods of bone analysis. Many well-conducted studies were reported in the late 1980s and 1990s that tested methods objectively for percentage of correct placement. Numerous individual methods involving midfacial measurements, femur traits, and so on are over 80 percent accurate alone, and in combination produce very high levels of accuracy. No forensic anthropologist would make a racial assessment based upon just *one* of these methods, but in combination they can make very reliable assessments, just as in determining sex or age. In other words, multiple criteria are the key to success in all of these determinations.

Gill's position is a fair summery of (by his own estimation) the majority of physical anthropologists' findings — although he concedes that it is a slim majority. Those who do not accept the utility of racial classification from skeletal remains fall into two categories (and sometimes both) of objectors. One is an argument already reviewed — that race as a concept is fundamentally flawed and therefore regardless of what empirical measures show, it is only demonstrating a chimera. The second argument is that the claim of a "high degree of accuracy" in racial identification of skeletal remains is itself questionable — that the accuracy becomes "high" only under very controlled conditions. This criticism point to the fact that techniques purported to measure racial traits of skeletons do not hold up well under various challenges, that they are easy to confound, and that they are so contextual as to limit their utility beyond extremely localized geographies and time frames.

A popular tool used to perform racial analysis of skeletal remains is the FORDISC computer program. The most recent version (v 2.0) uses regression statistics to identify skeletal remains by sex and race. It relies upon cranial measurements and is alleged to be able to identify white, black, Japanese, and Amerindian males and females — and also to distinguish among males who are of Hispanic, Chinese, and Vietnamese ancestry.

Wienker (2005, p. 3) notes that "FORDISC utilizes a set of measurements taken from an unidentified skull and creates a unique multiple discriminant function formula that classifies the skull with regard to percentage likelihood that it falls into any of the specific previously-mentioned demographic categories that the user selects. It also gives a statistical indication of how typical the skull is of those in the selected demographic categories in the known database program." One can assume that Gill, in his defense of racial identification by forensic anthropology, would include FORDISC as one of the tools that can be used to "attain a high degree of accuracy" in determining accurate racial identity (others might include: the demarking of the femoral head, the formation of the lower border of the nasal aperture, odontological features, etc.). While no common standard appears to exist for "high accuracy," in the literature a correct racial or gender identification in the 70-80% range is considered of sufficient accuracy to be "of value" in forensic identification (Sejrsen et al., 2005).

However, there are a number of questions that can be raised about the putative value of this approach to both racial and gender identity. The first is the generalizability and utility of these tools, most especially FORDISC. While a number of evaluators have credited FORDISC with high degrees of accuracy, there is far from a unanimous agreement on this point. Weinker, for example, reported that FORDISC correctly classified only 56% of 35 known skull specimens ("white, Cuban males"), attributing 16 of the skulls (46%) as being from "subcontinental India." It also failed to classify 16 of the 21 "white, Cuban skulls" as Hispanic. Wienker notes that the "frequently low typicality statistics, below 50% . . . is an indication that the skulls are statistically unlike those of known racial identity in the data base of FORDISC."

In their assessment of FORDISC analyses on ancient Nubian crania (an ethnic minority in Eastern North Africa), Williams et al. (2005, p. 343) reported high levels of misclassification: "Nubian crania were overwhelmingly misclassified . . . . FORDISC 2.0 classified the Nubian crania over an enormous geographic range, including North and Central Europe, Easter Island, the Andaman Islands, Japan, Taiwan, South Africa, Australia, and North America." They concluded that:

> Our results suggest . . . that FORDISC 2.0 is fundamentally flawed not only because these types are culturally mediated but because statistically defined populations cannot adequately represent the biological variation that characterizes individuals within each purported group . . . We suggest that skeletal specimens or samples cannot be accurately classified by geography or by racial affinity because of

(1) the wide variation in crania of the known series that crosscuts geographic populations (polymorphism), (2) the clinal pattern of human variation, and (3) cultural and environmental factors. Even a presumably homogeneous population such as the Meroitic Nubians shows extensive variation that preclude its classification as a geographic group. (pp. 344-45)

A similar outcome was reported by Ubelaker et al. (2002), who employed FORDISC 2.0 to classify the race and sex of Spanish cranial sample from the 16th and 17th centuries from the towns of Villanubla and Valladolid. Two FORDISC data bases were employed: the Howells and the Forensic Data Bank. FORDISC correctly classified the 37 female crania as female, but of the 58 male crania, 33 (approximately 57%) were classified as female by the Forensic Data Bank, and 52% were misclassified using the Howells data. Also of the 96 European Spaniards, 42 (44%) were classified as "white," 34 (35%) as "black," and only 8 (9%) as Hispanic. Of further interest was that FORDISC classified 4% as "Japanese," 4% as Native American Indians, and three as Chinese and Vietnamese. When the Howells data were used, FORDISC identified 21 different classification groups. The single most frequent identification was "Egyptian" and the second most frequent identification was "medieval Hungarian."

These results indicate that a major weakness in generating classifications from a FORDISC type of regression analysis is that it is captive to whatever the underlying data the researcher employs. In effect, it is the equivalent of measuring distances, but without any agreement on a metric. One would hardly expect uniformity of results. And the attempt to capture the complex human variation in phenotype to historic skeletal collections is likely to fail a rigorous test of identifying human morphological variation, regardless of the precision of the actual physical measures.

If there has been a theme repeatedly echoed in the literature attempting to validate this general methodology — the creation of a reference or ideal type — it is that such systems are strictly bounded to the core sample. It seems almost universally true that the application of discriminant function analysis to determine categories of sex and race "lose accuracy when applied to statistical populations which differ in some systematic way" from their base comparator populations (Meindl et al.,1985; Ramsthaler et al., 2007). The issue at hand is what the differential is, and how many differentials exist? At one extreme is the absolute differential that every human is unique, so the potential differentials are limited only by the number of humans. On the other extreme is the notion that these differentials fall reasonably neatly into three or four "racial groups." In addition to a simplification of the number of "natural groups" is the persistence of the idea that the assignments themselves are relatively easy. Consider Brues (1958), who has characterized racial groups typified by characteristics of the face and crania — she notes that they include "contours around the root and bridge of the nose — an area in which racial differences are especially well-developed" (p. 559). She also notes that "race determination may be greatly aided by even a small sample of hair; in fact typical Negro hair can make a race diagnosis without anything else." This argument of simplicity is really an appeal to "common sense" — which, as Posel points out, was one of the primary characterizations of racial differentiation under Apartheid as expressed in debates of the South African National Registration Bill, which established the legal basis for racial classification: "It is obvious to all: we know the native and if we see a white man, we know he is a white man . . . We have never experienced any difficulties in distinguishing between Europeans and non-Europeans" (Posel, 2001, p. 56).

Conclusion: Far from Simplicity

Over time the idea of racial divisions as a taxonomic concept has receded and been superseded by an appeal to the "common sense" assumption that "whatever it is, race helps us identify and categorized remains. It works and is therefore of value." One aspect of this heuristic approach is the view that those who deny the reality of biological race are at best "academic" in their objections (i.e., the arguments are technical and not central to the reality of race) or at worst sophists, who will forever argue for the sake of argument and are toying with a world which has always seen the "obvious reality" of racial division.

This chapter has argued that while race may sometimes play a useful role in identifying individuals (or forensic remnants of individuals), it does so at some larger cost. Additionally, it may not do so with the commonly claimed accuracy ascribed to it. The cost comes in the form of reification of racial identities. These reifications also have a "common sense" outcome that goes far beyond skeletal protuberances, hair textures, and complexion hues. Even in contemporary times the reification of all manner of "racial traits" converges into a false consciousness regarding race itself. "Common sense" is in the eye of the beholder, and quantitative metrics potentially open the door to all manner of claims when the underlying population basis of the metric is vague and often indefinable — consider, for example, as one consequence the works of J. Philippe Rushton or William Shockley (Lynch, 2000).

In anthropometric measurement, for example, there is complex and poorly defined terminology that makes it difficult to sort out the empirical verification of the various physical criteria applied to racial typing. Asala (2002), for example, describes the use of measures of the femoral head for skeletal sexing and racial identification purposes, as having "an overall success rate of 32% for both white and black populations, but the accuracy of sexing was 100%." From an external layperson's point of view the idea that a procedure with a "32% success rate" is "100% accurate" is difficult to comprehend. So when forensic anthropologists describe "highly accurate" methods of identification, it leads one to throw up a cloak of caution. The "success rate" or reliability is 32% — while the accuracy is "100%." What this really says is that there is no Type I error (we never see the trait when it is not there), but there is very high Type II error (we don't see the trait when it is there). How these two numbers relate to each other is important.

Metrics associated with an identification criteria are established by sampling and measuring characteristics from known groups (e.g., female Caucasoids; male Caucasoids, etc.). These measures become the type identifiers. In Asal's study, for example, a series of bone measurements were carried out on a sample of bones from donors whose sex and race were known. This information was used by a second examiner to assign a gender to a new sample based on measurements of identified "markers" for gender derived from the earlier sample. The examiner's assignments were then compared to the known sample, and correct identification (or reliability) and "accuracy" values were calculated. In the Asal study, for example, the findings were that 47% of the male femurs had "male metrics" (51 out of 108), and these results were "100% accurate." In effect, this means that when gender was assigned (47% of cases), it was assigned correctly (in 100% of cases, only males were identified as males), but that gender could not always be assigned (53% of cases) because a large number of male bones fell outside the metric. (Reliability for female bones was much lower, 14% or 13 out of 92.)

There is something of a tautology in this approach. The boundary between the identifiers and the identified can become blurry when a group identified as gender "x" or race "y" is defined by a metric derived from a group identified by social convention. For example, we utilize a sample from a racial group to characterize the metrics for typing, then we identify and categorize individuals into those groups based on those metrics. In recent times, the defense of skeletal identification has been defended as much on "practical" and heuristic grounds as on any sort of hypothetical taxonomic basis — a practice associated with earlier thinking about racial groupings. Often there is an appeal to "common sense," and, as Sauer (1992) has pointed out, the identification by race inevitably returns to the "big three" — white, black, and Asiatic. And, in effect, the assignment of one of these racial types takes a somewhat fuzzy metric and assigns one of these racial labels to skeleton or skeletal remnants. Sauer says:

> To be of value the race categories used by forensic anthropologists must reflect the everyday usage of the society with which they interact. In ascribing a race name to a set of skeletonized remains, the anthropologist is actually translating information about biological traits to a culturally constructed labeling system that was likely to have been applied to a missing person . . . Forensic anthropologists may be very good at matching a set of remains to the race label ascribed to a missing person, but the practice has little if anything to with the taxonomic question about the natural existence of races. (1992, p. 110)

In closing, it is important to remember that the forensic identification of race is difficult and fraught with complexities. Often, forensic racial identities overlap, making accurate identification of race difficult. In addition, the science of race has, throughout history, been contaminated by prejudice and social practices that threaten the objectivity of the science of race and its uses in forensics.

NOTES

1. By parametric values we mean the true value of the measure which would be obtained if an entire population could be measured. It is the value we attempt to infer from parametric statistical analysis.

2. Ideal types are hypothetical sociological constructs, first defined by Max Weber. Weber described them as distortions or "accentuations" of characteristics synthesized from a series of actual social interactions, circumstances, and observations. They constitute a form which then is utilized to order or classify, by transference, the variety of an individual's social experiences (Weber,1997).

3. The cephalic index is a ratio calculated by comparing the maximum width of the head to its maximum length. Based on this ratio (and other measures) persons were identified as belonging to specific racial groupings — races being demarcated as having specific ranges of values for the index. First used by Retzius in the early 19th century it has historically been identified with the hyper-racial anthropology of the nineteenth century

4. See, for example, the commentary in: Ida McLearn, G. M. Morant and Karl Pearson (1928). "On the Importance of the Type Silhouette for Racial Characterisation in Anthropology." *Biometrika*, Vol. 20B, No. 3/4 (Dec.), pp. 389-400.

5. This term simply means the likelihood that any given scientific process can produce an erroneous result.

11. The Neglect of Race and Class in Environmental Crime Research

Paul Stretesky

Criminologists have lately begun to pay greater attention to the study of environmental crime and deviance. Recent research, for instance, has examined the etiology of environmental crime, the enforcement of environmental laws, and the punishment of environmental offenders (Cohen, 1992; Lynch, 1990; Lynch and Stretesky, 2001; O'Hear, 2004; Pearce and Tombs, 1998; Rebovich, 1998; Seis, 1999; Shover and Routhe, 2005; Simpson and Piquero, 2002; South and Beirne, 1998). While criminologists have made great strides in studying environmental issues, there is still much work to be done. Specifically, the study of race and class are largely neglected in most studies of environmental crime and deviance.

The purpose of this review is to examine the role of race and class within criminological research on environmental issues, with the hopes of stimulating additional research on these important issues. This review is divided into three parts. First, I summarize the current state of environmental crime research in criminology and criminal justice, focusing on the definition of environmental crime and the popularity of the rational choice perspective in the study of environmental crime. Second, I provide an overview of existing studies of environmental crime and deviance that address issues of race and class. This section also examines research on the distribution of environmental hazards. Third, I conclude by looking at the role that race and class may play in future environmental crime research.

Environmental Crime and Deviance Research

In recent years, criminologists have published several books on environmental crime as well as chapters devoted to environmental crime within textbooks on corporate crime (Beirne and South, 2007; Burns and Lynch,

2004; Clifford, 1998; Frank and Lynch, 1992; Friedrichs, 1992; Lynch et al., 2008; Pearce and Tombs, 1998; Simon and Hagan, 1999; Situ and Emmons, 2000). Moreover, research on environmental crime is beginning to find its way into mainstream criminology journals (Halsey, 2004; Stretesky, 2006; Walters, 2006). Still, there is a considerable lack of environmental crime research in the criminological literature. A recent study (Lynch et al., 2004) discovered that only 4% of all articles published in mainstream criminology journals (e.g., *Criminology, Justice Quarterly, Journal of Criminal Justice, British Journal of Criminology*) dealt with toxic waste and environmental harm. Most of those articles were published in one journal (*Crime, Law, and Social Change*). Environmental crime issues are also typically absent from general criminology and criminal justice textbooks. For instance, consider that among the top 16 best selling criminology and criminal justice textbooks, approximately 1 in 1,568 pages were related to environmental crimes (Lynch et al., 2004). It is clear that criminology and criminal justice have been slow to embrace issues of environmental crime and deviance. However, as noted above, things are beginning to change (Zilney et al., 2006).

Environmental crime research can be broadly divided into two categories. The first line of research examines the causes of environmental crime, while the second examines the process of identifying and punishing environmental criminals. As will be discussed below, both lines of research have implications for race and class.

The Definition of Environmental Crime

A discussion of the etiology of environmental crime would not be complete without examining the "definition of crime" controversy. This controversy focuses on the way that power relations in society impact criminal labels (Box, 1989; Clifford and Edwards, 1998; Lynch and Michalowski, 2006; Lynch and Stretesky, 2003; Quinney, 1970; Schwendinger and Schwendinger, 2001; Spitzer, 1975). Quinney (1970), for example, popularized the idea that crime is a "social construction" that reflects class inequality. The idea that crime is socially constructed means that crime is a human creation that is dependent on social conditions. Thus, definitions of crime can vary across societies and can change within the same society over time. The social construction of crime perspective is opposed to the perspective that crime is inherent in the bad act and therefore universal across time and place. Consistent with the notion that crime is a social construction, studies of environmental crime often focus on the role that corporate and political elites play in determining which environmental harms will be treated as crimes. The chemical industry, for instance, has actively opposed environmental regulations designed to limit the production of dangerous chemicals such as PCBs, lead, and asbestos (Ehrlich and Ehrlich, 1996; Fagin and Lavelle, 1999).

Oftentimes, the rules that identify chemical harms as violations of law — as crimes — involve regulatory and civil laws. Some criminologists object to studies of regulatory and civil laws because they believe that these rules are qualitatively different than criminal violations. More recently, even the most mainstream criminologists are beginning to recognize that the difference between criminal and regulatory law is artificial or socially constructed (Clifford, 1998). In many instances, the same violation may be treated as a criminal, civil or administrative violation depending on how the agency in charge of the investigation and prosecution decides to proceed (Simpson, 2002; Stretesky, 2006). It is for this reason that the study of environmental crime must take power relations within society into account, and not just accept the state's definition of environmental crime when investigating the scope of environmental harms.

One way that criminologists interested in the study of environmental crime account for power relations is to incorporate issues of race and class into their research. One example of such an approach is "green criminology." In the first discussion of green criminology, Lynch (1990) argued that green criminology should emphasize how race, class, and gender structures impact the definition of environmental crime and influence law and social control mechanisms. The major point that green criminologists make is that the difference between a regulatory law and a crime is not found in the degree of harm, but in how effectively opposing interests — through political donations, lobbyists, industry politicians, labor unions, non-profit interest groups, and grassroots political groups — express their will in the lawmaking process (Lynch and Stretesky, 2003). Thus, because law results from a political process that unequally represents the interests of various groups in society, it cannot be taken as an objective measure of harm. From this point of view, environmental harms that primarily take place in poor and minority neighborhoods are the least likely to be regulated and/or criminalized. Accordingly, green criminologists advocate the development of independent models of harm to highlight race, class and gender inequality.

Rational Choice and Environmental Crime

While green criminologists focus on how social inequality influences environmental law, other criminologists concentrate on explaining the etiology or causes of environmental crime, often employing "rational choice" assumptions about offending that are based on free-market principles (Shover and Routhe, 2005; Stretesky, 2006; Lynch et al., 2008). Rational choice theory suggests that an environmental crime will occur when the anticipated benefits of committing the act outweigh the perceived costs (Zimring and Hawkins, 1973). It would not be an exaggeration to say that rational choice theories of environmental crime are widely accepted.

There are, however, both cultural and structural constraints on rational choice, suggesting that cost-benefit calculations are not always identical (Simpson, 2002). For instance, there are variations in organizational culture that may change an employee's perceptions of the costs and benefits of engaging in a potential environmental risk. For example, in their study of the Bhopal disaster, Pearce and Tombs (1998) note that the organizational culture of Union Carbide was clearly characterized by a tradition of "profits over safety" that caused employees at various plants to take risks that were simply not rational. Over the years this "profits over safety" culture was responsible for several chemical accidents, including the horrific accident at Union Carbide of India Limited in Bhopal that resulted in 10,000 deaths and 20,000 permanent injuries (Pearce and Tombs, 1998, p. 192). Others suggest that the personalities of corporate executives and characteristics of management teams appear to shape decisions about whether to engage in environmental crime (Daboub et al., 1995; Piquero et al., 2005). In short, the perceptions of the costs and benefits of engaging in environmental crime are likely to vary across firms and employees.

Deterrence theory employs rational choice assumptions to explain crime (Tittle and Paternoster, 2000). The idea behind deterrence is that the greater the certainty, severity, and celerity (or speed) of punishment, the more likely it is that crime will be prevented. People avoid breaking the law because they fear the law, legal consequences, or perceive a high probability of detection and punishment. Some researchers suggest that corporations are more rational than individuals and, therefore, are more likely to be deterred from crime (Paternoster and Simpson, 1996). Similarly, Vaughan (1998) points out that enforcement personnel often falsely believe that punishment effectively reduces corporate crime because corporations are more likely to be rational in their calculations of violative behavior. In a free-market system, however, the efficiency rather than the effectiveness of deterrence is often debated. As Shover and Routhe (2005, p. 321) note: " . . . if the economic costs of a regulatory program exceed the putative fiscal benefits it is deemed inefficient." Thus, in a free market, the best possible outcome occurs when individuals pursue their own interests and companies have no social responsibilities other than to maximize returns and comply with the law (Friedman, 1970). From an environmental perspective, a major problem with a free-market system is that it places socially disadvantaged communities in a position where they are more likely to become the victims of environmental crime and deviance. Even when communities rise up to stop corporations from violating environmental laws, corporations simply conduct business as usual in other disadvantaged communities (Schelly and Stretesky, forthcoming). This may occur because the penalties associated with environmental crime are small compared to the benefits associated with engaging in environmental crime.

Race, Economics, and Environmental Crime

Criminologists have been examining issues of race and class in criminal justice for some time, and research on the American criminal justice system suggests that race and class biases exist in dispensing justice (Lynch and Patterson, 1991, 1996). For instance, blacks and Hispanics are more likely than whites to be stopped by the police for the same traffic infraction, even when all stop characteristics are identical (Engle and Calnon, 2004; Warren, et al., 2006). In addition, with other factors held constant, blacks have a higher probability of being arrested for simple assault compared to whites (Eitle et al., 2005). Finally, blacks are more likely to be given harsher prison sentences than whites, even when all other sentencing factors are held constant (Mitchell, 2005).

While much of the research on racial discrimination is focused on the offender's race, the race of the victim may also influence how cases are processed. Several researchers have pointed out that blacks are devalued as victims (Eitle et al., 2005). For example, Williams et al. (2007) discovered that murderers (regardless of their race) are afforded the greatest leniency for their crime when they kill black males. Research on environmental crime also suggests that race matters. Black and low income communities may also be devalued when it comes to identifying and punishing corporate polluters. This issue is examined in greater detail below.

The issue of discrimination in environmental enforcement gained national attention in Warren County, N.C., in the early 1980s when protesters sparked a call for racial equality in the enforcement of environmental laws (Bullard, 1990, 1994; McGurty, 2000). The Warren County protests were a response to criminal violations of the federal Toxic Substance Control Act by the Ward Transformer Company. Ward, one of the largest transformer companies in the United States, purchased used transformers to rebuild and resell (New York Times, 1982). The oil in the used transformers contained high concentrations of Polychlorinated Biphenyls (PCBs), a thick liquid used in electric fluids, heat transfer fluids, and hydraulic fluids (Erickson, 2001). Unfortunately, PCBs have a variety of adverse health effects for the human immune, reproductive, nervous, and endocrine systems (DeRoos, et al., 2005). The dangers associated with PCBs caused Congress to prohibit their manufacturing, processing, and distribution in 1976 (§6[e], Toxic Substances Control Act; U.S. Environmental Protection Administration [EPA], 2006).

Ward built up an enormous stockpile of PCB-laced oil, and the president of the company, Robert "Buck" Ward, hired his friend, Robert Burns, to illegally dispose of the PCBs at a low cost to Ward. Ward and Burns planned to dump the hazardous waste along the roadside. To carry out the roadside dumping, Burns and Ward built a "special" truck out of a Ryder box van purchased to carry out the dumping. They installed a 750-gallon tank to store the PCB waste, and attached a hose to the tank that was concealed under the truck and directed at the side of the road. The PCB waste could be released onto the side of the road by means of a valve that the van's passenger controlled (New York Times, 1982). Randall and Timothy Burns (Robert Burns's sons) used the Ryder van to dump 31,000 gallons of PCB wastes along 243 miles of deserted North Carolina roadways.

These illegal disposal activities were eventually discovered by the authorities, and Burns and Ward were arrested, tried, and sentenced to prison. Robert Ward was also fined $200,000 to aid in the cleanup of the PCBs. The company later paid nearly $3.5 million to help offset the cleanup costs. This is the beginning of the story, however, rather than its end.

In order to clean up the PCBs, North Carolina officials dug up the PCB-contaminated soil and disposed of it on a 142-acre tract of land that the state purchased in Afton, a predominantly (84%) black community

(Bullard, 1990, 1994) with an elevated poverty rate (20% of residents lived below the poverty level). Residents protested the placement of the hazardous waste site, and argued that the site's placement not only appeared biased, but would threaten the health of residents when PCBs leached from the site. The residents were assured that the use of "dry tomb" waste methods would prevent PCB leakage into the surrounding buffer zone (more than 100 acres) and the local water supply. Despite these assurances (which later proved to be false), residents organized a protest against the state for disposing the illegal waste in their community. The Warren County protests were the first protests against racial discrimination in the siting of hazardous waste in America. Residents lined the roadways to the site, and laid down in the road to prevent trucks carrying the PCB laden waste from entering the site. In all, more than 500 protestors were arrested. The story of Warren County shows how environmental crime and enforcement can be linked to issues of race and class. However, it took nearly ten years for researchers to examine issues of discrimination in environmental enforcement more systematically.

In 1992, Lavelle and Coyle conducted the first study on this issue, published in a groundbreaking article entitled "Unequal Protection: The Racial Divide in Environmental Law." The researchers looked at the U.S. Environmental Protection Administration's (EPA) Civil Enforcement Docket (DOCKET) database to determine whether race and class biases existed in the distribution of monetary penalties for violations of the federal Clean Air Act, Clean Water Act, Safe Drinking Water Act, Comprehensive Environmental Response, Compensation, and Liability Act, and the Resource Conservation and Recovery Act (see Burns and Lynch, 2004, for a review of these laws). The DOCKET is an EPA database that tracks civil cases that were filed by the Department of Justice. The database contains information about the type, location, and outcome of each violation. Lavelle and Coyle used the facility addresses in DOCKET to obtain census data on the demographic characteristics surrounding each facility that violated an environmental law. Next, they ranked each case of environmental crime according to median household income in the zip code and the percentage of the zip code that was white. Zip codes that were ranked in the top 25% of all zip codes on the variable "percent white" were labeled "white," while zip codes that ranked in the bottom 25% of all zip codes on the variable "percent white" were labeled "minority." The same procedure was used to code "high" and "low" income zip codes. Lavelle and Coyle then compared penalties across zip codes.

Their findings revealed that the mean fine for violating federal environmental laws was higher in white ($153,067) zip codes compared to minority zip codes ($105,028). They also found that mean penalties were larger in high income zip codes ($146,993) than in low income zip codes ($95,564). When types of violations were examined separately, results varied. For instance, in violations of the Comprehensive Environmental Response, Compensation, and Liability Act (which governs the cleanup of contaminated sites), polluters in white zip codes were fined less than the polluters in minority zip codes. Finally, monetary penalties were greater in high income zip codes than in low income zip codes for the Clean Water Act, but lower in high income zip codes than low income zip codes in all other cases.

Several criticisms have been made of Lavelle and Coyle's (1992) study of inequality in environmental enforcement. The most relevant criticisms are that the researchers did not examine variables other than race and income, and that they use zip codes rather than census tracts or blocks as their unit of analysis. Additional research on monetary penalties (examined below) suggests that Lavelle and Coyle's results cannot be fully replicated in a multivariate study that includes measures of case characteristics (such as seriousness of violation) and examines spatial units that more closely approximate neighborhood communities. A more detailed description of the weaknesses of Lavelle and Coyle's work is presented by Atlas (2001). While not a criticism of Lavelle and Coyle's study, it is important to emphasize that the study of the distribution of monetary penalties is based on a rational choice perspective of crime and deviance that suggests undesirable behavior will occur when the anticipated benefits of the behavior outweigh the perceived costs. Thus, the implication of Lavelle and Coyle's work is that corporate executives are sent the message that the chances of a harsh penalty are greater if they violate environmental laws in a white community. The researchers observe:

> [T]here is a racial divide in the way the U.S. government cleans up toxic waste sites and punishes polluters. White communities see faster action, better results and stiffer penalties than communities where blacks, Hispanics and other minorities live. This unequal protection occurs whether the community is wealthy or poor. As the Journal report reveals, discrepancies exist in the enforcement of environmental laws, such as penalties imposed, and in the pace of cleanup. (Lavelle and Coyle, 1992, p. S1)

Two researchers reanalyzed the Civil Enforcement Docket database in an effort to replicate Lavelle and Coyle's findings of racial and economic discrimination. First, Ringquist (1998) examined DOCKET cases adjudicated between 1974 and 1991 to test the proposition that "penalties in these cases disadvantage poor and minority areas." Similarly to Lavelle and Coyle, Ringquist used zip codes to represent communities. In contrast to Lavelle and Coyle, however, Ringquist examined (1) the total fine assessed in each case, and (2) the mean (average) fine per violation. Ringquist also controlled for competing explanations of penalty variation through the use of ordinary least squares regression. Several variables, most of which are related to political behavior, are included in Ringquist's analysis. Unlike Lavelle and Coyle, Ringquist found little evidence of racial discrimination in the enforcement of environmental laws. Ringquist did find, however, that case characteristics — such as the type and number of violations, size and type of company, and the number of locations where the violations occurred — consistently mattered when determining the size of the monetary penalty.

Atlas (2001) also examined DOCKET to see if there was discrimination against poor and minority communities in environmental enforcement actions. Atlas, like Ringquist, also conducted a multivariate analysis to examine the relationship between penalty amounts and demographic characteristics using 1-mile buffers around each violation site to derive the race and income characteristics of the community. Atlas examined both single and multi-location cases separately, and controlled for relevant case characteristics such as type of violation. Atlas discovered that the proportion of minority residents in the community around environmental violations was positively related to penalties across EPA's civil judicial cases (1985 though 1991). Since the relationship was positive, this indicated that penalties for violating environmental laws were higher in minority neighborhoods. Notably, minority census-tract areas received mean fines of $133,808, while white areas received mean fines of $113,791. Atlas (1991:675) concluded that there is no "basis for concluding that penalties are lower in disproportionately minority or low-income areas."

While both Atlas and Ringquist found little support for the proposition that racial discrimination exists in the enforcement of environmental laws, the results of more recent research suggest that this conclusion may not be generalizable across all industries and datasets. For instance, Lynch et al. (2004) examined fines against petroleum refineries according to the demographics of the neighborhood in which the offending companies were located. The researchers focused on the petroleum industry because it produces a great deal of pollution, placing about 78 million pounds of regulated chemicals into the environment annually. Many of the releases from these refineries are carcinogenic, and studies indicate that there is an increased mortality rate and cancer rate among refinery workers and residents living near refineries. Using a sample of 153 operable petroleum refineries identified from the 2001 U.S. Department of Energy's *Petroleum Supply Annual*, and combining that data with compliance information from the EPA's Enforcement and Compliance System Online (ECHO), they discovered that enforcement actions were taken against 99 of the 153 facilities in the sample.

Next, Lynch et al. employed both census tract and zip code analysis to assess the association between community characteristics and penalties. Results indicated little evidence of racial discrimination at the census tract level of analysis. However, in the zip code model, a 1 standard deviation increase in median income across zip codes resulted in an 11% increase in the penalty amount, while a 1 standard deviation increase in the proportion of Hispanic residents across zip codes resulted in a 95% decrease in the penalty amounts. Other factors that appeared to be associated with penalty amounts, regardless of the area used to measure race, class, and income, included the type of law violated, the agency responsible for taking the lead in the enforcement action, the size of the company, and the value added by the petroleum refinery industry. Lynch et al., (2004, p. 345) noted: "After controlling for enforcement history, case characteristics, company characteristics, and political/economic climate, we discovered evidence of inequality in the case of Hispanics and low-income communities — but only if zip codes rather than census tracts are used to obtain the demographic data." Thus, the study by Lynch et al. suggests that the relationship between penalties and ethnicity at the zip code level could be the result of aggregation bias.

The four studies reviewed above specifically examine the issue of race and class discrimination in the enforcement of environmental laws and regulations. While current evidence of racial discrimination in the distribution of monetary penalties is mixed, the study of discrimination in the enforcement of environmental laws is still in its infancy. Thus, what is important about these studies to the study of race and class in environmental enforcement is not the specific statistical findings of each study but the focus on environmental enforcement as an outcome of race and class demographics. Together these studies provide a good starting point for research on disparate environmental enforcement conducted by those criminologists interested in environmental crime and inequality. In addition to the study of monetary penalties, issues of race and class bias in environmental protection can be generally be extended within the field of criminology to include: (1) hazardous waste sites; (2) treatment, disposal and storage facilities; and (3) air pollution. If evidence of the unequal distribution of environmental hazards is found, it might signal potential areas of research to be pursued by criminologists interested in the unequal enforcement of environmental laws.

The Unequal Distribution of Hazardous Waste Sites

Several researchers have examined the geographic associations among race, ethnicity, economic indicators, and areas that contain hazardous substances in the form of active, inactive, uncontrolled, or abandoned disposal sites. For example, shortly after the Warren County protests (see above), the U.S. General Accounting Office (USGAO, 1983) released a study of the distribution of offsite landfills in EPA's Region 4 (Alabama, Florida, Georgia, Kentucky, Mississippi, North Carolina, South Carolina, and Tennessee). The GAO researchers determined that, of the four off-site hazardous waste sites located in Region 4, three were located in communities whose populations were predominately black. Moreover, approximately one-quarter of the residents living near these waste sites were considered poor, and most of these poor residents were African-American (USGAO, 1983).

Also in 1983, Robert Bullard published a study on the geographic distribution of hazardous waste sites in Houston, Texas. The data used in Bullard's study were obtained from Houston's Solid Waste Management Division and Houston's Air Quality Board. Bullard's (1983:281) findings indicated that 11 of the 21 hazardous waste permits granted by the Texas Department of Health in the Houston area were located in predominately (i.e., over 50%) black neighborhoods. Moreover, five of the six municipal landfills in the Houston area were also sited in predominately black neighborhoods. The landfills and waste sites that Bullard studied were located near 47 schools. Thirty-one of those 47 schools were predominately composed of black students. Thus, hazardous waste regulations were used by the state of Texas to help both public and private entities site Houston's environmental hazards in predominately black communities and near predominately black schools.

More recent research by Stretesky and Lynch (2002) has confirmed Bullard's findings. Stretesky and Lynch (2002) studied the proximity of

84 public grade schools to hazardous waste sites in Hillsborough County (Florida) between 1987 and 1999. Controlling for the percentage of students eligible for free lunch (a poverty measure), they found that grade schools closer to environmental hazards (i.e., "Superfund" sites or disposal facilities) became disproportionately black and Hispanic over time, while grade schools situated farther from environmental hazards became disproportionately white. (Superfund is the name of the federal program to pay for the cleanup of toxic waste sites.) In California, Pastor et al. (2002) also found an association between ethnicity and cancer-causing air pollution. In that study the researchers discovered that Hispanic students were more likely than white students to attend schools in areas with the highest levels of toxic air pollution.

A number of studies have examined the relationship between neighborhood racial and class characteristics and proximity to hazardous waste sites. In the 1970s, as the environmental movement began to grow and people became worried about environmental hazards, President Carter and Congress established the Comprehensive Environmental Response Compensation and Liability Act (CERCLA). The purpose of CERCLA is to authorize the EPA to identify and evaluate the thousands of hazardous waste sites across the country by listing them in the Comprehensive Environmental Response Compensation Liability Information System or CERCLIS. The EPA must prioritize CERCLIS sites and put the most threatening sites on the National Priority List (NPL), where they can receive federal Superfund monies to be cleaned up.

In 1987, the United Church of Christ released the first national-level study of the location of abandoned and uncontrolled hazardous waste sites (CERCLIS) sites (UCC, 1987). The researchers found that CERCLIS sites were most often located in zip codes where the population was disproportionately black and poor. Using multivariate discriminate analysis, the UCC determined that race was more strongly related to the location of CERCLIS sites than to residents' income levels. Kreig's (1995) study of Superfund sites in the greater Boston area replicated the UCC's results. However, Kreig found that race was more strongly related to the location of Superfund sites in older industrial areas. Kreig hypothesized that new industrial growth attracted many workers from inner-city areas where old industrial jobs were declining. Those individuals who were able to take advantage of more technical and higher-paying jobs were also able to make the move with industry. Since many poor blacks were unable to move or were unqualified for these jobs, they remained in the older industrial areas where jobs were scarce and incomes relatively low. Industries that fled these older industrial areas also left their waste behind. As Kreig explained, the relationship between race and Superfund sites, then, is a product of industry abandoning its waste in central cities, combined with high-income whites leaving those areas for the suburbs.

Stretesky and Hogan (1998) examined the geographical correlates of Superfund sites across Florida between 1970 and 1990. They discovered that blacks and Hispanics were more likely to reside near Superfund sites, and that the association between race, ethnicity and proximity to Superfund sites was increasing over time. While illustrating both racial and ethnic disparities, this study revealed little evidence of income inequality. However, other studies examining the relationship between race, economic indicators, and Superfund sites have not been so definitive. For example, Hird (1994) also used census data to examine the residential, political, and economic characteristics of areas surrounding NPL sites. He discovered that Superfund sites were more likely to be found in affluent counties that were disproportionately nonwhite. Anderton et al. (1997) also examined the spatial distribution of CERCLIS and NPL sites across 1990 census tracts, and discovered that the percentages of blacks and Hispanics were significantly lower in tracts containing CERCLIS sites when compared to tracts containing no sites. These comparisons were roughly the same for CERCLIS and NPL tracts.

O'Neil's (2007) findings may help explain several discrepancies in hazardous waste studies. Specifically, O'Neil examined the likelihood that any given CERCLIS site would be listed on NPL and be eligible for Superfund funds to help with clean up. O'Neil discovered that the seriousness of the site, as measured through the hazard ranking score (HRS), was inversely related to NPL listings. Thus, more hazardous sites (those with high HRS scores) were *less* likely to be placed on the NPL. O'Neil claims that the reason for this finding is that less serious CERCLIS sites are easier to clean up and thus more likely to make Superfund look successful. Moreover, it is also hard to identify principally responsible parties (PRPs) in serious contamination cases. Because the identification of PRPs is also a factor in deciding whether to clean up a site, more serious sites are less likely to be cleaned up. Thus, there is likely to be a racial bias in cleaning up serious abandoned waste sites.

The Unequal Distribution of Treatment, Storage and Disposal Facilities

Researchers have also examined the distribution of treatment, storage, and disposal facilities (TSDFs). The term TSDF suggests an operation that temporarily stores waste in order to treat it for the purposes of neutralizing the hazard prior to disposing of "harmless" leftovers into the environment. In reality, however, TSDFs can do one or all of these functions. Many TSDFs are run by private companies that must obtain permits from government in order to operate their facilities. Because of the nature of the permitting process, research on TSDFs is highly controversial. Specifically, TSDF research highlights the issue of equal enforcement of environmental laws in the form of permits. For instance, Been (1994) discovered that a majority of the TSDF facilities were sited in areas that can be classified as disproportionately African American. However, Been (1994) also found that areas around these sites became disproportionately African American over time. Other researchers have also found evidence that TSDF siting can be traced to intentional discrimination (Hamilton, 1995; Hurly, 1997; Pastor et al., 2001).

There are studies, however, that find little evidence of racial discrimination in TSDF siting (e.g., Mitchell et al., 1999). Oakes et al. (1996) studied the siting of hazardous waste facilities in the 1960s, 1970s, and 1980s. When they examined the demographics of census tracts at the time of siting, they found that tracts with facilities did not have greater minority percentages or poverty rates when compared to tracts without hazardous waste sites (see Been and Gupta, 1997). The drawback of this study, however, is that it does not account for changes in the public's perception of hazardous waste that can occur over time, such as the NIMBY or "not in my backyard" syndrome (public opposition to siting hazardous waste sites near their homes). Moreover, changing perceptions that drive environmental movements can also help mobilize local environmental organizations to oppose the siting of hazardous waste producing facilities. Thus, changes in the relationship between the siting of TSDFs and the racial demographics of neighborhoods might be expected over time given the growth of the environmental movement in the 1970s.

Recent research by Saha and Mohai (2005) suggested that contradictory studies of discriminatory siting can be explained because people did not worry about TSDFs in the early 1970s, so that those facilities were simply sited near polluting industries, which were often located in white working-class neighborhoods. Saha and Mohai suggested that the relationship between TSDF locations and race makes more sense in light of the NIMBY movement. They point out that the location of hazardous waste producing facilities in the 1950s and 1960s was viewed as a tradeoff for economic growth. They found that in Michigan, facilities were often placed in predominantly white, middle-class neighborhoods, with little thought given to the potential health effects associated with various environmental hazards. However, during the 1970s, a greater public awareness of environmental hazards emerged and people did not want to live near TSDFs (Szasz, 1994; Taylor, 2000). This shift in public thinking was fueled by revelations like Love Canal, which became a top news story in 1978 and made "toxic" and "hazardous waste" household words. Love Canal was a residential community located in Niagara Falls, New York that was built upon a toxic waste dump. When the residents of Love Canal became disproportionately sick, and nearly half of all Love Canal children were born with birth defects, President Jimmy Carter declared the area a federal emergency and relocated its residents (Gibbs, 1998). After Love Canal, people were no longer comfortable allowing hazardous wastes to be placed in their neighborhoods. Saha and Mohai (2005) explained that as more attention was focused on toxic waste and environmental hazards, NIMBY protests by white middle-class grassroots activists made the siting of hazardous waste processing facilities in Michigan difficult. Some researchers, such as Szasz (1994), showed that surveys of hazardous waste facility operators during the mid-1970s indicated that less than 50 percent of operators believed that public opposition was a problem during the facility siting stage. However, by 1979 nearly all of the operators reported public opposition as a serious barrier to facility siting (Szasz, 1994). Thus, the siting of hazardous waste facilities followed a "path of least (political) resistance," which often meant locating facilities in socially disadvantaged neighborhoods where the residents were unwilling or unable to effectively combat the siting of hazardous wastes (Saha and Mohai, 2005, p. 618).

The Unequal Distribution of Air Pollution

Researchers have also examined the unequal distribution of air pollution. For instance, as early as 1973, Freeman used monitoring station data to examine the relationship between particulates and sulfates in the air and the percentage of minority residents across census tracts in three cities (Kansas City, Missouri; St. Louis; and Washington, D.C.). Freeman (1973) found that minorities in each city were exposed to higher levels of EPA-regulated particulates in the air (Asch and Seneca, 1978; Kruvant, 1975). Gelobter (1987) also used air-monitoring data to examine the distribution of air quality over time and space. He found that between 1970 and 1986 there was an overall improvement in air quality, but that minority communities consistently experienced elevated levels of air pollution when compared with white communities. Finally, Wernette and Nieves (1992) discovered that blacks were overrepresented in areas designated by the Environmental Protection Agency as non-attainment areas (that is, areas out of compliance with national ambient air quality standards).

Unfortunately, studies that rely solely on air monitoring data are geographically limited. Even in large urban areas, air-monitoring stations are relatively spread out and may not produce sufficient data for analysis. This limitation has been addressed through the use of self-reported data on chemical releases contained in the Toxics Release Inventory (TRI). Approximately 25,000 facilities submit TRI reports to the EPA during each reporting period. Many of these reports disclose chemical releases into the air, and the TRI has been widely used to study the unequal distribution of environmental hazards (Allen, 2001; Arora and Cason, 1999; Perlin et al., 1999). One of the first studies to use TRI data was carried out by Bowen et al. (1995), who examined reported toxic air releases across Ohio counties and across census tracts in Cuyahoga County. They determined that reported air releases were not associated with the racial composition of the counties or tracts (Cutter and Solecki, 1996).

However, Daniels's and Friedman's (1999) study of the distribution of TRI air releases across counties found evidence of racial bias even when they controlled for a variety of economic factors, urban/rural differences, manufacturing processes, and urbanization processes (see Perlin et al., 1995). Other localized TRI studies have replicated the results of Daniels and Friedman. For example, Downey (1998) used TRI data to study air, water, and land chemical releases across Michigan zip codes, and found that racial composition was one of the strongest predictors of the volume of toxins released.

Recently, TRI data have been used to examine specific air pollutants rather than air pollution in general. Hird and Reese (1998) looked at TRI data to examine the distribution of 29 environmental hazards across all U.S. counties. The researchers focused on the distribution of carbon monoxide, lead, nitrogen dioxide, ozone, and sulfur dioxide. They discovered an association between a county's racial composition and each specific hazard examined.

Several additional studies have examined the distribution of estimated air pollution. These estimates are based on air monitoring data, known pollution point sources, and meteorological conditions. Brajer and Hall (1992) developed a statistical model to estimate distributions of ozone across subpopulations in southern California (see Korc, 1996). The results suggest that exposure to particles was above average in young people and blacks. Liu (1996) sought to determine whether ozone pollution and accompanying industry were more likely to be present in black residential areas in New York and Philadelphia. However, Lui (1996,p. 213) found that, " . . . the rich and whites are more likely to live in the source areas." Moreover, demographic patterns were relatively stable, as county census data failed to confirm that the racial composition of neighborhoods downwind of ozone-producing manufacturing plants was changing over time. Based on these results, Lui suggested that people are not as worried about air pollution as they are about other types of environmental hazards. Moreover, Lui asserted that unlike toxic waste facilities, which are often highly visible and attract a great deal of public attention, air pollution is likely to be tolerated and viewed as being fairly distributed, largely dispersed, and a chronic rather than acute problem.

Morello-Frocsh et al. (2001) used air pollution data to estimate cancer potency values in 2,560 census tracts in the South Coast Air Basin of California (which includes Los Angeles, Orange, Ventura, San Bernardino, and Riverside counties). They discovered that in the case of air pollution only that the " . . . probability of a person of color in Southern California living in high cancer-risk neighborhood is nearly one in three, but the probability for an Anglo resident is about one in seven" (Morello-Frocsh et al., 2001, pp. 564-565).Their probability estimates included controls for population density, home ownership levels, and income. Unfortunately, the researchers did not adjust their estimates of high-risk cancer neighborhoods to account for environmental hazards other than air pollution.

Cumulative Impact Assessments

Most studies that examine the distribution of environmental hazards consider one hazard at a time. Researchers, however, have begun to consider the cumulative impact of environmental hazards. Krieg and Faber (2002;

Faber and Krieg 2004), for example, examined the cumulative impact of environmental hazards in Massachusetts. Their measure of cumulative exposure included 17 different environmental hazards (i.e., Department of Massachusetts waste sites, Environmental Protection Superfund sites, large power plants, small power plants, proposed power plants, municipal incinerators, resource recovery facilities, demolition landfills, illegal sites, tire piles, municipal solid waste landfills and trash transfer stations). The researchers found that across all 268 Massachusetts communities, there were, on average, 10.4 hazards per square mile. Moreover, the relationship between the racial composition of the community and the average number of hazards was nearly linear. For example, communities that were less than 5% non-white had an average of 6 hazards per square mile; communities that were 5 to 14.99% non-white had an average of 19 hazards per square mile; communities that were 15 to 24.99% non-white had an average of 43 hazards per square mile; and, communities that were more than 25% non-white had an average of 55 hazards per square mile. Krieg and Faber found similar relationships for income when examining chemical emissions per square mile. The researchers concluded that racial discrimination exists on " . . . a remarkably consistent continuum for nearly all communities" (Krieg and Faber, 2004, p. 667).

Taken together. studies examining the distribution of environmental hazards suggest that these types of hazards are generally located in poor and minority communities. Over all, most studies that examine environmental inequality suggest that inequality appears to be largely attributable to social forces that shape demographics around environmental hazards after those hazards are sited (except see Bullard, 1990) in cases where the hazard is highly visible. This suggests that environmental inequality is largely a product of institutionalized forms of discrimination, which tend to be less direct than the intentional siting of environmental hazards in poor and minority neighborhoods. For instance, once a noxious facility is built, minorities and the poor living near that hazard may not have the same ability as whites to move away from that threat because of other social disadvantages that limit residential mobility, such as income inequality, housing discrimination, educational opportunities, and/or unequal employment prospects.

The fact that social forces play a role in shaping demographics around environmental hazards may have implications for the enforcement of environmental laws. In the case of environmental enforcement, direct forms of discrimination are likely to be relevant to the issue of environmental inequality. For instance, the studies of monetary penalties reviewed above focus largely on discrimination by administrative and civil law judges. However, environmental crime researchers studying enforcement patterns would be wise to examine other discretionary points in the criminal justice system. Thus, researchers might ask whether high levels of community resources in neighborhoods around a polluting facility attract more inspections and more careful scrutiny by regulatory agencies. Or, researchers interested in environmental corporate crime might also ask whether companies are more likely to violate environmental laws if their operations are located in minority and poor communities.

THE FUTURE OF RACE AND CLASS IN THE STUDY OF ENVIRONMENTAL CRIME

One way that communities are fighting back against the inequalities they perceive in environmental enforcement is through calls for environmental justice. As the Warren County protests demonstrated, communities have the power to demand justice. Environmental justice is defined as "the fair treatment of all races, cultures, incomes, and educational levels with respect to the development, implementation, and enforcement of environmental laws, regulations and policies" (United States Environmental Protection Agency, 1998, p. 1). Environmental justice groups have sprung up all over the country and, according to the *People of Color Environmental Groups Directory* (Bullard, 2000), there are nearly 400 such organizations fighting against environmental injustice (Bullard, 2000). The environmental justice movement has consequences for enforcement agencies and has pushed them to take equity concerns more seriously. For example, the EPA has adopted a policy on environmental justice to ensure equal protection for everyone. While environmental justice has impacted the distribution of environmental enforcement, equity concerns have not disappeared and, in some cases, appear to have intensified.

One implication of the unequal distribution of environmental enforcement is that race, ethnic, and class concentrations determine the extent to which communities are protected. The implications of this assertion are truly profound — especially for researchers interested in the causes of crime. Not only does discrimination in environmental enforcement have implications for higher rates of death, disease, and illness among the socially disadvantaged, but it also has implications for crime rates. For instance, studies strongly suggest that environmental exposure to heavy metals such as lead, cadmium, and mercury has a direct and indirect causal influence on criminal behavior (Denno, 1990). Needleman (1990), for instance, noted that as much as 20% of crime is likely to be associated with environmental lead exposure. Further, Needleman et al. (1996) found a significant relationship between bone-lead levels and adolescent delinquency and behavioral problems. In a study of prison inmates, Phil and Ervin (1990) observed elevated levels of lead among violent inmates compared to those who committed property crime.

These individual-level associations have also been discovered at higher levels of aggregation. Using time-series data, Nevin (2000) discovered a relationship between preschool blood lead levels and subsequent violent crime rates in the United States between the years of 1941 and 1998. Nevin (2007) also reported that the relationship could be replicated for other countries, including Britain, Canada, France, Australia, Finland, Italy, West Germany and New Zealand. Similarly, Stretesky and Lynch (2001) have suggested that U.S. counties with higher lead levels in the atmosphere also had higher homicide rates, even when controlling for several other types of air pollution. More recent research by Stretesky and Lynch (2004) argued that variations in air lead levels may help explain higher crime rates in poor and minority communities (see also, Bullard and Wright, 1987; Kraft and Scheberle, 1995; Stretesky, 2003). That is, rates of crime may be higher in minority communities, in part, because residents in these communities are more likely to be exposed to lead, a known neurotoxin that affects tendencies toward violence and aggression, various learning disabilities, and attention deficit disorders. In short, enforcement efforts aimed at corporate polluters in disadvantaged communities may not only improve the health of surrounding residents, but may also reduce the rates of street crime within those communities.

In sum, research examining the unequal enforcement of environmental laws is still underdeveloped. More research is needed to determine the best course of action in determining the nature of the problem and potential solutions. If criminologists want to be part of that discussion, it is imperative that they continue to expand the study of environmental crime to specifically address issues of race and class.

Court Cases Cited

Blakely v. Washington, 542 U.S. 296. (2005).

District of Columbia, et al. v. Heller, Dick A. (2008).

Furman v. Georgia, 408 U.S. 238 (1972).

Gregg v. Georgia, 428 U.S. 153 (1976).

In re: Claims of Racial Disparity v. Commissioner of Corrections, Docket No. CVO-4000632S, State of Connecticut, Tolland Judicial District Court (2008).

Jurek v. Texas, 428 U.S, 262 (1976).

Lockett v. Ohio, 438 U.S. 586 (1978).

Kimbrough v. U.S., 552 U.S. (2007).

Marshall v. State, 130 N.J. 109; 613 A.2d 1059 (1992).

Maxwell v. Bishop, 398 U.S. 262 (1970).

McCleskey v. Kemp, 481 U.S. 279 (1987).

McCleskey v. Zant, 580 F. Supp. 338, 379 (N.D. Ga. 1984).

McGautha v. California, 402 U.S. 183 (1971).

McKoy v. North Carolina, 494 U.S. 433 (1990).

Plessy v. Ferguson, 163 U.S. 537 (1896).

Proffitt v. Florida, 428 U.S. 242 (1976).

State v. Cobb, 663 A.2d 948 (Conn. 1995).

State v. Loftin, 157 N.J. 253, 724 A.2d 129 (1999)

State v. Marshall, 130 N.J. 139 (N.J. 1992).

Turner v. Murray, 476 U.S. 28 (1986).

U.S. v. Booker, 543 U.S. 220 (2005).

Washington v. Davis, 426 U.S. 229 (1976).

Woodson v. North Carolina, 428 U.S. 280 (1976).

References

Adamson, C. 1983. "Punishment after Slavery: Southern State Penal Systems, 1865–1880." *Social Problems* 30: 555–569.

Adamson, J. 2000. *The Denny's Story: How A Company in Crisis Resurrected Its Good Name and Reputation.* New York: John Wiley & Sons.

Akers, R. 1994. *Criminological Theories: Introduction and Evaluation.* Los Angeles: Roxbury Publishing Company.

Akins, S. 2007. "Racial Residential Segregation and Crime." *Sociology Compass* 1(1): 81–94.

Albonetti, C.A. 1990. "Race and the Probability of Pleading Guilty." *Journal of Quantitative Criminology* 6:315–334.

———. 1991. "The Integration of Theories to Explain Judicial Discretion." *Social Problems* 38:247–266.

———. 1997. "Sentencing under the Federal Sentencing Guidelines: Effects of Defendant Characteristics, Guilty Pleas, and Departures on Sentence Outcomes for Drug Offenses, 1991–1992." *Law & Society Review* 31:789–822.

———. 1998. "The Role of Gender and Departures in the Sentencing of Defendants Convicted of a White Collar Offense under the Federal Sentencing Guidelines." In J. Ulmer (Ed.), *Sociology of Crime, Law and Deviance.* Greenwich, CT: JAI Press.

Allen, D. 2001. "Social Class, Race, and Toxic Releases in American Counties, 1995." *Social Science Journal* 38:13–25.

Allen, B. and J. Adams. 1992. "The Concept of 'Race': Let's Go Back to the Beginning." *Journal of Social Behavior and Personality* 7(1):163–168.

Allport, G. 1954. *The Nature of Prejudice.* Reading, MA: Addison-Wesley.

Allport, G.W. and L.J Postman. 1947. *The Psychology of Rumor.* New York: Russell and Russell.

Alvarez, A. and R. Bachman. 1996. "American Indians and Sentencing Disparity: An Arizona Test." *Journal of Criminal Justice* 24:549–561.

American Anthropological Association. 1998. *Statement on Race.* (http://www.aaanet.org/stmts/racepp.htm).

American Bar Association Death Penalty Moratorium Implementation Project. 2007. *State Death Penalty Assessments: Key Findings.* ABA: Chicago. http://www.abanet.org/moratorium/assessmentproject/keyfindings.do c).

American Civil Liberties Union (ACLU) . 2005. *Broken Justice: The Death Penalty in Alabama. ir>(http://www.aclualabama.org/WhatWeDo/BrokenJustice_report.pdf).*

———. 2007. *The Persistent Problem of Racial Disparities in the Federal Death Penalty.* (http://www.aclu.org/capital/general/30237pub20070625.html).

References

Amnesty International. 2003. *United States of America Death by Discrimination — The Continuing Role of Race in Capital Cases.* AI Index: AMR 51/046/2003.

Anderton, D., J. Oakes, and K. Egan. 1997. "Environmental Equity in Superfund: Demographics of the Discovery and Prioritization of Abandoned Toxic Sites." *Evaluation Research* 21:3–26.

Annan, S.O. 1995. *National Survey of Community Policing Strategies, 1992–1993.* Washington DC: The Police Foundation.

"Another push vowed for racial justice law." The News & Observer, Raleigh, NC., August 8, 2008.

Antonio, Michael E. (2006) "I didn't know it'd be so hard": Jurors' emotional reactions to serving on a capital trial." *Judicature*, 89, 282–288.

Arkin, S. 1980. "Discrimination and Arbitrariness in Capital Punishment: An Analysis of Post- Furman Murder Cases in Dade County, Florida, 1973–1976." *Stanford Law Review* 3:76– 101.

Arora, S. and T.N. Cason. 1999. "Do Community Characteristics Influence Environmental Outcomes? Evidence from the Toxics Release Inventory." *Southern Economic Journal* 65:691–716.

Asala, S. 2002. "The Efficiency of the Demarking Point of the Femoral Head as a Sex Determining Parameter." *Forensic Science International* 127:114–118.

Asch, P. and J.J. Seneca. 1978. "Some Evidence on Distribution of Air Quality." *Land Economics* 54:278–297.

Asquith, J.L. and D.N. Bristow. 2000. "To Catch a Thief: A Pedagogical Study of Retail Shoplifting." *Journal of Education for Business* 75:271–276.

Atlas, M. 2001. "Rush to Judgment: An Empirical Analysis of Environmental Equity in U.S. Environmental Protection Agency Enforcement Actions." *Law and Society Review* 35:633–682.

Austin, T. 1981. "The Influence of Court Location on Type of Criminal Sentence: The Rural-Urban Factor." *Journal of Criminal Justice* 9:305–316.

Austin, J. 1986. "Using Early Release to Relieve Prison Overcrowding: A Dilemma in Public Policy." *Crime & Delinquency* 32:404–502.

Austin, J. and J. Irwin. 2001. *It's about Time: America's Imprisonment Binge.* Belmont, CA: Wadsworth.

Baime, D. 2001. *Report to the New Jersey Supreme Court Systemic Proportionality Review Project.* Trenton, NJ: New Jersey Supreme Court.

———. 2005. *Report to the New Jersey Supreme Court Systemic Proportionality Review Project (2004–2005 Term).* Trenton, NJ: New Jersey Supreme Court.

Baldus, D.C., C. Pulaski, and G. Woodworth. 1983. "Comparative Review of Death Sentences: An Empirical Study of the Georgia Experience." *Journal of Criminal Law and Criminology* 74:661– 673.

Baldus, D.C. and G. Woodworth. 2003. "Race Discrimination and the Death Penalty: An Empirical and Legal Overview." In J. Acker, R. Bohm, and C. Lanier (Eds.), *America's Experiment with Capital Punishment*, 2nd Edition. Durham: Carolina Academic Press.

———. 2003. "Race Discrimination in the Administration of the Death Penalty: An Overview of the Empirical Evidence with Special Emphasis on the Post-1990 Research." *Criminal Law Bulletin* 39:194–226.

References

————. 2004. "Race Discrimination and the Legitimacy of Capital Punishment: Reflections on the Interaction of Fact and Perception." *DePaul Law Review* 53:1411–1487.

Baldus, D.C., G.G. Woodworth, and C.A. Pulaski. 1990. *Equal Justice and the Death Penalty: A Legal and Empirical Analysis*. Boston: University Press.

————. 1994. "Reflections on the Inevitability of Racial Discrimination in Capital Sentencing and the 'Impossibility' of its Prevention, Detection, and Correction." *Washington and Lee Law Review* 51:359–428.

Baldus, D., G. Woodworth, C. Grosso, and R. Newell. 2006. "Equal Justice in the Administration of the Death Penalty: The Experience of the United States Armed Forces (1984–2005)." Unpublished work in progress.

Baldus, D.C., G. Woodworth, C. Grosso, and A. Christ. 2002. "Arbitrariness and Discrimination in the Administration of the Death Penalty: A Legal and Empirical Analysis of the Nebraska Experience (1973–1999)." *Nebraska Law Review* 81:486–756.

Baldus, D.C., G. Woodworth, N. Weiner, and B. Broffit. 1998. "Racial Discrimination and the Death Penalty in the Post-*Furman* Era: An Empirical and Legal Overview, with Recent Findings from Philadelphia." *Cornell Law Review* 83:1683–1770.

Bamshad, M., S. Wooding, B. Salisbury, and J. Stephens. 2004. "Deconstructing the Relationship between Genetics and Race." *Nature* 5(August): 598–609.

Bandura, A. 1994. "Self-efficacy." In V.S. Ramachaudran (Ed.), *Encyclopedia of Human Behavior, Volume 4*. New York: Academic Press.

Barlow, D.E. and M.H. Barlow. 2002. "Racial Profiling: A Survey of African American Police Officers." *Police Quarterly* 5:334–358.

Barkaan, E. 1992. *The Retreat of Scientific Racism: Changing Concepts of Race in Britain and the United States between World Wars*. Cambridge: Cambridge University Press.

Barnes, K., D. Sloss, and S. Thaman. 2008. "Life and Death Decisions: Prosecutorial Discretion and Capital Punishment in Missouri." *Arizona Legal Studies*, Discussion Paper No. 08–03 (http://papers.ssrn.com/sol3/papers.cfm?abstract_id= 1107456).

Barnett, A. 1986. "Some Distribution Patterns for the Georgia Death Sentence." *University of California Davis Law Review* 18(4):1327–1374.

Baumer, D.C., S.F. Messner, and R.B. Felson. 2000. "The Role of Victim Characteristics in the Disposition of Murder Cases." *Justice Quarterly* 17:281–307.

Beck, A.J. and D.K. Gilliard. 1995. "*Prisoners in 1994*." (NCJ-151654). Washington, DC: U.S. Department of Justice.

Beck, J.C. and R. Shumsky. 1997. "A Comparison of Retained and Appointed Counsel in Cases of Capital Murder." *Law and Human Behavior* 21:526–538.

Becker, H. 1963. *Outsiders: Studies in the Sociology of Deviance*. New York: Free Press.

Beckett, K. and T. Sasson, T. 2000. *The Politics of Injustice: Crime and Punishment in America*. Thousands Oaks, CA: Pine Forge Press.

Bedau, H. 1964. "Death sentences in New Jersey, 1957–1960." *Rutgers Law Review* 14:1–41.

Bedau, H. 1965. "Capital punishment in Oregon, 1903–1964." *Oregon Law Review* 45:1–55.

Been, V. 1994. "Locally Undesirable Land Uses in Minority Neighborhoods: Disproportionate Siting or Market Dynamics?" *Yale Law Journal* 103:1383–1411.

Been, V. and F. Gupta. 1997. "Coming to the Nuisance or Going to the Barrios? A Longitudinal Analysis or Environmental Justice Claims." *Ecology Law Quarterly* 24:1–56.

Beirne, P. and N. South. 2007. *Issues in Green Criminology: Confronting Harms against Environments, Other Animals and Humanity.* Devon, UK: Willan Publishing.

Bell, J. 2005. "A Solvable Problem: Reducing the Disproportionality of Youths of Color in Juvenile Detention Facilities." *Corrections Today* 67(5):80–83.

Bensing, R.C. and O. Schroeder. 1960. *Homicide in an Urban Community.* Springfield, Illinois: Charles C. Thomas.

Bentele, U. and W.J. Bowers. 2001. "How Jurors Decide on Death: Guilt is Overwhelming, Aggravation Requires Death, and Mitigation is No Excuse." *Brooklyn Law Review* 66:1013–1080.

Berk, R. and J. Lowery. 1986. "Factors Affecting Death Penalty Decisions in Mississippi." (unpublished manuscript).

Berk, R.M., Western, R.E. and Weiss, R.E. 1995. "Statistical Inference for Apparent Populations." *Sociological Methodology*, 25, 421–458.

Berk, R., R. Weiss, and J. Boger. 1993. "Chance and the Death Penalty." *Law & Society Review* 27(1):89–110.

Berk, R., A. Li, and L. Hickman. 2005. "Statistical Difficulties in Determining the Role of Race in Capital Cases: A Re-analysis of Data from the State of Maryland." *Journal of Quantitative Criminology* 21(4):365–390.

Bienen, L.B., N. Weiner, D. Denno, P. Alison, and D. Mills. 1988. "The Reimposition of Capital Punishment in New Jersey: The Role of Prosecutorial Discretion." *Rutgers Law Journal* 41:327–372.

Bird, D.G. 2003. "Life on the Line: Pondering the Fate of a Substantive Due Process Challenge to the Death Penalty." *American Criminal Law Review* 40:1329–1386.

Bisbing, R. 2002. "The Forensic Identification and Association of Human Hair." In R. Saferstein (Ed.), *Forensic Science Handbook, Volume 1.* New Brunswick, New Jersey: Prentice Hall.

Bishop, D. 2005. "The Role of Race and Ethnicity in Juvenile Justice Processing." In D. Hawkins and K. Kempf-Leonard (Eds.), *Our Children, Their Children: Confronting Racial and Ethnic Differences in American Juvenile Justice.* Chicago: The University of Chicago Press.

Bishop, D. M., and C. E. Frazier. 1990. "A Study of Race and Justice Processing in Florida." In D.H Wagner (Ed.), *Where the Injured Fly for Justice: Report and Recommendations of the Florida Supreme Court Racial and Ethnic Bias Study Commission.* Tallahassee, FL: Office of the State Courts Administrator.

Blalock, H. 1967. *Toward a Theory of Minority-Group Relations.* New York: John Wiley and Sons.

Blume, J., T. Eisenberg, and M.T. Wells. 2004. "Explaining Death Row's Population and Racial Composition." *Journal of Empirical Legal Studies* 1(1):165–297.

Blume, J., S. Johnson, and T. Eisenberg. 1998. "Post- *McCleskey* Racial Claims in Capital Cases." *Cornell Law Review* 83:1771–1810.

Blumstein, A. 1993. "Racial Disproportionality of U.S. Prison Populations Revisited." *University of Colorado Law Review* 64:743–760.

———. 1995. "Youth Violence, Guns and the Illicit-Drug Industry." *Journal of Criminal Law and Criminology* 86:10–36.

Bohn, R.M. (Ed.). 1991. *The Death Penalty in America: Current Research.* Cincinnati, OH: Anderson Publishing Co.

Bohm, Robert M. 1994. "Race, Ethnicity, and the Law." *Law and Human Behavior,* 18:3:319–338.

Bonczar, T. 2003. *Prevalence of Imprisonment in the U.S. Population, 1974–2001.* Washington, DC: Office of Justice Programs, Bureau of Justice Statistics.

Bonczar, T.P. and A.J. Beck. 1997. *Lifetime Likelihood of Going to State or Federal Prison.* Bureau of Justice Statistics Bulletin, NCJ 160092. Washington DC: U.S. Department of Justice.

Bortner, P. and A. Hall. 2002. *Arizona First-Degree Murder Cases Summary of 1995–1999 Indictments: Dataset II Research Report to Arizona Capital Case Commission.* Phoenix: Arizona Capital Case Commission.

Bourdua, F. and L. Tifft. 1971. "Citizen Interviews, Organizational Feedback, and Police Community Relations Decisions." *Law & Society Review* 6(2):155–182.

Bowen, W., M. Salling, K. Haynes, and E. Cryan. 1995. "Toward Environmental Justice: Spatial Equity in Ohio and Cleveland." *Annals of the Association of American Geographers* 85:641–663.

Bowers, W. 1983. "The Pervasiveness of Arbitrariness and Discrimination under Post-Furman Capital Statutes." *Journal of Criminal Law & Criminology* 74(3):1067–1100.

———. 1995. "The Capital Jury Project: Rational, Design, and Preview of Early Findings." *Indiana Law Journal* 70:1043–1102.

Bowers, W.J. and W.D. Foglia. 2003. "Still Singularly Agonizing: Law's Failure to Purge Arbitrariness from Capital Sentencing." *Criminal Law Bulletin* 39:51–86.

Bowers, W. and G. Pierce. 1980. "Arbitrariness and Discrimination under Post-Furman Capital Statutes." *Crime and Delinquency* 26:563–632.

Bowers, W.J., M. Sandys, and T.W. Brewer. 2004. "Crossing Racial Boundaries: A Closer Look at the Roots of Racial Bias in Capital Sentencing when the Defendant is Black and the Victim is White." *DePaul Law Review* 53:1497–1538.

Bowers, W.J., M. Sandys, and B.D. Steiner. 1998. "Foreclosed Impartiality in Capital Sentencing: Jurors' Predispositions, Guilt Trial Experience, and Premature Decision Making." *Cornell Law Review* 83:1474–1557.

Bowers, W., B. Steiner, and M. Sandys. 2001. "Death Sentencing in Black and White: An Empirical Analysis of the Role of Jurors' Race and Jury Racial Composition." *University of Pennsylvania Journal of Constitutional Law* 3:171–274.

Box, S. 1989. *Power, Crime, and Mystification.* London: Routledge.

Brace, C.L. 2000. *Does Race Exist? An Antagonist's Perspective.* (http://www.pbs.org/wgbh/nova/first/).

Brajer, V. and J. Hall. 1992. "Recent Evidence on the Distribution of Air-Pollution Effects." *Contemporary Policy Issues* 10:63–71.

Brandl, S., J. Frank, R. Worden and T. Bynum. 1994. "Global and Specific Attitudes toward the Police: Disentangling the Relationship." *Justice Quarterly* 11(1):119–133.

Bridge, F.M. and J. Mosure. 1961. "Capital Punishment. Staff Research Report No. 26." Columbus, Ohio: Ohio Legislature Service Commission.

Bridges, G. S., D. Conley, G. Beretta, and R.L. Engen. 1993. *Racial Disproportionality in the Juvenile Justice System: Final Report.* Olympia, WA: State of Washington, Department of Social and Health Services.

Bridges, G., D. Conley, R. Engen, and T. Price-Spratlen. 1995. "Racial Disparities in the Confinement of Juveniles: Effects of Crime and Community Social Structure on Punishment." In K. Kempf- Leonard, C.E. Pope, and W. Feyerherm (Eds.), *Minorities in Juvenile Justice*. Thousand Oaks: Sage.

Bridges, G. and R. Crutchfield. 1988. "Law, Social Standing, and Racial Disparities in Imprisonment." *Social Forces* 66:699–724.

Bridges, G., R. Crutchfield, and E. Simpson. 1987. "Crime, Social Structure and Criminal Punishment: White and Nonwhite Rates of Imprisonment." *Social Problems* 34:345–361.

Bridges, G.S. and S. Steen. 1998. "Racial Disparities in Official Assessments of Juvenile Offenders: Attributional Stereotypes as Mediating Mechanisms." *American Sociological Review* 63: 554–570.

Brigham, J.C. 1993. "College Students' Racial Attitudes." *Journal of Applied Social Psychology* 23:1933–1967.

Bright, S.B. 1995. "Discrimination, Death and Denial: The Tolerance of Racial Discrimination in Infliction of the Death Penalty." *Santa Clara Law Review* 35:433–483.

Brock, D., N. Cohen, and J. Sorensen. 2000. "Arbitrariness in the Imposition of Death Sentences in Texas: An Analysis of Four Counties by Offense Seriousness, Race of Victim, and Race of Offender." *American Journal of Criminal Law* 28:43–71.

Brudney, J. and R.E. England. 1983. "Toward a Definition of the Co-Production Concept." *Public Administration Review*. 43:59–65.

Brues, A. 1958. "Identification of Skeletal Remains." *The Journal of Criminal Law, Criminology, and Police Science* 48(5): 551–563.

———. 1993. "Racial Concepts: The Objective View of Race." In C. Gordon (Ed.), *Race, Ethnicity and Applied Bioanthropolgy*. Arlington, VA: American Anthropology Association.

Brunson, R., and J. Miller. 2006. "Young Black Men and Urban Policing in the United States." *British Journal of Criminology* 46:613–640.

Bullard, R. 1983. "Solid Waste Sites and the Black Houston Community." *Sociological Inquiry* 53:273–288.

———. 1990, 1994. *Dumping in Dixie: Race, Class and Environmental Quality*. Boulder, CO: Westview.

———. 2000. *People of Color Environmental Groups 2000 Directory*. Atlanta, GA: Environmental Justice Research Center at Clark Atlantic University.

Bullard, R. and B. Wright. 1987. "Environmentalism and the Politics of Equity: Emergent Trends in the Black Community." *Mid-American Review of Sociology* 12:21–38.

Bureau of Justice Assistance. 1996. *National Assessment of Structured Sentencing*. Washington, DC: Bureau of Justice Statistics, Department of Justice.

Bureau of Justice Statistics. 2006. *Prisoners in 2005*. Washington, DC: Bureau of Justice Statistics, Department of Justice.

———. 2007. *Prisoners in 2006*. Washington, DC: Bureau of Justice Statistics, Department of Justice.

Burkhead, M. and J. Luginbuhl. 1994. "Sources of Bias and Arbitrariness in the Capital Trial." *Journal of Social Issues* 50:103–124.

References

Burns, R. and M.J. Lynch. 2004. *Environmental Crime: A Sourcebook.* New York: LFB Scholarly Publishing.

Butler, B.M. and G. Moran. 2002. "The Role of Death Qualification in Venirepersons' Evaluation of Aggravating and Mitigating Circumstances in Capital Trials." *Law and Human Behavior* 26(2):175–184.

Butterfield, F. 2000. "Settling Suit, Louisiana Abandons Private Youth Prisons." *New York Times,* September 8.

Byars, P. and J. Wilcox. 1991. "Focus Groups: A Qualitative Opportunity for Researchers." *Journal of Business Communication* 28(1):63–77.

Cahalan, M.W. 1986. *Historical Corrections Statistics in the United States, 1850–1984.* U.S. Department of Justice, Bureau of Justice Statistics. (NCJ 102529). Washington, DC: US Department of Justice.

Calder, B. 1977. "Focus Groups and the Nature of Qualitative Marketing Research." *Journal of Marketing Research* 14:353– 364.

Campbell, A. and H. Schuman. 1972. "A Comparison of Black and White Attitudes and Experiences in the City." In C. Harr (Ed.), *The End of Innocence: A Suburban Reader.* Glenview, IL: Scott Forseman.

Carnoy, M. 1994. *Faded Dreams: The Politics and Economics of Race in America.* NY: Columbia University Press.

Carroll, J. 1978. "Causal Attributions in Expert Parole Decisions." *Journal of Personality and Social Psychology* 36:1501–1511.

Carroll, J. 2004. "Iraq Support Split Along Racial Lines." (http://www.gallup.com/poll/13012/Iraq-Support-Split-Along-Racial- Lines.aspx).

Carroll, J. 2005. "Who's Proud to Be an American? Republicans More Likely than Democrats to Say They are 'Extremely Proud.' " (http://www.gallup.com/poll/14860/Whos-Proud-American.aspx).

Clayton, L.A. and W.M. Byrd. 2001. "Race: A Major Health Status and Outcome Variable, 1980–1999." *Journal of the National Medical Association* 93(3): 35–54.

Castells, M. 1996. *The Rise of the Network Society.* Oxford: Blackwell.

Chambliss, W. 1995. "Crime Control and Ethnic Minorities: Legitimizing Racial Oppression by Creating Moral Panics." In D. Hawkins (Ed.), *Ethnicity, Race, and Crime: Perspectives across Time and Place.* Albany, NY: State University of New York Press.

Chambliss, W.J. and R.B. Seidman. 1971. *Law, Order, and Power.* Reading, Massachusetts: Addison-Wesley.

Chamlin, M.B. 1990. "Determinants of Police Expenditures in Chicago, 1940–1958." *Sociological Quarterly* 31:485–494.

Chiricos, T.G. and C. Crawford. 1995. "Race and Imprisonment: A Contextual Assessment of the Evidence." In D. Hawkins (Ed.), *Ethnicity, Race, and Crime.* Albany: State University of New York Press.

Cicourel, A. 1968. *The Social Organization of Juvenile Justice.* New York: John Wiley.

Clark, S.H. and S.T. Kurtz. 1983. "The Importance of Interim Decisions to Felony Trial Court Dispositions." *The Journal of Criminal Law and Criminology* 74:476–518.

Clear, T.R. 2007. *Imprisoning Communities: How Mass Incarceration Makes Disadvantaged Neighborhoods Worse.* New York: Oxford University Press.

Clear, T.R., D.R. Rose, E. Waring, and K. Scully. 2003. "Coercive Mobility and Crime: A Preliminary Examination of Concentrated Incarceration and Social Disorganization." *Justice Quarterly* 20(1):33–64.

Clifford, M. 1998. *Environmental Crime: Enforcement, Policy, and Social Responsibility.* Gaithersburg, MD: Aspen.

Clifford, M. and T.D. Edwards. 1998. "Defining 'Environmental Crime'." In M. Clifford (Ed.), *Environmental Crime: Enforcement, Policy, and Social Responsibility.* Gaithersburg, MD: Aspen.

Close, B.R. and P.L. Mason. 2006. "After the Traffic Stops: Officer Characteristics and Enforcement Actions." *Topics in Economic Analysis & Policy* 6(1): Article 24 http://www.bepress.com/bejeap/topics/vol6/iss1/art24).

———. 2007. "Searching for Efficient Enforcement: Officer Characteristics and Racially Biased Policing," *Review of Law & Economics* 3(2): Article 5. http://www.bepress.com/rle/vol3/iss2/art5.

Cohen, M.A. 1992. "Environmental Crime and Punishment: Legal/Economic Theory and Empirical Evidence on Enforcement of Environmental Statutes." *The Journal of Criminal Law and Criminology* 82:1054–1108.

Cohen, R. 1993. "Common Ground on Crime." *Washington Post* December 21.

Cohen, L. and J. Kluegel. 1978. "Determinants of juvenile court dispositions: Ascriptive and achieved factors in two metropolitan courts." *American Sociological Review* 43:162–176.

———. 1979. "Selecting Delinquents for Adjudication: An Analysis of Intake Screening Decisions in Two Metropolitan Juvenile Courts." *Journal of Research in Crime and Delinquency* 10:143–163.

Cone, E. and R. Joseph. 1996. "The Potential for Bias in Hair Testing for Drugs of Abuse." In P. Kintz (Ed.), *Drug Testing in Hair.* Boca Raton, FL: CRC Press.

Conley, D. 1994. "Adding Color to a Black and White Picture: Using Qualitative Data to Explain Racial Disproportionality in the Juvenile Justice System." *Journal of Research in Crime and Delinquency* 31:135–148.

Cooper, J. 1980. *The Police and the Ghetto.* Port Washington, NY: Kennikat.

Cooper, Michael. 1999. "Officers in Bronx Fire 41 Shots, and an Unarmed Man Is Killed." *New York Times,* February 6, A1.

Cordner, G. 1999. "Elements of Community Policing." In L. Gaines and G. Cordner (Eds.), *Policing Perspectives: An Anthology.* Los Angeles, CA: Roxbury Publishing.

Cordner, G., B. Williams, and M. Zuniga. 2000. *Vehicle Stops for the Year 2000: Executive Summary.* San Diego, CA: San Diego Police Department.

Correll, J., B. Park, C.M. Judd, and B.W. Wittenbrink. 2002. "The Police Officer's Dilemma: Using Ethnicity to Disambiguate Potentially Threatening Individuals." *Journal of Personality and Social Psychology* 33:541–560.

Crawford, C., T. Chiricos, and G. Kleck. 1998. "Race, Racial Threat, and Sentencing of Habitual Offenders." *Criminology* 36:481–512.

Crockett, D., S.A. Grier, and J.A. Williams. 2003. "Coping with Marketplace Discrimination: An Exploration of the Experiences of Black Men." *Academy of Marketing Science Review* 7(4):1–18.

Crump, D. 1996. "How Do the Courts Really Discover Unenumerated Fundamental Rights? Cataloguing the Methods of Judicial Alchemy." *Harvard Journal of Law and Public Policy* 19(3):795–917.

Cuomo, A.M. 2005. "Fighting the Rockefeller Drug Laws is the Next Frontier of Civil Rights Movement." *New York Amsterdam News* 96(5):13–41.

Cutter, S. and W. Solecki. 1996. "Setting Environmental Justice in Space and Place: Acute and Chronic Airborne Toxic Releases in Southeastern United States." *Urban Geography* 17:380–399.

Dabney, D.A., L. Dugan, V. Topalli, and R.C. Hollinger. 2006. "The Impact of Implicit Stereotyping on Offender Profiling: Unexpected Results from an Observational Study of Shoplifting." *Criminal Justice and Behavior* 33:646–674.

Dabney, D.A., R.C. Hollinger, and L. Dugan. 2004. "Who Actually Steals? A Study of Covertly Observed Shoplifters." *Justice Quarterly* 21:693–728.

Daboub, A., A. Rasheed, R. Priem, and D. Gray. 1995. "Top Management Team Characteristics and Corporate Illegal Activity." *Academy of Management Review* 20:138–170.

Daly, K. 1989. "Re-Thinking Judicial Paternalism: Gender, Work-Family Relations, and Sentencing." *Gender and Society* 3:9–35.

Daly, K. and M. Tonry. 1997. "Gender, Race and Sentencing." *Crime and Justice* 22:201–252.

D'Amico-Samuels, D. 1990. *Access to Adult Basic Education: African-American Perspectives on Program Guidelines for Recruitment and Retention.* Albany, NY: New York Department of Education.

Daniels, B. and S. Friedman. 1999. "Spatial Inequality and Distribution of Industrial Toxic Releases: Evidence from the 1990 TRI." *Social Science Quarterly* 80:244–262.

Dannefer, D. and R. Schutt. 1982. "Race and Juvenile Justice Processing in Court and Police Agencies." *American Journal of Sociology* 87:1113–32.

Dasgupta, N. and T.L. Banaszynski. 2003. "Believing is Seeing: The Effects of Racial Labels and Implicit Beliefs on Face Perception." *Personality and Social Psychology Bulletin* 29: 360–370.

Death Penalty Information Center (2008). Retrieved January 2008 from: http://www.deathpenaltyinfo.org/Fact.

Demuth, S. and D. Steffensmeier. 2004. "Ethnicity Effects on Sentencing Outcomes in Large Urban Courts: Comparisons among White, Black, and Hispanic Defendants." *Social Science Quarterly* 85:995–1011.

Denno, D. 1990. *Biology and Violence: From Birth to Adulthood.* Cambridge: Cambridge University Press.

DeRoos, A.J., P. Hartge, J.H. Lubin, J.S. Colt, S. Davis, J.R. Cerhan, R.K. Severson, W. Cozen, D.G. Patterson, L.L. Needham, and N. Rothman. 2005. "Persistent Organochlorine Chemicals in Plasma and Risk of Non-Hodgkin's Lymphoma." *Cancer Research* 65:11214–11226.

Devine, P.G. 1989. "Stereotypes and Prejudice: Their Automatic and Controlled Components." *Journal of Personality and Social Psychology* 56:5–18.

Devine, P.G. and A.J. Elliot. 1995. "Are Racial Stereotypes Really Facing? The Princeton Trilogy Revisited." *Personality and Social Psychology Bulletin* 21:1139–1150.

Dieter, R. 2004. *Innocence and the Crisis in the American Death Penalty.* (http://www.deathpenaltyinfo.org/article.php?scid=45&did=1149#Sec 02a).

Dixon, J. 1995. "The Organizational Context of Criminal Sentencing." *American Journal of Sociology* 100:1157–1198.

Donohue, J.J., III. 2007. *Executive Summary, Capital Punishment in Connecticut, 1973–2007: A Comprehensive Evaluation from 4600 Murders to One Execution.* http://standdown.typepad.com/weblog/2007/12/more-on-the-yal.html.

Dorin, Dennis D. 1993. "Far Right of the Mainstream: Racism, Rights and Remedies from the Perspective of Justice Antonin Scalia's *McCleskey* Memorandum." *Mercer Law Review,* 45, 1035–1088.

Dovidio, J.F., N. Evans, and R. Tyler. 1986. "Racial Stereotypes: The Contents of Their Cognitive Representation." *Journal of Experimental Social Psychology* 22:22–37.

Dovidio, J.F., K. Kawakami, and S.L. Gaertner. 2000. "Reducing Contemporary Prejudice: Combating Explicit and Implicit Bias at the Individual and Intergroup Level." In S. Oskamp (Ed.), *Reducing Prejudice and Discrimination.* Mahwah, NJ: Lawrence Erlbaum.

Downey, L. 1998. "Environmental Injustice: Is Race or Income a Better Predictor?" *Social Science Quarterly* 79:766–778.

Drakeford, W. and J.M. Staples. 2006. "Minority Confinement in the Juvenile Justice System: Legal, Social, and Racial Factors." *Teaching Exceptional Children* 39:52–58.

Duncan, B.L. 1976. "Differential Social Perception and Attribution of Intergroup Violence: Testing the Lower Limits of Stereotyping Blacks." *Journal of Personality and Social sychology* 34:590–598.

Durkheim, E. 1964. *The Division of Labor in Society.* New York: Free Press.

Eberhardt, J., P. Davies, P. Purdie-Vaughns, and S.L. Johnson. 2006. "Looking Deathworthy: Perceived Stereotypicality of Black Defendants Predicts Capital-Sentencing Outcomes." *Psychological Science* 17(5):383–386

Eberhardt, J.L., P.A. Goff, V.J. Purdie, and P.G. Davies. 2004. "Seeing Black: Race, Crime, and Visual Processing." *Journal of Personality and Social Psychology* 87:876–893.

Eckland-Olsen, S. 1988. "Structured Discretion, Racial Bias and the Death Penalty: The First Decade after *Furman* in Texas." *Social Science Quarterly* 69:853–873.

Ehrlich, P.R. and A.H. Ehrlich. 1996. *Betrayal of Science and Reason: How Anti-Environmental Rhetoric Threatens our Future.* Washington, DC: Island Press.

Eisenberg, T. 2005. "Death Sentencing Rates and County Demographics: An Empirical Study." *Cornell Law Review* 90:347–373.

Eisenberg, T., S.P. Garvey. and M.T. Wells. 2001. "The Deadly Paradox of Capital Jurors." *Southern California Law Review* 74:371–399.

Eisenhauer, E. 2001. "In Poor Health: Supermarket Redlining and Urban Nutrition." *Geojournal* 53(2): 125–133.

Eisenstein, J., R. Flemming, and P. Nardulli. 1988. *The Contours of Justice: Communities and Their Courts.* Boston: Little Brown.

Eisenstein, J. and H. Jacobs. 1977. *Felony Justice: An Organizational Analysis of Criminal Courts.* Boston, MA: Little Brown.

Eitle, D., S.J. D'Alessio, and L. Stolzenberg. 2002. "Racial Threat and Social Control: A Test of the Political Economic, and Threat of Black Crime Hypotheses" *Social Forces* 81(2):557–576.

Eitle, D., L. Stolzenberg, and S.J. D'Alessio. 2005. "Police Organizational Factors, the Racial Composition of the Police, and the Probability of Arrest." *Justice Quarterly* 22:30–57.

References

Engen, R.L., R.R. Gainey and J.W. Crutchfield. 2003. "Discretion and Disparity under Sentencing Guidelines: The Role of Departures and Structured Sentencing Alternatives." *Criminology* 41:99–130.

Engle, R.S., J. Calnon, and T. Bernard. 2002. "Theory and Racial Profiling: Shortcomings and Future Directions in Research." *Justice Quarterly* 19(2):250–273.

Engle, R.S. and J.M. Calnon. 2004. "Examining the Influence of Drivers' Characteristics during Traffic Stops with Police: Results from a National Survey." *Justice Quarterly* 21:49–90.

————. 2004. "Comparing Benchmark Methodologies for Police- Citizen Contacts: Traffic Stop Data Collection for the Pennsylvania State Police." *Police Quarterly* 7(1):97–125.

Erickson, M.D. 2001. "PCB Properties, Uses, Occurrence, and Regulatory History." In L.W. Robertson and L.G. Hansen (Eds.), *PCBs- Recent Advances in Environmental Toxicology and Health Effects.* Lexington, KY: The University Press of Kentucky.

Everett, R. and R. Wojkiewicz. 2002. "Difference, Disparity and Race/Ethnic Bias in Federal Sentencing." *Journal of Quantitative Criminology* 18:189–211.

Ewen, S. 1996. *PR! A Social History of Spin.* New York: Basic Books.

Faber, D. and E. Krieg. 2002. "Unequal Exposure to Ecological Hazards: Environmental Injustices in the Commonwealth of Massachusetts." *Environmental Health Perspectives* 110:277–288.

Fagin, D. and M. Lavelle. 1999. *Toxic Deception: How the Chemical Industry Manipulates Science, Bends the Law, and Endangers Your Health.* Monroe, ME: Common Courage Press.

Fagan, J. and F. Zimring (Eds.). 2000. *The Changing Borders of Juvenile Justice: Transfer of Adolescents to the Criminal Court.* Chicago: University of Chicago Press.

Farnworth, M. and P. Horan. 1980. "Separate Justice: An Analysis of Race Differences in Court Processes." *Social Science Research* 9:381–399.

Farnworth, M., R. Teske, and G. Thurman. 1991. "Ethnic, Racial, and Minority Disparity in Felony Court Processing." In M. Lynch and E.B. Patterson (Eds.), *Race and Criminal Justice.* Albany: Harrow and Keston.

Farrell, A. 2004. "Measuring Judicial and Prosecutorial Discretion: Sex and Race Disparities in Departures from the Federal Sentencing Guidelines." *Journal of Research and Policy* 6:45– 78.

Farrell, R. and M. Holmes. 1991. "The Social and Cognitive Structure of Legal Decision-Making." *The Sociological Quarterly* 32:529–542.

Farrell, R. and V. Swigert. 1978. "Legal Disposition of Inter-Group and Intra-Group Homicides." *Sociological Quarterly* 19:565–576.

Feagin, J.R. 1991. "The Continuing Significance of Race: Antidiscrimination in Public Places." *American Sociological Review* 56:101–116.

Fearn, N. 2005. "A Multilevel Analysis of Community Effects on Criminal Sentencing." *Justice Quarterly* 22:452–487.

Feeney Amendment. 2003. Title IV of S. 151, Public Law 108–21.

Feinman, C. (Ed.). 1986. *Women in the Criminal Justice System.* New York: Praeger.

Feld, B. 1991. "Justice by Geography: Urban, Suburban, and Rural Variations in Juvenile Justice Administration." *Journal of Criminal Law and Criminology* 82:156–210.

————. 1999. *Bad Kids: Race and the Transformation of the Juvenile Court.* NY: Oxford University Press.

Fellner, J. and M. Mauer. 1998. *Losing the Vote: The Impact of Felony Disenfranchisement Laws in the United States.* Washington, DC: The Sentencing Project.

Feyerherm, W.H. 1995. "The DMC Initiative: The Convergence of Police and Research Theme." In K. Kempf-Leonard, C.E. Pope, and W. Feyerherm (Eds.), *Minorities in Juvenile Justice.* Thousand Oaks, CA: Sage Publications.

Fifield, A. 2001. "Shopping While Black." *Good Housekeeping* 233:129–136.

Flagg, B.J. 1993. "Was Blind but Now I See: White Race Consciousness and the Requirement of Discriminatory Intent." *Michigan Law Review* 91:952–1126.

Fogelson, R. 1968. "From Resentment to Confrontation: The Police, the Negroes, and the Outbreak of the 1960's Riots." *Political Science Quarterly* 83(2):217–247.

Foglia, W.D. 2001. *Report on Bias in Capital Juror Decision- Making in Pennsylvania.* Submitted in response to request by the Supreme Court of Pennsylvania's Committee on Racial and Gender Bias in the Justice System.

Foley, L. 1987. "Florida after the Furman Decision: The Effect of Extralegal Factors on the Processing of Capital Offense Cases." *Behavioral Sciences & the Law* 6(4):467–465.

Foley, L. and R. Powell. 1982. "The Discretion of Prosecutors, Judges, and Juries in Capital Cases." *Criminal Justice Review* 7(2):6–22.

Forensic Bioinformatics. 2007. *Insights into Race from DNA Profiles.* http://www.bioforensics.com/conference07/Racial_Identification/in dex.html).

Frank, N. and M.J. Lynch. 1992. *Corporate Crime, Corporate Violence: A Primer.* New York, NY: Harrow and Heston.

Frankel, M. 1973. *Criminal Sentences: Law without Order.* New York: Hill and Wang.

Frazier, E.F. 1957. *Black Bourgeoisie: The Rise of a New Middle Class in the United States.* Glencoe, IL: The Free Press.

Frazier, C. and D.M. Bishop. 1995. "Reflections on Race Effects in Juvenile Justice." In K. Kempf-Leonard, K., C.E. Pope, and W. Feyerherm (Eds.), *Minorities in Juvenile Justice.* California: Sage Publications.

Frazier, C., D.M. Bishop, and J. Henretta. 1992. "The Social Context of Race Differentials in Juvenile Justice Dispositions." *The Sociological Quarterly* 33:447–458.

Free, M.D. 1997. "The Impact of Federal Sentencing Reforms on African Americans." *Journal of Black Studies* 28:268–286.

Freeman, M. 1973. "The Distribution of Environmental Quality." In A. Kneese and B. Bower (Eds.), *Environmental Quality Analysis.* Washington, DC: Resources for the Future.

Fridell, L. 2005. "Improving Use-of-Force Policy Enforcement and Training." In J.A. Ederheimer and L.A. Fridell (Eds.), *Chief Concerns: Exploring the Challenges of Police Use of Force.* Washington, DC: Police Executive Research Forum.

Fridell, L. and M. Scott. 2005. "Law Enforcement Agency Responses to Racially Biased Policing and the Perceptions of its Practice." In R.G. Dunham and G.P. Alpert (Eds.), *Critical Issues in Policing,* 5th Edition. Prospect Heights, IL: Waveland Press.

Fridell, L., R. Lunney, D. Diamond, and B. Kubu. 2001. *Racially Biased Policing: A Principled Response.* Washington, DC: The Police Executive Research Forum.

Friedman, M. 1970. "The Social Responsibility of Business is to Increase its Profits." *The New York Times Magazine* September 13.

Friedrichs, D.O. 1992. *Trusted Criminals: White Collar Crime in Contemporary Society.* Belmont, CA: Wadsworth.

Frohmann, L. 1997. "Convictability and Discordant Locales: Reproducing Race, Class and Gender Ideologies in Prosecutorial Decision Making." *Law & Society Review* 31: 531–556.

Gabbidon, S.L. 2003. "Racial Profiling by Store Clerks and Security Personnel in Retail Establishments: An Exploration of 'Shopping While Black.' " *Journal of Contemporary Criminal Justice* 19:345–364.

Gabbidon, S.L., L. Marzette, and S.A. Peterson, S.A. 2007. "Racial Profiling and the Courts: An Analysis of Federal-Level Cases, 1991–2006." *Journal of Contemporary Criminal Justice* 23(3):226–238.

Gaines, L.K. 2006. An Analysis of Traffic Stop Data in Riverside, California. *Police Quarterly* 9:210–233.

Garfinkel, H. 1949. "Research Notes on Inter-and Intra-Racial Homicides." *Social Forces* 27:369–381.

Garvey, S.P. 1998. "Aggravation and Mitigation in Capital Cases: What Do Jurors Think?" *Columbia Law Review* 37:27–168.

Garvey, S.P. (2000). "The Emotional Economy of Capital Sentencing." *New York University Law Review,* 75, 26–73.

Garvey, S.P., Johnson, S.L. and Marcus, P. (2000). "Correcting Deadly Confusion: Responding to Jury Inquiries in Capital Cases." *Cornell Law Review,* 85, 627–655.

Gates, H.L. 1997. *Thirteen Ways of Looking at a Black Man.* New York: Random House.

Gelobter, M. 1987. "*The Distribution of Outdoor Air Pollution by Income and Race: 1970–1984.*" Master's Thesis, University of California at Berkeley, Berkeley, CA.

Georges-Abeyie, D. 1990. "The Myth of a Racist Criminal Justice System?" In B. MacLean and D. Milovanovic (Eds.), *Racism, Empiricism and Criminal Justice.* Vancouver: Collective Press.

Gibson, C. and K. Jung. 2002. "Historical Census Statistics on Population Totals by Race, 1790 to 1990, and by Hispanic Origin, 1970 to 1990, for the United States, Regions, Divisions, and States." Working Paper Series, No. 56. Washington, D.C: Population Division, U.S. Census Bureau: Washington.

Gibbs, L.M. 1998. *Love Canal: The Story Continues.* Stony Creek, CT: New Society Publishers.

Gill, G. 2000. "Does Race Exist? A Proponent's Perspective." (http://www.pbs.org/wgbh/nova/first/).

Girard, J. 2008. *Criminalistics: Forensic Science and Crime.* Sunbury, MA: Jones and Bartlett Publishers.

Gladwell, M. 2005. *Blink: The Power of Thinking Without Thinking.* New York, NY: Little, Brown and Company.

Glasser, I. 2006. "Drug Busts = Jim Crow." *Nation* 283(2):24–26.

Goffman, I. 1963. *Stigma: Notes on the Management of Spoiled Identity.* New York: Simon and Schuster.

Goldsmith, S. and W. Eggers. 2004. *Governing by Network: The New Shape of the Public Sector.* Washington, DC: Brookings Institution.

Goodman, A. and G. Armelagos. 1996. "The Resurrection of Race: The Concept of Race in Physical Anthropolgy in the 1990's." In L. Reynolds and L. Leiberman (Eds.), *Race and Other Misadventures.* Dix Hills, NY: General Hall.

Gorton, J. and J. Boies. 1999. "Sentencing Guidelines and Racial Disparity across Time: Pennsylvania Prison Sentences in 1977, 1983, 1992, and 1993." *Social Science Quarterly* 80:37– 54.

Gossett, Thomas F. 1963. *Race: The History of an Idea in America.* New York: Oxford University Press.

Gottschall, J. 1983. "Carter's Judicial Appointments: The Influence of Affirmative Action and Merit Selection on Voting on the U.S. Court of Appeals." *Judicature* 67:165–173.

Gould, S.J. 1993. "American Polygeny and Craniometry before Darwin." In S. Harding (Ed.), *The Racial Economy of Science: Toward a Democratic Future.* Bloomington, IN: Indiana University Press.

———. 2002. "Studying Inequality with One Eye: A New Agenda for Evaluating Disparate Treatment in the Courts." *Justice System Journal* 23(3):317–344.

Graines, S. and J. Wyatt. 2000. "The Rehnquist Court, Legal Process Theory, and *McCleskey v. Kemp.*" *American Journal of Criminal Law* 28:1–40.

Greenwald, A.G. and M.A. Oakes. 2002. "Targets of Discrimination: Effects of Race on Responses to Weapons Holders." *Journal of Experimental Social Psychology* 39:399–405.

Greenwald, A.G., M.A. Oakes, and H. Hoffman. 2003. "Targets of Discrimination: Effects of Race on Responses to Weapons Holders." *Journal of Experimental Social Psychology* 39:399–405.

Gross, S. 1998. "Lost Lives, Miscarriages of Justice in Capital Cases." *Stanford Law Review* 61:125–152.

Gross, S. and R. Mauro. 1984. "Patterns of Death: An Analysis of Racial Disparities in Capital Sentencing and Homicide Victimization." *Stanford Law Review* 37:27–153.

———. 1989. *Death and Discrimination: Racial Disparities in Capital Sentencing.* Boston: Northeastern University Press.

Gruhl, J., S. Welch, and C. Spohn. 1984. "Women as Criminal Defendants: A Test for Paternalism." *Western Political Quarterly* 37:456–467.

Guzman, B. 2001. *"Census 2000 Brief: The Hispanic Population, 2000."* (C2 KBR/ 01–3). Washington, DC: U.S. Census Bureau.

Hacker, J. 1995. *Two Nations: Black and White, Separate, Hostile and Unequal.* New York: Ballentine.

Hagan, J. 1974. "Extra-Legal Attributes and Criminal Sentencing: An Assessment of a Sociological Viewpoint." *Law & Society Review* 8:357–383.

———. 1975. "The Social and Legal Construction of Criminal Justice: A Study of the Presentencing Process." *Social Problems* 22:620–637.

———. 1987 "Review Essay: A Great Truth in the Study of Crime." *Criminology* 25:421–428.

Hagan, J. and K. Bumiller. 1983. "Making Sense of Sentencing: A Review and Critique of Sentencing Research." In A. Blumstein, J. Cohen, S. Martina and M. Tonry (Eds.), *Research on Sentencing: The Search for Reform, Volume 2.* Washington: National Academy Press.

Hagan, J., J.D. Hewitt, and D.F. Alwin. 1979. "Ceremonial Justice: Crime and Punishment in a Loosely Coupled System." *Social Forces* 58:506–527.

Hagan , J., C. Shedd, and M.R. Payne. 2005. "Race, Ethnicity, and Youth Perceptions of Criminal Injustice. *American Sociological Review* 70:381–407.

Hahn, H. 1971. "Ghetto Assessments of Police Protection and Authority." *Law and Society Review* 6:183–194.

Hahn, R., J. Mulinare, and S. Teutsch. 1992. "Inconsistencies in Coding of Race and Ethnicity between Birth and Death in U.S. Infants." *Journal of the American Medical Association* 267(2):259–263.

Haller, J. 1971. *Outcasts from Evolution.* Urbana, IL: University of Illinois Press.

Halsey, M. 2004. "Against 'Green' Criminology." *British Journal of Criminology* 44:833–853.

Hamilton, J. 1995. "Testing for Environmental Racism: Prejudice, Profits, Political Power?" *Journal of Policy Analysis and Management* 14:107–132.

Hamparian, D. and M. Leiber. 1997. *Disproportionate Confinement of Minority Juveniles in Secure Facilities: 1996 National Report.* Champaign, IL: Community Research Associates, Inc.

Hannaford, I. 1996. *Race: The History of an Idea in the West.* Baltimore: The Johns Hopkins University Press.

Haney, C. 1997. "Violence and the Capital Jury: Mechanisms of Moral Disengagement and the Impulse to Condemn to Death." *Stanford Law Review* 49:1447–1486.

———. 2004. "Condemning the Other in Death Penalty Trials: Biographical Racism, Structural Mitigation and the Empathic Divide." *DePaul Law Review* 53:1557–1586.

Harcourt, B.E. 1995. "Imagery and Adjudication in the Criminal Law: The Relationship between Images of Criminal Defendants and Ideologies of Criminal Law in Southern Antebellum and Modern Appellate Decision." *Brooklyn Law Review* 61:1165–1247.

Harris, A.G. 2003. "Shopping While Black: Applying 42 U.S.C. § 1981 to Cases of Consumer Racial Profiling." *Boston College Third World Law Journal* 23:1–56.

Harris, D.A. 1997. "Driving While Black and All Other Traffic Offenses: The Supreme Court and Pretextual Traffic Stops" *Journal of Criminal Law & Criminology* 87:544–582.

———. 1999. *Driving While Black: Racial Profiling on Our Nation's Highways.* (www.aclu.org/profiling/report/index/html).

———. 2002. *Profiles in Injustice: Why Racial Profiling Cannot Work.* New York: The New Press.

Harris, A.G., G.R. Henderson, and J.D. Williams. 2005. "Courting Customers: Assessing Consumer Racial Profiling and Other Marketplace Discrimination." *Journal of Public Policy & Marketing* 24:163–171.

Harrison, P. and A.J. Beck. 2003. *Prisoners in 2002.* Washington, DC: U.S. Department of Justice.

———. 2006. *Prisoners in 2005.* (NCJ 215092). Washington, DC: U.S. Department of Justice.

Hartley, M. and C. Spohn. 2007. "Concerning Conceptualization and Operationalization." *Southwest Journal of Criminal Justice* 4(1):58–78.

Hausman, L. 1925. "A Comparative Racial Study of the Structural Elements of Human Head- Hair." *The American Naturalist* 59:529–538.

Hawkins, D. 1987. "Beyond Anomalies: Rethinking the Conflict Perspective on Race and Criminal Punishment." *Social Forces* 65:265–277.

Heckscher, C. 1994. "Defining the Post-bureaucratic Type." In C. Heckscher and A. Donnellon (Eds.), *The Post Bureaucratic Organization: New Perspectives on Organizational Change.* Thousand Oaks, CA: Sage.

Helmer, J. 1975. *Drugs and Minority Oppression.* New York: Seabury Press.

Helms, R. and D. Jacobs. 2002. "The Political Context of Sentencing: An Analysis of Community and Individual Determinants." *Social Forces* 81(2):577–604.

Henderson, T.P. 2001. "Perception that Some Merchants Practice Racial Profiling Generates Debate." *Stores* 83. (http:stores.org/archives /jun01edit.asap).

Herring, C. 2002. "Bleaching of the Color Line? The Skin Color Continuum and the Tripartite Model of Race." *Race and Society* 5:17–31.

Hickman, M. and Reaves, B. 2001. *Community Policing in Local Police Departments, 1997 and 1999.* Washington, DC: US Department of Justice.

Hilton, J.L. and W. Von Hippel. 1990. "The Role of Consistency in the Judgment of Stereotype-Relevant Behaviors." *Personality and Social Psychology Bulletin* 16:430–448.

Hime, A. 2005. "Life or Death Mistakes: Cultural Stereotyping, Capital Punishment, and Regional Race-based Trends in Exoneration and Wrongful Execution." *University of Detroit Mercy Law Review* 82:181–218.

Hindson, S., H. Potter, and M. Radelet. 2006. "Race, Gender, Region and Death Sentencing in Colorado, 1980–1999." *University of Colorado Law Review* 77(3):549–594.

Hird, J. 1994. *Superfund: The Political Economy of Environmental Risk.* Baltimore, MA: Johns Hopkins University Press.

Hird, J. and M. Reese. 1998. "The Distribution of Environmental Quality: An Empirical Analysis." *Social Science Quarterly* 79:693–716.

Hoeffel, J.C. 2005. "Risking the Eighth Amendment: Arbitrariness, Juries, and Discretion in Capital Cases." *Boston College Law Review* 46:771–824.

Hoffman, J.L. 1995. "Where's the Buck? Juror Misperception of Sentencing Responsibility in Death Penalty Cases." *Indiana Law Journal* 70:1137–1160.

Holcomb, J.E., Williams, M.R. and Demuth, S. 2004. "White Female Victim and Death Penalty Disparity Research." *Justice Quarterly,* 21:4:877–902.

Holmes, M.D., H.M. Mosch, H.C. Daudistel, D.A. Perez, and J.B. Graves. 1993. "Judges' Ethnicity and Minority Sentencing: Evidence Concerning Hispanics." *Social Science Quarterly* 74:496–506.

Holowinski, I.A. 2002. "Inherently Arbitrary and Capricious: An Empirical Analysis of Variations among State Death Penalty Statutes." *Cornell Journal of Law and Public Policy* 12:231– 268.

Houck, M. 2004. *Trace Evidence Analysis: More Cases in Mute Witnesses.* Amsterdam: Elsevier Academic Press.

Howe, S.W. 2004. "The Futile Quest for Racial Neutrality in Capital Selection and the Eighth Amendment Argument for Abolition based on Unconscious Racial Discrimination." *William and Mary Law Review* 45:2083–2166.

References

Hsia, H. 2006. *A Disproportionate Minority Contact (DMC) Chronology: 1998 to Date.* (http://www.ojjdp.ncjrs.gov/dmc/about/chronology.html).

Human Rights Watch. 2000. *Punishment and Prejudice: Racial Disparities in the War On Drugs.* NY: Human Rights Watch.

Hurly, A. 1997. "Fiasco at Wagner Electric: Environmental Justice and Urban Geography in St. Louis." *Environmental History* 2:460–481.

Iceland, J. and R. Wilkes. 2006. "Does Socioeconomic Status Matter? Race, Class and Residential Segregation." *Social Problems* 53(2): 248–273.

Iceland, J., C. Sharpe and E. Steinmetz. 2004 "Class Differences in African American Residential Patterns in U.S. Metropolitan Areas, 1990–2000." *Social Science Research* 34(1): 252–266.

Jacob, H. 1971. "Black and White Perceptions of Justice in the City." *Law and Society Review* 6: 646–668.

Jarrett, R. 1993. "Interviewing with Low-Income Minority Populations." In D.L. Morgan (Ed.), *Successful Focus Groups: Advancing the State of the Art..* Newbury Park, CA: Sage.

Jenkins, M. 1995. "Fear of the Gangsta: African-American Males and the Criminal Justice System." Paper presented at the Annual Meeting of the Academy of Criminal Justice Sciences, Boston, MA.

Johnson, B. 2005. "Contextual Disparities in Guidelines Departures: Courtroom Social Contexts, Guidelines Compliance and Extralegal Disparities in Criminal Sentencing." *Criminology* 43:761–796.

Johnson, E.H. 1957 "Selective forces in capital punishment." *Social Forces 36*:165–199.

Johnson, G. 1941. "The Negro and Crime." *Annals of the American Academy of Political and Social Science* 217:93–104.

Johnson, O.C. 1951. "Is the Punishment of Rape Equally Administered to Negroes and Whites in the State of Louisiana?" In W.L. Patterson (Ed.), *We Charge Genocide.* New York: International Publishers.

Joint Legislative Audit and Review Commission of the Virginia Assembly (JLARC), (2002). "Review of Virginia's System of Capital Punishment." *Capital Defense Journal,* 14, 349.

Jones, D.R. 2001. "Get Rid of Discriminatory Drug Laws." *New York Amsterdam News* 92(52):5.

Jones, R. 2007. "In Louisiana, A Tree, A Fight, and A Question of Justice." *New York Times,* September, 18.

Josserand, E., S. Teo, and S. Clegg. 2006. "From Bureaucratic to Post-Bureaucratic: The Difficulties of Transition." *Journal of Organizational Change Management* 19(1):54–64.

Judson, C.J., J.L. Pandell, J.B. Owens, J.L. McIntosh, and D. Matschullat. 1969 "A Study of the Penalty Jury in First Degree Murder Cases." *Stanford Law Review* 21:1297–1431.

Kalven, H. and H. Zeisel. 1966. *The American Jury.* Boston: Little, Brown and Company.

Kautt, P. 2002. "Location, Location, Location: Interdistrict and Intercircuit Variation in Sentencing Outcomes for Federal Drug- Trafficking Offenses." *Justice Quarterly* 19:633–671.

Kautt, P. and C. Spohn. 2002. "Cracking Down on Black Drug Offenders? Testing for Interactions among Offenders' Race, Drug Type and Sentencing Strategy in Federal Drug Sentences." *Justice Quarterly* 19:1–37.

Kawakami, K. and J.K. Dividio. 2001. "The Reliability of Implicit Stereotyping." *Personality and Social Psychology Bulletin* 27:212–225.

Keil, T. and G. Vito. 1989. "Race, Homicide Severity, and Application of the Death Penalty: A Consideration of the Barnett Scale." *Criminology* 27(3):511–535.

———. 1990. "Race and the Death Penalty in Kentucky Murder Trials: An Analysis of Post-Gregg Outcomes." *Justice Quarterly* 7(1):189–207.

———. 1995. "Race and the Death Penalty in Kentucky Murder Trials, 1976–1991: A Study of Racial Bias in Capital Sentencing." *American Journal of Criminal Justice* 20:105–112.

———. 2006. "Race and Prosecutorial Decisions to Seek the Death Penalty in Kentucky." *Journal of Ethnicity in Criminal Justice* 4(3):27–49.

Keita, S. 2007. "On Meroitic Nubian Crania, Fordisc 2.0, and Human Biological History." *Current Anthropology* 48(3):425– 427.

Kempf, K. and R. Austin. 1986. "Older and More Recent Evidence on Racial Discrimination in Sentencing." *Journal of Quantitative Criminology* 2:29–47.

Kennedy, E. 1979. "Toward a New System of Criminal Sentencing: Law and Order." *American Criminal Law Review* 16:353–382.

Kennedy, R.L. 1988. "*McCleskey v. Kemp*: Race, Capital Punishment, and the Supreme Court." *Harvard Law Review* 101:1388–1443.

———. 1997. *Race, Crime, and the Law.* New York: Pantheon Books.

———. 1999. "Suspect Policy." *New Republic* 221(1/2):30– 35.

King, N.J. 1993. "Postconviction Review of Jury Discrimination: Measuring the Effects of Jury Race on Jury Decisions." *Michigan Law Review* 92:63–104.

Kirchmeier, J.L. 1998. "Aggravating and Mitigating Factors: The Paradox of Today's Arbitrary and Mandatory Capital Punishment Scheme." *William and Mary Bill of Rights Journal* 6:345–459.

Kleck, G. 1981. "Racial Discrimination in Sentencing: A Critical Evaluation of the Evidence with Additional Evidence on the Death Penalty." *American Sociological Review* 43:783–805.

Klein, J., R. Berk, and L. Hickman. 2006. *Race and the Decision to Seek the Death Penalty in Federal Cases.* Technical Report prepared for the National Institute of Justice www.rand.org).

Klein, S. 1989. "Relationship of Offender and Victim Race to Death Penalty Sentences in California." Unpublished manuscript, The Rand Corporation.

Klein, S. 1991. "Racial Disparity in Sentencing Decisions." Unpublished Manuscript of Testimony before the Subcommittee on Civil and Constitutional Rights hearing on Race and Arbitrariness in Capital Sentencing, Committee on the Judiciary, U.S. House of Representatives, July 10, 1991. RAND, Santa Monica, CA.

Klein, S., A, Abrahamse, and J. Rolph. 1987. "Racial Equity in Prosecutor Requests for the Death Penalty." Unpublished manuscript, The Rand Corporation.

Klein, S.P. and J. Rolph. 1991. "Relationship of Offender and Victim Race to Death Penalty Sentences in California." *Jurimetrics* 32:33–48.

Klein, S., S. Turner, and J. Petersilia. 1988. *Racial Equity in Sentencing.* Rand Corporation.

Klemm, Margaret F. 1986. "The Determinants of Capital Sentencing in Louisiana, 1975–1984." Dissertation, University of New Orleans

Knepper, P. 2000. "The Alchemy of Race and Crime Research." In M. Markowitz and D. Jones-Brown (Eds.), *The System in Black and White: Exploring the Connections Between Race, Crime, and Justice.* Westport, CT: Praeger.

Knodel, J. 1993. The Design and Analysis of Focus Group Studies: A Practical Approach. In D. L. Morgan (Ed.), *Successful Focus Groups: Advancing the State of the Art.* Newbury Park, CA: Sage.

Korc, M. 1996. "A Socioeconomic Assessment of Human Exposure to Ozone in the South Coast Air Basin of California." *Journal of the Air and Waste Management Association* 46:547–557.

Kozol, J. 2005. *The Shame of the Nation: The Restoration of Apartheid Schooling in America.* New York: Crown Publishers.

Kraft, M.E. and D. Scheberle. 1995. "Environmental Justice and the Allocation of Risk: The Case of Lead and Public Health." *Policy Studies Journal* 23:113–122.

Kramer, J.H. and D. Steffensmeier. 1993. "Race and Imprisonment Decisions in California." *Science* 247:812–816.

Kramer, J.H. and J.T. Ulmer. 1996. "Sentencing Disparity and Departures from Guidelines." *Justice Quarterly* 13:81–106.

———. 2002. "Downward Departures for Serious Violent Offenders: Local Court Corrections to Pennsylvania's Sentencing Guidelines." *Criminology* 40:897–932.

Kremling, J., M.D. Smith, J.K. Cochran, B. Bjerregard, and S.J. Fogel. 2007. "The Role of Mitigating Factors in Capital Sentencing Before and After *McKoy v. North Carolina.*" *Justice Quarterly* 24(3):357–381.

Krieg, E. 1995. "A Socio-Historical Interpretation of Toxic Waste Sites." *The American Journal of Economics and Sociology* 54:1–14.

Krieg, E. and D. Faber. 2004. "Not So Black and White: Environmental Justice and Cumulative Impact Assessments." *Environmental Impact Assessment Review* 24: 667–694.

Krippendorf, K. 1980. *Content Analysis: An Introduction to its Methodology.* Beverly Hills, CA: Sage.

Krueger, R. 1988. *Focus Groups: A Practical Guide for Applied Research.* Newbury Park, CA: Sage.

Kruvant, W. 1975. "People, Energy, and Pollution." In D. Newman and D. Day (Eds.), *The American Energy Consumer.* Cambridge, MA: Ballinger.

LaFree, G.D. 1980. "The Effect of Sexual Stratification by Race on Official Reactions to Rape." *American Sociological Review* 45: 842–854.

———. 1985. "Official Reactions to Hispanic Defendants in the Southwest." *Journal of Research in Crime and Delinquency* 22:213–237.

———. 1989. *Rape and Criminal Justice: The Social Construction of Sexual Assault.* Belmont, CA: Wadsworth.

Lamberth, J. 1996. *A Report to the ACLU.* New York: American Civil Liberties Union.

Langan, P. 1985. "Racism on Trial: New Evidence to Explain the Racial Composition of Prisons in the United States." *Journal of Criminal Law and Criminology* 76:666–683.

———. 1994. "No Racism in the Justice System." *Public Interest* 117:48–51.

Lavelle, M. and M. Coyle. 1992. "Unequal Protection: The Racial Divide in Environmental Law." *National Law Journal* 21:S1–S11.

Lawrence, C.R., III. 1987. "The Id, the Ego, and Equal Protection: Reckoning with Unconscious Racism." *Stanford Law Review* 39:317–388.

Leach, E. 1975. "Cultural Components in the Concept of Race." In F.J. Ebling (Ed.), *Racial Variations in Man*. London, Blackwell Press.

Lee, C. 2007. "Hispanics and the Death Penalty: Discriminatory Charging Practices in San Joaquin County, California." *Journal of Criminal Justice* 35:17–27.

Lee, H., T. Palmbach, and M. Miller. 2001. *Henry Lee's Crime Scene Handbook*. Amsterdam: Elsevier Academic Press.

Lee, J. 2000. "The Salience of Race in Everyday Life: Black Customers' Shopping Experiences in Black and White Neighborhoods." *Work and Occupations* 27:353–376.

Leiber, M.J. 1994. "A Comparison of Juvenile Court Outcomes for Native Americans, African Americans, and Whites." *Justice Quarterly* 11:257–279.

———. 1995. "Toward Clarification of the Concept of 'Minority' Status and Decision Making in Juvenile Court Proceedings." *Journal of Crime and Justice* 18:79–108

———. 2003. *The Contexts of Juvenile Justice Decision Making: When Race Matters*. Albany, NY: State University of New York Press.

Leiber, M.J. and A.N. Blowers. 2003. "Race and Misdemeanor Sentencing." *Criminal Justice Policy Review* 14(4):464–485.

Leiber, M. and K. Fox. 2005. "Race and the Impact of Detention on Juvenile Justice Decision Making." *Crime & Delinquency* 51(4):470–497.

Leiber, M.J. and K. Jamieson. 1995. "Race and Decision-Making within Juvenile Justice: The Importance of Context." *Journal of Quantitative Criminology* 11:363–388.

Leiber, M. and J.Johnson. In press. "Being Young and Black: What are their Effects on Juvenile Justice Decision Making?" *Crime & Delinquency*.

Leiber, M., J. Johnson, K. Fox, and R. Lacks. 2007. "Differentiating among Racial/Ethnic Groups and Its Implications for Understanding Juvenile Justice Decision Making" *Journal of Criminal Justice* 35: 471–484.

Leiber, M. and K. Mack. 2003. "The Individual and Joint Effects of Race, Gender, and Family Status on Juvenile Justice Decision-Making." *Journal of Research in Crime & Delinquency* 40(1):34–70.

Leiber, M. and J. Stairs. 1999. "Race, Contexts, and the Use of Intake Diversion." *Journal of Research in Crime and Delinquency* 36:56–86.

Lenhardt, R.A. 2004. "Understanding the Mark: Race, Stigma, and Equality in Context." *New York University Law Review* 79: 803–931.

Lenza, M., Keys, D. and Guess, T. (2005). "Prevailing Injustices in the Application of the Missouri Death Penalty 1978–1996." 32 *Social Justice: A Journal of Crime, Conflict & World Order* 151–166.

Leopold, A. 1998. "Objective Tests and Subjective Bias: Some Problems of Discriminatory Intent in the Criminal Law." *Chicago-Kent Law Review* 73:533–558.

Lesman, A. 2005. "State Responses to the Spector of Racial Discrimination in Capital Proceedings: The Kentucky Racial Justice Act and the New Jersey Supreme Court's Proportionality Review Project." *Journal of Law and Policy,* 13:359–424.

Lewis, P., H. Mannle, and H. Vetter. 1979. "A Post-Furman Profile of Florida's Condemned: A Question of Discrimination in Terms of Race of the Victim and a Comment on *Spenkelink v. Wainwright.*" *Stetson Law Review* 9(1): 1-46.

Lieberman, L. and L.Reynolds. 1978. "The Debate over Race: An Empirical Investigation." *Phylon* 39(4): 333–343.

Liebman, J., J. Fagan, and V. West. 2000. *A Broken System: Error Rates in Capital Cases, 1973–1995.* (http://www2.law.columbia.edu/instructionalservices/liebman/).

Liska, A. 1992. *Social Threat and Social Control.* Albany: SUNY Press.

———. 1994 "Modeling the Conflict Perspective of Social Control." In G. Bridges and M. Myers (Eds.), *Inequality, Crime, and Social Control.* Boulder: Westview Press.

Liu, F. 1996. "Urban Ozone Plumes and Population Distribution by Income and Race: A Case Study of New York and Philadelphia." *Journal of the Air and Waste Management Association* 46:207– 215.

Lortz, R. and J.Hewitt. 1977. "The Influence of Legally Irrelevant Factors on Felony Sentencing." *Sociological Inquiry* 47:39–48.

Loury, G. 2002. *The Anatomy of Racial Inequality.* Cambridge, MA: Harvard University Press.

Lugginbuhl, J. and Burkhead, M. 1994. "Sources of Bias and Arbitrariness in the Capital Trial". *Journal of Social Issues,* 50:2:103–124.

Lyman, S. 1994. *Color, Culture, Civilization: Race and Minority Issues in American Society.* Chicago: University of Illinois Press.

Lynch, J. and W.J. Sabol. 2000. "Prison Use and Social Control." In J. Horney (Ed.), *Criminal Justice 2000: Policies, Processes and Decision of the Criminal Justice System.* Washington, DC: U.S. Department of Justice, National Institute of Justice.

Lynch, M.J. 1990. "The Greening of Criminology: A Perspective for the 1990s." *The Critical Criminologist* 2:11–12.

———. 1990 "Racial Bias and Criminal Justice: Definitional and Methodological Issues." B. MacLean, and D. Milovanovic (Eds.), *Racism, Empiricism and Criminal Justice.* Vancouver: Collective Press.

———. 1996. "Race, Class, Gender and Criminology: Structured Choices and the Life Course." In M. Schwartz and D. Milovanovic (Eds.), *Gender, Race and Class in Criminology* Hamden, CT: Garland.

———. 2000. "J. Phillippe Rushton on Crime: An Examination and Critique of the Explanation of Crime in 'Race, Evolution, and Behavior.' " *Social Pathology* 6(3):228–244.

———. 2002. "Misleading 'Evidence' and the Misguided Attempt to Generate Racial Profiles of Criminals: Correcting Fallacies and Calculations Concerning Race and Crime in Taylor and Whitney's Analysis of Racial Profiling." *The Mankind Quarterly* 42(3):313–330.

———. 2007. *Big Prisons, Big Dreams: Crime and the Failure of America's Penal System.* New Brunswick, NJ: Rutgers University Press.

Lynch, M.J., R.G. Burns, and P.B. Stretesky. 2008. *Environmental Crime, Law and Justice.* New York: LFB Scholarly.

Lynch, M.J., D. McGurrin, and M. Fenwick. 2004. "Disappearing Act: The Representation of Corporate Crime Research in Criminological Literature." *Journal of Criminal Justice* 32:389–398.

Lynch, M.J. and R.J. Michalowski. 2006. *A Primer in Radical Criminology, 4th ed..* Monsey, NY: Criminal Justice Press.

Lynch, M.J. and E.B. Patterson. 1990. "Racial Discrimination in the Criminal Justice System: Evidence from Four Jurisdictions." In B. MacLean and D.Milovanovic (Eds.), *Racism, Empiricism and Criminal Justice.* Vancouver: Collective Press.

———. (Eds). 1991. *Race and Criminal Justice.* New York, NY: Harrow and Heston.

———. 1996. *Justice with Prejudice: Race and Criminal Justice in America.* Monsey, NY: Criminal Justice Press.

Lynch, M.J. and A. Schuck. 2003. "Picasso as Criminologist: The Abstract Art of Racial Profiling." In M. Free (Ed.), *Racial Issues in Criminal Justice: The Case of African Americans.* Westport, CT: Praeger.

Lynch, M.J. and P.B. Stretesky. 2001. "Toxic Crimes: Examining Corporate Victimization of the General Public Employing Medical and Epidemiological Evidence." *Critical Criminologists* 10:153– 172.

———. 2003. "The Meaning of Green: Towards a Clarification of the Term Green and Its Meaning for the Development of a Green Criminology." *Theoretical Criminology* 7:217–238.

Lynch, M.J., P.B. Stretesky, and R.G. Burns. 2004. "Determinants of Environmental Law Violation Fines against Petroleum Refineries: Race, Ethnicity, Income, and Aggregation Effects." *Society and Natural Resources* 17:333–347.

MacDonald, H. 2003. *Are Cops Racist? How the War Against the Police Harms Black Americans.* Chicago: Ivan R. Dee.

MacLean, B. and D. Milovanovic. 1990. "The Anatomy of the No Discrimination Thesis." In B. MacLean and D. Milovanovic (Eds.), *Racism, Empiricism and Criminal Justice.* Vancouver: Collective Press.

Manderson, D. 1999. "Symbolism and Racism in Drug History and Policy." *Drug & Alcohol Review* 18:179–186.

Mangum, C.F. 1940. *The Legal Status of the Negro.* Chapel Hill: University of North Carolina Press.

Mann, C.R. 1993. *Unequal Justice: A Question of Color.* Bloomington, IN: Indiana University Press.

Maravelias, C. 2003. "Post-bureaucracy — Control through Professional Freedom." *Journal of Organizational Change Management* 16(5):547–566.

Marks, J. 2006. "The Realities of Race." The Social Science Research Council. http://raceandgenomics.ssrc.org/Marks/printable.html.

Marshall, G. 1993. "Racial Classifications: Popular and Scientific." In S. Harding (Eds.), *The Racial Economy of Science: Toward a Democratic Future.* Bloomington, IN: Indiana University Press.

Massey, D. and S. Denton. 1994. *American Apartheid: Segregation and the Making of the American Underclass.* Cambridge, MA: Harvard University Press.

Mauer, M. 1999. *Race to Incarcerate.* NY: New Press.

———. 2007."Racial Impact Statements as a Method of Reducing Unwarranted Sentencing Disparities." *Ohio State Journal of Criminal Law* 5:19–46.

Mauer, M. and R. King. 2007a. *Uneven Justice: State Rates of Incarceration by Race and Ethnicity.* Washington, DC: The Sentencing Project.

References

————. 2007b. "A 25 Year Quagmire: The War on Drugs and Its Impact on American Society. Washington, DC: The Sentencing Project.

McAdams, J.C. 1998. "Racial Disparity and the Death Penalty." *Law and Contemporary Problems* 61:152–170.

McCord, D. (2002). "A year in the life of death: Murders and capital sentences in South Carolina." *South Carolina Law Review,* 53, 249–360.

McGurty, E. 2000. "Warren County, NC, and the Emergence of the Environmental Justice Movement: Unlikely Coalitions and Shared Meanings in Local Collective Action." *Society and Natural Resources* 13:373–387.

McIntosh, P. 2006. "White Privilege, Color, and Crime: A Personal Account." In. C.R. Mann, M.S. Zata, and N. Rodriguez, N. (Eds.), *Images of Color, Images of Crime: Readings.* Los Angeles: Roxbury.

McKinnon, J. 2001. "*Census 2000 Brief: The Black Population, 2000.*" U.S. Census Bureau: Washington, DC.

McLaughlin, V. and M. Donahue. 1995. "Training for Community- Oriented Policing," In P. Kratcoski and D. Dukes (Eds.), *Issues in Community Policing.* Cincinnati, OH: Anderson Publishing, Co.

Meehan, A. and C. Ponder. 2002. "Race and Place: The Ecology of Racial Profiling African-American Motorists." *Justice Quarterly* 19(3):399–430

Meindl, R., C. Lovejoy, R. Mensforth, and I. Don Carlos. 1985. "Accuracy and Direction of Error in the Sexing of the Skeleton: Implications for Paleodemography." *American Journal of Physical Anthropology* 68:79–86.

Merton, R. 1957. *Social Theory and Social Structure.* Glencoe, IL: The Free Press.

Miethe, T.D. 1987. "Charging and Plea Bargaining Practices under Determinate Sentencing: An Investigation of the Hydraulic Displacement Theory." *The Journal of Criminal Law and Criminology* 78:155–176

Miethe, T.D. and C.A. Moore. 1985. "Socioeconomic Disparities under Determinate Sentencing Systems: A Comparison of Pre-Guideline and Post-Guideline Practices in Minnesota." *Criminology* 23:337–363.

Miller, J.G. 1996. *Search and Destroy: African-American Males in the Criminal Justice System.* New York: Cambridge University Press.

————. 2000. *American Gulag.* (http://www.yesmagazine.org/article.asp?ID=371).

Miller, L. and K. Hess. 1994. *Community Policing: Theory and Practice.* Minneapolis/ St. Paul, MN: West Publishing Co.

Mitchell, J., D. Thomas, and S. Cutter. 1999. "Dumping in Dixie Revisited: The Evolution of Environmental Injustices in South Carolina." *Social Science Quarterly* 80:229–243.

Mitchell, O.J. 2005. "A Meta-Analysis of Race and Sentencing Research: Explaining the Inconsistencies." *Journal of Quantitative Criminology* 21:439–466.

Mitchell, O. and D. MacKenzie. 2004. *The Relationship between Race, Ethnicity and Sentence Outcomes: A Meta-Analysis of Sentencing Research.* Washington, DC: National Criminal Justice Reference Services.

Molgaard, V., R. Spoth, and C. Redmond. 2000. "Competency Training Families Program: For Parents and Youth 10–14." *National Report Series Juvenile Justice Bulletin.* Washington, DC: U.S. Department of Justice, Office of Juvenile Justice and Delinquency Prevention.

References

Morant, G.M. 1939. *The Races of Central Europe.* London: Allen and Unwin.

Morello-Frocsh, R., M. Pastor, and J. Sadd. 2001. "Environmental Justice and Southern California's Riskscape: The Distribution of Air Toxic Exposures and Health Risks among Diverse Communities." *Urban Affairs Review* 36:551–578.

Morgan, D. 1988. *Focus Groups as Qualitative Research.* Newbury Park, CA: Sage.

Moskowitz, G. B., P.M. Gollwitzer, W. Wasel, and B. Schaal. 1999. "Preconscious Control of Stereotype Activation through Chronic Egalitarian Goals." *Journal of Personality and Social Psychology* 77(1):167–184.

Murphy, E. 1984. "The Application of the Death Penalty in Cook County." *Illinois Bar Journal* 93:90–95.

Murty, K., J. Roebuck, and J. Smith, J. 1990. "The Image of the Police in Black Atlanta Communities." *Journal of Police Science and Administration* 17(4):250–257.

Musto, D. 1999. *The American Disease: Origins of Narcotic Control.* New York: Oxford University Press.

Myers, M. and S. Talarico. 1986. "Urban Justice, Rural Injustice? Urbanization and Its Effect on Sentencing." *Criminology* 24:367–392.

———. 1987. *The Social Contexts of Criminal Sentencing.* New York: Springer-Verlag.

Nagel, I. and S. Schulhofer. 1992. "A Tale of Three Cities: An Empirical Study of Charging and Bargaining Practices under the Federal Sentencing Guidelines." *Southern California Law eview* 66:501–566.

Nakell, B. and K. Hardy. 1987. *The Arbitrariness of the Death Penalty.* Philadelphia: Temple University Press.

Nalla, M., M. Lynch, and M.J. Leiber. 1997. "Determinants of Police Growth in Phoenix, 1950–1988." *Justice Quarterly* 14:115–143.

National Advisory Commission on Civil Disorders. 1968. *The Report of the National Advisory Commission on Civil Disorders.* Washington, DC: Government Printing Office.

National Institute on Drug Abuse. 2003. *Drug Abuse among Racial and Ethnic Minorities: Revised.* Washington, DC: U.S. Department of Health and Human Services.

Nardulli, P., J. Eisenstein, and R. Flemming 1988. *Contours of Justice: Felony Courts and the Guilty Plea Process.* Bloomington, IL: University of Illinois Press.

Needleman, H. 1990. "The Future Challenge of Lead Toxicity." *Environmental Health Perspectives* 89:85–89.

Needleman, H., J.A. Riess, M.J. Tobin, G.E. Biesecker, and J.B. Greenhouse. 1996. "Bone Lead Levels and Delinquent Behavior." *Journal of the American Medical Association* 275:363–369.

Nelson, H. and R. Jurmain. 1991. *Introduction to Physical Anthropology,* 5th Edition. St. Paul, MN: West Publishing.

Nevin, R. 2000. "How Lead Exposure Relates to Temporal Changes in IQ, Violent Crime, and Unwed Pregnancy." *Environmental Research* 83:1–22.

———. 2007. "Understanding International Crime Trends: The Legacy of Preschool Lead Exposure." *Environmental Research* 104:315–336.

Newport, F., D.W. Moore and L. Saad. 1999. "The Most Important Events of the Century From the Viewpoint of the People." (http://www.gallup.com/poll/).

New York Times. 1982. "Carolinians Angry Over PCB Landfill." *The New York Times,* August 11.

————. 2008. "Toward Drug Case Justice." Editorial, *New York Times*, February 8.

Nunn, K.B. 2002. "Race, Crime and the Pool of Surplus Criminality: Or Why the 'War on Drugs' was a 'War on Blacks.' " *Journal of Gender, Race, and Justice* 6:381–445.

Oakes, J., D. Anderton, and A. Anderson. 1996. "A Longitudinal Analysis of Environmental Equity in Communities with Hazardous Waste Facilities." *Social Science Research* 23:125–148.

Odem, M. 1995. *Delinquent Daughters: Protecting and Policing Adolescent Female Sexuality in the United States, 1885–1920.* Chapel Hill: The University of North Carolina Press.

.Oettmeir, T. and M. Wycoff. 1997. *Personnel Performance Evaluation in the Community Policing Context.* Washington, DC: Police Executive Research Forum.

————. 1998. "Personnel Performance Evaluations in the Community-Policing Context." In G.P. Alpert and A. Piquero (Eds.), *Community Policing: Contemporary Readings.* Prospect Heights, IL: Waveland Press.

Office of National Drug Control Policy. 2006. *Drug Facts: Minorities and Drugs.* Office of the President of the United States. (www.whitehousedrugpolicy.gov/drugfact/minorities/).

Ogle, R. and M. Fox. 1999. *Atlas of Human Hair; Microscopic Characteristics*, Boca Raton, FL: CRC Press.

Ogletree, C.J., Jr. 2002. "Black Man's Burden: Race and the Death Penalty in America." *Oregon Law Review* 81:1–15.

O'Hear, M. 2004. "Sentencing the Green Collar Offender: Punishment, Culpability and Environmental Crime." *The Journal of Criminal Law and Criminology* 95:133–276.

O'Neil, S. 2007. "Evaluating the Impact of Executive Order 12898." *Environmental Health Perspectives* 115:1087–1093.

Osborne, N. and M. Feit. 1992. "The Use of Race in Medical Research." *Journal of the American Medical Association* 267(2):275–279.

Ossorio, P. and T. Duster. 2005. "Race and Genetics: Controversies in Biomedical, Behavioral, and Forensic Sciences." *American Psychologist* 60(1):115–128.

Partington, D.H. 1965. "The Incidence of the Death Penalty for Rape in Virginia." *Washington and Lee Law Review* 22:43–75.

Paternoster, R. 1983. "Race of Victim and Location of Crime: The Decision to Seek the Death Penalty in South Carolina." *The Journal of Criminal Law and Criminology* 74(3):754–785.

Paternoster, R. 1984. "Prosecutorial Discretion in Requesting the Death Penalty: A Case of Victim-Based Racial Discrimination." *Law & Society Review* 18(3):437–478.

Pager, D. 2003. "The Mark of a Criminal Record." *American Journal of Sociology* 108:937–75.

Park, R. 1950. *Race and Culture.* Glencoe: The Free Press.

Partridge, A. and W. Eldridge. 1974. *The Second Circuit Sentencing Study: A Report to Judges and Justices of the Second Circuit.* Washington, DC: Federal Judicial Center.

Pastor, M., J.L. Sadd, and R. Morello-Frosch. 2002. "Who's Minding the Kids? Pollution, Public Schools, and Environmental Justice in Los Angeles" *Social Science Quarterly* 83:263–280.

Pastor, M., J. Sadd, and J. Hipp. 2001. "Which Came First? Toxic Facilities, Minority Move-In, and Environmental Justice." *Journal of Urban Affairs* 23:1–21.

Pastore, A.L. and K. Maguire. 2006. *The Sourcebook of Criminal Justice Statistics* http://www.albany.edu/sourcebook/.

Paternoster, R. 1984. "Prosecutorial Discretion in Requesting the Death Penalty: A Case of Victim-Based Discrimination." *Law and Society Review* 18:437–478.

Paternoster, R. and R. Brame. 2003. "An Empirical Analysis of Maryland's Death Sentencing System with Respect to the Influence of Race and Legal Jurisdiction." http://www.urhome/newsdesk.umd.edu.pdf.finalrep.pdf).

Paternoster, R. and L. Iovanni. 1989. "The Labeling Perspective and Delinquency: An Elaboration of the Theory and Assessment of the Evidence" *Justice Quarterly* 6:359–394.

Paternoster, R. and M. Kazyaka. 1988. "The Administration of the Death Penalty in South Carolina: Experiences over the First Few Years." *South Carolina Law Review* 39(2):245–414.

Paternoster, R. and S. Simpson. 1996. "Sanction Threats and Appeals to Morality: Testing a Rational Choice Model of Corporate Crime." *Law and Society Review* 30:549–584.

Patrick, P.A. and S.L Gabbidon. 2006. "*Bowden v. Caldor:* A Case Study of the Intersection of Racial Animus and Private Security Misconduct." *Journal of Ethnicity in Criminal Justice* 4:51–64.

Patterson, O. 2007. "Jena, O.J. and the Jailing of Black America." *New York Times* September 30.

Patterson, E.B. and M.J. Lynch. 1991. "The Biases of Bail: Race Effects on Bail Decisions." In M.J. Lynch and E. B. Patterson's (Eds.), *Race and Criminal Justice* Albany. NY: Harrow and Heston.

Patterson, E.B. and L.A. Patterson. 1996. "Vice and Social Control: Pre-dispositional Detention and the Juvenile Drug Offender." In M.J. Lynch and E.B. Patterson (Eds.), *Justice with Prejudice: Race and Criminal Justice in America.* New York: Harrow and Heston.

Payne, B.K. 2001. "Prejudice and Perception: The Role of Automatic and Controlled Processes in Misperceiving a Weapon." *Journal of Personality and Social Psychology* 81:1–12.

Pearce, F. and S. Tombs. 1998. *Toxic Capitalism: Corporate Crime and the Chemical Industry.* Brookfield, VT: Ashgate.

Pearson, F.S. and A.G. Harper. 1990. "Contingent Intermediate Sentences: New Jersey's Intensive Supervision Program." *Crime & Delinquency* 36:75–86.

Pennsylvania Juvenile Court Judges' Commissión. 2002. Juvenile Court Delinquency Disposition Database.

Pennsylvania State Data Center. 2006. "2005 Detailed Population Estimates Released." Harrisburg, PA: Penn-State- Harrisburg, Institute of State and Regional Affairs. (www.pasdc.hbg.psu.edu/pasdc/data_and_information/briefs/RB080406.pdf).

Pettit, B. and B. Western. 2004. "Mass Imprisonment and the Life Course: Race and Class Inequality in US Incarceration." *American Sociological Review* 69:151–169.

Perlin, S., W. Seltzer, J. Creason, and K. Sexton. 1995. "Distribution of Industrial Air Emissions by Income and Race in the United States: An Approach using the Toxic Release Inventory." *Environmental Science and Technology* 29:69–80.

Perlin, S., K. Sexton, and D. Wong. 1999. "An Examination of Race and Poverty for Populations Living Near Industrial Sources of Air Pollution." *Journal of Exposure Analysis and Environmental Epidemiology* 9:29–48.

Peruche, B.M. and E.A. Plant. 2006. "The Correlates of Law Enforcement Officers' Automatic and Controlled Race-Based Responses to Criminal Suspects." *Basic and Applied Social Psychology* 28:193–199.

Petersilia, J. 1983. *Racial Disparities in the Criminal Justice System*. Santa Monica: Rand.

———. 1985. "Racial Disparities in the Criminal Justice System: A Summary." *Crime & Delinquency* 31:15–34.

Peterson, R. and J. Hagan, J. 1984. "Changing Conceptions of Race: Towards an Account of Anomalous Findings of Sentencing Research." *American Sociological Review* 49:56–70

Pettigrew, T.F. 1997. "Generalized Intergroup Contact Effects on Prejudice." *Personality and Social Psychological Bulletin* 12:173–185.

Phil, R.O. and F. Ervin. 1990. "Lead and Cadmium Levels in Violent Criminals." *Psychological Reports* 66:839–844.

Phillips, S. In press. "Racial Disparity in the Capital of Capital Punishment." *Houston Law Review.*

Pierce, G. and M. Radelet. 2002. "Race, Region, and Death- Sentencing in Illinois, 1988–1997." *Oregon Law Review* 81:39– 85.

———. 2004. "Empirical Analysis: The Impact of Legally Inappropriate Factors on Death Sentencing in California: 1990– 1999." *Santa Clara Law Review* 46:1–47.

Pierce, G., M. Radelet, and R. Paternoster. 2006. Racial and Geographic Disparities in Death Sentencing in Georgia, 1989–1998. *Evaluating Fairness and Accuracy in State Death Penalty Systems: The Georgia Death Penalty Assessment Report, An Analysis of Georgia's Death Penalty Laws, Procedures, and Practice, Appendix A.* Chicago, IL: American Bar Association. (http://www.abanet.org/moratorium/).

———. 2007a. Racial and Geographic Disparities in Death Sentencing in Tennessee, 1981–2000. *Evaluating Fairness and Accuracy in State Death Penalty Systems: The Tennessee Death Penalty Assessment Report, An Analysis of Tennessee's Death Penalty Laws, Procedures, and Practice, Appendix C.* Chicago, IL: American Bar Association. (http://www.abanet.org/moratorium/).

———. 2007b. Racial and Geographic Disparities in Death Sentencing in Indiana, 1981–2000. *Evaluating Fairness and Accuracy in State Death Penalty Systems: The Indiana Death Penalty Assessment Report, An Analysis of Indiana's Death Penalty Laws, Procedures, and Practice, Appendix C.* Chicago, IL: American Bar Association. (http://www.abanet.org/moratorium/).

———. 2007c. Racial and Geographic Disparities in Death Sentencing in Ohio, 1981–2000. *Evaluating Fairness and Accuracy in State Death Penalty Systems: The Ohio*

References

Death Penalty Assessment Report. Chicago, IL: American Bar Association. http://www.abanet.org/moratorium/).

Piquero, N., L. Exum, and S. Simpson. 2005. "Integrating the Desire-For-Social Control and Rational Choice in a Corporate Crime Context." *Justice Quarterly* 22:252–280.

Plant, E.A. and B.M. Peruche. 2005. "The Consequences of Race for Police Officers' Responses to Criminal Suspects." *Psychological Science* 16:180–183.

Plant, E.A., B.M. Peruche, and D.A. Butz. 2005. "Eliminating Automatic Racial Bias: Making Race Non-Diagnostic for Responses to Criminal Suspects." *Journal of Experimental Social Psychology* 41:141–156.

Pope, C.E. 1976 "Social Structure and Social Control: Modeling the Discriminatory Execution of Blacks in Georgia and North Carolina, 1925–1935." *Social Forces* 65:458–475.

Pope, C.E. and W.H. Feyerherm. 1990. "Minority Status and Juvenile Justice Processing." *Criminal Justice Abstracts* 22: 327–336, 527–542.

———. 1993. *Minorities and the Juvenile Justice System: Research Summary*. Washington, DC: Office of Juvenile Justice and Delinquency Prevention (OJJDP).

Pope, C.E., R. Lovell, and H. Hsia. 2002. *Disproportionate Minority Confinement: A Review of the Research Literature from 1989 through 2001*. Washington, DC: U.S. Department of Justice, Office of Juvenile Justice Delinquency and Prevention.

Posel, D. 2001. "What's in a Name? Racial Categorizations under Apartheid and Their Afterlife." *Transformation* 47: 50– 74.

Poveda, T. 2006. "Geographic Location, Death Sentences and Execution in Post-*Furman* Virginia." *Punishment and Society* 9(4):423–442.

Powell, Janet E. (2001). *The Kentucky Racial Justice Act: A Policy Analysis*. Retrieved December 9, 2007 from http://www.google.com/search?hl=en&q=Racial+Justice+Act+Kentucky&btnG=Search.

Price, S.D. 2007. "Jury Takes 90 Minutes to Clear Boot-Camp Defendants in Teen's Death." (http://tallahassee.com/apps/pbcs.dll/article?AID=/20071012/CAPIT ALNEWS/7101201).

Pruit, C.R. and J. Wilson. 1983. "A Longitudinal Study of the Effects of Race on Sentencing." *Law and Society Review* 17:613–35.

Public Agenda. (2008). "RACE: People's Chief Concerns." (http://www.publicagenda.org/issues/pcc_detail.cfm?issue_type=rac e&list=4).

Quinney, R. 1970. *The Social Reality of Crime*. Boston, MA: Little Brown.

Radelet, M. 1981. "Racial Characteristics and the Imposition of the Death Penalty." *American Sociological Review* 46:918– 927.

———. 2001. "Gregg vs. Georgia: The Beginning of the Modern Era of America's Death Penalty." (http://www.amnestyusa.org/abolish/greggvgeorgia/).

———. 2002. "Recent Developments in the Death Penalty in Florida." (http://www.fadp.org/pad/apage4.html#race).

Radelet, M. and G. Pierce. 1985. "Race and Prosecutorial Discretion in Homicide Cases." *Law and Society Review* 19(4):687–621.

————. 1991. "Choosing Those Who Will Die: Race and the Death Penalty in Florida." *Florida Law Review* 43:1–34.

————. 2002. "Wayne Morse Center for Law and Politics Symposium: The Law and Politics of the Death Penalty: Abolition, Moratorium, or Reform?_Race, Region, and Death Sentencing in Illinois, 1988–1997." *Oregon Law Review* 81:39–96.

Radelet, M. and M. Vandiver. 1983. "The Florida Supreme Court and Death Penalty Appeals." *Journal of Criminal Law and Criminology* 74(3):913–926.

Rafter, N. H. 1990. *Partial Justice: Women, Prison and Social Control.* Boston: Northeastern University Press.

Ramirez, O., J. McDevitt, and A. Farrell. 2000. *A Resource Guide on Racial Profiling Data Collection Systems: Promising Practices and Lessons Learned.* Washington, DC: Department of Justice.

Ramsthaler, F., K. Kreutz, and M. Verhoff. 2007. "Accuracy of Metric Sex Analysis of Skeletal Remains using Fordisc Based on a Recent Skull Collection." *International Journal of Legal Medicine* 121(6):477–482.

Rebovich, D.J. 1998. "Environmental Crime Research." In M. Clifford (Ed.), *Environmental Crime: Enforcement, Policy, and Social Responsibility.* Gaithersburg, MD: Aspen.

Reskin, B. and Visher, C. 1986. "The Impacts of Evidence and Extralegal Factors in Jurors' Decision." *Law & Society Review* 20:423–438.

Riedel, M. 1976. "Discrimination in the Imposition of the Death Penalty: A Comparison of the Characteristics of Offenders Sentenced Pre-Furman and Post-Furman." *Temple Law Quarterly* 49(2):261–287.

Ringquist, E.J. 1998. "A Question of Justice: Equity in Environmental Litigation, 1974–1991." *Journal of Politics* 60:1148–1165.

Rojek, J., R. Rosenfeld, and S. Decker. 2004. "The Influence of the Driver's Race on Traffic Stops in Missouri." *Police Quarterly* 7(1):126–147.

Rook, A. 1975. "Racial and Other Genetic Variations in Hair Form." *The British Journal of Dermatology* 92:599–600.

Roscoe, M. and R. Morton. 1994. *Disproportionate Minority Confinement.* http://www.ncjrs.gov/textfiles/fs-9411.txt.

Rose, D. and T. Clear. 1998. "Incarceration, Social Capital and Crime: Implications for Social Disorganization Theory." *Criminology* 36:441–480.

Rossi, P., R. Beck, and B. Eidson. 1974. *The Roots of Urban Discontent.* New York, NY: John Wiley.

Rotter, J.B. 1966. "Generalized expectancies for internal and external control of reinforcements." *Psychological Monographs* 80:1–28.

Rubin, P.J. 2003. "Square Pegs and Round Holes: Substantive Due Process, Procedural Due Process, and the Bill of Rights." *Columbia Law Review* 103:833–894.

Ruchelman, L. 1989. *A Workshop in Redesigning Public Services.* Albany: State University of New York Press.

Russell, K.K. 1998. *The Color of Crime: Racial Hoaxes, White Fear, Black Protectionism, Police Harassment, and Other Macroaggressions.* New York: New York University Press.

Saferstein, R. 2004. *Criminalistics: An Introduction to Forensic Science,* 8th Edition. Upper Saddle River, New Jersey: Pearson Publishers.

Sagar, H.A. and J.W. Schofield. 1980. "Racial and Behavioral Cues in Black and White Children's Perceptions of Ambiguously Aggressive Acts." *Journal of Personality and Social Psychology* 39: 590–598.

Saha, R. and P. Mohai. 2005. "Historical Context of Hazardous Waste Facility Siting: Understanding Temporal Patterns in Michigan." *Social Problems* 52:618–648.

Sabol, W. J., H.Couture, and P.M. Harrison. 2007. "*Prisoners in 2006.*" (NCJ 219416). Washington, DC: U.S. Department of Justice:

Sabol, W.J., T.D. Minton, and P.M. Harrison. 2006. "Prison and Jail Inmates at Midyear 2006." *Bureau of Justice Statistics Bulletin.* (NCJ-217675). Washington DC: U.S. Department of Justice.

Sampson, R. 1986. "Effects of Socioeconomic Context on Official Reaction to Juvenile Delinquency." *American Sociological Review* 51:876–885.

Sampson, R. and J. Laub. 1993. "Structural Variations in Juvenile Court Processing: Inequalities, the Underclass, and Social Control." *Law and Society Review* 27:285–311.

Sampson, R. and J. Lauritsen. 1997. "Racial and Ethnic Disparities in Crime and Criminal Justice in the United States." In M. Tonry (Ed.), *Ethnicity, Crime and Immigration: Comparative and Cross-National Perspectives.* Chicago: University of Chicago Press.

Sampson, R.J., S. Raudenbush, and F. B. Earls. 1997. "Neighborhoods and Violent Crime: A Multilevel Study of Collective Efficacy." *Science* 277:918–24.

Sampson, R. and W.J. Wilson. 1995. "Toward a Theory of Race, Crimes, and Urban Inequality." In J. Hagan and R. Peterson (Eds.), *Crime and Inequality.* Stanford: Stanford University Press.

Sandys, M. 1995. "Cross-Overs — Jurors Who Change Their Minds about the Punishment: A Litmus Test for Sentencing Guidelines." *Indiana Law Journal* 53:475–527.

Sandys, M., and McClelland, S. (2003). "Stacking the Deck for Guilt and Death: The Failure of Death Qualification to Ensure Impartiality." In James R. Acker, Robert M. Bohm, and Charles S. Lanier (Eds.), *America's Experiment with Capital Punishment: Reflections on the Past, Present, and Future of the Ultimate Penal* Sanction (2nd ed.), pp. 385–411. Durham, NC: Carolina Academic Press.

Sarri, R. 1986. "Gender and Race Differences in Criminal Justice Processing." *Women's Studies International Forum* 9:89–99.

Sauer, N. 1992. "Forensic Anthropology and the Concept of Race: If Races Don't Exist, Why are Forensic Anthropologists So Good At Identifying Them?" *Social Science and Medicine* 34(2):107–111.

———. 1993. "Applied Anthropology and the Concept of Race: A Legacy of Linnaeus." In C. Gordon (Ed.), *Race, Ethnicity and Applied Bioanthropolgy.* Arlington, VA: American Anthropology Association.

Savas, E.S. 1986. "Alternative Structural Models for Delivering Urban Services." In A. Swesey and E. Ignall (Eds.), *Studies in Management Sciences: Delivery of Urban Services* Beverly Hills, CA: Sage.

Scaglion, R. and R. Condon. 1980. "Determinants of Attitudes toward City Police." *Criminology* 17(4):486–489.

Schalock, R. 2001. *Outcome-Based Evaluations,* 2nd Edition. New York: Kluwer Academic/Plenum Publishers.

Schalock, R. and G.Bonham. 2003. "Measuring Outcomes and Managing for Results." *Evaluation and Program Planning* 26(3):229–235.

Schelly, D. and P. Stretesky. forthcoming. "An Analysis of the 'Path of Least Resistance' Argument in Three Environmental Justice Success Cases." *Society and Natural Resources.*

Scherer, N. 2004. "Blacks on the Bench." *Political Science Quarterly* 119:655–674.

Schiraldi, V. and J. Ziedenberg. 2002. *Cellblocks or Classrooms? The Funding of Higher Education and Corrections and Its Impact on African American Men.* Washington, DC: The Justice Policy Institute.

Schmidt, P. 2007. *Color and Money: How Rich White Kids are Winning the War Over College Affirmative Action.* NY: Palgrave Macmillan.

Schneider, V. and J. Smykla. 1991. "A Summary Analysis of Executions in the United States, 1608–1987: The Epsy File." In R. Bohm (Ed.), *The Death Penalty in America: Current Perspectives.* Cincinnati, OH: Anderson.

Schwendinger, H. and J. Schwendinger. 2001. "Defenders of Order or Guardians of Human Rights?" In S. Henry and M. Lanier (Eds.), *What is Crime?* New York: Rowman and Littlefield.

Sears, D.O. 2004. "A Perspective on Implicit Prejudice from Survey Research." *Psychological Inquiry* 15:293–297.

Seis, M. 1999. "A Community-Based Criminology of the Environment." *Criminal Justice Policy Review* 10:291–317.

Sejrsen, B., N. Lynnerup, and M. Hejmadi. 2005. "An Historical Skull Collection and Its Use in Forensic Odontology and Anthropology." *Journal of Forensic Odontostomatology* 23(2): 40–44.

Selected North Carolina Death Penalty Statutes. 2003. *Chapter 15A-2000,* North Carolina General Statutes. (www.ncga.state.nc.us/gascripts/Statutes/Statutes.asp).

Sellin, T. 1935. "Race Prejudice in the Administration of Justice." *American Journal of Sociology* 41:212–217.

Sherif, M. and C.W. Sherif. 1969. *Social Psychology.* New York: Harper and Row.

Shih, M., T.L. Pittinsky, and N. Ambady. 1999. "Stereotype Susceptibility: Identity Salience and Shifts in Quantitative Performance." *Psychological Science* 10:80–83.

Shipman, P. 1994. *The Evolution of Racism.* New York: Simon and Schuster.

Shover, N. and A.S. Routhe. 2005. "Environmental Crime." *Crime and Justice: A Review of Research* 32:321–371.

Simon, D. and F. Hagan. 1999. *White Collar Deviance.* Needham Heights, MA: Allyn and Bacon.

Simpson, S. 2002. *Corporate Crime, Law, and Social Control.* Cambridge, UK: Cambridge University Press.

Simpson, S. and N. Piquero. 2002. "Low Self-Control, Organizational Theory and Corporate Crime." *Law and Society Review* 36:509–548.

Situ, Y. and D. Emmons. 2000. *Environmental Crime: The Criminal Justice System's Response in Protecting the Environment.* Thousand Oaks, CA: Sage.

Skolnick, J. 1975. *Justice without Trial.* New York, NY: Wiley.

Slobogin, C. 1995. "The Capital Jury Project: Should Juries and the Death Penalty Mix? A Prediction about the Supreme Court's Answer." *Indiana Law Review* 70:1249–1273.

Small, D. 2001. "The War on Drugs is a War on Racial Justice." *Social Research* 68(3):896–903.

Smith, M.D. 1987. "Patterns of Discrimination in Assessments of the Death Penalty: The Case of Louisiana." *Journal of Criminal Justice* 15:279–286.

Smith, B. and K. Damphhouse, K. 1998. "Terrorism, Politics, and Punishment: A Test of Structure-Contextual Theory and the Liberation Hypothesis." *Criminology* 36:67–92.

Smith, E.L. and M.R. Durose. 2006. *Characteristics of Drivers Stopped by the Police, 2002.* Washington, DC: Bureau of Justice Statistics.

Smith, M. and G. Allpert. 2002. "Searching for Direction: Courts, Social Science, and the Adjudication of Racial Profiling Claims." *Justice Quarterly* 19:673–703.

———. 2007. "Explaining Police Bias: A Theory of Social Conditioning and Illusory Correlation." *Criminal Justice Behavior* 34(10):1262–1283.

Smith, M. and M. Petrocelli. 2001. "Racial Profiling? A Multivariate Analysis of Police Traffic Stop Data." *Police Quarterly* 4:4–27.

Snell, T.L. 1995. *Correctional Populations in the United States, 1993.* (NCJ-156241). Washington, DC: U.S. Department of Justice.

Sommers, S. and P.C. Ellsworth. 2003. "The Jury and Race: How Much Do We Really Know about Race and Juries? A Review of Social Science Theory and Research." *Chicago-Kent Law Review* 78:997–1032.

Songer, M. and I. Unah. 2006. "The Effect of Race, Gender, and Location on Prosecutorial Decisions to Seek the Death Penalty in South Carolina." *South Carolina Law Review* 58:161–209.

Sorensen, J. and D. Wallace. 1999. "Prosecutorial Discretion in Seeking Death: An Analysis of Racial Disparity in the Pretrial Stage of Case Processing in a Midwestern City." *Justice Quarterly* 16:559–579.

Sourcebook of Criminal Justice Statistics. 2005. "Table 6.28: Number and Rate of Sentenced Prisoners under Jurisdictions of State and Federal Correctional Authorities on December 31."

South, N. and P. Beirne. 1998. "Special Issue: Green Criminology." *Theoretical Criminology* 2:147–285.

Sowell, T. 2005. *Black Rednecks and White Liberals.* San Francisco: Encounter Books.

Spitzer, S. 1975. "Toward a Marxian Theory of Deviance." *Social Problems* 22:638–651.

Spohn, C. 1990. "The Sentencing Decisions of Black and White Judges: Expected and Unexpected Similarities." *Law & Society Review* 24:1197–1216.

———. 2000. "Thirty Years of Sentencing Reform: The Quest for a Racially Neutral Sentencing Process." In J. Horney (Ed.), *Criminal Justice 2000: Policies, Processes and Decisions of the Justice System.* Washington, DC: Department of Justice.

Spohn, C. and J. Cederblom. 1991. "Race and Disparities in Sentencing: A Test on Liberation Hypothesis." *Justice Quarterly* 8(3):305–327.

Spohn, C. and D. Holleran. 2000. "Research Note: The Imprisonment Penalty Paid by Young, Unemployed Black and Hispanic Male Offenders." *Criminology* 38:501–526.

Spohn, C., J. Gruhl, and S.Welch. 1981. "The Effect of Race on Sentencing: A Re-Examination of an Unsettled Question." *Law and Society Review* 16:71–88.

Squires, G.D. 2007. "Demobilization of the Individualistic Bias: Housing Market Discrimination as a Contributor to Labor Market and Economic Inequality." *The Annals of the American Academy of Political and Social Science* 609(1): 200–214.

Squires, G.D. 2003. "Racial Profiling, Insurance Style: Insurance Redlining and the Uneven Development of Metropolitan Areas." *Journal of Urban Affairs* 25(4): 391–410.

Stahl, A., T. Finnegan, and W. Kang. 2007. *Easy Access to Juvenile Court Statistics: 1985–2004.* http://ojjdp.ncjrs.gov/ojstatbb/ezajcs/.

Stapleton, V., D. Aday, and J. Ito. 1982. "An Empirical Typology of American Metropolitan Juvenile Courts." *American Journal of Sociology* 88:549–564.

Stauffer, A.R., M.D. Smith, J.K. Cochran, S.J. Fogel, and B. Bjerregard. 2006. "The Interaction between Victim Race and Gender on Death Sentencing Outcomes: A Further Exploration." *Homicide Studies* 10(2):98–117.

Steen, S., R. Engen, and R. Gainey. 2005. "Images of Danger and Culpability: Racial Stereotyping, Case Processing, and Criminal Sentencing" *Criminology* 43(2):435–469.

Steffensmeier, D. 1980. "Assessing the Impact of the Women's Movement on Sex-Based Differences in the Handling of Adult Criminal Defendants." *Crime and Delinquency* 26:344–357.

Steffensmeier, D. and C. Britt. 2001. "Judge's Race and Judicial Decision Making: Do Black Judges Sentence Differently?" *Social Science Quarterly* 82:749–764.

Steffensmeier, D. and S. Demuth. 2000. "Ethnicity and Sentencing Outcomes in the U.S. Federal Courts: Who is Punished More Harshly?" *American Sociological Review* 65:705–729.

———. 2001. "Ethnicity and Judges' Sentencing Comparisons." *Criminology* 39:145–178.

Steffensmeier, D., J. Kramer, and R. Streifel 1993. "Gender and Imprisonment Decisions." *Criminology* 31:411–446.

Steffensmeier, D., J. Ulmer, and J. Kramer. 1998. "The Interaction of Race, Gender, and Age in Criminal Sentencing: The Punishment Cost of Being Young, Black, and Male." *Criminology* 36:763–798

Steggerda, M. and H. Seibert. 1941. "Size and Shape of Head Hair from Six Racial Groups." *The Journal of Heredity* 32:315–318.

Stepan, N. 1982. *The Idea of Race in Science.* London: The MacMillan Press.

Stewart, D. and P. Shamdasani. 1990. *Focus Groups: Theory and Practice.* Newbury Park, CA: Sage.

Stith, K. and J. Cabranes. 1998. *Fear of Judging: Sentencing Guidelines in the Federal Courts.* Chicago: IL: University of Chicago Press.

Stout, D. 2007. "U.S. Panel Cuts Jail Time for Crimes Tied to Crack Cocaine." *New York Times*, December 11.

Stretesky, P.B. 2003. "The Distribution of Air Lead Levels across US Counties: Implications for the Production of Racial Inequality." *Sociological Spectrum* 23:91–118.

———. 2006. "Corporate Self-Policing and the Environment." *Criminology* 44:671–708.

Stretesky, P.B. and M.J. Hogan. 1998. "Environmental Justice: An Analysis of Superfund Sites in Florida." *Social Problems* 42:268–287.

Stretesky, P.B. and M.J. Lynch. 2001. "The Relationship between Lead Exposure and Homicide." *Archives of Pediatrics and Adolescent Medicine* 155:579–582.

———. 2002. "Environmental Hazards and School Segregation in Hillsborough County Florida, 1987–1999." *Sociological Quarterly* 43:553–573.

———. 2004. "The Relationship between Lead and Crime." *Journal of Health and Social Behavior* 45:214–229.

Stults, B.J. and E.P. Baumer. 2007. "Racial Context and Police Force Size: Evaluating the Empirical Validity of the Minority Threat Perspective." *American Journal of Sociology* 113(2):507–46.

Sudnow, D. 1965. "Normal Crimes: Sociological Features of the Pearl Code in the Public Defender's Office." *Social Problems* 12:255–277.

Sundby, S. 1998. "The Capital Jury and Absolution: The Intersection of Trial Strategy, Remorse and the Death Penalty." *Cornell Law Review,* 83, 4.

Sundby, S.E. 2003. "The Capital Jury and Empathy: The Problem of Worthy and Unworthy Victims." *Cornell Law Review* 88:334– 381.

Sunderland, E. 1975. "Biological Components of the Races of Man." In F.J. Ebling (Ed.), *Racial Variation in Man.* London: Blackwell Press.

Sutton, L.P. 1978. *Variations in Federal Criminal Sentences: A Statistical Assessment at the National Level.* Washington, DC: U.S. Department of Justice, Law Enforcement Assistance Administration.

Swigert, V. and R. Farrell. 1976. *Murder, Inequality and the Law: Differential Treatment in the Legal Processes.* Lexington: D.C. Heath.

———. 1977. "Normal Homicides and the Law." *American Sociological Review* 45:16–32.

Szasz, A. 1994. *Ecopopulism: Toxic Waste and the Movement for Environmental Justice.* Minneapolis, MN: University of Minnesota.

Taylor, D.E. 2000. "The Rise of the Environmental Justice Paradigm: Injustice Framing and the Social Construction of Environmental Discourses." *American Behavioral Scientist* 43:508–580.

Tiffany, L.P., Y. Avichai, and G.W. Peters. 1975. "A Statistical Analysis of Sentencing in Federal Courts: Defendants Convicted after Trial, 1967–1968." *Journal of Legal Studies* 4:369–390

Timoney, J. 2004. Panelist at "Law Enforcement Use of Force." Webcast discussion sponsored by the Office of Community Oriented Policing Services at their 2004 National Community Policing Conference, June 22.

Tittle, C. 1980. "Labeling and Crime: An Empirical Evaluation." In W.R. Gove (Ed.), *The Labeling of Deviance,* 2nd Edition. Beverly Hills: Sage.

Tittle, C. and D. Curran. 1988. "Contingencies for Dispositional Disparities in Juvenile Justice." *Social Forces* 67:23–58.

Tittle, C. and R. Paternoster. 2000. *Social Deviance and Crime: An Organizational and Theoretical Approach.* Los Angeles: Roxbury.

Tolnay, S., E.M. Beck and J. Massey. 1989. "Black Lynchings: The Power Threat Hypothesis Revisited." *Social Forces* 67:605–623.

Tomkins, A.J., A.J. Slain., M.N. Halliman, and C.E. Willis. 1996. "Subtle Discrimination in Juvenile Justice Decision Making: Social Scientific Perspectives and Explanations." *Creighton Law Review* 29:1619–1651.

Tonry, M. 1995. *Malign Neglect: Race, Crime, and Punishment in America.* New York: Oxford University Press.

Tonry, M.H. 2004. *Thinking about Crime: Sense and Sensibility in American Penal Culture.* New York: Oxford University Press.

Toomer, J. 1993, 1923. *Cane.* NY: Liveright Publishing.

Tracy, P.E. 2002. *Decision Making and Juvenile Justice: An Analysis of Bias in Case Processing.* Westport: Praeger.

Turk, A. 1969. *Criminality and Legal Order.* Chicago: Rand McNally.

Ubelaker, D. 2002. "Application of Forensic Discriminant Functions to a Spanish Cranial Sample." *Forensic Science Communications* 4(3):1–5.

Uhlman, T. 1978. "Black Elite Decision Making: The Case of Trial Judges." *American Journal of Political Science* 22:884– 895.

Uhlman, T.M. and N.D. Walker. 1980. "'He Takes Some of My Time, I Take Some of His: An Analysis of Judicial Sentencing Patterns Injury Cases." *Law & Society Review* 14:323–341.

Ulmer, J. 1995. "The Organization and Consequences of Social Pasts in Criminal Courts." *The Sociological Quarterly* 36:587–605.

———. 1997. *Social Worlds of Sentencing: Court Communities under Sentencing Guidelines.* Albany: State University of New York Press.

Ulmer, J. and B Johnson. 2004. "Sentencing in Context: A Multilevel Analysis." *Criminology* 42:137–177.

Ulmer, J. and J. Kramer. 1996. "Court Communities under Sentencing Guidelines: Dilemmas of Formal Rationality and Sentencing Disparity." *Criminology* 34:383–708.

Ulmer, J.T. and J.H. Kramer. 1998. "The Use and Transformation of Formal Decision-Making Criteria: Sentencing Guidelines, Organizational Contexts, and Case Processing Strategies." *Social Problems* 45:248–267.

Unah, I. and J. Boger. 2001a. *Preliminary Report on the Findings of the North Carolina Death Penalty Study 2001.* North Carolina Council of Churches and the Common Sense Foundation: Durham, NC. (www.common-sense.org/pdfs/NCDeathPenalty2001.pdf).

———. 2001b. *Preliminary Report: Race and the Death Penalty in North Carolina - An Empirical Analysis: 1993–1997.* Commonsense Foundation of North Carolina: Durham, NC.

Uniform Crime Reports (annual). Washington, DC: Federal Bureau of Investigation (http://www.fbi.gov/ucr/ucr.htm).

United Church of Christ (UCC). 1987. *Toxic Wastes and Race in the United States: A National Report on the Racial and Socio- Economic Characteristics with Hazardous Waste Sites.* United Church of Christ, Commission for Racial Justice, New York.

United States Census Bureau. 2000. *Social and Demographic Statistics.* Washington, DC.

———. 2006. *Statistical Abstract of the United States: 2007, 126th* Ed. Washington, DC. (http://www.census.gov/statab/www/).

United States Census Bureau. 2007a. *Educational Attainment. Historical Tables, A-2.* (http://www.census.gov/population/www/socdemo/educ-attn.html.)

United States Census Bureau. 2007b. *Educational Attainment.* Historical Tables, A-3. (http://www.census.gov/population/www/socdemo/educ-attn.html.).

United States Census Bureau. 2007c. *Poverty Status in the Past Twelve Months.* (S1701). American Community Survey. Washington, D.C.: U.S. Census Bureau. (http://www.factfinder.census.gov/).

United States Department of Justice. 2000a. Justice Department Sues, Files for Emergency Relief to Protect Juveniles in Louisiana's Jena Juvenile Justice Center. (http://www.usdoj.gov/opa/pr/2000/March/155cr.htm).

———. 2000b. *The Federal Death Penalty System. Supplementary data, analysis and revised protocols for capital case review.* Washington, DC: U.S. Department of Justice.

United States Environmental Protection Agency (USEPA). 1998. *Final Guidelines for Incorporating Environmental Justice Concerns in EPAs NEPA Compliance Analysis.* Washington, DC: Office of Federal Activities.

———. 2006. "*Polychlorinated Biphenyls (PCBs),* Vol. 2006." Washington, DC: Environmental Protection Agency.

United States General Accounting Office. 1990. *Death Penalty Sentencing: Research Indicates Pattern of Racial Disparities.* Washington, DC: U.S. General Accounting Office.

United States Government Accountability Office (USGAO). 1983. *The Siting of Hazardous Waste Landfills and Their Correlation with Racial and Economic Status of Surrounding Communities.* Washington, DC: General Accounting Office.

United States Sentencing Commission. 2007. *Report to Congress: Cocaine and Federal Sentencing Policy.* Washington, DC: U.S. Sentencing Commission.

Unnever, J., Cullen, F.T. and Roberts, J. (2005). "Not Everyone Strongly Supports the Death Penalty: Assessing Weakly Held Attitudes about the Death Penalty." *American Journal of Criminal Justice,* 29:2:187–216.

Vaughan, D. 1998. "Rational Choice, Situated Action, and the Social Control of Organizations." *Law and Society Review* 32:23–61.

Vernall, D. 1961. "A Study of the Size and Shape of Cross Sections of Hair from Four Races of Men." *American Journal of Physical Anthropology* 19(4):345–350.

Vito, G. and T. Keil. 1988. "Capital Sentencing in Kentucky: An Analysis of the Factors Influencing Decision Making in the Post- Gregg Period." *Journal of Criminal Law & Criminology* 79(2):483–508.

Von Hirsch, A. 1976. *Doing Justice: The Choice of Punishments.* New York: Hill and Wang.

Walker, S. 1998. *Popular Justice: A History of American Criminal Justice.* New York, NY: Oxford University Press.

Walker, T. and D. Barrow. 1985. "The Diversification of the Federal Bench: Policy and Process Ramifications." *Journal of Politics* 47:596–617.

Walker, S., C. Spohn, and M. DeLone. 2004 (2000). *The Color of Justice: Race, Ethnicity, and Crime in America.* Belmont, CA: Wadsworth/Thomson Learning.

Walters, R. 2006. "Crime, Bio-Agriculture and the Exploitation of Hunger." *British Journal of Criminology* 46:26–45.

Ware, Leland (2007). "A Comparative Analysis of Unconscious and Institutional Discrimination in the United States and Britain." *Georgia Journal of International and Comparative Law*. 36, 89–158.

Warren, P., D. Tomaskovic-Devey, W. Smith, M. Zingraff, and M. Mason. 2006. "Driving While Black: Bias Processes and Racial Disparity in Police Stops." *Criminology* 44:709–738.

Webb, V. and C. Marshall. 1995. "The Relative Importance of Race and Ethnicity on Citizen Attitudes toward the Police." *American Journal of Police* 14:45–66.

Weber, M. 1969. *Max Weber on Law in Economy and Society*. Translated by M. Rheinstein. Cambridge: Harvard University Press.

Weber, Max. 1997. *The Methodology of the Social Sciences*. (Edward A. Shils & Henry A. Finch, Trans. & Eds.) New York: Free Press.

Weisburd, D. and Naus, J. (2001). *Report of Special Master Baime: Re Systemic Proportionality Review*. New Jersey Supreme Court.

Weiss, R. 1995. "The Influence of Variable Selection: A Bayesian Diagnostic Perspective." *Journal of the American Statistical Association* 90(430):619–625.

Weiss, R., R. Berk, and C. Lee. 1996. "Assessing the Capriciousness of Death Penalty Charging." *Law & Society Review* 30(3):607–626.

Weitzer, R. and S. Tuch. 1999. "Race, Class, and Perceptions of Discrimination by the Police." *Crime & Delinquency* 45(4):494–507.

———. 2002. "Perceptions of Racial Profiling: Race, Class and Personal Experience." *Criminology* 40:435–57.

Welch, S., M. Combs, and J. Gruhl. 1988. "Do Black Judges Make a Difference?" *American Journal of Political Science* 32:126–36.

Wernette, D.R. and L. A. Nieves. 1992. "Breathing Polluted Air: Minorities are Disproportionately Exposed." *EPA Journal* 18:16–17.

West, C. 1994. *Race Matters*. New York: Vintage.

Wienker, C. 2005. "Using Biological Data to Challenge the Reality of Race." *Journal of the American Association of Behavioral and Social Sciences* 8. http://aaabss.org/journal2005/AABSS%20Article%201%20USING%20BIOL. pdf.

Whitaker, G. 1980. "Co-production: Citizen Participation in Service Delivery." *Public Administration Review* 40(3):240–246.

Wilbanks, W. 1987. *The Myth of a Racist Criminal Justice System*. Monterey, California: Brooks/Cole Publishing Company.

———. 1987. *The Truly Disadvantaged: The Inner City, the Underclass, and Public Policy*. Chicago: University of Chicago Press.

———. 1990. "Response to the Critics of the Myth of a Racist Criminal Justice System." In B. Maclean and D. Milovanovic (Eds.), *Racism, Empiricism and Criminal Justice*. Vancouver: Collective Press.

———. 1990. "The Myth of a Racist Criminal Justice System." In B. Maclean and D. Milovanovic (Eds.), *Racism, Empiricism and Criminal Justice*. Vancouver: Collective Press.

References

Williams, B.N. 1998. *Citizen Perspectives on Community Policing: A Case Study in Athens, Georgia.* Albany: State University of New York Press.

———. 1999. "Perceptions of Children and Teenagers on Community Policing: Implications for Law Enforcement Leadership, Training, and Citizen Evaluations." *Police Quarterly* 2(2):150–173.

Williams, F., R. Belcher, and G. Armelagos. 2005. "Forensic Misclassification of Ancient Nubian Crania: Implications for Assumptions about Human Variation." *Current Anthropology* 46(2):340–346.

Williams, M.R., S. Demuth, and J.E. Holcomb. 2007. "Understanding the Influence of Victim Gender in Death Penalty Cases: The Importance of Victim Race, Sex-Related Victimization, and Jury Decision Making." *Criminology* 45:865–891.

Williams, J.D., A.M. Harris, and G.R. Henderson. 2006. "Equal Treatment for Equal Dollars in Illinois: Assessing Consumer Racial Profiling and Other Marketplace Discrimination." *Law Enforcement Executive Forum* 83–104.

Williams, M.R. and J.E. Holcomb. 2004. "The Interactive Effects of Victim Race and Gender on Death Sentence Disparity Findings." *Homicide Studies* 8:350–376.

Willison, D. 1984. "The Effects of Counsel on the Severity of Criminal Sentences: A Statistical Assessment." *Justice System Journal* 9:87–101.

Withrow, B.L. 2006. *Racial Profiling: From Rhetoric to Reason.* Upper Saddle River, NJ: Prentice-Hall.

Witt, H. 2007. "Juvenile Justice on Trial." *Chicago Tribune* March 27.

Wolf, E.D. 1964. "Abstracts of Analysis of Jury Sentencing in Capital Cases." *Rutgers Law Review* 19:56–84.

Wolfgang, M.E., A. Kelly, and H.C. Nolde. 1962. "Comparisons of the Executed and the Commuted among Admissions to Death Row." *Journal of Criminal Law, Criminology and Police Science* 53(3):301–311.

Wolfgang, M. and M. Riedel. 1973. "Race, Judicial Discretion, and the Death Penalty." *Annals of American Academy of Political and Social Science* 407:119–133.

Yee, A., H. Fairchild, F. Weizmann, and G. Wyatt. 1993. "Addressing Psychology's Problems with Race." *American Psychologist* 48(11):1132–1140.

Young, J.Z. 1971. *An Introduction to the Study of Man.* Oxford: Clarendon Press.

Zatz, M. 1987. "The Changing Forms of Racial/Ethnic Biases in Sentencing." *Journal of Research in Crime and Delinquency* 24:69–92.

———. 1990. "A Question of Assumptions." In B. MacLean and D. Milovanovic (Eds.), *Racism, Empiricism, and Criminal Justice.* Vancouver: Collective Press.

———. 2000. "The Convergence of Race, Ethnicity, Gender and Class." In J. Horney (Ed.), *Criminal Justice 2000: Policies, processes and decisions of the justice system.* Washington, DC: Department of Justice.

Zeisel, H. 1981. "Race Bias in the Administration of the Death Penalty: The Florida Experience." *Harvard Law Review* 95:451–468.

Ziemba-Davis, M. and B.L. Myers. 2002. *The Application of Indiana's Capital Sentencing Law: A Report to Governor Frank O'Bannon and the Indiana General Assembly.* www.in.gov/cji/home.html).

Zilney, L.A., D. McGurrin, and S. Zahran. 2006. "Environmental Justice and the Role of Criminology" *Criminal Justice Review* 31:47–62.

References

Zimbardo, P.G. 1985. *Psychology and Life*. Glenview, IL: Scott Forsman & Co.

Zimring, F.E., J. Eigen, and S. O'Malley. 1976. "Punishing Homicide in Philadelphia: Perspectives on the Death Penalty." *University of Chicago Law Review* 43:227–52.

Zimring, F.E. and G. Hawkins. 1973. *"Deterrence: The Legal Threat in Crime Control."* Chicago, IL: University of Chicago Press.

Zuckerman, M. 1990. "Some Dubious Premises in Research and Theory on Racial Differences: Scientific, Social, and Ethical Issues." *American Psychologist* 45(12):1297–1303.